IMAGES OF LIBERTY

The Modern Aesthetics of Great Natural Space

Richard Bevis

Order this book online at www.trafford.com
or email orders@trafford.com

Most Trafford titles are also available at major online book retailers.

Printed in Victoria, BC, Canada.

ISBN: 978-1-4269-2424-8 (sc)
ISBN: 978-1-4269-2425-5 (hc)

Library of Congress Control Number: 2009913325

Our mission is to efficiently provide the world's finest, most comprehensive book publishing service, enabling every author to experience success. To find out how to publish your book, your way, and have it available worldwide, visit us online at www.trafford.com

Trafford rev. 06/30/2010

 www.trafford.com

North America & international
toll-free: 1 888 232 4444 (USA & Canada)
phone: 250 383 6864 ♦ fax: 812 355 4082

Also by Richard Bevis:

Eighteenth Century Drama: Afterpieces. London: Oxford University Press, 1970.

The Laughing Tradition. Stage Comedy in Garrick's Day. Athens, GA: University of Georgia Press, 1980.

English Drama: Restoration and Eighteenth Century, 1660-1789. London and New York: Longman, 1988.

The Road to Egdon Heath. The Aesthetics of the Great in Nature. Montreal & Kingston, London and Ithaca: McGill-Queen's University Press, 1999.

Contents

To Starker and Betty
who recognized and taught the important issues early

Preface

Jorge Luis Borges, echoing Ecclesiastes, laments the "Desvarío laborioso y empobrecedor el de componer vastos libros," the 'arduous and impoverishing delirium of composing large books' (12); Max Oelschlaeger calls his *Idea of Wilderness* an "almost hopelessly vast undertaking" (ix). I have been enmeshed in such toils for many years. Lyndon Johnson was promoting the Great Society when my interest began; Vietnam was the burning issue and Pierre Trudeau the fresh new face in politics when I began to write about it. Friends who asked why the project was taking forever ended by asking, "But have you read ...?" To them be some of the credit and blame for two books having consumed four decades. Yet how could I *not* explore a subject that, once recognized, might be seen all around? One can hardly pick up a newspaper or magazine without finding stories of people drawn to Joseph Addison's "Great" and Thomas Hardy's "chastened sublimity": in the Himalayas, at the poles, in the Grand Canyon or the Sahara. Evidently something like what Hardy foresaw in *The Return of the Native* has been happening; a 2004 issue of *National Geographic* features a young Norwegian explorer marvelling at the "elemental forces" of the Patagonia icecap, which made him "feel small - but very alive" (Ousland 64).

The results of my addiction were *The Road to Egdon Heath* (1999), invoking Hardy's famous setting, and now *Images of Liberty*, alluding to Addison's founding description of the Great. The lapse of time suggests a sequel; in fact this is a continuation, the road *beyond* Egdon Heath. Any book that builds on a predecessor published years earlier, however, poses special problems. The author must construct a bridge of some sort between the two, a compromise structure that recognizes the disparate needs of different readers. Gerald Durrell explains the difficulties in the second volume of his *Corfu Trilogy*:

Writing something of this sort presents many pitfalls for the author. His new readers do not want to be constantly irritated by references to a previous book that they have not read, and the ones who have read the previous book do not want to be irritated by constant repetition of events with which they are familiar. I hope that I have managed to steer a fairly steady course between the two. (Durrell, 317)

I have also steered a middle course, but compromises by definition do not satisfy everyone.

Some readers of *Egdon Heath* remarked that it had as much quotation as an anthology. Actually I did consider the model used by Farley Mowat in his *Top of the World* trilogy: excerpts from important texts, with some annotation. The primary documents in this field often have a power and directness beside which most analysis pales, so I quote a good deal in this book as well, hoping to send more readers to the original accounts. They will then be in a better position to judge whether I have fairly represented my sources.

In the early 1990s, as I began organizing decades of research, it became clear that to do justice to the material I had gathered would require two volumes and a sharp focus on my topic: the changing modern aesthetics of nature first noted by Thomas Hardy. That there would be little room to discuss other scholars' views did not perturb me; I saw my project as quite original, having come across few helpful secondary sources. Also I was struck by the late Edward Said's comments on Erich Auerbach's statement in *Mimesis* that if he been at a good European research library instead of in wartime Istanbul, he might never have gotten past the criticism on so huge a subject and written his book. Maybe "the executive value of exile" - even a figurative one - would work for me as well (Said 8). If I had found secondary texts that elucidated my reading I would have used them gladly, but, absent a sufficiency of useful critical material, an author must make a way through untrodden fields by discussing mainly primary sources. This I take to be my situation.

Some early readers urged me to include "more theory." I did not reply that both books examine eighteenth- and nineteenth-century theories (Addison's and Hardy's, mainly), knowing that they meant twentieth-century Continental "Critical Theory" and its numerous spawn of "theorized" approaches. And readers for university presses grew more insistent. When *Egdon Heath* was submitted in the mid-1990s, my method was acceptable: a decade later, it was not. The ideological fissures that have split the humanities over the last few decades are clearly visible in this shift, and in the disparate responses to *Images of Liberty*. A traditional (probably older) critic who found it "worthy of publication" added, "If another assessment advocates 'more theory,' ignore it!" This comment was prescient but vain. Several readers objected that the coverage of secondary sources was inadequate for a university press. One stipulated, "I do not recommend publication *as an academic text* since it is too lacking in theory" (my italics). Thus it is "difficult to align it with any theoretical field." Outside the university, for "a general readership," it might pass, but on campus, no. Personally I am comfortable addressing general readers, for whom I have always tried to write, but it is clear that the theoretical orthodoxy now regnant in academe looks elsewhere.

Almost as soon as the first wave of Theory hit us in the 1960s there was Resistance to Theory. Said, who had theoretical credentials himself, sounded an early warning. In gathering his essays of the '70s for *The World, the Text, and the Critic* (1983), he added an introduction on "Secular Criticism" to remind advocates of pure textuality that texts are of this world ("secular"), as if that were a point that now needed to be made. Said also warned of Theory's penchant for obscurantist jargon, and of the way it reproduces the power relationships of society. It was no accident, he wrote, that its ascendancy coincided with the era of Reaganism. Halfway between Said and the present, Graham Good represented Theory as "dissolving" the study of literature through its doctrines of Textualism, Presentism and Categoryism, respectively the rejections of literature, history and individuality ("The Hegemony of Theory" [1996], 535). Literature and commentary have now traded places, he noted: "The citation of received authorities is more important than direct personal inquiry and independent verification" (543). Good also saw the similarities between the ideologies of Theory and of the New Right that Said had observed. At about the same time, several contributors to a collection of scientific writings took unfavourable note of this increasing hegemony - an unwelcome development for those early enthusiasts who hoped that Theory would give the humanities a harder empirical edge. Richard Dawkins objected that the very word "theory" had been hijacked, as if critical theory were the only kind; Steve Jones felt it necessary to point out that "Science is data-led, not theory-led" (Brockman 23, 118).

Recently, William Deresiewicz took the occasion of a review of books on literary Darwinism to consider the humanities' struggle for survival in our universities:

... a lot of this suffering is self-inflicted. In literary studies ... the last several decades have witnessed the baleful reign of "Theory," a mash-up of Derridean deconstruction, Foucauldian social theory, Lacanian psychoanalysis and other assorted abstrusiosities, the overall tendency of which has been to cut the field off from society at large and from the main currents of academic thought, not to mention the common reader and common sense. Theory, which tends towards dogmatism, hermeticism, hero worship and the suppression of doctrinal deviation - not exactly the highest of mental virtues - rejects the possibility of objective knowledge and, in its commitment to the absolute nature of cultural "difference," is dead set against the notion of human universals. Theory has led literary studies into an intellectual and institutional cul-de-sac, and now that its own energies have been exhausted (the last major developments date to the early '90s), it has left it there (27).

The final sentence's obituary for Theory may be premature - clearly it still has a strong hold on academic presses and humanities departments - but otherwise the passage coincides with my experience. The readers who judged *Images of Liberty* not a university book faulted it for being *apolitical* in its approach to the subject. Why was I not more sceptical of travellers' motives? How could I treat landscapes so "innocently"? Why did I not "problematize liberty"?[1] And why was I not *engagé* with a theoretical school? They could not "place" me in a category, and were being asked to read large amounts of primary material unmediated by any recognized ideology. But they did not agree on which one I should join. One reader thought the book "cried out" for deconstruction: a highly corrosive form of analysis that assumes the critic knows

---

[1] Actually, readers will note that I "problematize liberty" several times, as do some of the travellers. What is surprising - given the obstacles that mountains, deserts, and polar ice obviously present to freedom of choice or movement - is how seldom travellers complain of restriction, and how often they cite freedom of some kind as one of the most attractive attributes of Great space.

more about the author's (ulterior) motives and omissions than he or she ever could have. Another reader heard it cry out for post-colonial criticism: the easiest and most predictable of the new styles (obviously every British traveller was doing the Empire's work). But why stop there? The Marxists want to hear that travellers were rich and natives poor, feminists to hear why so few writers were women, and so on. One response is that Theory is constrictive. Said remarks, "criticism modified in advance by labels … is, in my view, an oxymoron" (28).

Most of the readers' specific suggestions led to dead ends. Gaston Bachelard's *La Poétique de l'espace* (1958), for example, was much recommended, though he says at the outset that his subject is attractive, "lived in" space; "hostile space is hardly mentioned in these pages" (1964, xxxii). "Hostile space" is, however, a fair description of my subject. For "images of immensity" he refers us to his *La Terre et les rêveries de la volonté* (1948), a psychoanalytic study of images of rocks, mountains, the moon, and so on. Bachelard is an interesting writer, but he did not help my study of aesthetic ideas about Great nature. I was also directed to Paul Carter, *The Road to Botany Bay* (only our titles are parallel); to Ezerim Kohak, *The Embers and the Stars* (plenty of space, but focused on philosophy and ethics); to post-colonial studies and essays on environmental politics. The moral: not *every* book about nature, aesthetics, or travel - and there are many - bears on my topic.

Those who object that I omit relevant secondary material have either misunderstood my topic, which is a modern history of natural aesthetics viewed from a particular angle, not "nature" in general; or are wedded to an approach in which the secondary is primary. In making a pioneer effort in a new field, you do not participate in an existing debate, but hope to start a new one. At several places in both books I reach out to fellow scholars, present and future, saying in effect, "I have just scratched the surface; you take it from here." That, I think, is the scholarly contribution suitable to this kind of book.

I have persisted in my study of aesthetic responses to Great nature despite some warning signs. In 2000 Jean-Marie Schaeffer actually bid *Adieu à l'esthétique*: a bit prematurely, as she knows, for she also includes useful advice, such as not to confuse "aesthetic" with "artistic" (43-4). And "in the modern age aesthetic consciousness itself is viewed as retrograde" by some (Oelschlaeger 22). True, although "retro" is a term employed rather facilely by those who, having no interest in a subject themselves, wish to move on to something else.

I have, however, benefited greatly from other kinds of assistance. Every scholar draws on the tradition of published scholarship; in my case, historians of ideas about nature from Alexandre Koyré, Marjorie Hope Nicolson, and Clarence Glacken, through Roderick Nash and Yi-Fu Tuan to Jonathan Bate and Lawrence Buell have been valuable sources of information, ideas, and inspiration. For gifts, loans, or suggestions of books I am indebted to (among others) Paddy Sherman, the late Bob Crumlin, Vivian Bevis, Linda Bevis, Virginia B. Littleton, William Bevis, Barbara R. Leamer, Shawn Malley, Jay Stansel, Wilda Dockery, David Gibson, Robert Weyeneth, and Burkhard Niederhoff. At an early stage of the project, Ian Ross, John Wilson Foster, and Daniel Klang helpfully vetted some ideas. Marcus Smith brought Said's discussion of Auerbach's scholarly exile to my attention. Gilbert Robinson and Norman Fischer of San Francisco provided interesting insights into the appeal and spread of Buddhism in the west. And G.R. Taneja of the University of Delhi kindly allowed me to expound my ideas in his journal *In-between* (Sept. 1997).

Thanks of a different kind are due to Kim Krohn, a guide with Black Feather Wilderness Adventures, for his lead up Mt. Nivko in Greenland to a vista of the central icecap where Nansen emerged from the first crossing (1888); to Lee Whitehead for his story about the woman he met in Ulan Bator awaiting the arrival of her daughter, who (unaware of the theory that women prefer enclosed places to open vistas) was hiking alone across Mongolia; and to the Englishman we met on Dartmoor one Sunday afternoon in 2000 who confided, "Dartmoor is my spiritual home." Exactly. To these and others who assisted in various ways, grateful thanks - and solemn assurances that I have now finished.

Richard Bevis
Vancouver, BC
2009

A NOTE ON DOCUMENTATION

My style of documentation is based on the *MLA Style Manual* (2nd edition, 1998), but introduces variations aimed at streamlining references to the minimum interruption consistent with clarity. For example, I follow the MLA system of parenthetical author-page references in the text, keyed to a Works Cited section; but if there is more than one work by an author, I use author-date-page rather than the MLA's short-title style, which is usually longer. In general, I choose the most economical style that is clear. Information given in my text is not repeated in the note. Subsequent references to the same work in the same paragraph consist of the (volume and) page number alone. Superscripted numbers keyed to footnotes are used for longer references. Single quotation marks surround my own translations from other languages. Published translators are credited in footnotes and Works Cited.

LOOKING UP: Telescope Peak (11,049')
from Death Valley (below sea level), CA.

LOOKING DOWN: Death Valley from Telescope Peak.

Looking southeast from Mt. Shasta towards Lassen Peak (68 miles away) and the Sierra Nevada, CA.

Overlooking the Plain of Guweira from Ras al Naqab in southern Jordan.

Mt. Hermon from Mt. Sannine, Lebanon.

The Takhini River and mountains of the coast ranges in March.
Yukon Territory, Canada.

Lago Nordenskiold, Paine Grande, and the southern end of the Andes.
Parque Nacional Torres del Paine, Chile.
Photo: Vivian Bevis

The Rocky Mountains in November. Banff National Park, Alberta, Canada.

Cathedral Lakes Provincial Park, BC, Canada.

The Artist and the Great. Keele River, Northwest Territories, Canada.
Photo: Carrie Nolan.

Introduction:
The Largeness of a Whole View

A PLEASING ASTONISHMENT

When Londoners opened #412 of *The Spectator* on Monday, June 23, 1712, they found that Mr Spectator was continuing his series on "the pleasures of the imagination." His topic that day was natural aesthetics, particularly the inadequacy of the term "beauty" to describe the psychological impact of the grandest phenomena in nature. Vistas of "open Champian country [extensive plains], a vast uncultivated Desart, of huge Heaps of Mountains, high Rocks and Precipices, or a wide Expanse of Waters," he said, excite in us a "pleasing Astonishment" quite different from the sensation aroused by orthodox beauty, which is smaller, a matter of pretty details in a face, a statue, a garden. Scenes offering "the Largeness of a whole View" constitute a distinct aesthetic category, "the Great," with its own pleasure, a "delightful Stilness and Amazement in the Soul"; thus "a spacious Horizon is an Image of Liberty" (Addison 209).

Most readers probably then laid aside the paper and made a start on the week's work. They would have been surprised to hear that #412 would become a major document of English aesthetics. In *The Spectator*? A middle-brow periodical with an urbane interest in manners and literature was hardly the place to publish serious work. And who was "Mr Spectator," anyway?

The foundations of modern western culture's secular, non-utilitarian aesthetics of nature had been laid on a base of Renaissance science in seventeenth-century Europe.[1] Influential writers -

---

[1] The material summarized in the next few paragraphs is presented at length in the early chapters of my first volume, *The Road to Egdon Heath* (1999).

1

Nicholas of Cusa, Giordano Bruno, Galileo - suggested that infinity and eternity (hitherto understood as attributes of God alone) might be glimpsed or felt in the largest, wildest manifestations of the natural world. The first area considered was space, whose vast emptiness terrified Pascal and fascinated de Fontenelle in France and Henry More in England. This blend of religion and science remained in the background of all discussions of the Great, a belief that did not need to be mentioned. While the size of the cosmic void remained a matter of dispute, some writers began to investigate how earth's mountains and deserts might fit into the Divine Plan. Longinus, the Hellenistic author who wrote a treatise on sublimity, was translated into French (1674) and English (1712). The Third Earl of Shaftesbury argued in 1709 that oceans and stars may provide images of God, and are part of His goodness: the philosophy of Deism, implicit in Henry More. Even in deserts, says Shaftesbury, "The wildness pleases."

One of More's students at Cambridge was Thomas Burnet, who (like Shaftesbury) travelled in the Alps, and wrote vividly of their emotional impact in *Telluris theoria sacra* (1680-1) or *The Sacred Theory of the Earth*, a controversial and influential book. For Burnet, the greatest objects in nature (such as mountains) give us an idea of infinity that makes us think of God, much as More had written. Burnet went on to teach at Cambridge, where he tutored a student named Joseph Addison, who went on to become Mr Spectator. Playwright, essayist, improver of taste, popularizer of philosophy and literature to the middle class, he may seem an unlikely contributor to aesthetic history, but he too had crossed the Alps and been greatly impressed. Nothing comes *ex nihilo*: Addison's enlarged view of nature was born of his experience and his studies. And everything goes somewhere: "The Great" became "the sublime" in Edmund Burke's *Philosophical Enquiry into the Origin of Our Ideas of the Sublime and the Beautiful* (1757), and reached the nineteenth century in this form.

Considerable parts of that story have already been told by earlier scholars such as A.O. Lovejoy, Alexandre Koyré, Samuel Holt Monk, and Marjorie Hope Nicolson. In *The Road to Egdon Heath*, I examined the antecedents of the idea of the Great in science, philosophy, theology, literature, and travel; traced it through its Victorian darkening to Thomas Hardy; and tried to assess its status as an interpretation of humanity's relationship to nature in the late nineteenth century.

2

In *The Return of the Native* (1878), Hardy proposed that a "vast tract of unenclosed wild" land, Egdon Heath, might well represent a new standard of natural beauty, reflecting a shift in his culture's aesthetic response to nature. His central argument was that modern attitudes towards nature had changed from classical times, such that grand, "haggard," mostly barren lands were now more highly valued than verdant pastoral vales:

> Smiling champaigns [meadows] of flowers and fruit ... are permanently harmonious only with an existence of better reputation as to its issues than the present. ... Fair prospects wed happily with fair times; but alas, if times be not fair! Men have oftener suffered from the mockery of a place too smiling for their reason than from the oppression of surroundings oversadly tinged. Haggard Egdon appealed to a subtler and scarcer instinct, to a more recently learnt emotion, than that which responds to the sort of beauty called charming and fair. (Hardy 1980, 2)

In other words, an austere stretch of country such as Egdon Heath could dull what he later called "the ache of modernism" by reflecting our mood of disillusion (it is "a place perfectly accordant with man's nature"). This declaration of interest in nature's great barrens had many precedents - including Addison - though not all share Hardy's view of their meaning.

Hardy went on, however, to extrapolate from his historical generalizations to the probable future of our responses to nature. That "our" is problematic, of course; who are "we"? To what group(s) do his remarks apply? Humanity? Middle-class Englishmen? The adventurous? I cannot wish away Hardy's vagueness here. In any case, the appeal of Egdon Heath, he believed, was a harbinger of things to come:

> Indeed, it is a question if the exclusive reign of this orthodox beauty is not approaching its last quarter. The new Vale of Tempe may be a gaunt waste in Thule: human souls may find themselves in closer and closer harmony with external things wearing a sombreness distasteful to our race when it was young. The time seems near, if it has not actually arrived, when the chastened sublimity of a moor, a sea, or a mountain will be all of nature

that is absolutely in keeping with the moods of the more thinking among mankind. And ultimately, to the commonest tourist, spots like Iceland may become what the vineyards and myrtle-gardens of South Europe are to him now; and Heidelberg and Baden be passed unheeded as he hastens from the Alps to the sand-dunes of Scheveningen. (Hardy 1980, 2)

Hardy's meaning resides in the nature of these places. The Vale of Tempe (a river valley near Mount Olympus) was the Graeco-Roman standard of natural beauty, celebrated by poets for verdure and birdsong. Its modern counterparts, spas like Heidelberg and Baden-Baden (which Hardy had recently visited), however, were losing their hold on humanity, now sadder and wiser, he thought. Thus the *new* Tempe "may be a gaunt waste in Thule" (the mythic north of the ancient geographers, successively identified as Norway, Iceland, and Greenland as exploration moved west). But Hardy clearly intends more than the Arctic here; the "chastened sublimity of a moor, a sea, or a mountain" - Addison's Great - will be the new desideratum in nature, at least for "the more thinking among mankind." Pastoral vales now please only the thoughtless, ignorant of the burdens that spiritual maturation has brought. "Sublimity" or spiritual uplift was associated with a Romantic response to great mountains: a reaction severely "chastened" (both "disciplined" and "purged of impurities"), in his view, by what the nineteenth century had disclosed.

In time the new attitude will filter down to "the commonest tourist," who will forsake lush spas and adopt the "thinking" itinerary, the Thulean Great, of moors (Egdon Heath), ocean beaches (Scheveningen on the Dutch coast), and mountains (the Alps), regarding them with "chastened," post-Romantic eyes. By then, even ordinary folks will find such sombre contexts "accordant" with their natures.

The second, prophetic part of Hardy's meditation on Egdon Heath - which my earlier book could not compass - is the starting point here. The hypothesis to be examined is that, after 1878, classical natural beauty ("Tempe") loses ground to a new "gaunt" type found on moors or deserts, seas, and mountains ("Thule"); and that this happens first among the "more thinking," then among the population at large. To what degree and in what sense, I ask, have "we" moved in this direction, and why? For Hardy includes a rationale in his prediction: *since times have become grim, chastened* sublimity is more attractive. So, to the extent that people *have* sought out barren wastes, has it been for the reasons, and with the responses, that he posits?

In some respects Hardy is as vague as most prophets (making their work easier and that of commentators more challenging). He gives no time-scale for this development, and indicates no cultural boundaries, as if he were speaking universally, yet his geographical and cultural references are European. How wide a net should we cast, then? My choice has been to concentrate on areas that were at the centre of his consciousness, western Europe and North America, and places that travellers from these regions went repeatedly (e.g. the Middle East, the Himalayas, the poles), while making occasional reference to other cultures.

Why should we care what Hardy wrote on this subject? For two reasons, I suggest. One is historical importance: his poems and novels form a recognized part of early modernist literature. In his "Study of Thomas Hardy," D.H. Lawrence calls Egdon Heath the "great, tragic power" of *The Return of the Native*, one before which humans are transients, and compares Hardy to Sophocles, Tolstoi, and Shakespeare in this regard (1972, 415). If a writer of that stature thinks that he has identified a type of landscape with particular appeal to a "recently learnt emotion," he is at least entitled to a hearing. The other reason is the prescience of Hardy's remarks. Some of what he writes, especially his respectful interest in "waste" lands, anticipates twentieth-century developments in natural philosophy: a quaint-sounding phrase now, but ecology and environmentalism are systems of thought about nature, resting on a base of science, as classical natural philosophy was. If his prophecy had not struck so many sympathetic vibrations and resonated so widely since his time, I would not have undertaken a critique of it.

No investigation of a Tempe-Thule dialectic, however, can confine itself to Hardy's terms. His remarks, though provocative, are too limited and general to suffice. He does not, for example, mention the escapist motive for going to the Great, though it can be inferred as early as Byron and Burton. Hardy's mentor Leslie Stephen wrote in 1871 - before overpopulation became a popular issue - that English Alpinists were fleeing London's crowds. Nor does Hardy discuss literature's role in the evolution of a new aesthetic, though the "thinking" people would include writers like himself. We must allow those who have written of "Thule" to speak for themselves, not only when they sound joyless and spent, but whatever their mood. I am not a commentator on scripture, but a researcher into the validity of a theory about what had happened by 1878, and would happen, to attitudes toward physical nature in European and North American culture.

Images of Liberty continues on smoother pavement the narrative of *The Road to Egdon Heath*, which had to introduce a subject and rough out its intellectual history from materials in several disciplines. It treated the palaeo-history of the Great (up through the eighteenth century), its reworking by the Romantics, and its further evolution under the influence of Victorian science. With that foundation for an "aesthetic of Thule" in place, the subject emerges into the light. This book carries the story of our engagement with Great barren spaces to the present, noting its changes and its impact on twentieth-century literature, and connecting the previous book's history of ideas about nature to modern developments such as the emergence of ecology and the conservation movement. *Images of Liberty* is about the various (mainly) aesthetic ways in which people regard, understand, and represent "chastened sublimity."

My data extend along several axes. Chronologically, there are three main periods - the halcyon age before the Great War, an interbellum era, and the decades since World War Two - each with its own character. Generically, reports on travel and exploration are supplemented by treatments of the subject in the creative arts. Geographically, mountains, deserts, and the poles have their own distinct though related narratives. Ideologically, clusters of ideas or aesthetic attitudes may either respect or overstep the preceding divisions. My choice has been to treat authors and ideas within types of landscape within genres within periods. Each part has three chapters exploring the motives and reactions of some of those who have been drawn to Hardy's expanded Great (Addison's plus the polar regions), and a fourth treating some of the imaginative art associated with "Thule," whose creators may or may not have been travellers.

Part One:
From Hardy to the Great War
The More Thinking Among Mankind

That the mid-1870s saw Thomas Hardy imagine "Egdon Heath" out of a few Dorset moors and present it as the modern standard of natural beauty; Charles Doughty go wandering in the Arabian desert; John Muir begin to write about his climbs in the Sierra Nevada; John Wesley Powell affirm the arid reality of the American west; and Herman Melville publish a long poem about the wilderness of Judaea while explorers were probing the polar oceans, is not likely to have been mere coincidence. Though Hardy, who predicted that such regions would increasingly attract "the more thinking among mankind" and eventually "the commonest tourist," did not know about *all* of these explorers and writers, he could certainly see - from books, periodicals, lectures, and personal contacts - that mountains, deserts, and the Arctic had more appeal than ever before.

The Franklin expedition and the years of searching for it had, after all, been the stuff of his boyhood, and the English press followed the progress of polar exploration assiduously throughout the 1870s. Leslie Stephen, Hardy's editor and mentor, could talk of mountain climbs, the French and English Alpine clubs, and books such as Whymper's *Scrambles Among the Alps*, Tyndall's *Hours of Exercise in the Alps*, and his own *The Playground of Europe* (all published in 1871). Richard Burton's desert books were well known, and the French expedition to Timbuktu received press attention when it was wiped out in 1874. To Hardy, the idea of Egdon Heath as the new "vale of Tempe" may have seemed a simple statement of fact, and his prophecy mere extrapolation. The wind was full of straws: for various reasons - science, ambition, empire, curiosity - men (mainly) were being drawn to the great empty places, the world's "vast edges drear" (Matthew Arnold, "Dover Beach").

Just what wind *was* blowing all this straw is a point of great interest. Hardy suggested that such wanderers were seeking congruence between inner and outer: the times were "not fair," (his) culture had entered a period of gloom, and sensitive souls felt more comfortable surrounded by natural "sombreness" and "chastened sublimity." In *The Road to Egdon Heath* I argued that while this mood and motive fit some travellers and writers, many others, moved by a love of adventure, fame, or knowledge, were not gloomy at all. Roderick Nash has advanced an economic theory of the "intellectual revolution" that by 1900 began to send (and still sends) city dwellers to the wilderness, when once the traffic went the other way: nations who have a surplus of wild nature "export" it (or the experience thereof) to those who lack and want it, for money (1982, 343-7).

Every monolithic theory fails, however, because more than one wind was blowing through the numerous cultures (even within "western culture") of the late nineteenth and early twentieth centuries. Views of nature comparable to Hardy's appear independently in several other writers of his period who do not otherwise resemble him or each other. Even George Meredith, another late Victorian poet and novelist with a keen interest in nature, exhibits a *joyful* acceptance of evolution very different from Hardy's gloom. In America, Walt Whitman exclaimed over the "simple, unornamented space ... fascinations ... in sea and shore!", wondered "What is it in us, arous'd by those indirections and directions?" ("Winter Day on the Sea-Beach"), found "the law of [his] own poems" in the Rocky Mountains, and seemed far from depressed (2:91, 142).

Nor was this merely an Anglophone phenomenon: a German "North Pole Expedition" ship was crushed by ice off Greenland in the winter of 1869-70; Austrian explorers discovered Franz Josef Land in the Arctic (1873); and Baron Adolph Erik Nordenskiöld of Sweden, having drifted the Northeast Passage, ventured 75 miles onto the Greenland icecap in 1883. The German sage Friedrich Nietzsche, whose philosophical work would disturb so much traditional thought, admired the new spirit of "virile scepticism" evident in all this polar exploration (133). We moderns, Nietzsche wrote, yearn for "the thrill of the infinite" and are happiest when in danger (153): emotions regularly associated with exploration of

8

the Great. *Beyond Good and Evil* (1886) ends with an "Aftersong" titled "From High Mountains" (an "almost infinite" realm), whose speaker has "learned to dwell / Where no one lives, in bleakest polar hell" (241, 243). Nietzsche, said an English climber, may have been more influential on "mountain philosophy" than Leslie Stephen was (Noyce 1950, 127, 132).

From recognizing the human value of such experiences to acknowledging the value - and fragility - of the places where they might be gained was only a step. In 1903, the wealthy American sportsman, soldier, and president, Theodore Roosevelt, having talked with John Muir in Yosemite (already protected by law), visited the Grand Canyon and advocated similar treatment. "Leave it as it is," he urged; "The ages have been at work" here and "man can only mar it" with his development. We cannot "treat any part of our country as something to be skinned for two or three years." A few years later he asserted that "All civilized governments" recognize a "duty" to "preserve ... tracts of wild nature."[1] This preservationist note, rare in America then, echoed attitudes that had begun to be heard in Europe, inclinations away from human (ab)use, towards the land as it was, or had been: an almost misanthropic satiety with one's species, implicit in Burton's sojourns in the world's deserts, and explicit in Stephen's admission that some Englishmen climbed Swiss peaks to escape the hordes of London. And these are but a few of those who, in Hardy's time and later, were taking new interest in the planet's empty, barren, "wide waste spaces."[2]

Given all this diversity, it is prudent to be wary of any *a priori* assumption about why modern souls have become more interested in "Thule." Only through careful attention to individuals can we come to an understanding of motives; only by doing our homework may we earn the right to formulate a general theory of "Thule."

Of the contemporaries of Hardy named in the first paragraph of this section, Powell and Melville were discussed in *The Road to Egdon Heath*, but Doughty and Muir are new faces. Each in a sense stands at the head of a line of development: Doughty as an eloquent writer on the desert and a standard for later travellers, Muir as an inspiration for mountaineers, nature writers, and conservationists. They are thus natural starting-points for the modern period.

---

[1] Quoted in Krutch 1967, 18-21; Roosevelt 13.

[2] Roosevelt acknowledges "the strong attraction of the silent places" and "wide waste spaces of the earth, unworn of man, and changed only by the slow change of the ages" in *African Game Trails* (1910), xi.

9

1
Less Is More:
Minimalism and Desert Space

> A preference for the stark environment, bare as the
> desert ..., is contrary to the normal human desire for
> ease and abundance. Yet people are known to have
> sought, repeatedly, the wilderness .... What can be
> the positive appeal of asceticism?
>
> Yi-Fu Tuan, *Topophilia*

"Normal human desire" notwithstanding, more people were seeking
desert wilderness and praising its rewards in the late nineteenth
century than ever before: John Wesley Powell and Mary Austin
in America, Charles Doughty and Gertrude Bell in the Middle
East, Charles de Foucauld and Isabelle Eberhardt in the Sahara,
and so on. What - apart from the general interest in geography,
geology, and/or anthropology that many of them professed - was
attracting gifted people to such places? Yi-Fu Tuan suggests that
asceticism may be "a type of affirmation" of will over matter, "and
the desert the austere stage for epiphany." Early Christian hermits
went there, as do modern ascetics. Ultimately he pronounces this
urge mysterious: "Heroic minds are drawn to it for reasons that
common humanity finds difficult to understand" (Tuan 1974, 51-2).
"Common humanity," having normal human desires, would not see
the point. Later he suggested that the desert represents a yearning
for simplicity, intensity, and God (Tuan 1993, 144).

The same question is raised by David Hogarth in *The Penetration
of Arabia*. Enumerating the first explorers to enter its deserts -
Niebuhr, Burckhardt, Burton, Doughty, Blunt, and others "of too

serious mind to have been tempted by mere love of adventure or the forbidden thing" - he asks, "Why did such as these hazard themselves in a land so naked ... how should Arabia have mattered to them?" (Hogarth 1904, 6-7). He replies that Arabia was the cradle of Semitic religion and a cultural "island," but the query is broader and more resonant than that. We must seek our own answers.

When Richard Wollheim wrote the seminal article on minimal art in 1965, he traced it back fifty years. For him, the style meant dismantling the cluttered, and simplifying (Battcock 398). Others said that minimal art criticized society and reduced form to a "primary state, often related to basic structures in geology, physics and chemistry"; seeing the "puritan simplicity" of these forms, a spectator might feel like a visitor to "monuments of archaic culture" (Develing 11-14). Alan Leepa saw minimalism as a search for clarity, for "basic roots and meanings in a world that appears to have none," by artists unsure of their "position in the universe" (Battcock 206-8).

Such attitudes are not irrelevant to desert travel. The motives commonly attributed to minimalists and the qualities critics see in their art closely resemble impulses and traits discernible in the writings of those who have been drawn to the world's great deserts. If minimalism is taken as a general proclivity in psyche and culture, not just a narrow term in modern art history, the parallels between Doughty's portrait of Arabia, John Cage's short musical compositions, and Samuel Beckett's bare-bones drama become apparent.

Those connections are clear in recent work on minimalism. Warren Motte's *Small Worlds* (1999) treats it as a broad artistic movement with a pedigree as old as Heraclitus: a cyclical impulse in music (Satie, Schönberg, Webern, Glass, Pärt, etc.) and literature as well as in the plastic arts. John Barth wrote in 1986 that minimalism underlies "the most impressive phenomenon" in current North American literature: the short story (Motte 22). Tracing the French minimalist tradition from Pascal to Camus, Nathalie Sarraute, Beckett's speechless 35-second play *Breath*, and Alain Robbe-Grillet, Motte decides that "a minimalist tendency" exists "wherever literature flourishes" (22). He provides an extensive bibliography.

The qualities that critics use to define minimalist work - asceticism, simplicity, clarity, solitude, emptiness, freedom - also characterize many accounts of desert travel. If "Less is more" could be the motto of minimalism, as Barth suggested, it is also necessarily the mantra of those who venture into waste lands. They too must be "essentialists," and are often (at least implicitly) cultural critics: Doughty of flaccid Victorian English, W.S. Blunt of colonialism, Powell of imprudent attempts to settle the arid West, and so on (Motte 4-5, 23).

One clarification must be made: minimal art need not be short. Minimalism is a matter of approach, not length; Motte can "imagine 'long' minimalist narratives," characterized by a penchant for reduction and austerity (22). The point is vital when we confront Doughty's hefty two-volume record of his Arabian sojourn. It may take the minimalist some time to explain how little is needed, why less is more.

ISHMAELITES

Midway through the first volume of Charles Doughty's *Travels in Arabia Deserta*, he and Sheikh Zeyd, his host, go looking for a carved stone image on the desolate slopes of Ybba Moghrair. Eventually they find it near a pool at the head of a box canyon, "a long inlet in the mountain bosom, teeming green with incomparable freshness, to our sense, of rank herbage." The Englishman is so taken with this maternal nook that he asks Zeyd to let him have a milk camel and "abandon [him] here" (Doughty n.d. [1888], 1:349-50). It is a stunning moment: possessing so little on this journey (they have just broken their fast on dandelions and a handout of camel's milk from friendly herdsmen), already doing without most of what Europeans think they need, the narrator yearns for less. An "oozy slumbering pool" for water, a "garden of weeds" for pasturage and salad, a camel for milk, and a narrow ravine for shade will, he thinks, suffice. Omar Khayyam's request for wine, bread, and thou in Fitzgerald's poem seems relatively hedonistic. (Zeyd refused.)

This is only the most spectacular instance of Doughty's minimalist leanings. "Cheerful is the bare Arabic livelihood in the common air, which has sufficiency in few things snatched incuriously as upon a journey!" he exclaims (Doughty 1:582). In the second volume - having suffered extended privations - "Khalil" (i.e. Charles) still endorses a nomadic existence, twice assuring his hosts that it is "the best life" (2:252, 262). This might have been tact or strategy, of course, but the author does not turn to us and gainsay his persona on this point, for the ideal of "sufficiency in few things" was his, too.

While Charles Montagu Doughty stands apart from all other desert writers stylistically, in many respects he represents typical impulses of his period. The son of a clergyman in southeast England, he grew up a good Victorian: pious, patriotic, interested in natural science. His first life-defining moment came when he left Caius College, Cambridge - in whose evangelical atmosphere his devotion to "the new studies" (evolution) was unwelcome - for the more liberal air of Downing, which had instituted a Natural Science Tripos. Doughty (like Hardy) belonged to the first generation brought up on Charles Lyell's *Principles of Geology* (1830-34), which contended that natural forces still operating could explain the earth's formation, and these you could "go and see." Doughty promptly went to Norway, saw its glaciers in action, and published a monograph on them that elicited a visit from Lyell himself.

After graduation, Doughty studied independently for four years, concentrating on the early literary history of "the British race," rather like John Milton. During this interval, however, his family lost most of its money. Henceforth poor, he left England for eight years of "studious travel" in poorer countries, going to Italy, where he examined Vesuvius (then erupting) and Etna, to the Sahara, and eventually to the Mideast. (He apparently preferred deserts to mountains, of which he took the old view that they were deformities of the earth's crust.) Doughty geologized through the Sinai and visited Petra in Jordan, looking for traces of the Biblical past. At Ma'an he heard about Nabatean inscriptions at Medain Sâlih in northern Arabia and arranged to accompany the annual *hajj* (pilgrimage from Damascus to Mecca) that far, despite a lack of money and diplomatic protection. Thus, in his messianic year of 33, Doughty, clad as a Persian, riding a camel, carrying medicines, a barometer, and writing materials, began the nearly two years of hard knocks that would produce *Travels in Arabia Deserta*.

Our primary source for what happened there is a set of notebooks in the Fitzwilliam Museum in Cambridge. Consisting mainly of scrawled jottings on topography and the weather, they have more about geography and geology than about people or religion, and hardly any "style" at all. Of course it was difficult to write anything under those conditions. The *hajj* left Doughty at Medain Sâlih, where he busied himself with nearby monuments and inscriptions until it reappeared. Then came his second life-shaping decision: he did not return to Damascus as planned, but set off into the desert with Zeyd's tribe. Why? He never really explains, leaving us to speculate. Perhaps Doughty was fascinated by the past, as his English studies suggest; or he was escaping modern civilization; or it was some unique personal combination of religious and scientific motives. He himself may not have been altogether sure.

Travels in Arabia Deserta cost Doughty a decade to write and publish. T.E. Lawrence called the book "a bible of its kind," and like the Bible it contains a wealth of material that will support many opinions. On the question of motive, however, it is usually silent or playful, though it begins with an old friend asking him (afterwards), "How couldst thou take such journeys in the fanatic Arabia?" The two volumes constitute an extended answer. When a nomad inquires "What did I there in the wilderness, and wherefore had I banished myself from all the world's good?" Khalil replies with a casual Arabic idiom, "I take the air" (Doughty 1888, 1:377). Accused of being a spy, he labels himself instead "*Sâiehh* ... a walker about the world ... God's wanderer, who betakes himself to the contemplative life's pilgrimage" (1:315-16). This mantle fits; "it is pleasant to recede from the town to the silent desert," he observes (1:195).

In such exchanges, Doughty was trying to translate his motives into terms his hearers would understand or to deflect their curiosity; he is reporting what he told them. In the preface to the 2nd edition of *Arabia Deserta* (1920), however, speaking to us, he says that "the Story of the Earth" (a gloss of "geo-logy") is "Of surpassing interest." Also, he valued "all that pertains to Biblical research," and the Semitic nomads of Arabia, living "as it were beyond the World," suggested the Hebrew patriarchs in the wilderness. The preface to the 3rd edition (1921) points to the same attraction: a primitive people in an ancient land, hence time travel to the Mosaic world, separated from us, after all, by only "a moment of geological time." Educated late-Victorian travellers knew that geology had lengthened the time-scale enormously.

These are only the first steps to understanding Doughty; when we think we have him, he slips away. "I was as much Geologist as Nasrâny" (Christian), he wrote: "the Story of the Earth" again. Yet his geology has been attacked as elementary and unimaginative, too vague to be scientific. As for religion, he matured into "an agnostic Humanitarian," holding that "Humanity is the ultimate Religion of man" (Hogarth 1929, 133, 169). In fact, neither a scientific nor a religious label quite fits; like many Victorians, Doughty combined these modes. What he knew of geology actually made him feel closer to God through keener appreciation of His works (as Lyell said it should): a form of Deism, which treated nature as a scripture. Doughty had strong feelings for the earth, especially its deserts, whose bareness brought out all the piety and idealism of his nature. If his geology lacked empirical rigor, it offered spiritual and emotional dimensions rare in scientific literature.

Above and beyond all questions of motive are the qualities of the book. Its length and weighty style, full of archaisms, inversions, and borrowings from Arabic, have meant relatively few - but devout - readers. Open it almost anywhere and you find resonant descriptive phrases of a baroque splendour: "the sun's great rundle" (from roundel); the nomads' "worsted booths [tents] leak to this fiery rain of sunny light" while their "camels waver dispersedly" on the plain, with "Mountains looming like dry bones through the thin air"; at night "the spirit [seems] to waver her eyas [nestling] wings unto that divine obscurity." Doughty laboured over such sentences, which were integral to his mission as the English Vergil, leading his compatriots back to the primitive virtues, including purity of language (which for him meant Spenser). Potential publishers who asked for revisions learned that the style was not negotiable.

He was right to hold out: W.S. Blunt thought it "the best prose written in the last two centuries" (1:273); John Middleton Murry found an "ascetic purity" in the book (1926, 662); Anne Treneer called Doughty's prose rhythms "sectional drawings of the desert" (131). Not only does *Arabia Deserta* imitate the desert, aspects of life there being traits of the prose as well, but environment and experience are permeable to each other. Human feelings are projected onto "sweet lemon groves" and the "sickly climate," while empty space and natural desolation can slip inside the weary, hungry nomads.

Several of the book's themes arise from both: the land and the lives of its inhabitants. The simplicity of Arabian life and the raw, bare-bones character of the land speak to Doughty the primitivist, who notes that the Beni Sokhr tribe are literally "children of sandstone"; the desert-dweller must perforce be ascetic. Some see a masochistic streak in Doughty, to endure all this voluntarily, albeit for the sake of spiritual cleansing. Khalil attributes that trait (perhaps ironically) to "many" pilgrims, "whom their old pain so enamours of the sacred way" to Mecca that they take it repeatedly, considering the pain an integral part of the *hajj* (Doughty 1888,

1:102, 106). His nomad friends keep asking why he absents himself from worldly felicity to wander in the empty waste. Apparently he too finds these pains to be purifying, and is happy. Arabia is for him a divine scourge that makes him a better man, a crucible in which to purge his gold of its dross.

Doughty never sentimentalizes the desert, many of whose traits are unattractive or double-edged. His "word notes" for the book begin with "void waste"; "Desert" will be "infinite," "inhuman," and "desolate" (Tabachnick 1981, 45-6). Infinity was at first a divine attribute, only later applied to the universe. "Inhuman" originally defined desert; by the 1880s that was not a wholly negative attribute for Europeans. Arabia Deserta is, in fact, profoundly ambiguous. Negative qualities are generally balanced by positive ones. If desolate, it is a "Titanic desolation" with the grandeur of immensity (Doughty 1888, 1: 427). Its bareness is pleasing. "Bare of all things of which there is no need, the days of our mortality are so easy" refers to the nomads' lives, and the terrestrial bareness facilitates geologizing (1:490). If there is anarchy, there is also freedom. Khalil describes nomadic life as "a long holiday, wedded to a divine simplicity," adding "but with this often long tolerance of hunger in the khala" (1:82, 490): empty in the emptiness.

Doughty's is a real desert, which he wants to know as the geographer and geologist do, but *Arabia Deserta* has figurative deserts, too. People can be "desertic": the venal surveyor at Medain Sâlih lives in "the deserts of his corrupt mind" (Doughty 1888, 1:132); Prince Mohammed's sterile life at Hayil partakes of the barrenness of the surrounding waste. For Khalil, "the world" is a "moral desolation," which ups the ante considerably, relating Arabia to European civilization (1:305). We can infer that someone who sees society in this way will be (more) comfortable in landscapes that reflect the moral reality of "the world," much as Hardy had suggested. Doughty's Arabia is a darker version of Addison's Great, with some of the "chastened sublimity" of Egdon Heath.

Murry viewed Doughty - for whom the nomads were "Ishmaelites" - as himself "veritably an Ishmael, who would find a home for his soul in the desert, or nowhere at all" (1926, 658). This is a dangerous image to deploy, with its connotations of "a wild man," his hand against every man and vice versa; even during his worst times in Arabia, this was not Doughty's case. But in the broader sense of a desert-dweller, it will do. That Doughty found spiritual food in Arabia can hardly be doubted, nor did he think the phenomenon peculiar to himself: "in truth," he wrote, "if one live any time with the Aarab, he will have all his life after a feeling of the desert" (1888, 2:481). He would prove the truth of this a generation later in his poem *Adam Cast Forth*, discussed in Chapter Four.

Doughty and the Blunts missed each other in Hayil by about a year. Wilfrid S. Blunt and his family had crossed the Alps on sledges when he was 12; in his teens he hiked in Scotland and Switzerland, climbed Monte Rosa, and crossed the Col du Géant. Joining the diplomatic service, he met Richard Burton in Buenos Aires, rode the pampas, read Palgrave's Arabian travels. In 1869 he married Lady Anne Noel, Byron's adventurous grand-daughter. Three years later an inheritance enabled them to indulge a penchant for rough travel, beginning with a ride through Asia Minor; both were skilled equestrians. They were drawn to the desertic margins of Victorian adventure: the Algerian Sahara, Egypt (where they used camels), the Sinai Peninsula. Blunt was deeply impressed by the holiness of Mt. Sinai (E. Finch 68-9); his family, converts to Catholicism, had sent him to a Jesuit school. Though he lost his faith (to Darwin and *Essays and Reviews*) in the 1860s, he always hoped it would return.

In 1878 the couple rode from Aleppo to Baghdad and back. Lady Anne, an extraordinary woman by any standards, published her journals ("edited by W.S.B.") as *Bedouin Tribes of the Euphrates*. They found the Syrian desert clean, and "more attractive" than Algeria or Egypt; the Euphrates valley seemed "a garden of Eden" (A. Blunt 1879, 1:79, 85). After following the river to Baghdad, they set out on camels across Mesopotamia. "Wilfrid is perfectly happy" to be "free" again and "in his own tent," she reports; "Liberty ... is the greatest of all blessings," and not found in Europe "in its perfect form" (1:223, 229). The Blunts never wavered in this view. From Deyr, they rode again into "*our own* desert" and felt "more at home" (2:17). South of Palmyra they sought the Roala tribe, to whom they had an introduction. Coming over a ridge and seeing the "wonderful spectacle" of their camp - ten thousand tents stretching across a plain to a large lake - she "felt an emotion almost of awe, as when one first sees the sea": a kindred area of the Great (2:136).

The connections they formed among the Bedu enabled them to ride into Arabia, ostensibly to arrange a marriage, the following winter. Anne's account, again edited by Wilfrid, is called *A Pilgrimage to Nejd*, because (he explains in the preface) Nejd "seems no unworthy object of a religious feeling." His biographer writes that the couple thought of central Arabia as a romantic "holy land" (E. Finch 92). They rode south from Damascus over the stony Hauran plain, glad to leave squalid villages for open desert. From the rim of a crater, Anne declared the volcanic Harra "a wonderful sight," adding, "There is always something mysterious about a great plain" (A. Blunt 1881, 1:68). The vagueness is typical; the Blunts never tried, as Doughty did, to elucidate that mystery. Yet their feelings were hardly less keen. Blunt was also a poet, and Anne felt the "black wilderness" of the Harra as nightmarish (1:75).

They continued south, noting the geological changes, towards the Nefud, "the object of our dreams" and *"ne plus ultra* of deserts in the world" (A. Blunt 1881, 1:148). The Blunts had become connoisseurs; the first dune-field was "not really the Nefud," merely the sort of thing you can see in the Sahara. The *real* Nefud was of red sand, and by no means wholly barren. Crossing it took ten days, some of them hard, but "Blunt [is] happy now," Anne recorded (E. Finch 98). They made a point of enjoying their last few days of travel, admiring the growing beauty of Jebel Shammar, the local mountain. Welcomed by Ibn Rashid in Hayil, they wondered what European calling himself Khalil could have visited there the previous year. Anne Blunt found the clarity of the desert mornings at four thousand feet exhilarating. They then followed the Persian *hajj* route to Baghdad, perhaps the first Europeans to do so.

Whatever attracted the Blunts to the Middle East, they came to admire Arabic culture. Wilfrid began to write in favour of Islam and against the British Empire. The deserts by then seemed "a sort of shell of protection" around an Arabia "uncontaminated by Western civilization," which had tarnished much of Africa and Asia (Assad 63). They bought a garden on the desert's edge near Cairo, wintering there in the 1880s and 1890s. The couple made their last joint expedition in 1896 through the Eastern Desert, a little-known region, which Blunt considered "a great additional charm" (W. Blunt 1:168). He retraced the journey in 1898 without his wife to make a map - but not for the Royal Geographical Society, which he feared would use it for imperial purposes (E. Finch 294). Blunt is a difficult figure for post-colonialism to swallow.

In 1897 he fulfilled a long-held wish to ride to the historic Siwa oasis, Anne staying behind with their daughter. It would be an arduous trip, 400 miles of desert, requiring some 40 days. Blunt was seeking a "better tradition of Islam" among the Senussi, maybe even "that true desert hermitage I had so often dreamed of" (1:247-

8). It was the old urge for a more intense spiritual life, a return to faith - Muslim this time - now with a touch of solipsism, a desire to exist as an individual soul. On the trail he again mentions his "wish for a hermit's life in the desert"; Lake Sittarah would be "the best" place, "*never* visited by man" (1:255, 262). But in the end it all fell apart: attacked and briefly imprisoned at Siwa, he rode straight home without meeting the Senussi sheikh. His ideas about a purer religion deep in the desert now seemed self-deluding, "a romance," and he gave up, not only on Islam but on all religion, of which "The less ... the better" (1:276).

LANDS OF LITTLE RAIN

Other deserts were receiving more attention by now. In America, cowboys, settlers, professors, and tourists fanned out over the western plains. John Wesley Powell, who led the first run of the Grand Canyon of the Colorado and wrote a book about it, went on to broader concerns, warning in an 1878 government report that settlement of the west, to be rational, must be minimal, but never forgot the great adventure of his younger years. In 1895 he published *Canyons of the Colorado*, a popular account based on his 1875 narrative. Originally "interested only in the scientific results," the geology professor fondly recalls "the most sublime spectacle on earth" (Powell iv, 389-90). The Indians, for whom it was a trail to a "happier land," had "woven the mysteries of the canyon" into their religion (35, 37). In his final chapter Powell adopts this spiritual reading: the Grand Canyon, "a stairway from gloom to heaven," affords "a concept of sublimity ... never again to be equaled on the hither side of Paradise" (386, 397).

Geology brought many to the Great. Clarence Dutton studied for the ministry before becoming a geologist; like Doughty, Powell, and John Muir, he shifted from Biblical to natural studies without losing spiritual intensity. Titles like *Geology of the High Plateaus of Utah* (1880) and *Tertiary History of the Grand Cañon District* (1882) sound dry and anaesthetic, but Dutton was an ardent desert-lover with literary leanings.[1] In the preface to *Tertiary History* he admits to having "found the temptation irresistible to wander far outside the

---

[1]   Wallace Stegner, who wrote a thesis and a book on Dutton, refers to his "Geological Aesthetics": 1954, 158. On his literary bent, see Stegner 161.

limits of my prescribed field" (northern volcanoes), and to winter in "milder regions ... beyond the foot of the great stairway of terraces which leads down from the heights." Nor would the "severe ascetic style" of scientific writing be appropriate: at the Grand Canyon, the imagination *must* be allowed rein "to exalt the mind sufficiently to comprehend the sublimity of the subjects" (C. Dutton vii-viii).

The monograph - published by the US Geological Survey, whose head was Powell, Dutton's boss - develops the theme of "EROSION upon a grand scale," combining travel narrative with geological maps and sections (C. Dutton 1). The view from Point Sublime is only one of many panoramas "sublime in the highest degree," he says, but "even the least imposing portions of the cañon are in their general effects upon the sensibilities as impressive as any scenery ... in the world" (6). This is late in the history of the term "sublime," which had been overgrazed by then. The chapter on "The Terraces" emphasizes their vastness. A salient of the Markagunt Plateau offers a "magnificent spectacle": one sees over "the calm of the desert platform" to various ranges, a hundred miles of elevated land. The Kaibab escarpment extends until "the curvature of the earth" hides it (26). This is just the kind of scene that Addison defined as "Great" and Hardy said would attract thoughtful moderns.

Later Dutton devotes a chapter to "The Panorama from Point Sublime," trying to analyze its power. The Point provides "the most sublime and awe-inspiring spectacle in the world," even "the smallest" of the views into the canyon being "tremendous and too great for comprehension" (C. Dutton 140). But the Grand Canyon is "a great innovation in modern ideas of scenery, and in our conceptions of the grandeur, beauty, and power of nature." At first you may react with "shock" or "horror," for you will not see that which you have learned to call "beautiful and noble" (141). Only gradually, over time, will you realize that this is "the sublimest thing on earth" (143). The magnitude of the scale is the problem; in that vastness there is no rest for the mind, since "Everything is superlative, transcending the power of the intelligence to comprehend it" (150). It is fascinating to watch a nineteenth-century American geologist working out the formulae of eighteenth-century European aesthetics on his own. Stegner remarks that this area, "the Plateau Province," required a new geology and "new aesthetic perceptions" (1954, 164).

Educated men might assign the Arizona landscape to an existing category of experience; others had to devise a vocabulary to express their feelings. In his youth, John B. Fletcher saw a two-thousand mile stretch of the high plains east of the Rockies while helping drive cattle from Texas to Montana in 1879. Fletcher recalled the joy of leaving settled south Texas for the "uninhabited wilderness" northwards: "no more lanes, no more obstructing fences, but one grand expanse of free grass," that is, "free from all the restraints and annoyances of civilization" (J. Fletcher 29, 31). Naïve sources, with no agenda beyond telling what they saw and felt, represent primary data at its purest, which may contradict but often dovetails with formal aesthetics; liberty had been an attribute of the Great since 1712. Yet the "monotony" and silence of the treeless plains grew "oppressive," and when the Rockies appeared on the horizon, a hundred miles west, "I feasted my eyes for several days on the backbone of America" (103-04, 60).

Robert Louis Stevenson took the railroad from New York to California that same summer. The well-educated Stevenson was a self-aware traveller ("Out of my country and myself I go") and reporter, but not an aesthete. "I travel for travel's sake," he wrote, "to come down off this feather-bed of civilization, and find the globe granite underfoot and strewn with cutting flints" (R.L. Stevenson 1912, 63), a mood shared by Whitman and Muir. In 1892 Stevenson published a memoir of his journey "Across the Plains." Ohio gave him "long aerial vistas" over a "flat paradise" (Stevenson 1966, 108-9). In Nebraska, where he felt "at sea," his reactions grew complex: the train was like a snail on an "infinity" of green plain; then it seemed "huge," and he himself (surprisingly) "a great thing in that emptiness." Stevenson contrasts his "exhilaration in this spacious vacancy" with the reactions of the first settlers, imagining how the pioneer's eye "quails before so vast an outlook" (123-4) - the more traditional response to encountering great space.

Nebraska eventually makes him homesick for mountains, but the Black Hills seem "sad," and the Rockies equal them in "misery of aspect." After the "grandeur" of the plains, "mountain gloom" is all he feels there (R.L. Stevenson 1966, 127). His sensitivity to landscape perhaps heightened by illness, Stevenson finds the long canyons "sterile," "deadly," and "horrible." This might be the deprivation of long vistas, yet when Nevada opens, it is only "deserts ... horrible to man" (128-9, 144), and he greets the mountains of California with joy and relief. What Stevenson appreciates, then, is arable sweep; both barren desolation and close-ups of contorted rocks horrify him.

Others stopped, however, and found the desert interesting. In 1888, young Mary Hunter, brought up on Keats, Shelley, Ruskin, Poe, Emerson, and Melville - authors central to the literary expression of the Great - moved with her family from Illinois to the arid Tejon district of southern California. There and in the Owens Valley after her marriage, Mary H. Austin gained the knowledge of and feeling for the desert that she turned into an essay, "A Land of Little Rain," and a book, *The Land of Little Rain* (1903), considered a classic of American nature writing. Both convey a keen sense of what is *not* there, of absences and limitations. The desert ("land that supports no man") is a "Country of Lost Borders" and a "land of lost rivers" as well as of little rain. Austin confirms Powell's main point: "Not the law, but the land sets the limit" (Austin 1903, 3). Hardly able to sustain life, it is "the loneliest land that ever came out of God's hands" (16). As in Doughty, the reader starts to wonder why anyone stays.

Austin tackles the question head on, giving many examples of how far a little can go, of the desert's rewards and secrets. This is country "with little in it to love; yet a land that once visited must be come back to inevitably" (Austin 1903, 6). It seizes your affections: you mean to leave but don't, or curse it and return. Salty Williams came back to the Death Valley-Mohave run, ninety miles of salt desert lined with graves, because "The land had called him" (19). But whence this power? To start with, its air is the cleanest, most divine on earth, and above that is the great sweep of the heavens; at night the stars "make the poor world-fret of no account" (Austin 1996, 38). This note was often heard in the seventeenth and eighteenth centuries, when telescopes, Galileo, and Newton made astronomy an adjunct of religion. In the desert, says Austin, you feel that awe nightly, and also discover that the "lifeless" desolation around actually supports a number of remarkably adapted life forms.

Yet this is only the start of a desert education: one must learn, from nature or the natives, its ambiguities. Southeast from the Sierra Nevada stretches "a lonely, inhospitable land, beautiful, terrible" (Austin 1903, 68). Travellers to the Great had used oxymoron for centuries, but Austin moves beyond that. Among the "broken ranges" and "pure desertness" of the Shoshone lands she finds "room enough and time enough" for spirituality (86-7). Her sonorous style becomes more Biblical here; these deserts lie "eastward from Eden" and give an idea of heaven (90). "Somehow the rawness of the land favors the sense of personal relation to

the supernatural" might be Melville writing about Judaea, but the
idea that "a certain indifference, blankness, emptiness" in the land
gives us "the courage to sheer off what is not worthwhile" sounds
more like a minimalist or a desert father (120-1). Though the land
is her protagonist, "the physical environment" is not her "primary
reality," notes Buell (80-1), for she is a transcendentalist.

   The Land of Little Rain is, in fact, a remarkably pious book for a
woman who wrote about religion humanistically ("The Man Jesus,"
1915) and made a career of social and political advocacy. The mesa's
"treeless spaces uncramp the soul" (Austin 1903, 144). And what
then? Austin's religion was personal, a blend of natural science,
Shoshone spirituality, and Christianity. In the mountains bordering
the desert, she saw canyons "scored out by the glacier ploughs of
God" - lacking everything but "beauty and madness and death and
God" - and the "pure bleak beauty" of granite cliffs (183-4, 187).
They are "high altars," and their pines "tall priests" (191); most
of her overt religious allusions are to mountains. Weather is "the
visible manifestation of the Spirit moving itself in the void" (247).

   Meeting John Muir, Robinson Jeffers, and other writers in
Carmel from 1904 onwards, Austin became an environmentalist.
She opposed Los Angeles's plans to use the Owens River as its own
aqueduct, exposed mismanagement on government lands (attracting
Pres. Roosevelt's attention), and fought Hoover Dam. Later, in
London and New York, she met more writers and her interests
broadened, but she finally settled in Santa Fe, produced another
desert book, *The Land of Journey's Ending*, and her autobiography,
Earth's Horizon. Indeed, some think that she never really left the
desert, which, wrote John Farrar, "made her life articulate. It has
never failed her since nor freed her" (Austin 1996, 17). Reuben Ellis,
detecting a sneer hidden in this view, argues that her socialist and
feminist "vision was rooted in her sense of the western American
landscape" and the "spiritual process of discovery" involved in
adapting to it (Austin 1996, 4). Austin put it this way: "Man is not
himself only .... He is all that he sees ... he takes it in and gives it
forth again ... as a prevailing tone of thought" (1996, 12).

DEATHS IN THE DESERT

The harsh face of French military conquest in North Africa was
somewhat softened by the passions, sacred and profane, stirred by

the desert in the breasts of civilians. Actually Charles, Vicomte de Foucauld, first went to Algeria as a soldier, one so dissolute that he was broken for misconduct. Years later he settled in the Sahara as a priest and began the martyr's career that caught T.S. Eliot's attention. Foucauld re-enacted the archetypal Christian paradigm of the sinner who emerges from moral night to holy day, as well as the broader myth of the privileged man who renounces all for the spiritual life (Buddha).

Foucauld's whole life pointed towards a home in the desert. As a young orphan, he loved the quiet peace of his grandfather's woods. Losing his faith early, despite (or because of) his Jesuit preparatory school, he went to military academy, still fond of solitude. In his second year, his grandfather died and he fell apart, losing his stripes and finishing low in his class. He also inherited his fortune, which made little difference to his career. At cavalry school he was idle and dissipated, not yet having found "liberation in the immensity and the austerity of the desert and in a life of the spirit bound up with the desert both as a place and as a symbol" (Hamilton 40-1). Barely graduating, Foucauld kept a mistress, whom he took along when posted to Algeria. He could not bear army discipline but, fascinated by North Africa, resigned to explore it. Posing as a Jewish doctor, possibly spying as well as map-making, he was greatly impressed by the Atlas Mountains. Returning to France, Foucauld wrote and published *Reconnaissance au Maroc* (1888).

The book was well received, but its author kept searching. In 1886, Foucauld (re)accepted Catholicism and was seen sleeping on the floor of a Paris apartment in his *burnous*. Interested in the desert fathers, he visited the Holy Land; then became a Trappist monk at Notre Dame des Neiges (the highest, coldest monastery in France) and later in Syria. Yet the Trappists were not poor or austere enough for him; "striving towards the infinite," he wanted to be a priest (Hamilton 111), so left the order and went to Nazareth to prepare himself. His meditation on Luke 4.12, the Temptation in the Wilderness, has Jesus say, "on est plus tenté au désert qu'ailleurs"[2]: a pertinent remark in view of his later career. In 1899, still at Nazareth, he urges that we attach no importance to the transitory things of this life. If we see in the light of faith, we are lifted up "en plein soleil, ... dans un calme serein, dans un

---

[2] 'One is more tempted in the desert than elsewhere': 1966, 97.

paix lumineuse" without stormclouds.[3] Foucauld was ready for the desert.

Ordained in 1901, he went to Beni-Abbès, an oasis on the Algeria-Morocco frontier, ministered to the French garrison, and built a hermitage commanding long horizons. "*A hermit ought to stay in the desert,*" Foucauld had emphasized (1964, 132). There he looked for the silent solitude that the desert fathers had found. In 1903, however, after talking with Major Laperrine about the Tuareg people of the deep Sahara, Foucauld felt called there. He made an exploratory trip to study the language and the nomads. Thereafter he gradually shifted his base to Tamanrasset in the Hoggar district. This was almost the place, yet "only by looking out beyond this world" can we find "true joy" and satisfy our spiritual thirst,[4] and the town of Tamanrasset was still "the world." Subsequently he built a hermitage at Asekrem, 35 miles away on top of a 7800-foot mountain, near a nomad encampment. Into this austere, primeval, lonely place, "une bien belle solitude," Foucauld moved in 1911 and remained for the rest of his life: the early apostle *redivivus*.

And what did Frère Charles find on his mountain? He had said that it was good to live alone in the land and return to "Christian simplicity."[5] Busy with his ministry and meditations, Foucauld wrote relatively little that has survived from the Asekrem years, as if, having at last come to the place, he need not discuss it with "the world." A biographer notes his affinity with the desert as "a symbol of the spiritual solitude in which the soul communes with its Creator," citing his thoughts on Psalm 104 ("God leads us into the desert, where he feeds us on celestial food") and his echo of St John of the Cross, that the desert is a "state ... of soul, through which all must pass" (Hamilton 228). T.S. Eliot, drawn to the idea of "a death in the desert," said that Harry in *The Family Reunion* might imitate Foucauld. He would not be alone. A member of a Sahara trek in 1979 took Foucauld's "You must go by way of the desert and live there to receive God's grace" for his epigraph (Woodrow): the

---

[3]   'In full sunlight, ... in a serene calm, in a luminous peace': 1966, 143.

[4]   1964, 169. In the original: "Ce n'est qu'en regardant au-delà de ce monde ... qu'est la vraie joie dans l'espérance d'une autre vie dont celle-ci n'est que le prélude; ... ou la lumière, le vérité, l'amour dont ont soif nos esprits et nos coeurs, seront pleinement et éternellement satisfaits" (1966, 193).

[5]   1964, 173, 188; 1966, 196, 210.

adventure tourist as pilgrim. The thinkers, then the tourists, said Hardy.

At the other pole from his asceticism stands Isabelle Eberhardt's life-long affair with the Sahara. The natural daughter of Russian emigrés in Geneva, she became interested in desert life as she studied Arabic and read "eastern" novels, especially those of Pierre Loti.[6] "I was already a nomad as a young girl," she wrote (Kobak 17). Influenced by her father/tutor (of Turkish-Armenian descent), Eberhardt grew up considering herself a Muslim, and often dressed as a boy. Two of her brothers ran off to join the French Foreign Legion in Algeria, firing her imagination. A romantic anarchist, she hoped to find happiness with "simple people" in "the vast spaces of the desert," and began to write, publishing her first story at 18 (28). In 1897 she and her mother moved to Bône, Algeria; after her mother died, Isabelle went south to the Sahara, where she sometimes lived until killed by a flash flood in 1904. Usually attired as a man, "Mahmoud Saadi," she had many (male) Arab lovers, one of whom she married: a Muslim Algerian *spahi* (French soldier) and fellow-member of a mystical Sufi order.

Meanwhile she wrote novels and sensitive vignettes, some of which have been translated as *Prisoner of Dunes* (1995). A strong need to know what was over the horizon made Eberhardt declare that running away is an act of courage and "vagrancy is emancipation" (17-18). Emancipation from what? From the bonds of modern life, she says. But we should travel poor, so as not to be weighed down by material goods, and alone, for "true freedom depends on solitude" (17). In theory it does not matter where we go; in practice Eberhardt was strongly attracted to the "melancholy charm" of "the magnificent, mournful Sahara" (33). The desert's "mysterious [or "inchoate"] sadness" was part of its appeal: one reason that she "loves" it (74, 90, 91). This dark turn of mind seems to date particularly from her mother's death, which brought both sadness and anger.

---

[6] She knew at least *Aziyade* (1879) and *Le Roman d'un Spahi* (1881). Several of his other novels have "oriental" settings and disguise motifs. His travel books are also relevant here: *Au Maroc* (1889), *Le Désert* (1895), narrating a camel-ride across the Sinai, *Vers Ispahan* (1904, travels in Persia), etc. Loti was a popular writer; *Le Désert* influenced John C. Van Dyke's book about the American southwest, *The Desert* (1901), itself very influential. See Kobak 26-7.

Like other expatriates of that time, Eberhardt found that the rapid changes and "sterile tumult" of Europe died away in the "great, immutable silence" of the desert, an "archaic, ageless landscape"; the "harsher and wilder" the terrain, the greater her joy (92, 46, 65, 44). After all, the Beduin herdsman praying towards "splendid desert horizons" is "superior to the pseudo-intellectual" of the north (123-4: Eberhardt loved Rousseau). On her many crossings, the Mediterranean reminded her of the Sahara's space, and she felt like a homesick exile. "O Sahara," she cries, "hiding your beautiful, grave soul under your bleak, desolate emptiness" (Kobak 128). Just how she became "attached to" something "violent" and "too bare" is not explained, but no other place has so "captivated" her (Eberhardt 73). To write about the desert, though, she must leave, for its lulling voice, favourable to meditation and the blessed "annihilation of ego," is sterile creatively as well as botanically (93).

Two themes of Eberhardt's life and work have particular interest here. One is *le néant* or "the Void," a recurrent preoccupation of late nineteenth-century French poets. In 1896, a Tunisian correspondent wrote her that science leaves us with only *le néant*. When Isabelle made her own analysis ("l'Age du néant," 1900), however, she blamed not science but modern society (Kobak 46, 102-3). Like Foucauld, she reacted to the sense of personal void by going to the largest topographical void she could reach. And she went there as a minimalist, "interested in fulfilment through reduction"; she would isolate herself, she wrote, and "put into practice my theory of diminishing my needs as much as possible" (122-3). It is a Wordsworthian strain, the world too much with us, crossed with *fin de siècle* disgust at decadent materialism - things as Void - and carried to its logical conclusion by a primitivist. The flood waters of Ain Sefra robbed us of what might have been an interesting modernist voice.

UPROOTED

By the end of the nineteenth century, improvements in modes of transport, more flexible social structures in Europe, and in some cases imperial concerns were encouraging more travellers and diversifying their itineraries. Many showed a penchant for Great venues: in W.H. Hudson's case, the spacious horizons of South America's pampas.

Hudson grew up on an Argentine sheep ranch. In *Idle Days in Patagonia* (1893), an extended inquiry into the "strange feelings" that the "unmarred desert" of Argentina awakened in him, Hudson asks repeatedly why empty plains have such a strong and lasting appeal (1979, 4). Their "ancient quiet" and "peace, untouched by man" are sweet, the feeling of "absolute freedom" in a "vast solitude" is delightful, and the pure air is healthy (4, 6-7). Still, he wonders why he misses these scenes, and how they please. In "Plains of Patagonia," confessing that he was often drawn to a "barren plateau … stretching away into infinitude" (with "nothing to delight the eye") "as if to a festival," he can say only that nature moves us more deeply in such a place than elsewhere (204-6). At times Hudson saw "old ocean-washed pebbles" there, giving the sense of great geological time-spans that struck Darwin. In that huge silence he reverted to a "primitive" mental state that produced "elation" (210, 215). As infinite as the sea, as ancient and desolate as the desert, Patagonia sounded what Jack London would soon term "the call of the wild." And, Hudson insists, something in us answers.

Gertrude Bell - the fourth remarkable woman in the desert literature of this period - seems to have been born to travel, learn languages, enjoy people of other cultures, and write books about her experiences. From her first summer in Europe at the age of 18 she wanted to see the world, and her family were well off, so time and means were never lacking. Graduating from Oxford with a First in Modern History, Bell toured Bucharest, Paris, and Istanbul, but found her vocation while visiting relatives in Teheran, studying Farsi, and riding about the countryside (1892). She also became engaged to an Englishman there, whose early death generated the travel-as-sublimation theory of her life.

From that trip came a translation of classical Persian poetry and a travel book. If *Safar Nameh. Persian Pictures* (1894) is fragmentary and rather slight, it is also finely written, with a saving light touch. Bell knows that she has only *excursions* to chronicle, yet narrates them so sensitively that readers are charmed, not minding that this young woman presumes to speak for them, and hardly noticing that she tells fellow-tourists, "your presence is a blot on the wild surroundings, a hint of desecration" (1928, 76). Go home, she says; you do not belong here (advice she never took, becoming, ironically, a servant of empire). Bell knows the attractions of wandering - "the great free sunlight," the "boundless plain," even "the cold kisses of the wind that flies before the dawn" - but farther afield, on bare tableland encircled by mountains, she is horrified by the loneliness and silent desolation (69-70). "We are not accustomed to finding ourselves face to face with nature" of this kind, she realizes: "here there is nothing" (72). Still, as we are only "playing at nomads, after all," we then go home (75-6).

Bell continued to travel, and took up mountain-climbing. She voyaged around the world; then focused on the Mideast, studying languages in Jerusalem and riding into desert Syria (1899-1900), apparently wanting more of the "nothing" that had repelled her at first. On her second round-the-world trip, the "wild, desolate" Khyber Pass seemed "a wonderful thing" (Burgoyne 1:149). A three-month ride led to another book, *Syria: The Desert and the Sown* (1907), a title taken from Fitzgerald's *Omar Khayyam*. The nomads were the great attraction (hearing the gossip of the desert again, she "wept for joy"), but Bell also responds to the changing face of the land. Though the Jordan valley feels bare and inhuman, east of the mountains of Moab the great undulant plains open out: "swell and fall, fall and swell, as though the desert breathed quietly under the gathering night" (Bell 1907, 37). On a misty dawn it is beautiful, "like waking in the heart of an opal." Nor is this, for the Arabs, an empty, desolate wilderness, but rather a home. "See the desert on a fine morning and die – if you can," she counsels (60, 64).

Between trips Bell would return to England (where important people would ask her political questions about the Middle East), but soon she would set off again, being "a vagabond, happier on the road than anywhere else" (Burgoyne 1:242). In Egypt, she met Lady Anne Blunt and admired the landscape. *Amurath to Amurath* (1911) recounts another long ride through Syria and Asia Minor. By the time it appeared she was riding from Damascus to the Euphrates, a two-week trip. "I loved it all," she wrote: the people, the land (Burgoyne 1:276). Having become interested in archeology, Bell visited the excavation at Carchemish, meeting young T.E. Lawrence there. She had also fallen in love with a married man, Maj. Doughty-Wylie, Charles Doughty's nephew. This untenable situation made her want to flee and take the road again. An Arabian trip seemed politically possible, yet she started for Hayil in 1913 without government protection (like Doughty), keeping a diary and letter-journal for Doughty-Wylie. The war broke out before she could write a book about the trip; the journals were not published until 2000.

They reveal that she had by then somehow largely assimilated the nothingness that had appalled her at first. It was not pretty or pleasant land, not to be romanticized: Arabia Petraea looked "terrible from without," flint desert was "bare and forbidding," Nejd seemed "terrifying in its desolation," and Syria was "weary dull desert" (Bell 2000, 44, 51, 77, 113). Yet there were moments when her responses surprised her. Climbing a hill gave a "glorious view" of sand desert, volcanic cliffs, and arid hills. "I wonder why one takes pleasure in such a landscape," she muses, "but the fact remains that one does" (52-3; Addison, Burke, and Hardy had addressed just this point). Bell keeps returning to the idea: an "incredible desolation," she notes, "sets its seal upon you, for good or ill," and will change the traveller. She herself was in good spirits. "In spite of the desolation and the emptiness, it is beautiful - or is it beautiful partly because of the emptiness?" she asks, and does not answer, only adding, "At any rate, I love it" (65).

She reached Hayil using *Arabia Deserta*'s map and feeling like a pilgrim to a Doughty shrine. Detained there, then sent away without seeing the Amir, Bell rode up to Baghdad and across to Damascus again. At first, near the Euphrates, it was grassy, not desertic; still, "it is out under the open sky again and at once my heart leaps to it" (Bell 2000, 110). When genuine desert came later, she was ready, writing "I like the *khala*," the emptiness (123). Safely in Damascus, she penned a valediction to the wasteland: "I must try to forget it for a little … it looms too big, out of all proportion to the world, and too dark, unbelievably menacing." The power could not be denied: "I can't forget it yet" (133). The *khala* had set its seal upon her.

After receiving the Royal Geographical Society's medal for her "last and greatest journey," losing Doughty-Wylie at Gallipoli, and doing war work in Cairo, she settled in Iraq and became part of the "Official East," despite doubts about conveying Europe's broken civilization to the Arabs (Burgoyne 2:13, 48).

The motives of desert travellers were almost as various as they themselves. Sven Hedin grew up reading Fenimore Cooper, Jules Verne, and tales of Arctic and African adventure. At 15 he witnessed Nordenskiöld's triumphant return to Stockholm after making the Northeast Passage and was hooked; at 20 a tutorship in Baku on the Caspian Sea pointed him in the direction of his own destiny. The book titles - *Through Asia, A Conquest of Tibet, Across the Gobi Desert, My Life as an Explorer* - tell the rest. Hedin was drawn to wild, unmapped country in general: deserts, old style. When he mentions motive, it is to acknowledge an instinctive love of "endless wilderness," a *"desiderium incogniti"* (lust for the unknown), and an ambition to be the first European to see vast tracts of Asia and do "geographical research" (Hedin 1991, 5, 118, 176). When, after an unusually long stay in Stockholm (1902-05), "the desert winds lured [him]" back, that means blank spaces on the map of Tibet (332). He rarely records an aesthetic reaction to geographical deserts, reserving his lyrical flights for the mountains.

Alongside Sven the Indefatigable (who gained the support of the King of Sweden, the Tsar of Russia, and Emanuel Nobel), most other travellers look tame. Arthur Weigall, Inspector-General of Upper Egypt, (British) Department of Antiquities, was no explorer; most of his *Travels in the Upper Egyptian Deserts* (1913) were made over Roman roads. But Weigall loved that austere, empty landscape, seeing its "beauty" and missing its "splendour" as he wrote (27). The solitude and silence, such as one might find on the moon, awed him, especially at sunset, when the desert was "magnificent" (11, 105). Roman ruins were time machines, dissolving the present and carrying him back two thousand years: "but an hour" in earth history (130). "Only those who have travelled in the desert can understand the joy" of being where "there are no cares ... no fretfulness," and, he adds, with a touch of misanthropy, "no irritation, for man, the arch-irritant, is absent" (150). Like most Edwardian travellers, Weigall knew his *Omar Khayyam*, and declared that "the wilderness is indeed Paradise ... here one may find true happiness" (166).

Norman Douglas is a more problematical writer, preserving some colonial attitudes - anti-Arab, anti-Muslim - for posterity, but *Fountains in the Sand* (1912) also conveys detailed impressions of the Tunisian edge of the Sahara. At first Douglas seems to dislike the desert, but this response gradually evolves. Even from the train its colours and vastness are worth evoking, and at sunset the scene is magical: particularly if you are smoking *kif* (N. Douglas 73, 26). Dawn can have a spiritual quality that promotes religion or myth. Later he sees an analogy with another Great landscape: the northern tundra, with palms and sand instead of firs and snow. But Douglas is most interesting when, seeing the "hostile face" of the *chotts* (salt lakes), he admits that "There is a charm, none the less - a charm that appeals to complex modern minds - in that picture of eternal, irremediable sterility" (118): very nearly what Hardy says of Egdon Heath. Douglas finds a "deep peace" in seeing the *chotts* "stretching into infinity," and opines that "man disencumbers himself" here, "discarding much that seems inconsiderable" (129).

This minimalist note brings us back to Doughty and the theme of disencumbrance. What is most striking about the desert literature of this period is how quickly and variously it burgeoned, moving from marginal to mainstream around the turn of the century. Along the road *to* Egdon Heath were found few who sought out and fewer who appreciated deserts; most early visitors (Burton and Fromentin were notable exceptions) repeated Biblical expressions of disapproval or horror. Beginning with Melville, Powell, and Doughty in the 1870s, however, a succession of western travellers described deserts in terms compatible with the aesthetic category of the Great descending from Addison. The words shift somewhat - there is less of "the sublime," and more melancholy - but we hear enough of awe, grandeur, and vast solitudes to recognize the lineage.

What caused this phenomenon? Improved transportation may have helped, but does not by itself explain the changing attitudes; more people *might* have come with the old views, and some notable desert travellers - Doughty, the Blunts, Bell, Hedin - made a point of avoiding modern transport. The travellers themselves give answers in trying to explain the appeal of the desert. One, we have seen, was minimalism: the urge to simplify and focus a cluttered existence. Another was the desire to escape overcrowding at home, first voiced by Richard Burton and Leslie Stephen in the 1850s and 1860s. As Europe and North America filled up, more found the desert's emptiness attractive. Some also found a religion there that they did not find (or live) at home. It might be a place to practice Christianity more intensely (Foucauld); a kind of substitute for orthodox Christianity, such as we sense in Doughty; or a non-Christian sense of being in touch with the earth and its indigenous peoples, as in Austin and Bell. The desert served as a *tabula rasa* upon which they could write what they needed.

2
Mind Has Mountains

> O the mind, mind has mountains; cliffs of fall
> Frightful, sheer, no-man-fathomed. Hold them cheap
> May who ne'er hung there.

G.M. Hopkins, Sonnet 42

Metaphorical mountains are at least as old as Dante's *Purgatorio*, and though by Hopkins's time a century's worth of literature about real mountains had accumulated, their referential meanings were always available. Whether a mountaineer chose to make those metaphors central, hint at them occasionally à la Leslie Stephen, or studiously ignore them, he could be sure that most readers understood what mountains meant, or could mean. Non-climbing mountain writers such as John Ruskin or Guy De Maupassant usually dealt more with symbols or qualities than with facts, while climbers were apt to operate toward the other end of the spectrum. *National* generalizations are hazardous, here as elsewhere; the major natural categories consist of writers on Europe's well-known mountains, and those introducing readers to new ranges in Asia and the Americas.

Several of the major English mountain writers treated in *The Road to Egdon Heath* were still active, though less important.[1] John Ruskin, whose *Modern Painters* (1843-56) had contributed substantially to the aesthetic philosophy of mountains as spiritual entities, fought against the evolutionary thrust of Victorian science. In *Deucalion* (1875-83), a diverse collection of lectures and articles

---

[1] Ruskin is discussed in chs. 11, 12, and 19 of *The Road to Egdon Heath*; Stephen in chs. 15 and 19; and Whymper in ch. 19.

on geology, glaciology, mountaineering, et cetera, he attacks some of the major scientists and climbers of the day: Charles Lyell for his doctrine of "continuing creation," John Tyndall (and by implication Louis Agassiz) for their theories of glacial flow, Leslie Stephen for encouraging an athletic approach to the Alps. Ruskin, nostalgic for de Saussure, Humboldt, Forbes - the reverent and revered sages of his youth - re-issued the geological material from *Modern Painters* as *In Montibus Sanctis* (1884), reminding his public that the Alps were still holy, whatever heretics might say or do.

Edward Whymper, a conqueror of the Matterhorn and the leading English Alpinist of his day, turned to Greenland and then to the Andes, devoting ten months in 1879-80 to Ecuador. He made many first ascents, described in *Travels Amongst the Great Andes of the Equator* (1892). Any hopes that the reticent Whymper of *Scrambles Among the Alps* (1871) might have become more expressive are dashed. He says in his introduction that "the main object of the journey was to observe the effects of low pressure" at high altitude. His modern editor, Loren McIntyre, believes that "zest for high adventure" was "his chief motivation," but admits that "Whymper did not own up" to it (Introduction to the 1987 edition). Without a fatal accident to move him (as on the Matterhorn), Whymper keeps his feelings to himself, other than distaste for Andean Ecuador as a primitive, storm-swept place. He did not like the *paramo*, a "bleak, uncultivated moorland" (the elevated equivalent of Egdon Heath) "which it would be too complimentary to term a howling wilderness" (Whymper 386). His prevailing mood is dyspeptic; he may have been suffering from the altitude sickness that he had come to study.

Leslie Stephen, by 1890 past his own climbing days and writing less about mountains, still kept up. His 1894 review of *Climbing in the Karakoram - Himalayas* by W.M. Conway seems to pass the torch, with some doubts, to the next generation. The romance of early Alpine climbing, a creation of de Saussure, Rousseau, Byron, Forbes, and Ruskin, has gone, he writes; now they are for tourists, so Conway has found himself a new, larger sphere of action. Stephen sounds half-jocular, as usual, though his preference for day hikes in the semi-civilized Alps over campaigns in the savage Himalayas or Rockies seems sincere. These raw new ranges, unsoftened by culture, suggest "the deathly solitudes of the moon"; he is sure that he would find their "huge, frigid images of death" monstrous, not sublime. Give me Land's End, not the "appalling ... solitudes of the mid-ocean," says Stephen (shifting momentarily to another area of the Great), give me "the eternal Alps" (211-12). To an aging climber, the Alps felt comfortably familiar, and Asia's untamed peaks lay beyond the pale of his inherited aesthetic.

GOING HOME: JOHN OF THE MOUNTAINS

The most famous American mountaineer of the period, John Muir, loving mountains equally as facts and as symbols, combined science, religion, and poetry in his approach. A strong, agile, daring climber, schooled in geology and glaciology, he wrote eloquently about all aspects of wild nature. Muir, like Doughty, seems to support Hardy's thesis that moderns are drawn to deserts and mountains; arriving in San Francisco for the first time, he asked directions to the Sierra Nevada and started walking. Yet no one could be farther from Hardy's "*chastened* sublimity," the quiet of Egdon Heath, the vaguely post-Christian ethos. Joy, excitement, and a deep reverence for God's creation pervade all that Muir wrote about wilderness, the only gloom arising from human depredations. He had none of the trouble others had in reconciling religious feeling with nature and science. To him, Lyell's "continuing creation" meant that God was still with us; faulting and glaciers were simply divine tools.[2]

Muir's career had a Platonic curve, from a physically active youth to a literary and political maturity. His major writings date from the 1890s, two decades after his Sierra adventures began. Emigrating from Scotland with his family as a boy, he grew up in Wisconsin under the thumb of a tyrannical, fundamentalist-Presbyterian father who believed that nature was evil. Few men can have failed so utterly to indoctrinate their children in their ideas. At the University of Wisconsin, Muir studied classics and natural science, read Wordsworth, Thoreau, Emerson, Humboldt, Darwin, and Agassiz, but left early for the "university of the wilderness." This included a *Thousand-Mile Walk to the Gulf* (as he titled his journal), and voyages to Cuba, New York (where he did not even disembark), and California, henceforth his base. Working his way into the mountains as a sheepherder, Muir built a cabin in Yosemite

---

[2]   Max Oelschlaeger writes that Muir came to equate nature with divinity (182) and developed a "wilderness theology" (192).

Valley (1869) and began the journals that formed the basis of his books.

He soon became known as a solo mountaineer, a field geologist, and a philosophical resident of Yosemite. Joseph Leconte, a geology professor at Berkeley, visited Muir in 1870 (they agreed on the glaciation of the Sierras) and Ralph Waldo Emerson came to call in 1871. Muir was disappointed that the elderly sage would not camp with him; he felt that Emerson and Thoreau were not as excited by wild nature as they should be. Muir continued to explore the region and revel in the wholeness of his life. The letter called "Prayers in Higher Mountain Temples, or a Geologist's Winter Walk," dates from 1873; like Doughty, Muir could be called a "spiritual geologist." He described himself as "hopelessly and forever a mountaineer" in 1874, but that soon changed (Ewart 5). The damage being done to mountains and forests by "hoofed locusts" (sheep) and lumbermen horrified him, and in 1875 he began to advocate protection: the cause that occupied the rest of his life.

It is here, when Muir's articles and meetings with lawmakers begin, that efforts to shelter wild nature from human depredation enter this story. There are precedents in the fears of some European climbers that the Alps were becoming crowded and overdeveloped, but in America, where there was more unspoiled country and the developers were less restrained by law or custom, the issues were even graver. Muir argued for parks to save the Sierras, as Yellowstone had been protected in 1872; the Yosemite Act was passed in 1890. He founded the Sierra Club (1892) and served as its president until his death. America's conservation movement soon split between "wise use" and strict preservation. Muir was at first willing to admit some forestry, but in 1896 he lost faith in the good will of the other side and became a preservationist (Nash 1982, 129-38). Guiding President Roosevelt around Yosemite in 1902, Muir lobbied for new or larger parks in the Sierra and the Grand Canyon.

What does all this have to do with the aesthetics of nature? The expansion of mechanized western society in the later nineteenth century had begun to change the terms of aesthetic discourse by affecting the web of ideas associated with natural beauty. Technological advances, industrialization, and growing populations could be seen impinging on some areas of the Great, starting with the more accessible mountain ranges. Vestigial ideas that a quasi-divine entity, Nature, stood above and beyond human interference were being undermined in Hardy's time as farms and fences cut into real-world heaths, and forests fell. In Muir, damage and loss first emerge as themes in the work of a major nature writer. One aesthetic aspect of this phenomenon is clearly expressed in Keats's "Ode on Melancholy" (1819). "Ay, in the very temple of Delight / Veil'd Melancholy has her sovran shrine," he wrote; "She dwells with Beauty - Beauty that must die." Gloom had been a fairly common response to Great landscapes before Hardy; now the perception of their vulnerability gave a new, more objective reason for melancholy.

In connection with the struggle to gain support for wild nature, Muir was persuaded to come down from the Sierras - a major sacrifice for a man who felt that "going to the mountains is going home" - and write books such as *The Mountains of California* (1894), *My First Summer in the Sierra* (1911), and *The Yosemite* (1912). His Alaska writings, *The Cruise of the* Corwin (1881) and *Travels in Alaska* (1915), also attack the abusers of wilderness. Since his death, Muir's growing status as a cult figure has brought forth a succession of more or less hagiographic biographies, theses, collections, and new publications: *Steep Trails*; *John of the Mountains: Unpublished Journals of John Muir*; *John Muir's Views of Nature*; *Sacred Summits: John Muir's Greatest Climbs*, and so on.

Two aspects of Muir's work are especially notable: his euphoria (despite many incentives to gloom), and the consistency of outlook from work to work. He is much of a piece throughout. In his 1869 journal, Muir already loves whatever is wild and natural: the "serene beauty" and peace of a "majestic landscape," the "spiritually fine" light that clothes the mountains, the sense that "everything is flowing."[3] Some critics have found an oriental cast, even a touch of Zen, in such remarks - an interest Muir might have acquired from the New England Transcendentalists..But his sense of the oneness of things is firmly grounded in knowledge of the natural sciences and in classical and Christian beliefs about an orderly cosmos. Atop Mt. Dana, he can see the "unity" of this "Godful wilderness" (Muir 1997, 9-10). On Cathedral Peak in the "Sierra Cathedral," he is "at church" for the first time in California, with mountains for altars, his surroundings as "wild as the sky and as pure" (12, 19, 21). Here, nature is still divine.

---

[3]   Muir 1997, 4-6. The influence of Thomas Carlyle is likely. The journal
       was revised for publication in 1911.

At the end of his career, forty-five years later, the Muir of *Travels in Alaska* is clearly the same witness, sensing a "harmony" beneath the "bewildering variety" of the Inland Passage's scenery, a path to paradise (1979b, 14, 16). He recalls the Sierra Nevada's light as "pure spiritual essence," but Alaska's mountains are also "the word of God" and part of "Nature's Bible" (42, 57). Muir was a Deist (without its agnostic connotations), devoutly reading Nature as God's words and music. The Sierra felt as "holy as Sinai"; and the Fairweather Range, "ineffably chaste and spiritual," towers over an "icy wilderness unspeakably pure and sublime" (Muir 1979a, 92; 1979b, 149). Ignoring physical discomfort to camp alone on a glacier's "silent icy prairie," Muir remains the eager, pious iron man of science who kept the Sierra journals.

Given this homogeneity, we can take Muir's aesthetic palette as a whole, though different works are variously shaded. He uses many of the same basic colours as other writers on the Great, but tends to emphasize the more reverent and positive emotions. That mountains, and wild nature in general, are spiritual and holy is his leading theme. "Prayers in Higher Mountain Temples" finds God's "words of love" in every part of these "mighty temples of power" (Muir 1997, 61). "God's glacial-mills" ground the Sierras into their "predestined" forms, whose darkest sections are illumined with "bright passages of love" (Muir 1977, 55, 57; 1962, 147). Like Thomas Carlyle, Muir saw nature as the garb of Spirit. Cruising Arctic coastal waters on a calm, clear summer day, he finds that "God's love is manifest in the landscape as in a face" (Muir 1974, 51).

Three qualities often mentioned by nineteenth-century Alpine travellers - grandeur, beauty, and sublimity - are also important components of Muir's world-view; in fact, his lavish use of them made him sound old-fashioned by the 1890s. Grandeur (or majesty, or magnificence) was originally such a common attribute of the Great in nature as virtually to define it. Muir tells us repeatedly that Yosemite valley is a revelation of "grand objects" such as El Capitan and Cathedral Peak (1962, 6), though it is only a special case of the prevailing majesty of the Sierras and Alaska's mountains. Nor is it just high peaks that have this attribute: both California's Mono Lake and Siberia's "Plover Bay," a channel to the Bering Sea, are "magnificent" (Muir 1979a, 157; 1974, 87).

The eighteenth-century distinction between beauty and sublimity, also used by some nineteenth-century writers, does not concern Muir, who may find both in the same scene and rarely analyzes them into their factors. Mt. Shasta possesses "sublime beauty" (a phrase that would have puzzled Edmund Burke) and the clouds seen from the summit are "sublime and beautiful" (Muir 1997, 70, 77), as is Half Dome in Yosemite.[4] Mt. Rainier is another composite: at a distance it seems both "awful" (in the old sense, awe-full, a "sublime" trait) and "beautiful," while the view from the summit has "sublimity and grandeur" (Muir 1999, 146, 148). Burke (for whom the sublime was by definition grand) might have asked, if told that the Sierra Nevada has both "beauty and grandeur," which features of the scene had which; and why Siberian mountains viewed over a smooth sea were beautiful rather than sublime (1979a, 205; 1974, 62).

Elsewhere Muir shows an awareness of the old distinction. To call the cliffs of Yosemite "awful in stern majesty, types of permanence, yet associated with beauty of the frailest and most fleeting forms" is to acknowledge that awe and majesty are usually sublime, not beautiful (Muir 1977, 6). And the "sublime whirl of planets around their suns" is exactly how the term was first used (267). What Muir did (most clearly in his journals) was to redefine both adjectives by expanding their meanings towards each other. He can speak of the Inland Passage's "infinite beauty" because it is "God's eternal beauty"; the restriction to small prettiness is not for him (Muir 1979a, 261, 299). As beauty gains in scope, sublimity is domesticated. Burke associated it with fear and awe, while Muir finds "Much that is tranquil and joyous" within the "vast sublimity" of Yosemite valley (51). Thus his beautiful and sublime can share the same landform; a "sublime beauty" is simply a higher, larger beauty than you will find in your garden.

Beyond this group, the frequency of aesthetic responses falls off sharply. Vastness - as in the glaciers' "vast job of rockwork" (Muir 1977, 17) - is mentioned much less often than holiness: spirituality ranks far above size, though Muir enjoyed imagining great expanses of space and time. Awe, an emotion associated with vastness, also appears, usually in the form "awful," which had not yet lost its connotations of "awe." Thus at a pass, "the view is awful - a vast wilderness of rocks and canyons" (Muir 1979a, 179). Muir feels "peculiar awe" among the "mansions of the icy North" (glaciers),

---

[4]   1962, 10. Muir was not the first to discover the valley's sublimity. In 1865, Sam Bowles called it "grand," "majestic," and "sublime." Albert Bierstadt's painting "Looking Down Yosemite Valley" in the same year shows it as a portal to radiant glory.

which is "the natural effect of appreciable manifestations of the presence of God" (1979b, 64). No one contradicts the stereotype of the Victorian robbed of faith by science - or Hardy's image of the joyless modern drawn to the barren - as emphatically as John of the Mountains does.

For Muir, the oneness of nature - the ancient idea of cosmos, refined by his geological studies - is as important as awe. His journals show him working out the aesthetics of this credo. "In what is termed awful, ... terrific, ... etc.," he insists, "there is order and tranquillity," and a strong sense of unity in canyons, mountains, trees, flowers: "they are made one, unseparate" (Muir 1979a, 51, 82). On the Inland Passage he sees the "design" within the beauty of the coast, "a finished stanza"; in Glacier Bay he hears the "harmony of the storm" (251, 312). In *The Mountains of California* this theme appears as the "harmonious sequence" within the "eternal flux of nature" as she carves canyons, and the microcosm of a thunderstorm's "big transparent drops, each a small world in itself, - one unbroken ocean without islands hurling free through the air like planets through space" (Muir 1977, 69-70, 132-3).

"Glory" to Muir means not only Ruskin's "mountain glory," but the glory of God felt in wild nature. It is related both to his keen enjoyment of the Great, and to his recognition that wilderness can be severe, like Yosemite's cliffs, "awful in stern majesty." But glorious wildness is threatened by human greed: his version of "mountain gloom." Seeing the "destruction of the forest about Shasta" in 1888, Muir notes that "the glory is departing" (1979a, 289). In the Sierra, loggers join sheep-herders, trail-builders, and (lower down) farmers in an orgy of wastage. "The money-changers were in the temple" reveals the spiritual stakes (1977, 116). The theme of loss, strong in Muir's late writings and near the ends of books, darkens earlier idylls, making them ironic. "The Bee-Pastures" chapter in *The Mountains of California* presents the "sad havoc" *before* closing with his "balmy, dissolving days" in the now-departed Eden (333, 352). Such losses elicit an occasional misanthropic statement, and point directly to his crusade to protect wild lands.

Muir often alludes to geology; like Lyell and many other nineteenth-century geologists, he wanted to "Go and see!" In Alaska he climbed a slope of "calcareous slates," mostly "fossiliferous" (Muir 1974, 132). His forte, though, was glaciology, which he - unlike most scientists - related directly to aesthetics. "The Ancient

Yosemite Glaciers: How the Valley Was Formed" shows that the prehistoric ice-flow, thousands of feet thick, produced today's "sublime relief" (Muir 1962, 131). Any science that teaches the age of the earth sounds the theme of Antiquity. Glaciers ruled Alaska and the north for "unnumbered centuries," writes Muir; their work has lasted tens of thousands of years, helping us visualize the "colossal ice-flood grinding on" for hundreds of thousands of years (1974, 236, 257), and erosive forces have been shaping the Sierras for even longer. Like Darwin in Patagonia, Muir uses geology to bring the earth's innumerable millenia home to our imaginations.

Atop Mt. Shasta, he moves directly from the antiquity of the mountain-building process to its immediacy: the fact that it "is still going on" (1977, 14-15). Geology, by telling of earth's secular changes, introduces the idea that poets call mutability - Lyell's continuing creation. In 1870, Joseph Leconte reported that Muir believed Yosemite to have been "formed by causes still in operation" (Muir 1979a, 35). This evolutionary gospel, which had excited Lyell and Darwin in the 1830s, moved Muir to his most lyrical passages. "We live in 'creation's dawn,'" he wrote as a young man. "The morning stars still sing together, and the world, though made, is still being made and becoming more beautiful every day" (1979a, 72). He repeated this passage almost verbatim *re* the fjords of British Columbia at the end of his life: "the world, though made, is yet being made; ... this is still the morning of creation" (Muir 1979b, 67). The man who should have gone camping with Muir was William Blake.

Most of the other notes that Muir hits in his writings also have precedents in earlier travel literature and aesthetic philosophy. He remembers fondly the silence, solitude, and purity of the wilderness, its power to move us, its freedom and intimations of eternity. Glacier Bay, Mt. Rainier, Lake Tenaya by moonlight: each is "another world," distinct from the mundane. He acknowledged the gloom of some barren areas, usually in a context of "brighter passages" of nature and of feeling joyfully, intensely alive and conscious of God's presence there. Such responses do not significantly alter the larger picture sketched above, dominated by spiritualized grandeur and "sublime beauty." While Muir's Deism and his echoes of Romantic poets connected him with pre-Victorian modes of thought, his geology was quite up to date, and his concern for protecting the environment placed him in the vanguard of a twentieth-century movement.[5]

Muir's contributions to mountain literature tend to overshadow others', but a number of good writers were being drawn to the world's great ranges by then. More and more young climbers warmed up on the Alps in preparation for greater things. As early as 1868, England's Alpine Club arranged an expedition to the Caucasus led by Douglas Freshfield and A.W. Moore, both of whom returned later. Albert Mummery moved on after making some daring Alpine ascents in the 1880s; by the time *My Climbs in the Alps and Caucasus* was published (1895), he was in the Himalayas. Gertrude Bell settled for some exciting climbs in the Alps around 1900, but the tendency was for mountaineers to train there and then leave them to tourists, artists, and the various Alpine Clubs: French, Italian, English Ladies, et cetera.

Mark Twain's *A Tramp Abroad* (1880), narrating his second trip to Europe, gives some idea of what a bright, well-travelled tourist of that time might feel in the Alps. He describes the mountains seen from Lucerne, and sunset from the top of the Righi, conventionally enough as "magnificent" (Twain 190). Most of the book is jokes, but (like his contemporaries, Gilbert and Sullivan) he sometimes slips into unexpectedly lyrical strains. Seeing the Jungfrau at night - that "silent and solemn and awful presence," "a spirit, not an inert mass" - is "meeting the eternal face to face and feeling trivial" (222). Mark Twain?! Romantic poetry, especially Byron's and Shelley's, was one of the lenses through which late-nineteenth-century visitors viewed the Alps. Twain thinks he now understands why people yearn for them, return repeatedly without knowing why, and find "rest and peace" there, "before the visible throne of God" (223). This response, like his apprehension of "sublimity" at Mont

---

[5] Another "old-fashioned" source, the English adventurer Isabella Bird, travelled in the Sierras and Rockies in 1873; *A Lady's Life in the Rocky Mountains* was published serially in 1878 (in book form, 1879). For her too, grandeur, beauty, sublimity, and spirituality were the main feelings associated with great mountains. She lacks the knowledge of geology that enables Muir to see order in landforms, and the sense of loss that made him a conservationist.

Blanc (306), is closer to what one of the Alpine Club's more pious climbers might say than to the satirist's usual mode.

A new climber-writer who emerged in the 1880s, Clinton Dent, described life *Above the Snow Line* (1885), but *Mountaineering* (1892), his collection of articles on its history, craft, and future in which several generations of climbers explain why they do it and how things have changed, had more influence. Published in The Badminton Library of Sports and Pastimes, it reached a 3rd edition in 1901. Dent wrote about half the pieces, mainly technical advice and primers on relevant sciences such as meteorology and geology. Alfred Wills, who made some Alpine first ascents in the 1850s and wrote well about them, notes the "rapid growth of interest" in climbing, but warns that the "playground" (as Leslie Stephen had called the Alps) may become a "field of death" if treated casually (Dent 1901, xviii-xix). Frederick Pollock's "The Early History of Mountaineering" defines it as going to the mountains "for the sake of something that is to be found there," not just passing through. In this sense, it is "only a few generations old," dating from Wills, Tyndall, and the Alpine Club's journal in the 1860s.[6]

In that time, however, English mountaineers had pretty well covered the Alps and wanted new challenges. Douglas Freshfield, saluting "mountain exploration as the noblest form of sport," argues that its "highest perfection" is first ascents, so climbers should head for Norway, the Caucasus, the Himalayas, the Americas, and New Zealand (Dent 1901, 300, 291). The Alps have lost their "primitive charm," he writes: now that tourism is an industry, it is harder every year to avoid Shelley's "polluting multitude" (292-3). Dent's 3rd edition contains James Bryce's 1900 update of Freshfield's 1892 article. In the interim there had been three British Himalayan expeditions, plus Sven Hedin's. Noting what has been achieved recently by the English in South America, the Italians in Alaska, Mackinder on Mt. Kenya, et cetera, Bryce surveys what chiefly remains to be done outside Europe. He even informs young climbers who have not done their aesthetics homework that "vastness of scale" produces "grandeur," but not necessarily "beauty" (325).

The volume closes with a retrospective by C.E. Mathews, another old hand, that echoes Freshfield's dislike of tourism and recalls earlier critiques by Ruskin and Stephen. "Recollections of a

---

[6]   Dent 1901, 1, 4-5, 36-7. For later treatments of this material see Marjorie H. Nicolson, *Mountain Gloom and Mountain Glory*, and *The Road to Egdon Heath*, especially ch. 15.

Mountaineer" deplores most changes in the Alps since the 1850s: roads and railways now deface once-peaceful valleys, "small mountain inns are dying out ... climbing is made easy" by expensive guides, yet accidents proliferate as fools rush in (Dent 1901, 370). Amidst his nostalgia, Mathews pauses to ask why mountains attract the brightest:

How is it that the mountains appear to have fascinated chiefly those persons whose general intellectual endowments have been so high? It is certain that the English makers of mountaineering had already climbed high in the paths of literature and science before they prospected in the new field. How is it that men like [Tyndall, Wills, Stephen, etc.] should have gravitated to the mountains? ... Bishops, Deans, ... men of letters and men of science, have sought and found among the glories and beauties of the Alps the most true rest and the most perfect form of recreation. (380-1)

It is the question that David Hogarth posed about the Arabian desert (ch. 1). Mathews never answers directly - he has already placed this situation in a departed Golden Age - but his peroration on the joys of climbing at least clarifies his own motives. Mountaineering is, he says, "the noblest pastime" for its freedom from "over-civilisation," its camaraderie, the "glorious natural beauty," the extraordinary experiences and happy memories it provides, and the peace, vitality, and rejuvenation we find there (Dent 1901, 394-5). Not a word, note, of anguished moderns seeking "chastened sublimity" - unless all that is to be read into the dig at "over-civilisation."

Another climbing writer whose work documents the expansion beyond Europe was William Conway, one of the few climbers with professional expertise in aesthetics: no other president of the Alpine Club has also been Slade Professor of Fine Art at Cambridge. Conway climbed in the Alps, Andes, Himalayas, and elsewhere. *The Alps from End to End* (1895) is a narrative, not a guidebook. A quarter-century of rapid, radical changes in mountaineering had left Conway, like other veterans, with much to regret. Hoping to recover the ideal of early exploration and get a sense of the whole range, he devoted an entire summer to a thousand-mile walk, "the Alps from end to end," pausing to climb several major peaks.

His interest in the components of beauty is apparent; both his eye and his vocabulary are trained. Trying to "analyze the nature of panoramic beauty," he finds it in "the uninterrupted travel of

the circumambient eye," which sounds like a technical version of
Addison's original description of the Great as a "spacious horizon"
(Conway 1895, 259). Occasionally one hears the art critic in Conway.
A connoisseur of views, he critiques them like paintings, and is
not easily pleased: Monte Viso has an aspect of "sheer desolation,
with forms not large enough to be grand, not graceful enough for
beauty" (36). But he can no more resist the sight of mists dissolving
to reveal a "celestial vision" of Mont Blanc than can anyone else:

Seldom have I been in lovelier surroundings than those afforded
by the rippled nevé and the glittering mist. ... we seemed to be
in a world of gossamer and fairy webs. Presently there came an
indescribable movement and flickering above us, as though our
bright chaos were taking form. Vague and changeful shapes
trembled into view and disappeared. ... At last, to our bewildered
delight, there spread before us in one long range the whole mass of
Mont Blanc and the Grandes Jorasses, a vision of sparkling beauty
beheld through a faint veil, which imperceptibly dissolved and
disappeared. (69)

As is natural in wilderness travel, such visions alternate with
"utter desolation and dreariness," nor can we appreciate one without
the other (Conway 1895, 52). But there are also moments of disgust
with humanity as tourist developments are sighted. For Conway,
the Aiguille du Géant, first climbed in 1882, "has lost its mystery. It
is hung with a cable from top to bottom, so that the veriest tiro may
swarm up it in an hour. Thus does the glory of a peak pass away.
All the dragons are driven from the Alps and maiden tourists sport
in their dens" (73). One often hears variations of "The world is too
much with us" in late-Victorian Alpinists, who would give much
for a glimpse of the tutelary deities, even dragons.

On Conway's traverse of Mont Blanc the pendulum swings
both ways. His ascent is given lyric and Homeric touches: "Greys
and faint purples began to overspread the distant view; then dawn
swept her rosy wing over all and the golden day appeared, full
armed, on the margin of the east." Higher up are "cavernous blue
crevasses, and schrunds half-opening their icicle eyelids to the
heavens. Cold curdled nevé poured down on all sides between
jutting walls of splintered rock" (Conway 1895, 80). The summit,
however, formerly an "unbroken curve of snow, aloof from man,"
is now "disfigure[d]" by a hut (82). And so it goes: swinging

between doom and hope like a Biblical prophet, Conway balances complaints about fixed ropes, new huts, and ugly mines with noble views, beautiful clouds, and geological notes.

Conway's main interest is the aesthetic quality of each place and the emotion it produces. He sometimes shares the work of assessment with his Swiss guide, to broaden the cultural perspective and allow a simpler, more direct emotion into the text than he will express himself. Atop the Wildhorn, Aymonod says (in Conway's translation), "Here it is good to come. What beauty!" (Conway 1895, 107). Conway is cooler, more empirical: what is the form of this glacier's curve? What made that valley seem so wild? How are the Himalayas similar and different? Instead of exclaiming "What beauty!" he pronounces the Weisskugel at dawn "beautiful beyond words" - and then proceeds to find them: "Softly undulating fields of snow surrounded us, breaking here and there into mazes of sérac, whose tops the sun was brushing. There was a delicacy in the mist-filled and sparkling air that manifested with unusual detail the complex curvatures of the whitest névé" (204).

There is also a streak of the moralist in Conway, for whom climbing symbolizes living. "The troubles of mountaineering seldom last long, and intervals of ease are frequent," he notes. "Each difficulty has to be ... surmounted in turn and serves as contrast to what may follow. Thus, distributed through a day, they resemble the troubles ... whereby life is relieved from the boredom of unbroken peace. Only when the long day's work is done ... does featureless repose possess its perfect charm" (Conway 1895, 76). A tough day on Monte Rosa seems in retrospect highly stimulating, because "struggles with nature produce a moral invigoration of enduring value. ... They bring a man in contact with cold stony reality and call forth all that is best in his nature. They act as moral tonics" (129). Some twentieth-century climbers who would not touch the Victorian vocabulary have said essentially the same thing.

Yet Conway did not welcome established religion as an adjunct to the morality of climbing and the holiness of mountains. He was displeased to learn that Catholic masses were being said on some Alpine summits, and though he admits Aymonod's dissent into the text ("I don't see anything improper in that, for Holy Scripture tells us that God has always manifested Himself amongst the mountains. ... Christ himself was crucified a little way up-hill"), it is only to display his simplicity (Conway 1895, 74). The Swiss guide may be an aesthetic ally, but is out of his depth on religious matters.

Aconcagua and Tierra del Fuego (1902) is valedictory, even elegiac:
Conway's farewell to decades of writing about mountains, and to
friends who have died on climbs. Steaming to Chile with two Swiss
guides, he reflects that romance has moved from Europe to South
America (by this time he had also been to the Himalayas, British
Columbia, Alaska, and Spitsbergen). Aconcagua, at over 23,000 feet
the summit of the Andes and the Americas, had been climbed for the
first time in 1897, the year before Conway arrived. On the approach,
besides describing glaciers and strata, he goes off by himself for
a day to taste "the joy of solitude" in "the loneliest place" he can
find, where earth and heaven gaze at each other (Conway 1902, 64).
Altitude sickness keeps the party from enjoying the views at their
first camp, but at dawn they are "magnificently recompensed" by
the sight of the peak's shadow reaching 200 miles to the Pacific
horizon (91). On top, besides the Pacific, they see the Argentine
pampas extending to the east "like another ocean" - a vista that
Addison might well have accepted as defining "the Great" (96).

But the book's main interest resides in Conway's response to
the remote lands farther south, described by Darwin in the 1830s.
As they work their way down to Tierra del Fuego, Conway climbs,
enjoys scenic beauty, records geological structure, and pays homage
to Darwin. Smyth Channel, majestic and ghostly in the twilight,
affords an impressive vista of land and sky. A Pisgah-sight of a
winding waterway "suggests more powerfully than any other
natural phenomenon the sense of the Beyond," Conway notes,
while "The glory of an ocean prospect is in the sense it gives of
immensity ... beyond the reach even of imagination" (1902, 155).
This is straight Addison: a "spacious horizon" transcending mere
beauty to liberate the soul. Conway does find some "lovely" scenes,
but the "desolate" lands bordering Magellan Strait seem "grander"
(159). They make him "solemn," a mood that culminates in the
epiphany of Mt. Sarmiento at sunset: "there stood before us as it
were a mighty pillar of fire," a mountain "like a pale ghost illumined
by some earthly light" (200-1).

They dare to climb this revelation, in a mood of due reverence, on
the last day of 1898. Conway describes the view from the summit as
one of "indescribable solemnity" - before wind, snow, and hail blot
it out and drive them down (1902, 206). Crossing to the Argentine
mainland, the party rides north to "boundless pampa," which feels
joyous, "free and fresh after the forest" (216). Open country near
Otway Water also produces "exhilaration" (230). Conway does not

say *why* this long vista elates him when those of Magellan Strait made him grave, but a few pages later remarks that he enjoyed seeing "these wide and beautiful lands as nature made them," prior to the arrival of civilization (233-4). The mode has shifted from the Great to dread of the gathering human threat.

Douglas Freshfield was both an avid climber and a fine writer on mountain exploration who published an account of his and A.W. Moore's *Travels in the Central Caucasus* in 1869, and wrote on *The Italian Alps* (1875). He kept being drawn farther afield: twice back to the Caucasus, generating a second book, and to the Himalayas in 1899. When John Ruskin suggested that he write a biography of the eighteenth-century Swiss Alpine scholar H.B. de Saussure, he did so, and served as president of the Alpine Club. The quintessential Victorian Alpinist, learned and literate, Freshfield sprinkled his books with classical quotations, and supplemented his own experiences with references to works by climbers of other nations.

Freshfield tried to coax English mountaineers out of western Europe. In *The Exploration of the Caucasus* (2nd edition, 1902), based on visits in 1868, 1887, and 1889, he presents the area as more romantic and sublime than the Alps - which had almost defined those qualities for his culture since Rousseau and Byron. Freshfield uses the Romantic association as a basis for frequent comparisons: the Caucasus is to the Alps as Shelley's poetry is to Scott's, he suggests (1902, 1:72). The Caucasus lacks inns and paths, yet can lift us to "a higher sphere" of happiness. He agrees with Conway that "the Alps are almost exhausted"; even their literature has become "technical" and "minute." Alpinists seeking novelty would be well advised to investigate this "new playground" (1:76, 78; Leslie Stephen had popularized the term *The Playground of Europe* for the Alps in his 1871 book).

Freshfield found in Caucasia several qualities that visitors to the mountain Great had been reporting since the eighteenth century - sublimity, vastness, grandeur, purity - and had used to define it as a category of aesthetic experience. He tries to show that the Caucasus can provide what the Alps are prized for, and more. Parts of it actually outdo them by combining "sublimity with softness" of atmosphere (Freshfield 1902, 1:183). Its longer vistas make Switzerland seem confined; most people "prefer ... broader landscapes" to "high mountain walls" (1:239). The standards of the Great were rising. Still, his paeans to wildness, simplicity, beauty, "stern magnificence," and a sense of order derived from the mountain cosmos are all staples of mainstream Alpine literature (1:140).

But a darker theme (also being heard in Alpine dirges) is audible in the bass. The first assertion that unpopulated country is beautiful seems casual, perhaps ambiguous: beautiful though - or because - empty? We cannot miss Freshfield's drift, however, when he regrets that "progress" is coming to the region in the form of a train (1902, 1:116). Nor is it just mechanization that will sully the idyll. In 1868 he liked passes as well as peaks; twenty years later, with more people around, he feels that high "undiscovered country no human eye had ever before seen" is best (1:133). This may not be misanthropy, but there is no mistaking a wish to escape other men, particularly young climbers: the failings of the new breed preoccupy him. The modern fashion is to "ignore the view," to be technical and specialized, turning travel into sport (2:172, 218). These *nouveaux* need to be reminded that we go to mountains for "spiritual help," and to be lifted above the everyday world (2:219). The passage could have been written by Ruskin.

There is a sense of human loss, too, counterpointing the wish for solitude and giving some of the elegiac mood of Conway's *Aconcagua*. The volume is dedicated to a climber who died in the Caucasus (Freshfield contributes a Latin elegy for him). The text mentions other mountaineers who have passed on: A.W. Moore, his companion in 1868, died 1887; A.F. Mummery, who had disappeared on Nanga Parbat. Like Whymper, Freshfield presents climbing as a serious business with potentially fatal consequences, yet one that is still worthwhile, for reasons rarely spelled out. In 1889, he and others searched for traces of two climbers missing for a year. They found their last camp, high on Koshkantau, in superb surroundings like "solemn and sympathetic music," but no trace of the mountaineers, who probably fell into a crevasse: their "high tomb, ... watched only by the stars" (Freshfield 1902, 2:85, 88). Like those who located the Scott party in Antarctica a few years later, Freshfield makes a verbal tomb, emphasizing the grandeur of the final resting place.

A self-assured young man named Arnold Lunn anthologized the work of English mountain writers on the eve of the Great War, editing *The Englishman in the Alps* (1913). His own adventure books would come later; first he wanted to present a tradition as old as John Evelyn in prose and Wordsworth in poetry. Lunn offers glimpses of pioneers like William Windham and James Forbes, early climbers such as Wills, Whymper, Stephen, and Tyndall, and lyrical passages from nineteenth-century poetry. Here, too, are recent names: Mummery on "The Educative Value of Danger" and "The Rewards of the Climber"; Dent on the Aiguille du Dru; Freshfield in the Lombardy Alps, "in harmony with the soul of the universe" (Lunn 1913, 148); Conway recalling his "First Vision of the Snows," a "vast, majestic, ... mysterious ... wall of white" (159); Hilaire Belloc, viewing his first "Revelation of the Alps" with bated breath; and G. Winthrop Young, a sensitive writer on Alpine subjects. Lunn is worried, though, that "the old charm is vanishing"; neither the romance of Alpine climbing nor the descriptions are now what they were (viii).

A GLANCE AT THE CONTINENT

After the accident on the first ascent of the Matterhorn (1865) left four dead, public opinion swung against mountaineering as a dangerous and useless pastime. European climbers responded by developing new techniques that enabled them to complete hitherto impossible routes, making winter ascents, going without guides, and enlarging their territory. Like the English, they spread out over the world as the main Alpine problems were solved toward the end of the century; Freshfield's *Exploration of the Caucasus* acknowledges fellow-climbers from France, Italy, Switzerland, Germany, Hungary, and Russia. Europe did not, it is said, develop a mountain *literature* comparable to England's (nor show much interest in English climber-writers), as if l'*alpinisme*, the sport or science itself, absorbed all the available energy.[7] Thus most of Europe's *fin de siècle* climbers remain obscure. Emile Javelle, a Swiss who found "the mystery ... of beauty," an "eternal rhythm," and "God's infinity" in the mountains, constitutes a rare exception (Engel 1971, 151).

Still, a few European writers on mountains in this period require acknowledgment. Abate Achille Ratti would have received less attention had he not become Pope Pius XI, but his work shows an Italian Alpinist expressing some familiar emotions. For Ratti, climbing meant a love of the "secret," "awful," and "sublime ...

---

[7] Engel 1930, 240, 244, 248-51. On the new techniques and the daring of climbers, see Engel 1971, 140-1, 145-7, 157, 170.

beauties" of nature (33). He goes farther, however. To climb is to assert "spiritual energy" against "lifeless matter," to follow the "sacred instinct" to learn more of creation, and perhaps to fulfil the "ambition of the lord of the earth" to "seal ... his relationship with the Infinite, on the highest point" (34). Low on a glacier, Ratti feels dwarfed by the "vast theatre of lifeless nature," but high up on the peaks, he revels in silence, a "revelation" of God's majesty, and "sublime solitude" (74, 60, 101). *"Del mondo consacrò Jeova le cime,"* 'God has consecrated the world's peaks,' he quotes (60). Ratti is one of Wilfrid Noyce's "scholar mountaineers," exemplifying pious modern climbers who find in the Alps an "inspiring revelation of the omnipotence and majesty of God" (Noyce 1950, 143).

Ratti's work gained prominence only when he was chosen pope, long after his last climb. By contrast, Sven Hedin was acknowledged as a major explorer in mid-career, patronized by royalty, read by the general public, sought out by scientists and other explorers. If he had formed an expedition company and sold shares, it would have been a blue-chip stock. (Hedin also appears in chapter one, because his Asian expeditions took him through great deserts as well as mountainous regions.)

His love of mountains dated from a journey through the Caucasus, Persia, and Kurdistan at the age of 20. Five years later Hedin returned to Persia as an interpreter at the Swedish Embassy, climbed Mt. Demavend, a "glorious wild landscape," and rode east to Bokhara, Samarkand, and Tashkent, where, from a pass, he saw a "magnificent landscape" of "wild mountain ranges" stretching east (1991, 53, 75). In 1893 he began an ambitious expedition into central Asia, crossing the Pamirs, "Roof of the World," in mid-winter, and making four attempts on Mustagh-Ata, 25,500 feet, the "Father of Ice-Mountains." All were defeated by bad weather. Camping at 20,000 feet on the last, just "a step ... from the stars," he found the night scene one of "wild and fantastic beauty" (106). While his aesthetic vocabulary does not (in translation) include "sublime," Hedin's idea of beauty encompasses rugged wilderness: he calls the shores of Rakas-Tal, the Devil's Lake, "rocky, savage, but beautiful" (421).

The Conquest of Tibet narrates his journeys of 1896 and 1906. Hedin felt Tibet's mountain wilderness - its pure air, "majestic grandeur," and natural music of wind and lakes - as a spiritual place, both in itself and from the worship of Buddhist lamas (1941, 84). "In these magnificent surroundings," though it be only a "naked, sterile, desolate wilderness," he noted, "one experiences the same attunement to worship as in entering a cathedral" (28). On his second trip, he joined a pilgrimage around the Holy Ice Mountain, navel of the earth, with paradise on its top. At a pass higher than any mountain in Europe, "awed into silence" by the distant Himalayas, he felt his own "insignificance" (240). Hedin illustrates as well as Doughty or Muir the displacement of religious feeling from church to land that occurred for many in the nineteenth century, as well as the diffusion and usefulness of the aesthetic ideas enunciated by Addison and Hardy.

*

It is not difficult to account for the popularity of mountain literature in this period: mountains, the first terrestrial foundation of Great aesthetics, an earthly sample of the Divine Work, simply retained their well-established attraction. The burgeoning of desert books between Hardy and the present is more surprising. Before 1878, nearly twice as much mountain as desert literature demands a researcher's attention; since then, the latter has moved ahead. There are many more books on the desert in my second volume than in my first, and fewer on mountains. By the 1880s mountaineering had been around for a century, and familiarity may have bred apathy. Deserts were more novel and exotic, requiring a trip outside Europe, and offered more space with less population than the Alps. And the literary and philosophical mood that eventually gave us existentialism was tending to favour the desertic over the mountainous metaphor for the human condition, as Hardy suggests. In any case, deserts were gaining ground, figuratively as well as literally.

3
The Worst Journeys:
The Polar Heroic Age

Polar regions came to be considered "Great" or sublime belatedly. Joseph Addison did not list them among his "spacious horizons" in 1712, though mariners were reporting the marvels of northern oceans by the late seventeenth century. Captain Cook's Antarctic voyage in the 1760s made the high latitudes interesting to writers (e.g. Coleridge, Mary Shelley); Parry's voyages in the 1820s and the search for the Franklin expedition in the 1850s brought Arctic scenery to the notice of a broad public in Europe and North America. By the time Hardy wrote *The Return of the Native* (1878), it was natural to include Iceland among the areas where "chastened sublimity" might be found, and to represent all those places where an aesthetic of bareness ruled by "a gaunt waste in Thule." Thule is now a place in northwest Greenland, but for Hardy's readers it connoted the far north in general, as exotic in its way as Tahiti or Timbuktu.

Hardy probably did not have the Victorian poet and artist William Morris in mind when he used Iceland as an example of the landscapes to which "the more thinking among mankind" were being drawn: though Morris visited Iceland in 1871 and 1873, his poem "Iceland First Seen" (ch. 4) was not published until 1891, nor his journals until the *Collected Works* (1911). *Journals of Travels in Iceland* shows that the North Atlantic world evoked strong if elusive feelings in him. Sailing west from the Faroe Islands in the midnight dusk seemed stranger than any dream; "nothing I have ever seen has impressed me so much" (Morris 8:xvii). The Faroes themselves, though empty and barren, had "something ... poetic and attractive about them" (8:11-12). Morris was also "deeply impressed" with Straumey, "yet can scarcely tell you why," he wrote his wife (8:13-14). It is this enigmatic appeal that Hardy tries to explain in historical terms as a *modern* affinity for "gaunt wastes" such as Egdon Heath.

Morris found Iceland "terrible but beautiful" - a familiar oxymoron in Great venues - and said that a "true instinct for what [he] needed" took him there (8:xxxiii-iv). He describes the island's topography in detail, noting what emotion each part evoked and analyzing his reactions. Why, he asks, should such desolation be "impressive and exciting"? For one thing, "there was nothing mean or prosaic to jar upon one" (8:42): an obvious contrast with industrial England. Then there was the thrill of knowing that the mediaeval sagas were set here - Grettir haunted these woods, Njal lived there - tinged by sadness that this world had passed. It is a land of aesthetic paradox: riding through "horrid" or "dismal" country, he can feel "exaltation" (8:53-4). Several times Morris uses "awful" in the old sense: evoking wonder, reverence, fear. "Ah, what an awful place!" he exclaims of a mountain wilderness, "so barren and dreadful ... and yet has a kind of beauty" (8:203). "And yet" is significant: Iceland challenged traditional western aesthetics. His daughter's introduction compares Icelandic travel to Arabian, and mentions that Doughty was one of his favourite authors.

Of course Morris was only a tourist on the edge of Thule; the real work was being done by explorers. Nansen, Amundsen, Peary, and Cook led the way into the Arctic at the end of the century, before Amundsen shifted his sights to Antarctica. These tough, competent men, at home in polar regions, were determined to expand geographical knowledge (and immortalize their own names) by venturing into new lands and waters.

LIFE ITSELF BECAME BEAUTY:
FRIDTJOF NANSEN

Nansen was naturally a loner. Despite the spirituality visible in his books he refused to join the State church. Edward Shackleton saw in his love of solitude a desire for self-knowledge; skiing over a pass at night, alone, as a young man, with "Nature all about ... vast and silent," he felt himself "high above the life of men" (1959, 4-5, 9). Nansen read about the Franklin expedition and was "strangely thrilled with longing for the scenery" (1897, 2:14). Trained as a zoologist, he first saw the Arctic while studying seals. When his ship was caught in the pack ice off Greenland in 1882 (the first "International Polar Year"), within sight of the "wild beauty" of peaks and glaciers, he was "drawn irresistibly to the charms and mysteries of this unknown world" (Nansen 1890, 1:2). He would have set off across the ice to shore then if the captain had not stopped him.

Over the next five years Nansen organized an expedition to land on the east coast of Greenland and cross the interior, then *terra incognita*. After leaving the ship, his party drifted for days on the ice before reaching shore, halfway through volume one of *The First Crossing of Greenland*. Nansen writes about sealers' lives, earlier explorations in the area, and the scenery. Beneath his tough hunter's skin and indifference to discomfort and danger he was sensitive to landscape, finding "savage beauty" in the coast's fjords, glaciers, mountains, and icebergs, and a "grand and simple beauty" on the icecap (Nansen 1890, 1:214, 431). He speaks of beauty, not sublimity, in which category Addison and Burke had placed grandeur. Like other early visitors to the Arctic, he found its pure air and desolate magnificence similar to areas that had already been classified as "Great." So the coast has its "Alps," and the icecap is the "Northern Sahara," or a "vast ... sea" (1:259, 494, 242).

They had trained to live comfortably in that environment, but Nansen knows that a landscape of grey rock and ice "would certainly not attract everyone in the same degree as it did us" (1890, 1:428-9). There is something of the ascetic in a man who can derive "divine" enjoyment from a stream of ice water on the glacier (1:444). Nansen was always open to the metaphysical: during their night marches, when the northern lights or moon and stars bathed the "dead frozen desert in a flood of silver light, the spirit of peace reigned supreme and life itself became beauty" (2:19). Yet he was glad, after weeks of the monotonous uniformity of mid-ice, to reach the other side, where he could geologize and shoot game. Nature's "true beauty" - mountains - and "the glories of barrenness" are best appreciated when you are warm and well-fed, he admitted (2:154).

Yet the book ends on a note of regret at having to re-enter civilization after all those "wonderful nights" out, during which they had been "thoroughly comfortable"; to Nansen, unsure that the change from tent to house is "altogether for the better," the etiquette of Danish Godthaab (modern Nuuk) seems "altogether incongruous" (1890, 2:166, 174, 179). This reaction virtually guaranteed that he would spend more time in the field.[1]

One of his companions on that trip, Otto Sverdrup, served as captain of *Fram*, a custom-built ship that they and their crew rammed into the ice north of Siberia and allowed to drift across the Arctic Ocean from 1893 to 1896. Why? Nansen states at the beginning of *Farthest North* that they sailed towards Helheim, the realm of death, Nåstrand (the shore of corpses), and the "mythic land" where frost-giants gambol, from a "thirst for knowledge" of Arctic currents (1897, 1:2, 67). He later expands this austere motivation to include a desire for achievement and a love of adventure and the unknown (1:338-9). Nansen hoped that *Fram* would drift close to the North Pole, but his account shows that the Arctic satisfied other and deeper instincts as well.

Our concern here is with the appeal of Great space, not theories of polar drift or zeal for the Pole; still, Nansen helps us. Shipboard life is generally more conducive to meditation and journal-keeping than is foot travel, yet few mariners have been as forthcoming about the feel of the Arctic. His refrain is that he sensed infinity and eternity there: qualities that the seventeenth century had reserved for God. An ecstatic page about winter's night (which Nansen preferred to the summerlong day) builds to the assertion that its "utter stillness" is "the symphony of infinitude"; even in their second winter his soul adores "the infinity of the universe" (1897, 1:153, 331). He rhapsodizes about "the great adventure of the ice, deep and pure as infinity," where we are "face to face with nature ... at the feet of eternity" (1:338-9). Feeling dwarfed by the spatial-temporal scale of the Arctic, Nansen writes that human souls disappear like ants in "the ocean of eternity" (2:48). Yi-Fu Tuan justifiably sees him as "almost a mystic" (1993, 149).

Nansen risks boring us with his philosophizing, but balances metaphysics with aesthetics. The "dreamland" of an Arctic winter, "wonderfully beautiful," has an "undercurrent of ... sadness ... all this beauty ... over a dead world. Why?" (Nansen 1897, 1:153, 161). And before winter's long night (like a "marvellously lovely woman") ends, it is "how tired I am of thy cold beauty!" (1:213). In the second winter the frigid Snow Queen has "the infinite loveliness of death - Nirvana" (1:336): an interesting gloss, repeated a few pages later.

---

[1] Arne Naess, the founder of "deep ecology," discusses Nansen's embrace of Norwegian *Friluftsliv* or "open air life" (178).

After that winter, Nansen and Frederik Johansen sledged north towards the Pole, reaching a record 86°13′ N. in 1895, and then had to retreat and winter on Franz Josef Land. By moonlight it had "A weird beauty, without feeling, as though of a dead planet, built of white marble" (2:263). This striking image resembles the end-of-the-world vision of H.G. Wells's *The Time Machine* (1895).

Nansen, like Wells, knew that a terminal ice age was one of the possible fates that scientists were predicting for the earth. "Some say the world will end in fire, / Some say in ice," as Robert Frost puts it: the Sahara or the (pre-global-warming) poles. Nansen was fascinated by this idea - which gave the Arctic a prophetic dimension - from the day in September 1893 when, *Fram* having been frozen into the icepack, he looked around and said, "*This* is the coming earth" (1897, 1:154). In April 1894 he exclaims, "The world that shall be! ... Again and again this thought comes back to my mind." He imagines the sun cooling, ice and snow covering the earth, the extinction of life, and finally the frozen globe rolling on "in her path through eternity" while "northern lights flicker over the desert, icy plain" (1:270) - as they were doing then. The last winter on Franz Josef Land also conjures up "the silence that shall one day reign, when the earth again becomes desolate and empty," and his "soul bows down before the majesty of night and death" (2:263-4).

Yet Nansen was not morose in the Arctic: he loved its purity and peace, and the health and sanity he found there. "This quiet, regular life suits me remarkably well," he says, reviewing their situation complacently: "it is as good as at home; there is not a thing we long for" (Nansen 1897, 1:216, 225). The lessons of nineteenth-century explorers from Parry on had been learned well. Storms may rage, *Fram* groan: they are *chez eux*. But this is the mood of the first winter, snug in the nautical womb, when gleaming icefields and magnificent nocturnal heavens seem a "temple" of worship. The "oppressive actuality" of summer's "eternal day" turns the temple into a desert of slush, and Nansen grows "tired of these endless, white plains" (1:301, 294). A "spacious horizon" will not *always* be felt as an "image of liberty," whatever Mr Spectator thinks.

Once out of the vastness and solitude of the High Arctic, Nansen was glad to see Norway's "beautiful barren coast" from the ship that took them off Franz Josef Land (1897, 2:352). A week later, Sverdrup brought *Fram* safely home, full of valuable scientific data, "the foundation of our knowledge of the great frozen ocean" (Mowat 1973, 237). Then, from 1898 until 1902, Sverdrup circumnavigated Ellesmere Island in *Fram*, discovering new lands and mapping 100,000 square miles of the Arctic (between 1893 and 1902 he spent only 1897 at home). Of all those who ventured south or north in the "heroic age," Sverdrup may have been the purest devotee of science; he barely glanced toward the North Pole.

Meanwhile Nansen, leaving the field work to others, eased into the roles of avuncular sage for young explorers, altruist (he won the Nobel Peace Prize for his work with refugees), and scholar. *In Northern Mists*, his history of Arctic exploration, begins with an interesting meditation on what drew the pioneers north. Nansen first says that desire for fame, knowledge, or wealth has been the spur. In glossing these motives, however, he adds that polar voyages show the "power of the unknown over the mind of man," and claims that the Arctic has been a school of manliness with joys and rewards, embodying noble ideals, teaching the will to conquer adversity, and feeding the imagination (Nansen 1911, 1:3-4). Only in this final point is Nansen true to his full experience.

LAND NOT MADE FOR MAN

The attraction of high latitudes for explorers increased from the 1870s until both poles were attained and world war broke out. In 1878, when Hardy made "Thule" a category of natural aesthetics, one expedition was attempting the Northeast Passage, a second was on Greenland's icecap, and a third was surveying Franz Josef Land. The USS *Jeanette* vanished while exploring the Bering Sea in 1879 (a US Army expedition under Adolphus Greely searched for her for three years, losing many men). The British Association formed an Antarctica Committee in 1885 to investigate ways of reaching the South Pole.

The traverse of Spitsbergen by the mountaineer W.M. Conway (ch. 2) and his party in 1896 was a comparatively modest affair. Articulate and keen on landscape, the art professor is a valuable source on the appeal of the north. In *The First Crossing of Spitsbergen*, Conway asserts that the journey was "worth while for the mere pleasure of it" (1897, 12). The pleasures begin in Norway on the way up; each time the ship stops he climbs the nearest hill for its panorama. One sunny evening stands out: "I can recall no more enjoyable hour of active life. ... Golden light flooded forth from the low sun, and enveloped the north in a glory as of the portals of heaven" (32). As in the Alps, halo-like "glories" of this kind are among Conway's favourite effects. "In other directions great reaches of water led the eye to distances so great and clear … as if we beheld all the area of the north at one sweep, with countless mountains, promontories, and secret places, all apparently aloof from and forgotten of man" (33).

Apart From Man is one of the book's themes. After seeing that visitors have defiled some of Spitsbergen's shoreline, Conway observes, "the vulgarisation … has begun," doubtless thinking of the Alps (1897, 70). The episode seems to heighten his pleasure in the vista of glaciers and snowy peaks from a mountaintop, "a region in which man has no abiding-place - a land not made for man, but mainly inimical to him. In such a world the human species would swiftly degenerate and presently disappear" (121). Conway does not seem appalled by the idea. Ivory Glacier gives "one of the greatest and most memorable prospects I have ever beheld," evoking a credo that is part aesthetics, part philosophy of nature: "oh! the glorious world, where man has no place and there is no sign of his handiwork, where Nature completes her own intentions unhindered and unhelped by him" (175). The Alps, says Conway, have not anything to show more fair, and he would know.

What intrigued him most was the island's kind of beauty. Once, at Mossel Bay, it is an undesirable quality ("What a cold dead world … lovely but undesired, like the beauty of the grave!"); elsewhere it is positive (Conway 1897, 293). It may seem paradoxical to call Spitsbergen bleak, barren, and beautiful, but "Arctic glory is a thing apart, wilder, rarer, and no less superb than the glory of any other region of this beautiful world" (175). Most northern travellers came to accept this coexistence of beauty and bareness, just as Hardy had posited. That there are almost as many references to "grandeur" and "melancholy" as to stark beauty does not indicate confusion: gloom attaches to certain places (usually in cloudy weather), which may or may not have the "lonely grandeur" of the Table Islands (280). Conway knew that the grand or sublime was aloof from humanity, and how it was related to the beautiful. Some glaciers had "blue grottoes of marvellous beauty," but "all the parts worked more admirably together to produce an effect of grandeur" there than anywhere else (285, 298).

The "dignity" that Conway finds in the area resides both in majestic landforms and in the knowledge that "great explorers" such as Parry and Nansen have been there. The nearby Seven Islands, even "bleaker, ... more desolate and aloof from man" than Spitsbergen, focus these associations (Conway 1897, 278). They stopped to see Salomon Andrée's balloon beside a bay among barren hills at the north end of Spitsbergen. With luck (a gentle south wind) the daring Swede hoped to fly to the North Pole and join the ranks of great explorers. Better still, at Hammerfest, Norway, they were in time to help welcome Nansen home.

Conway's verdict on the trip is positive: "Hither it was well to have come," he writes, translating his Alpine guide's eulogy after a good climb (1897, 298). Yet he closes oddly, recommending Spitsbergen as a summer resort - presumably for the Hardean tourist of the future. The true lover of nature, he insists, enjoys all her moods and places. His hope that science and tourism would work together in Spitsbergen, however, ran counter to his Alpine experience and data.

THE COMPLEAT EXPLORER

Conway's private venture was hardly noticed among a welter of national efforts in that decade and the next. Scandinavia, Italy, the US, Belgium, and Germany mounted polar expeditions, and at the turn of the century the British (after a long hiatus) sent Carsten Borchgrevink, then Scott, to Antarctica. Some explorers, like Peary and Scott, focused on one pole; others were driven to try both. Wintering in the Antarctic ice aboard the Belgian ship *Belgica* in 1898 were both Frederick Cook, who would claim the North Pole before Peary, and Roald Amundsen, who would drift the Northwest Passage and beat Scott to the South Pole.

Amundsen was in many ways the compleat explorer. Like Nansen, he traced his interest to reading about the Franklin expedition in his youth. What "appealed to me most strongly," he recalled, "was the sufferings he and his men endured. A strange ambition burned within me to endure those same sufferings" (Amundsen 1927, 2). Strange indeed. Most readers do not react this way, of course; from a social perspective, Amundsen looks ascetic or masochistic - neither of which is irrelevant to the Great. But the Norwegian's analysis is different. "Perhaps the idealism of youth ... found its crusade in me in the form of Arctic exploration," he continues. "I, too, would suffer in a cause - not in the blazing desert on the way to Jerusalem, but in the frozen North." The notion of spiritual quest ("crusade") here is surprising; spirituality is rare in his texts. Amundsen is rather the supreme pragmatist, who from boyhood prepared his body (through sports) and his mind (by reading explorers' journals) for his chosen profession.

He served two seasons on an Arctic sealer and two more as mate on the Belgian Antarctic expedition of 1897-99. Amundsen studied navigation and science so that he would not be dependent on others for crucial information, and met with explorers in England and Norway (Nansen lent support, and Sverdrup taught him about huskies). He bought a shallow-draft boat, *Gjöa*, which he hoped might be able to thread the channels of the Arctic archipelago where large vessels had failed; "Amundsen was an advocate of smallness" (Berton 534). Her crew was 7 men (Franklin had had 129), who would "go native" in order to survive, like John Rae, an Orcadian who travelled widely in northern Canada with Inuit companions (1846-54) and brought back news of the Franklin disaster. This crew came through the Northwest Passage (1903-06) without fatalities or serious hardship. Like Nansen, Amundsen had mastered the subject.

After completing the Passage, *Gjöa* was frozen in for a third winter off the Mackenzie River delta. Anxious to tell his story, Amundsen set off in October 1905 with the skipper of another icebound vessel and two Inuit on a 500-mile journey across the mountains to the first telegraph station in Alaska. Walking or running with the dogs along the rivers, they covered up to 30 miles a "day." Amundsen cabled Nansen (collect: he was penniless) and headed back to the ship with the Inuit in February. Without the other captain, it was "a picnic." Along the Porcupine River they met a Mr Darrell, dragging the mail on a toboggan from the Mackenzie River over the mountains to various trading posts. He was alone, without even a dog, hundreds of miles from anywhere in midwinter. "I could not believe my eyes," wrote Amundsen; "I was lost in admiration" (1927, 59) - praise worth having. He would have taken Darrell to Antarctica with him if the postman had not disappeared first on another of his runs.

As an author Amundsen is less impressive. He wrote a book about each of his major exploits - *The North-West Passage*, *The South Pole*, *The North-East Passage* - and a memoir, *My Life As an Explorer*, but human-interest stories like the mailman's are few and aesthetic responses minimal. The visual potential of the encounter with Darrell, for example - the travellers converging in the starlit, snowy waste - is not developed: they just meet, and the natural scene, having been mentioned earlier, is assumed. Admiration is the only emotion. The treatment is as flat as Daniel Defoe's when Robinson Crusoe, seeing a footprint after years alone on his island, says, "I was exceedingly surprised." Amundsen's books portray a man immersed in the practical, unsentimental about life forms, and preferring narration to description. Perhaps he felt that that had already been done, better than he could, by Nansen and others.

An expanse of ice and snow, however, always stirred him. In Antarctica he saw "imposing majesty" in the Great Ice Barrier, a "vast, mysterious" place (Amundsen 1912, 1:167, 169). He evokes the beauty of a summer evening on the Barrier, where the "bright, white, shining light, so intense that it dazzles the eyes," makes him speculative (1:178). Northward lies a darkness they know, but what does the luminous south conceal? "Inviting and attractive the fair one lies before us. Yes, we hear you calling, and we shall come. You shall have your kiss, if we pay for it with our lives" (1:179). The pole is the beautiful mysterious woman of myth, then, but which one: the *femme fatale*, the sleeping princess, or the Snow Queen? Amundsen thinks he knows. The path is opening; the castle looms in the distance. "The Beauty is still sleeping, but the kiss is coming, the kiss that shall wake her!" (1:194). After all, this is "fairyland" (1:254). Of course he wrote after the fact, but we note that Amundsen found the ice shelf beautiful, not God-forsaken and desolate.

Nansen's introduction to *The South Pole* evokes the tiny dots of men and dogs crossing an "endless white surface" as the wind erases their tracks from "the desert of snow" (Amundsen 1912, 1:xxxiv-v). He presumes visibility, which is required for the Great to work; when fog covers the polar plateau, there is no "spacious horizon" and no sense of liberation. In good weather, Amundsen admires the "perfect stillness" and "radiantly clear air" of the Barrier (1:283, 2:54). Like Nansen, he had solved enough of the problems of polar travel to win a modicum of comfort and see more in the environment than hostility. Filled with a sense of well-being in their hut *Framheim*, he anticipates winter "with pleasure" (1:259). The dogs, very much at home, accept the Barrier as their "native heath," while the men listen to Grieg's *Peer Gynt* on the gramophone "in the dark winter night on the vast wilderness of ice" (1:304, 338).

But this is at the coast, before the great trek south: surely that will stifle enjoyment? While Scott struggled with his "motors," ponies, plans, and personalities, the Norwegians executed their one plan, using the dogs and skis with which they were thoroughly familiar. Departing earlier, they also lucked into better weather than Scott. Out on the Ice Barrier, with the Queen Maud Range beginning to rise, Amundsen thinks he has never seen "a more beautiful or wilder landscape" (1912, 2:30). Reaching land, they ascend Axel Heiberg Glacier, a two-mile-high icefall through a notch in the mountains. The "grand and imposing" scenery, of a "wildness … not to be described," gave Amundsen the "impression that here Nature was too powerful for us" (2:56). To the Norwegians, however, that simply means not ascending "here"; the best route is over *there*. Higher up, at "The Devil's Glacier," the scenery lives up to Amundsen's daydreams, offering "a fairy landscape … a play of colours that defies description." As for Mt. Nilsen, "ah! Anything more beautiful … I have never seen" (2:87).

After the splendour of the mountains, Amundsen says little about the polar plateau. At the South Pole he notes ironically that the *North* Pole was his "life's goal" (Huntford 1987, 44). Reaching the coast again in good trim after 14 weeks, Amundsen remarks, "it was good outside, but still better at home" (1912, 2:174). He felt "melancholy" at leaving *Framheim*, where they had lived "undisturbed and untroubled" in their "thoroughly good and comfortable home" (2:176-7). Perhaps only Parry, Nansen, and a few mountaineers in huts had managed to exist so cosily within the Great. In fact, says Amundsen, "this spot exercised a strong attraction upon each of us"; they would gladly have postponed their return to the "great world," realizing that they would "look back with regret" on their happy Antarctic days (2:178) - a virtual outburst from the normally reticent explorer. Nor was it just Amundsen who said so: Lt. K. Prestrud reported that on the eastern sledge journey they were "happy and contented," and that the vista of the sea from the Barrier was "always grand," sometimes "beautiful" (2:230, 232).

THE BIG NAIL

The race for the poles per se is not part of my brief. The purposes that Hardy predicted would move "the more thinking among mankind" were not what brought *explorers* to Thule. Those men were driven mostly by combinations of curiosity, personal ambition, and national rivalries. Without them, of course, there would have been far fewer observers to report aesthetic reactions. And their reports suggest some affinity for those regions besides a zeal to plant their flags in new lands and their names in history.

At 26, Dr Frederick Cook volunteered as surgeon for Robert Peary's 1891 Greenland expedition, during which he set the leader's broken leg. After two more Arctic ventures, he joined the Belgian Antarctic Expedition, serving with Amundsen (who called him the expedition's brightest light) on the *Belgica*. They explored the coast of the Antarctic Peninsula and wintered in the icepack. Cook wrote a book about it, *Through the First Antarctic Night*, whose vague but sensitive descriptions of nature are typical of all his narratives. He was much taken with the "strange other-world scenic effects" of the Palmer Archipelago (such as mist with an inner light) and of the icepack, whose horizon is "not unlike ... ruined marble buildings" (Cook 1900, 145, 352). Cook found the extreme south a "hopeless icy-desolation," yet its mystery, "strange simplicity," and dreamlike weirdness were fascinating (170, 218). The wild beauty charmed him: late-summer nights had a transcendental quality that he felt raised his soul to the supernatural. Winter and spring, while "melancholy," could give "lofty thoughts," and he was "half sorry" to leave (370, 400-1).

But the north drew him back. He went with Peary again in 1901, and made two attempts on Alaska's Mt. McKinley (Denali), one, he said, successful, which he related in *To the Top of the Continent* (1908). Cook was on seven expeditions between 1891 and 1907. Then, with the aid of a wealthy backer, he and two Inuit made a "dash" for the North Pole that turned into a fourteen-month ordeal (1908-09). His claim to have reached the Pole (disputed, along with the Denali climb, by Peary's supporters) is set out in *My Attainment of the Pole* (1911).

Following the coast of Ellesmere Island north, Cook "found an inspiration in being thus alone [sic] at the world's end. The barren rocks, the waste of snow fields, the mountains stripped of earlier ice sheets ... There was a note of absolute abandon on the part of nature" (quoted Mowat 1973, 299). The arch-minimalist among polar explorers, Cook says he then headed north with two men, two sleds, 26 dogs, and 80 days of food: no waiting ship, no back-up. At latitude 82° north, their "strange white world" was "transformed into a land of magic" by mirages, which provided some diversion, whereas above 83° "life is devoid of pleasure" (304, 308). In the "mental bleach" of the barren icefields, only ambition kept him moving towards the "chilled flame of a new Hades" (309-10). Fighting off despair, they pressed on "through a mental desert" and, he says, reached the pole (311). The Inuit were polite but disappointed, and Cook himself wonders what all the fuss was about; for so many to have striven so long for this desolate non-place seems an allegory of futility.

His claim challenged, Cook explained that he had cached his instruments and records at Etah, Greenland, where (Peary having refused to bring them back on his ship) they were lost. What, said the world, you abandoned your proofs? Even his supporters shook their heads. Cook did not profit from his polar venture; one does not buck the favourite of Teddy Roosevelt, *The New York Times*, and *National Geographic* - Peary - with impunity. After a variety of activities, he was imprisoned for five years on dubious fraud charges. When he emerged at age 65, he burned to tell his story again, and spent five years writing *Return From the Pole*, published posthumously (1953). Here the quest for the Pole is only a short prologue to the drama of the return. Cook says disarmingly that "pinpoint accuracy" was impossible with the equipment he had, but that if they were not exactly at the Pole, they were very close (1953, 17).

Cook never romanticized the high Arctic, recalled as "Desert doom and icy desolation" (1953, 12). It is often a "lifeless desert of floating damnation," a "depressing Arctic Sahara" and "a world of paradoxes" where compass north may lie south and the environment, composed of "illusion, delusion, and misconception," is ambiguous (16, 30-1). In fog among islands, they moved in "a shining gloom of mystery" (51). The portrait of the North Pole in his 1911 book is confirmed and developed: it is "a negative area," a world of absences and "nothingness," a "dominion of zero world" (18, 22, 191).

Yet Cook (like other "desert" travellers) finds it also a world of spirit. His Inuit friends describe the aurora as the "people in the heavens above" dancing, or "seeking a way to eternal rest"; he himself comments that "in no part of the world is one so near the Creator and His methods as in the seeming chaos of polar regions" (Cook 1953, 189, 191). In order to survive, Cook lived as the natives lived, speaking no English for fourteen months, and he tries to include their point of view in his narrative. Etuq and Wela considered the trip to the pole a failure, since no new hunting grounds were found. Returning south, though, they were not depressed by absences, as he was, but detected signs of distant land and life, and felt the energy of storms and moving ice. Devon Island, rich in breeding animals, they called "Baby Land," and would gladly have stayed longer. Once home in Greenland, they were "ready to go back to colonize the new world," and "half of their friends were ready to follow" (207). All three, says Cook, became "new men" mentally and physically during the ordeal, so it offered more than futility and negation.

Hard on Cook's heels came Robert Peary, making his seventh or eighth try for the pole. If we take both men at their words, Peary reached "the Big Nail" (the Inuit thought the Pole must be iron for white men to value it so highly) in April 1909, a year after Cook. Peary's Arctic dossier began with an 1886 sally onto the Greenland icecap. After Nansen crossed it, Peary kept traversing Greenland at higher latitudes, learning his trade. A Peary Arctic Club was formed in 1898 and he became the semi-official US standard-bearer in the north. But he won few friends outside the American establishment; polar historians of other lands - Markham, Berton, Mowat - depict him as narrow, ungenerous or even underhanded with rivals, and a careless cartographer whose errors cost lives and whose claim to the pole is no more persuasive than Cook's. Even the US Congress, not entirely convinced that Peary had reached the pole, awarded him only a medal for lifetime achievement in the Arctic.

Most of this - Peary's character, conduct, treatment of associates, and the whole sordid Cook-Peary controversy, which dragged the Arctic epic down to the meanest level - is mercifully not our concern. Why Peary kept returning to the Arctic, and what he found there, are, and here we have no particular reason to distrust him. He begins *The North Pole* (1909) by evoking "The lure of the North," a "strange and a powerful thing" that brought him back repeatedly.[2] Each time he limped home from an expedition he found that within months he grew "restless" and began to long for "the silence and the vastness of the great, white lonely North" (Peary 10). Peary was not without emotion, then, even aesthetic emotion, about the Arctic, but he gets it all out of the way in the first pages. Of the attributes

---

[2]   Peary had written to his wife in 1899 that "there is something beyond me, something outside of me, which impels me irresistibly to the work ..." (quoted Berton 526).

noted above, only silence is ever mentioned again, and that is a memory of the "silent, eternal, immeasurable" Greenland icecap, seen in the distance years earlier (53).

Grandeur is the only other quality Peary mentions twice. He hails the "pure atmosphere" - once; and while "there is nothing so beautiful as the glittering Arctic on a sunlit summer day," he was usually "too busy ... to enjoy the beauty of the frozen wilderness" (Peary 74-5, 283): the explorer as responsible businessman and worthy recipient of grants. That his ship (the *Roosevelt*) looks "utterly insignificant" amid the icefields is only a passing thought (88). As for the aurora borealis, which excited Cook's party to discuss colours and myths, Peary had seen better displays in Maine. But northern expeditions have another interest for him: the frozen wastes reveal a man's true character for all to see. Mountaineers sometimes report that climbing promotes camaraderie or brings out truths by stripping away layers of appearance. Peary's formulation is characteristic: "if he is a man, the man comes out; and, if he is a cur, the cur shows as quickly" (19).

Peary was adept at logistics, executing his system with military precision. Without teams of support parties moving in relays, he said, one could not hope to win the Pole - a dig at Cook, whose book claimed otherwise. Matthew Henson, Peary's servant or assistant, was one cog in this machine. In a foreword to Henson's book *A Negro Explorer at the North Pole* (1912; repr. 1969 as *A Black Explorer at the North Pole*), Peary notes that Henson had been on all of his expeditions since 1891. Henson loyally seconds Peary's story, but is more sensitive to scenery. As they shift supplies northward from cape to cape during the fall, he finds a "somber magnificence" the land's dominant mood (Henson 53). Cape Columbia seems a "magnificent desolation," with a "beautiful blankness" that has an "irresistible fascination" for him (66). The mountains at Karnah are "sublime in their grandeur," and even the level snow-plain of the Arctic Ocean is "grand and sublime" in good weather (168, 109). He ends by professing to want more of the same, like Peary: "the lure of the Arctic is tugging at my heart" (188).

These pioneers' reports remind us of the relation between aesthetics and comfortable leisure. Frantically busy or suffering travellers have no time for beauty, sublimity, or philosophy; mountaineers from Leslie Stephen to Jon Krakauer have made this point. Compared to Nansen - meditating on the Arctic in the cosy *Fram* - Cook, Peary, and Henson provide only a few impressions in narratives with thin sensory content. The seeming exception, Cook's *Return From the Pole*, proves the rule, having been written after long years of (enforced) reflection.

HEARTS OF THE ANTARCTIC

The distinct narrative of the quest for the South Pole was proceeding during the same years, and this one at least had a clear outcome. Antarctica provided a different set of problems from the Arctic: once a ship breached the ice pack, the shore party did not have to face thin ice or open leads. While conditions could be terrible on the Great Barrier (an ice shelf larger than France), up ten thousand feet of icefalls, and on the wind-raked polar plateau, at least it would not be death by drowning, and the footing did not drift. On the other hand, there were no "helpful natives" to stalk game. British explorers, whose ranks have always included some highly literate people, are again prominent. Besides the sledging parties, who might have little opportunity to write, large expeditions left diarists and photographers at the coast in the relative comfort of ships or huts, recording their impressions.

Sir Clements Markham - respected Navy veteran (a sailor on the Franklin search), secretary of the Royal Geographical Society, writer on the Arctic, advocate of polar exploration - spotted Robert Falcon Scott as a young midshipman. Taking Scott's career in hand, he obtained for him the command of the British South Pole Expedition and HMS *Discovery* despite Scott's lack of relevant experience. Markham could inscribe his own views of polar travel on this *tabula rasa*. Unfortunately they were the ideas of Britain in the 1850s; ignoring a half-century of Arctic travel by several nations, Markham restricted *Discovery* to the equipment used in his youth (Spufford 288). A believer in exploration as a moral tonic, he convinced Scott that man-hauling loaded sledges was a "higher" mode of travel than dog-hauling (Markham 472).

As leader of the *Discovery* expedition (1901-04), Scott directed two seasons of sledging. Those were busy years in Antarctica: Germans, Swedes, and Scots were also at work there. Scott had a hut built on Ross Island, made an ascent in a tethered balloon for a better view, and led a three-man party 380 miles south. His *Voyage of the Discovery* (1905) increased public interest in the South Pole. One need not go so far as Francis Spufford, who presents Scott as an Imagist poet, to see him as a man of feeling. The explorer (whose wife was a sculptor) makes Antarctica's beauty and magnificence the dominant colours on his verbal canvas. The former usually arises from solar or lunar lighting, the latter from mountains, glaciers, or icebergs. Wilfrid Noyce surprisingly calls Scott one of the "fathers of our modern movement of mountaineering" because he fostered "a certain feeling in us" and strengthened "our appreciation and our exertions among hills" (1950, 9). Scott's sister said that he felt "keenly the call of the vast empty spaces; silence ... beauty ... liberty" (Spufford 6).

But darker hues - deception, gloom, fear - are as prominent in the book as scenic grandeur. Of course Antarctica's unknown terrain makes the "sense of its mystery" a fact as well as a feeling (Scott 1905, 1:156). Optical illusions (a recurrent motif in polar narratives) take several forms. Size and distance are difficult to guess because the scale is vast beyond anything in their experience: another of the book's themes. Afloat, Scott sees "how deceptive appearances may be," and on land "Curious illusions" make objects appear nearer than they are (1:159, 205). Shadowless days and whiteouts puzzle the men; phenomena such as fog-bows and mock suns intrigue them. Antarctica, writes Scott, displays "pictures of its own," being unique (2:43).

The scene where Scott's party turns back on the "western journey" during their second season is more daunting. There are no landmarks in sight, just "a further expanse of our terrible plateau ... all we have done is to show the immensity of this vast plain" (Scott 1905, 2:249). In every direction stretches "a scene so wildly and awfully desolate that it cannot fail to impress one with gloomy thoughts," especially if one imagines "thousands of miles" more over the horizon. *Gloom* had been a common response to polar wastes, deserts, and the Alps in the nineteenth century; Ruskin or Hardy could be his precedent here. Scott then produces another well-established trope: the "terrible limitless expanse of snow ... inspires awe" in the "little human insects [who] crawl over this awful desert" (2:249-50). Awe and feelings of insignificance often kept company (though "awful" may have its modern meaning here). "Could anything be more terrible than this silent, wind-swept immensity?" he wonders (2:250). Using "terrible" three times in three paragraphs is as close as Scott will come to admitting fear.

If nowhere on earth could be "less attractive" than Victoria Land (a "vivid but evil dream"), what consoles Scott for its hardships?

(1905, 2:251) Besides gratifying patriotism and ambition, it yields geographical knowledge, and the oft-attested brotherhood of shared pain and achievement. There is also an aesthetic interest. Like some imaginative writers - Coleridge, Poe, Melville - Scott revels in the emotions aroused by the dominant whiteness. The "pale white light and silence" of a moonlit night at the coast are "perfect," yet "so weird that it gives one a positively eerie feeling," perhaps because "the ship looks spectral": white as death (1:289). Three months later the wintry scene connotes magic and beauty. "The cold white light falls on the colder, whiter snow" of "our white world," with some black forms and lines for contrast. It is a "fairyland," under whose "enchantment" the dogs howl a dismal "accompaniment to the vast desolation without" (1:323-4).

Scott can sound like a less metaphysical Nansen, or Amundsen in his Sleeping Beauty mood, but another variation on the white theme is original. In the spring his sledging party passed 80° S. latitude, beyond which all charts "show a plain white circle": white as goal. "It has always been our ambition to get inside that white space," Scott writes, "and now that we are there the space can no longer be a blank" (1905, 2:39). Having parted the veil that Poe imagined hiding the pole, they have entered the void and begun substituting facts and details with human meaning for the weird, fatal, or beautiful whiteness that lured them. This, adds Scott with dry understatement, "compensates for a lot of trouble." *Voyage of the Discovery* lacks the tragic piquancy of *Scott's Last Expedition*, but, because Scott had a chance to work up his journals, offers a fuller range of aesthetic responses, as well as epigraphs from Thomson, Shelley, and Arnold.

Ernest Shackleton was one of Scott's lieutenants on this expedition. The first winter he edited *The South Polar Times*, which helped keep up morale, and accompanied Scott on the southward push the next summer. But he contracted scurvy, and Scott sent him home (much against his will) on the relief ship in 1903 as "not fitted." Disgruntled and hurt, Shackleton organized his own expedition (1907-09). First he requested permission of Scott, who asked him not to use Hut Point. So Shackleton built a hut 20 miles north at Cape Royds, from which six men made the first ascent of 13,000-foot Mt. Erebus. In the spring he led a party south across the Barrier, up the Beardmore Glacier, and onto the polar plateau for the first time. His decision to turn back only 97 miles from the Pole when the risks became unacceptable has earned him the respect of all subsequent explorers. When Amundsen's party reached that point two years later, they stopped to toast him.

Shackleton left Cape Royds in March 1909 (his men singing "Auld Lang Syne") and published *Heart of the Antarctic* in November. No wonder Scott asked him to edit the *South Polar Times*: Shackleton is articulate and literate, which partly explains his recent surge in popularity.[3] He is also forthcoming on major issues, speculating at once on why men journey to "the void spaces of the world": adventure, scientific knowledge, and "the mysterious fascination of the unknown"; somehow "the stark polar lands grip the hearts of the men who have lived in them" in ways not to be comprehended by stay-at-homes (Shackleton 1909, 1) - a remark that falls in the Addison-Kant-Hardy tradition of thought about the nature of the power that inhuman space has over human beings. Shackleton admits feeling all of these attractions, which produced a "keen desire to see more of the vast continent" of Antarctica (1). Vastness - of icebergs, of the Barrier, of the Beardmore Glacier - impresses him more than any other aspect of the southern continent.

Almost as often, he asserts that the place is "magnificent and awe-inspiring" in its "rugged grandeur" - qualities central to the Great - and that it is odd (Shackleton 1909, 114, 193). Like Amundsen and Scott, he felt an enchantment there, beginning in the pack ice, a "wonderful snowy Venice. Tongue and pen fail in attempting to describe the magic of such a scene" (40). Shackleton occasionally plays Othello ("Rude am I in my speech") before launching into a vivid description. "A stillness, weird and uncanny, seemed to have fallen upon everything when we entered the silent water streets of this vast unpeopled white city" (40). The Barrier too is "weird beyond description"; strange optical effects such as mock suns and fog-bows are seen on that "limitless waste" (165, 167). The Barrier strikes him as "a wonderful place," altogether "new to the world," though foreseen by Coleridge in "The Ancient Mariner." Mirages, astonishing colours, vast solitude: for Shackleton, as for Scott, Antarctica is "unlike anything else in the world" (171, 167).

It was not given to Scott to write a book about his last expedition, yet his journals are full until the polar journey: building a hut at Cape Evans, depot-laying, winter in the hut. On the march to One Ton Depot he noted "The eternal silence of the great white desert"

---

[3] Caroline Alexander explains how Shackleton "dictated" parts of both his books to a "collaborator," Edward Saunders (8, 191).

(Scott 1913, 1:120); he would revisit the desert image, minus the silence, when gales howled across the Barrier. During the winter, the party's experts lectured on their fields. Scott's sophisticated questions to Taylor about Antarctic geology show that he had studied the subject, by now a virtual prerequisite for any serious explorer. What stirred Scott most was the aurora australis; one display left him with "a sense of awe" and a feeling that "the appeal is to the imagination by the suggestion of something wholly spiritual, something instinct with a fluttering ethereal life" (1:257). To return to the hut and the Midwinter Day carouse seemed "profane."

The rough entries of Scott's last journal differ sharply from those of this studious, spiritual writer. Jotted at night with stiff gloved fingers in his sleeping bag in the freezing tent, they confirm that cold, hunger, and pain suppress the aesthetic sense. The most striking remark of the trip, his exclamation at the South Pole, "Great God! This is an awful place," contrasts ironically with the "awe" he felt under the aurora (Scott 1913, 1:424). The famous final sentences of the journal are moving as the last words of a brave, defeated man, but it was left to the relief party, who built a cairn over the tent and bodies, to provide a context. Dr Atkinson wrote, "There alone in their greatness they will lie without change or bodily decay" (1:468) - the idea of supernatural preservation often associated with mountains, deserts, and the poles.

The 1910-13 expedition produced a plenitude of commentary, both at the time and for years afterwards: books, diaries, or photographs by Cherry-Garrard, Edward Evans, Taylor, Ponting, Gran, and others, as well as by Scott. Historians rummaging through this material have given it new prominence, and published manuscripts. Francis Spufford calls attention to the piety of Dr Wilson, and his time spent amid Great landscapes in Switzerland and Norway before dying on the Barrier (261-2). Herbert Ponting, the expedition photographer, was excited by this "new world" but felt its loneliness; Bowers found it "grand beyond conception"; and Frank Debenham, a geologist, felt "dwarfed" by the vast and "magnificent" land (Spufford 309-10, 316, 326).

T. Griffith Taylor wrote "The Western Journeys" chapter for *Scott's Last Expedition*, and two books, *With Scott: The Silver Lining* (1916) and *Journeyman Taylor* (1958). All stress his interest in geology and the pleasures of friendship with men who became "closer than brothers" (Scott 1913, 2:198). Like Peary, he was too busy with his work to have "much eye for the beautiful scenery" (Taylor 1916,

92). But at the end of *With Scott*, Taylor admits that "pleasures ... more concentrated than those met with in times of ease" reward explorers, which leads to his parting advice: go to the Antarctic if you can, for "Only in Polar lands is to be found the joy of a 'real return to the primitive' ... There, if anywhere, is life worth while" (447). Perhaps he had a fuller emotional life than he has shown, and eventually realized that there had been more to the experience than science and camaraderie. The idea of a return to the primitive - a fairly common response to the Great - comes out of nowhere here.

South *With Scott* by Lt. (later Admiral) Edward Evans moves in the opposite direction. He is sensitive to scenery, enjoying the beauty of icebergs, moonlight, and the aurora, but also admits grimmer strains: the mountains in their "eternal ... loneliness" bid "silent defiance" to visitors; with the approach of winter, they look "sinister and relentless" (Evans 64-5, 106-7). Evans's feelings about Antarctica were radically mixed; "The view magnificent, though lonely and awful in its silence," recurs in various forms (208). He gazes at the Barrier scenery and admits that "it all had a dreadful fascination for me" (200-1). Sailing north at last, he can feel the lure that pulls explorers back and caused the dying Scott to write, "How much better has it been than lounging in too great comfort at home" (312-13). Yet, Evans concludes, Antarctica was "not meant for human beings to associate their lives with"; glad to be left alone, it seems to mock the departing ship (317-18).

Young Tryggve Gran, self-styled "the Norwegian with Scott," kept a careful journal (published in Norway, 1915; in England, 1984). He did not respond much differently from the British to Antarctic scenery. Like others in the party, Gran was most impressed by its beauty, often of a "strange" or "savage" kind (81). In fact, the fairy-tale quality of the place vies with beauty as his dominant response: a pairing also found in Scott, Shackleton, and Amundsen. Almost as strong are his sense of wonder at the continent's grandeur - the Barrier's "awesome desert," "majestic" mountains beneath a "superb" aurora - and his instinctive recoil from "the desolation of this icy, God-forsaken wasteland" (219, 39, 126, 115). His reactions to its vastness, emptiness, and wildness also resemble those of his British teammates. The main difference is that he thinks and hopes Amundsen will win the race to the Pole.

Apsley Cherry-Garrard's *The Worst Journey in the World* (1922) remains the most substantial and popular book by one of Scott's men. (The title was imposed by the publisher; the author feared that it would seem arrogant, tasteless, or overwrought if taken as applying to his winter journey to the Emperor penguins' nesting ground on Ross Island instead of to Scott's ordeal.) Cherry-Garrard's appeal lies in his gift for description and a judicious selection of the writings of his colleagues. As in many of their accounts, Antarctica's vast scale is the quality most often noted in his book. Beginning as the "chaotic immensity" of the icefalls on Mt. Erebus, it continues with the sweep of the Barrier, and culminates in the "grand ... vastness" of the Beardmore Glacier (Cherry-Garrard 228, 418).

But Cherry-Garrard, who always retains his own flavour, is equally taken with Antarctica's layers of purity. At the visual level, beauty, grandeur, and immensity are qualities that awe visitors to "this pure Land" (Cherry-Garrard 231). Purity also has invisible aspects, such as the "clean, open life" they lived on the Barrier, for which veteran sledgers in time grow nostalgic (274). The life demanded by this land has a refining action, as when the dross is skimmed off molten gold. In ordinary society we have "so many ways of concealment" that our true worth may go unknown. "Not so down South": its rigours will dis-cover a man's reality, as Peary said of the Arctic. So Wilson (to whom he was Assistant Zoologist) and Bowers, his companions on the winter journey who died with Scott, were assayed (tested) and found to be "gold, pure, shining, unalloyed" (294). The same idea permeates Doughty's narrative of desert travel.

The preservative qualities of the climate's dry cold also struck Cherry-Garrard; he and Raymond Priestley, a geologist, both note the freshness and edibility of food left over from Shackleton's 1908-09 expedition. Eighteenth-century visitors to deserts and Alpine glaciers, seeing that decay bacteria did not corrupt food and corpses there, read this as a secular version of immortality or eternity, the usual ravages of time being suspended. In this case, more than food seems to have been preserved: Priestley found Shackleton's Cape Royds hut "very eerie, there is such a feeling of life about it" (Cherry-Garrard 143). Both he and Lt. Campbell heard shouting in the night, which they decided must be seals. What else could it be?

Cherry-Garrard says, "We travelled for Science"; of all their motives, "the desire for knowledge" is the one that "really counts" (275, 643). Yet there is also much of spirit and emotion in his book. He often pays tribute to the way Antarctica's "wild desolate grandeur" bound them together (194). A fine auroral display moves him to exclaim "the spiritual veil is drawn," and to quote poetry suggesting that the aurora is God's garment (279). And his is the fullest and most eloquent account of finding the bodies of the polar party, tastefully combining veneration of the landscape with religious sentiment. Atkinson read out the Burial Service from Corinthians. "Perhaps it has never been read in a more magnificent cathedral," writes Cherry-Garrard, consecrating the Great Barrier and the Western Mountains; "it is a grave which kings must envy" (540). It was he who suggested the final line of Tennyson's "Ulysses" as the motto for the memorial erected on Observation Hill near Hut Point: "To strive, to seek, to find, and not to yield."

And these are only some high points of polar travel in the period. Of the expeditions to Franz Josef Land or the Russians' discovery of Novaya Zemlya; of the Italian Arctic Expedition or various European efforts in Greenland, including the first wintering on the icecap; of the discovery of the South Magnetic Pole during Shackleton's expedition or Vilhjalmur Stefansson's years in the Arctic (ch. 7), nothing has been said. As with mountain books, one simply cannot discuss them all. The poles would never be for the masses, in the Alpine sense: they demanded time, money, and large-scale organization. But from being the most neglected part of the Great, polar wastes became, in the two decades preceding the war, its most popular, most described area; and the terms in which visitors presented the Arctic and Antarctic often draw on the aesthetics of "chastened sublimity" found in nineteenth-century accounts of mountain and desert travel.

4
Nothing Is Made for Man:
Great Space and the Pre-War Arts

[T]he first time I ever felt the necessity or inevitableness of verse, was in the desire to reproduce the peculiar quality of feeling which is induced by the flat spaces and wide horizons of the virgin prairie of western Canada.

T.E. Hulme, "A Lecture on Modern Poetry" (1908)

Appraising Hardy's thesis that "the more thinking among mankind" would increasingly be drawn to "gaunt wastes" involves looking for this inclination among (other) writers and artists of his time and later: that is, seeking the imaginative counterpart of adventurous travel, wherein literary culture tries to assimilate the landscapes traversed by its bolder spirits. T.E. Hulme, the Modernist critic and poet, spent a year working on the Canadian prairies at age 22 before writing the sentence quoted above, which suggests a connection or parallel between mental states and the experience of "wide horizons."

SWALLOWED IN VASTNESS:
LATE VICTORIAN WRITERS

In the 1880s, a number of prominent English poets did turn to vast and barren nature for subject matter. Algernon Charles Swinburne's "By the North Sea" (1880), for example, might easily have been written for the purpose of illustrating Hardy's idea that the tourist of the future would be drawn to "the sand-dunes of Scheveningen." In surroundings "lonelier than ruin" (a "wan waste" that is "endless and boundless"), Death and the sea exchange "desolate speech" among "desolate hollows" beneath "the hoary / Wan sky" (Swinburne 193-4). The dark mood and sombre decor of the poem are consonant with many of Hardy's scenes on Egdon Heath.

The dean of Victorian poets, Alfred Tennyson, kept coming back to the natural sublime throughout his long poetic career.[1] Though he said that "there is nothing worth living for but to have one's name on the Arctic chart" and wrote the epitaph for Sir John Franklin's memorial, the North interested him less than did the largest aspects of space and time. Evolutionary geology is a major theme of *In Memoriam* (1850), and he was still grappling with the scale of the cosmos in his last decade. "Vastness" (1885) is similar in tone to some passages of the great elegy. Here Tennyson asks again that most resonant of nineteenth-century European questions: if science is right about the universe, what do human suffering and achievement finally mean? "What is it all but a trouble of ants in the gleam of a million million of suns?" (Tennyson 465, l. 4). We seem "Swallow'd in Vastness, lost in Silence" (467, l. 34). At the end a voice insists that the dead live in memory, but what happens as the remembering ants are swept away? In the seventeenth century, when Copernicus and the telescope began to raise these issues, the faithful found no easy answers, nor does Tennyson.

He continued to puzzle over the questions evolution raised. In "By an Evolutionist" (1889), a young man - or early man - wonders why, if he has the body of a brute, he should not *carpe diem*? An older (or evolved) man urges him to heed his better self. "I have climb'd to the snows of Age," he says, whence one looks down on the sloughs of desire. And there on "the heights of his life," untroubled by the inner beast, he has "a glimpse of a height that is higher" (Tennyson 486, ll. 17-20). It had become common practice for writers to treat mountains and climbing as allegories since Bunyan's popular *Pilgrim's Progress* (1678).

Gerard Manley Hopkins, a more sensory, less public poet, gives glimpses of remote rural districts of Britain in several poems. "Inversnaid" (1881) celebrates the course of a "darksome burn" as it falls from ridge to lake, leading to a question: "What would the world be, once bereft / Of wet and of wildness?" (Hopkins #56).

---

[1]   See *The Road to Egdon Heath*, 279-85.

The speaker's toast, "Long live the weeds and the wilderness yet," connects him to the dawning conservation movement of Thoreau and Muir in America. Hopkins also works natural allusions into poems about something else. In "No worst, there is none" (1885?), the grieving, comfortless speaker becomes a mountaineer in distress. "O the mind, mind has mountains," he exclaims, "cliffs of fall / Frightful, sheer, no-man-fathomed. Hold them cheap / May who ne'er hung there," the vivid details suggesting first-hand experience (#65). He finally creeps into a cave or under a bush; "a comfort serves in a whirlwind." For Hopkins, wild nature is a solace or a parallel, not a philosophical problem.

George Meredith's *Poems and Lyrics of the Joy of Earth* (1883) and *A Reading of Earth* (1888) illustrate how complex Victorian attitudes toward nature could be. He accepted Darwin and rejected Christianity early without becoming depressed, as Hardy had. Meredith was not drawn to *barren* nature particularly; "Sense and Spirit" (1883) affirms nature in general. He seems happiest among trees, though "The Woods of Westermain" grants that beneath Nature's song can be heard "the heart of wildness": earth's body under the skin of verdure (Meredith 1883, 196). And some of the 1888 poems are more austere. "Hard Weather," for example, is sent by nature "That she may give us edgeing keen" to survive the struggle for existence (1888, 320). But Meredith had already looked past woods and weather: while star-gazing, he said in 1878 (eight years before Nietzsche's book), "I saw beyond good and evil, to a great stillness" (quoted L. Stevenson 206).

Twenty years after his two visits to Iceland, William Morris finally gave his experiences poetic expression. "Iceland First Seen" (1891) suggests that the island appealed to him because it preserved antiquity (as Egdon Heath does for Hardy). Glimpsing barren mountains ("like the building of Gods that have been") from shipboard, Morris feels that here "Lives the tale of the Northland of old," which he accepts as part of English history (9:125-6, ll. 5, 14). Like Doughty, Morris went looking for his cultural roots but found much more. In both cases, however, the prose record of travel is fuller and in some respects more impressive than the poetic recollection.

Hardy's own early poetry is often wintry in tone and setting ("Neutral Tones," "The Farm-Woman's Winter," "The Darkling Thrush"). His "wintriness" is of the domestic variety: marital discontent, loss of faith. The reaction against his dark novels in the 1890s pointed Hardy towards verse; *Wessex Poems* (1898) and *Poems of the Past and Present* (1901) were his first collections. A visit to the Alps produced two lyrics. "The Shreckhorn" (1897) is mainly a reminiscence of his friend Leslie Stephen, who had climbed it, but "Zermatt: To the Matterhorn" (1897), setting its recent human history (four of seven on the first ascent died) against its great age, is vintage Hardy. "At a Lunar Eclipse" (1901) similarly contrasts the "torn troubled form" of earth and all that appears "immense" to us with our small, symmetrical shadow, "the stellar gauge of earthly show."

From time to time Hardy returned to the idea of "chastened sublimity" in his novels, not by explaining it, as in *The Return of the Native*, but by pitting characters against powerful natural realities. In *Two on a Tower* (1882, based on Fontenelle's *Entretiens sur la pluralité des mondes*, 1686), he "set the emotional history of two infinitesimal lives against the stupendous background of the stellar universe" (Hardy 1900a, v), much as Tennyson's "Vastness" does. The astronomer's message that "nothing is made for man" and his telescopic vistas "almost annihilate" Lady Constantine (33-4). Astronomy seems to her a "terrible" science, in that it "reduc[es] the importance of everything" else (36): exactly what John Stuart Mill feared when he warned against being overawed by the Great (in his essay "Nature," which Hardy had read).

Terrestrial nature can also undermine human comfort and dignity. Flintcomb-Ash farm in *Tess of the D'Urbervilles* (1891) is a grimmer place than Egdon Heath; the insights of Charles Lyell's evolutionary geology darken Hardy's account of the turnip field. Its "outcrop of siliceous veins in the chalk formation, composed of myriads of loose white flints" coloured a "desolate drab," has a "complexion without features," like the sky, which is "a white vacuity of countenance with the lineaments gone" (ch. 43, Hardy 1978, 360). Between these two faceless visages, Tess and Marian crawl "like flies," bearing a "forlorn aspect ... in the landscape" as they slave away through a storm (360-1).

Polar writers - Cook, Nansen, Shackleton - depict the puny figure that explorers cut in much this way. And indeed "strange birds from behind the North Pole began to arrive silently," their eyes "tragical" from having "witnessed scenes of cataclysmal horror in inaccessible polar regions," where sub-zero temperatures, crashing icebergs, terrible storms, and mirages are the norm (Hardy 1978, 363). Evidently conversant with some of the arctic narratives that burgeoned after Franklin disappeared, Hardy produces a snow of Biblical scope, which "had followed the birds from the polar basin as a white pillar of cloud"; its accompanying "blast smelt of icebergs, arctic seas, whales, and white bears" (364). This ice-age winter, an apt backdrop to Tess's labours and her pain at Angel's absence, harmonizes with her belief that we live on a "blighted" world (70).

In *The Well-Beloved* (1892), Hardy has the sea teach a young man and woman the power of nature as they try to walk the long "narrow thread of land" linking the Isle of Slingers to the mainland on a stormy night (1900b, 37; the frontispiece of the Wessex edition shows this spit curving out to the island). After sheltering beneath an upturned boat, they proceed towards solid land "like the children of Israel," with the sea close on either hand. Pedestrians have drowned here; rivulets run across the "frail bank of pebbles" from the open sea to the basin. Drenched with spray and buffeted by the wind, "They had not realized the force of the elements till now" (38). Hardy uses this experience to bring the two together: the familiar camaraderie of those who venture together into the Great put to dramatic use.

Other Victorian novelists worked similar veins. W.H. Hudson, best known for a jungle novel, *Green Mansions*, spent more time eulogizing the broad pampas where he grew up (ch. 1). *The Purple Land That England Lost* (1885), a story of love and loss in Uruguay, combines travel with fiction, both celebrating the land. Cipriano's song of the "grassy desert wide" and the "hills of God" ("My heart within the city pent / Pines for the desert's liberty") is Hudson's own (1887, 1:46). He spent his later life in England, remembering; "My life ended when I left the pampas," he would write. His preface sets the story around 1860, before progress destroyed the "archaic simplicity" that blooms only "in nature's waste places amidst barren thorns and nettles" (1:8). At the end, a vision of beauty on the plains produces a mood of religious veneration: "Face to face with nature on the vast hills at eventide, who does not feel himself near to the Unseen?" asks the narrator rhetorically (2:51-2).

Hudson's nostalgia for a lost "desert" differs sharply from the chill vision of H.G. Wells's *The Time Machine* (1895), but there too the Great is prominent. The narrator voyages into the future of scientific speculation, first to the time of the Eloi and Morlocks, where he finds comfort in the night sky. The heavens put decadence and predation in perspective: "Looking at these stars suddenly dwarfed my own troubles and all the gravities of terrestrial life. I thought of their unfathomable distance" (Wells 247-8). As in Fontenelle and Hardy, the celestial sublime gives a sense of space so vast that mundane problems hardly signify. Later the traveller goes thirty million years into the future to learn the earth's fate. The final scene is of a dying planet and sun, now huge but only red-hot; it seems the world will end in ice. Wells's snowy beach beside a dead sea in the silence and desolation of a twilit planet resembles the Arctic winter that Nansen imagined as earth's end during his *Fram* voyage. Cherry-Garrard liked one quotation from Wells enough to put it in *The Worst Journey in the World*: "Ordinary people snuggle up to God as a lost leveret in a freezing wilderness might snuggle up to a Siberian tiger" (493).

The turn of the century brought a fresh crop of novelists, some interested in the vast and barren. In Rudyard Kipling's *Kim* (1900), a Tibetan lama leads young Kim into the Himalayas (earlier, his advisor "the Baku" tells Kim to study Burke, and Wordsworth's *Excursion*, as preparation). The epigraph to chapter XII, noting that "hillmen desire their hills" as others do the sea - an old pairing - is elaborated in the epigraph to chapter XIII as the ascent begins (Kipling 19:338, 376). Since the hills are everyone's mother, the old lama, stretching his arms toward them, gains strength as he climbs. The mountain people, Buddhists or nature worshippers, are "freed" from the "visible temptations" of the "Wheel of Life" (380): one of the earliest appearances in English literature of Buddhists as real, sympathetic people, and the beginning of an important connection.

Kim thinks "the Gods live here" (repeating the oldest praise of mountains), while the narrator notes the "eternal snow" of the high peaks, "changeless since the world's beginning" (Kipling 19:384-5) - untrue, of course, but *apparent* permanence had always been part of the appeal of the Great. At Shamlegh, the lama's window looks out on "white peaks ... yearning" to the moon and the "darkness of ... space"; he calls it country where a man can be "above the world, ... considering vast matters" (411). The germ of this idea is in Plato's *Phaedo*, though it was the Enlightenment that brought together the feelings aroused by mountains and the night sky in the Great. What is new here is an English novelist assigning this emotion to a Tibetan lama.

THE GREAT SILENCE :

SOME CONTINENTAL EXAMPLES

European - especially French - literature had evinced a taste for "chastened sublimity" before 1878,[2] and later writers touch on all areas of the Great from a variety of angles. Alphonse Daudet's *Tartarin sur les Alpes* (1885) spoofs Alpine tourism; the scene of the epic first ascents of 1786-1865 has become a playground, like spas and beach resorts. Or so it seems as Tartarin, having "trained" by reading Whymper and Tyndall, arrives at the Grand Hotel on the Righi for a meeting of the "Tarascon Alpine Club," where Bompard assures him that *alpinisme* is all theatre. Two guides take him up the Jungfrau, in whose reality Tartarin never believes, though the "silence and solitude of the white desert" make him shiver (Daudet 191). And when he and Bompard try Mont Blanc, his friend admits en route that this is *not* just a show. They abandon the climb in a storm, get lost, and fall when the rope breaks. Tartarin disappears, but turns up at his own funeral. Though the book is primarily satirical, Daudet's Alps are, after all, real mountains.

Pierre Loti, who chronicled his desert travels at length (ch. 1, n. 6), was also, like Conrad, a mariner who wrote novels about the sea. In *Pêcheur d'Islande* (1886; *Iceland Fisherman*), the "astonishingly simple" circuit of ocean seen from the boat in calm weather is impressively vast, and has looked thus since the "beginning of time" (Loti 1935, 136). The "great empty horizons" glimpsed through rifts in storm-clouds earlier seem more terrible than the waves close by (62). At the end, the widow Gaud surveys from a clifftop the Atlantic's mysterious "great blue emptiness" (232). Several aspects of this portrait - antiquity, simplicity, a huge void, terror, mystery - are staples of other reports on the Great, including Loti's desert books.

Robert Adams argues that the "icy chill of the stars" and void of space in Guy de Maupassant's *Mont-Oriol* (1887) symbolize "death or loneliness" (65). It is also a very land-conscious novel, using the volcanic Auvergne region of central France (a battleground between old and new geology in the early nineteenth century) as a setting for adulterous love. The "grand pays ... si vaste qu'elle semblait grandir l'âme" is wild and exciting; in scenes at the gorge called "The End of the World" and inside a crater, de Maupassant

---

[2]   See chs. 6 and 17 of *The Road to Egdon Heath.*

connects the couple's primitive, illicit passion with ancient lava flows.[3] Paul declares his love beside the crater's lake as a full moon rises "au-dessus du cratère tout rond comme elle."[4] Later, when Christiane hears of Paul's engagement, a circle of moonlight on the floor recalls that scene, and she realizes that everyone is alone, "aussi loin l'un de l'autre que les étoiles."[5] Thus two areas of the Great - mountains and space - reflect two phases of the affair.

In Émile Verhaeren's verse, images of the Great sometimes constitute almost the entire poem, as if the setting were the message. The gravedigger in "Le Fossoyeur" (1895) toils steadily, digging in a dry cemetery while a stream of white coffins arrives from far out "dans la campagne immense."[6] This nightmare scene recalls Flaubert's vast, empty North African plains in *Salammbô* (1862) and *La Tentation de Saint Antoine* (1874), and prefigures some Salvador Dali paintings. The digger has been doing this forever ("Depuis toujours"), and as he realizes that the coffins are aspects of his own life, seems to be waiting for Beckett. Several poems in *Les Apparus dans mes chemins* (1891) also feature long gloomy vistas. "Dans ma plaine" is similar to "Le Fossoyeur," while "Celui du Rien" gives a view of Nothing. "Celui de l'horizon" and "Au loin" are set on ocean beaches; the speaker in the latter says, "Mon âme ... est aux sables de la mort."[7] For Verhaeren, the melancholy Great served as a theatrical backdrop that dominates his characters.

Jules Verne's *Le Sphinx des glaces* (1897; *The Sphinx of Ice*), a sequel to Edgar Allen Poe's *The Narrative of Arthur Gordon Pym of Nantucket* (1837), is further testimony to Poe's grip on the French imagination.[8] His truncated ending, which leaves so much dangling, begged for continuation; happy to accept, Verne dispatches another ship southward to search for survivors and find out what happened. Yet there is more than Poe here: Verne's book exploited public interest in the first landing on the Antarctic mainland and the International Geographical Congress's call for scientific study of Antarctica (both

---

3   'Huge country ... so vast it seemed to enlarge the soul' (De Maupassant 125).

4   'Above the crater as round as itself' (De Maupassant 141).

5   'As distant from each other as the stars' (De Maupassant 410).

6   'on the vast plain' (Verhaeren 259).

7   'My soul ... is on the sands of death' (Verhaeren 165).

8   Charles Baudelaire translated Poe's book in 1857.

1895). Nansen and Sverdrup returned from their Arctic drift in 1896, but Verne had already "done" the North.[9]

The Sphinx mixes speculation with exotic scenery. The ship crosses the Antarctic Circle, Poe's "region of Desolation and Silence," enters an "ocean of light ineffable," and slips between icebergs into open water (Verne 14:278). To the narrator it looks like the Ice Age. Finding relics from Pym's ship, they reach 86°33' S. latitude, sailing on "the vast sea with its desert horizon" (14:321). In a few more years everyone would know that this position is up on the polar plateau, but in 1897 Verne could fill the cartographic vacuum with his imaginings (based on the Arctic). They lose their ship at 88° S., float over the Pole on icebergs, then drift north to volcanic islands in the eastern hemisphere. At 75° S. the Sphinx is sighted on the coast: a huge lodestone that wrecks any ship containing iron. Pym is found dead against it, attached by his musket. Maybe it's the South Magnetic Pole! At any rate, "Alone on that vast plain it produced a sense of awe" - like Shelley's ruined statue of Ozymandias in Egypt - which is clearly its main purpose (14:385).

The Great makes occasional appearances in other European literatures of the period: for example, Henrik Ibsen's play *Little Eyolf* (1894). At the outset, Allmers returns from the mountains saying that he wants to go back "To the high peaks and the great wide spaces" (Ibsen 25). "Being alone in the mountains," he explains, "one feels that power" - theirs, and his (32). Loneliness greater than his own forms part of the appeal, as it does for many climbers: up there he reached "an infinite solitude" wherein he renounced his life work and took responsibility for Little Eyolf, who is disabled (35). When Rita cries, we are "flesh and blood," Allmers answers, "We are also kin with the sea and the sky" and again yearns for the mountains' "peace and serenity" (75-6). Feeling that "Our lives are empty wastes" seems to make the barren peaks more congenial, as Hardy predicted (76). Allmers and Rita decide to stay together. And where will they look for guidance? "Up towards the mountains. Towards the stars. And the great silence," says Allmers, lifting up his eyes unto the hills as the curtain descends (80).

---

[9]   In *The Adventures of Captain Hatteras* (1864).

INEXORABLE SPACES :

NORTH AMERICAN FICTION

Mark Twain and Jack London, classic American writers on the west, contribute surprisingly little on this topic because their literary styles work against aesthetic responses to nature. Twain, ever the humorist, reaches for a joke if the scenery threatens to become too impressive. His chapters on Lake Tahoe in *Roughing It* (1872) mention beauty and purity in passing, but quickly return to comedy. London's *idée fixe* is naturalism. A character may feel a momentary sense of purification on a summit, as in *Burning Daylight* (1910), but nature's iron laws soon reassert themselves. Though London writes about the call of the wild, the freedom of spacious horizons is not his point, and the chastening comes from what was always there to constrain us, not "the ache of modernism."

A Strange Manuscript Found in a Copper Cylinder (1888), on the other hand, offers unexpected bounty. James de Mille was a Canadian professor who died at 46, before his novel, a satirical utopia full of literary allusions, was published. The copper cylinder found by four Englishmen adrift on a yacht in the equatorial Atlantic contains a manuscript written by "Adam More" in a land from which escape is impossible. It recounts a voyage to the Antipodes during which he was driven far to the south; separated from his ship, he drifted in a dinghy to an island of cannibals, but escaped to an Edenic archipelago in a warm, placid ocean. There dwell a Semitic people who love death, darkness, and self-denial. Received as a prophet, he has had many adventures, including a love triangle with two princesses.

The well-educated De Mille brings in much of his reading. Filling the Antipodes with reversals of northern realities is a device as old as Elizabethan England. Adam ("man" in Hebrew) is loved by both Almah (Latin, "soul") and Layelah (Hebrew and Arabic, "night"). The satirical Kosekin Land echoes Thomas More's *Utopia*, Swift's *Gulliver's Travels*, and Samuel Butler's *Erewhon* (1872).[10] But the closest parallel is Poe's *Narrative of Arthur Gordon Pym*; de Mille re-entered that imaginative realm years before Jules Verne. *Strange Manuscript* is one more voyage to the open polar sea of eccentric speculation, complete with re-runs of Poe's geography of birth and his Tsalal Island (also inhabited by Semites and dominated

---

[10]   The last is discussed in *The Road to Egdon Heath*, 320-1.

by blackness). De Mille wrote during the long hiatus in Antarctic exploration when readers might still be invited to believe almost anything about the region.

Less exotic, Hamlin Garland's valuable records of pioneer life in the American midwest include reverent responses to the prairie. *Main-Travelled Roads* (1891) consists of stories about farm life, represented as bare and often harsh, but not void of beauty. His characters will pause before long vistas, especially at sunset: "silence was the only speech amid such splendors" (Garland 1956, 47). In "Up the Coolly," Howard stands under "the inexorable spaces of the sky," mindful of domestic tragedy, but knows that this mood will soon pass (75-6). Usually the Great is soothing; Seagraves finds a "weird charm" in the prairie, "infinite in reach as a sea" and "characteristically, wonderfully beautiful," though the wind's soughing has a "faint melancholy" (86). And when the wind off "the wide unending spaces of the prairie west" blew through Robert Bloom's office window in Chicago, "his heart turned back to nature" (192). In *Boy Life on the Prairie* (1899), a memoir, Garland hails the nobility of sky and plain, asserts our need for wildness, and writes a requiem for "the vanishing prairie" (1965, 233).

A more sophisticated midwestern writer, Willa Cather, drew in *The Song of the Lark* (1915) a Portrait of the Artist as a Young Woman whose development depends on coming to terms with the vast spaces of the west. In a Colorado desert, talk of the Grand Canyon and Death Valley stirs Thea, much as a windy ridge in Wyoming had. Her taste for Great nature awakened, she goes on to read about Adolphus Greely's and others' polar expeditions. Years later, while a music student in Chicago, Thea finds that Dvorak's *New World Symphony* calls up "that high tableland above Laramie ... the far-away peaks of the snowy range, the wind and the eagles"; its Largo especially evokes "the reaching and reaching of high plains, the immeasurable yearning of all flat lands" - and her own (Cather 1915, 198-9). One frosty night in a troubled time, she walks by Lake Michigan and the "great empty space" out there seems "restful," connoting "freedom" (264). Looking at the stars, Thea can only shake her head.

Riding a train back to Colorado, she sees how "the absence of natural boundaries gave the spirit a wider range"; larks and the heart sing "over flat lands like this," she thinks (Cather 1915, 219-20). Thea is an Addisonian: Hardy's *chastened* sublime seems not to touch her. On vacation in Arizona, she rediscovers her youthful love of the "solitudes of sand and sun," makes herself a nest in old cliff-dwellings in Panther Canyon, and thinks about art (296). Cather makes this interlude play a role in Thea's success as a singer. With her operatic career well underway, Thea says that she would not "have got anywhere without Panther Canyon," where she realized that art must be used as a vessel to convey the totality of life (463, 304).

IN THE FAR DISTANCE: MUSIC

The Song of the Lark raises an interesting question: is there a music of the Great? Two or more people will not soon agree on how to define that category, or what belongs to it. A soul like Thea might feel the high plains of the west in the *New World Symphony* when most auditors would not. Her reaction would have surprised Dvorak, as Edward Abbey's declaration that twelve-tone music expresses the austerities of Utah's slickrock desert surprised many admirers of both half a century later. Such associations are highly subjective, but other composers have overtly celebrated the Great in programmatic music. Though there are precedents in Vivaldi and Beethoven, the symphonic tone poem emerged in the nineteenth century, beginning, arguably, with Felix Mendelssohn's *Hebrides Overture* and especially "Fingal's Cave" (areas that were judged "sublime" in the eighteenth century). Russian composers took up the form enthusiastically, turning to spacious horizons for their subjects: Borodin to the steppes of Central Asia, and Ippolitov-Ivanov to the Caucasus, already popular with European climbers.

Composers can evoke place and space in non-verbal ways. High flutes over bass viols may suggest the idea of *distance between;* soft will seem distant, and loud, close. Some melodies and instruments connote certain locales (modal scales sound eastern to western ears, horns were used in mountain communication). Programmatic composers sometimes annoy purists by using verbal resources as well. Alexander Borodin wrote a detailed program note for *In the Steppes of Central Asia* (1880):

In the silence of the sandy steppes of Central Asia is heard the refrain of a peaceful Russian song. One hears, too, the melancholy sounds of Oriental music, and the approaching steps of horses and camels. A caravan, escorted by Russian soldiers, crosses the immense desert …. The caravan moves steadily onward. The songs of the Russians and of the natives mingle in harmony; their refrains are heard for a long time in the desert until they finally die out in the distance.[11]

He also tries to convey the scene musically. The violins first sound a soft high E (held, with one variation, for 90 measures); two flutes then enter on E an octave lower, creating a gap. Upon this simple ground, two clarinets offer the first theme ("a peaceful Russian song"), quietly. In measure 28, cello and viola begin the pizzicato walking bass of the camels' march. An English horn introduces the second, "oriental" theme (m. 44). Two reprises of the first theme are high and quiet, but the *tutti* at m. 123 has it played *ff* by flutes, oboe, horn, clarinets, bassoons, and cello. The caravan, first heard faintly in the distance, is now opposite the auditor and at its loudest.

Halfway through, the *tutti* ends and the walking bass can be heard *mezzo forte*. The violins resume their high E and the second theme returns, *piano* again; the strings give this melody in a new key, spaced in octaves. The two themes are played contrapuntally by oboe and violins at m. 193 - a political harmony. This counterpoint is given to other instruments in a second *tutti*, *mf*, and passed around. But now the caravan is moving off and its volume wanes: when the first theme returns, it is soft again, and soon the orchestra is told to play *sempre diminuendo poco a poco*. The walking bass fades out. At last we have only a solo flute, playing the first melody against the violins' high hold, starting *pp*, diminishing to *pppp*, and *perdendosi*: "losing itself" in the immense distance of the steppe.

Other composers tried to capture the feeling of mountainous country. Ippolitov-Ivanov, who became interested in folk music during his years in the Caucasus, produced *Caucasian Sketches* (1894), titling the first movement, with its wistful horn calls, "In the Mountain Pass." Frederick Delius, an English admirer of the Great in general, wrote incidental music for James Elroy Flecker's desert caravan drama *Hassan*, set Walt Whitman's words to music in *Sea-Drift*, and took walking holidays in Norway, sometimes with his friend Edvard Grieg, whose *Peer Gynt Suite* evokes mountains in the manner of a tone poem. Delius's "The Song of the High

---

[11]   Paul Affelder's translation on the jacket of the Dimitri Mitropoulos-New York Philharmonic recording (Columbia CL 751, 1953?), combined with my translation of the French note in the score. London: Ernst Eulenberg, n.d.

Hills" for orchestra and chorus (1911) represents an ascent. Near the midpoint, at the "summit," he wrote in the score, "The wide far distance - the great solitude." The chorus enters quietly and wordlessly, like an Aeolian harp or harmonious wind, "as if in the far distance," and with the orchestra builds to a mighty climax, trailing off into silence.

Richard Strauss made a larger contribution to this kind of music than any of them; *Eine Alpensinfonie*, a symphonic tone poem (1911-15), demands an orchestra of over a hundred instruments and lasts almost an hour. The subtitles of its 22 sections provide a running narrative. It begins at night, slowly and quietly, until rising horns signal sunrise and the start of the ascent (a lively march). Offstage hunting horns give a sense of distance. We follow a brook to a waterfall, where winds and strings suggest falling water, and string *glissandi*, a rainbow. After idyllic meadows and a detour into chromatic thickets, rising themes lead to a glacier, some perilous moments, and the summit, where a choir of winds and brass greets us. The music diminishes to *pp*, then builds to a majestic *ff* as we absorb the spectacle.

At this halfway point, a powerful vision of some kind brings in the organ for the first time. Then mists rise (quietly on the strings) and the sun dims, evoking a soft elegy. A clarinet solo is the calm before the storm; drums begin to mutter with distant thunder, a wind machine starts to whine, and raindrops fall. The music builds to a thunderstorm as we hasten down: a long, fast section with many descending passages, including an inversion of the ascent motif. Organ and wind machine yield to glockenspiel, celeste, and waltz time as we pass the waterfall, but they return, along with a thunder machine. After many a forte dies the storm, subsiding into sunset (stately passages for strings and brass). The epilogue's long falls and rises recapitulate the main motifs of the symphony. Night comes, descents pass from voice to voice, quiet chords move slowly, and the violins slide down to a final soft note of well-earned rest. It is difficult to imagine how music could go farther in imitating the experience of a mountain climb.

TERRIBLE SPACES: THE EDWARDIANS

In the decade before the First War, a number of British writers found employment for the Great. The ocean always means more than itself in the work of Joseph Conrad - a sailor writing about seafaring - but its meaning varies widely. He is too original a writer to confine himself to any one outlook, including Addison's. In *Lord Jim* (1900), the sea is a "vast surface" reflecting our glances (an image explored in *The Mirror of the Sea*, 1904); the "destructive element" in which Stein urges Jim to immerse himself; and the "unknown" into which Jim leaps (Conrad 1957, 101, 163, 175). The storm in *The Nigger of the 'Narcissus'* (1897) is an "avenging terror" against human sin; the calm sea is called "immortal" (Conrad 1947b, 340). At the height of "Typhoon" (1902), the elements attack the ship with human rage, "like a personal enemy" (1947b, 228). In "Heart of Darkness" (1902), the ocean links all the places on its shores - England, the Congo - and mariners of different times: Roman, Victorian (it thus shares Egdon Heath's aura of permanence). The sea also unites Leggatt and the captain in "The Secret Sharer" (1912). The Golfo Placido in *Nostromo* (1904) is an "enormous ... unroofed temple" with mountain walls (Conrad 1947a, 3).

Still, Conrad *describes* oceans less often than we might have expected, as if real sailors were too busy with the sea, or too close to it, to have aesthetic responses. Addison, Carlyle, and Hardy attest the ocean's Greatness from a clifftop or a beach; corroboration from mariners is rare. Has anyone conveyed the ocean's appearance more vividly than H.M. Tomlinson, a landlubber on his first voyage, in *The Sea and the Jungle* (1912)? An Atlantic storm wave is a "heaped mass of polished obsidian," the sea swirls past "in a vitreous flux," and the prow sinks into "drifts of lambent snow" (Tomlinson 32-3, 47). Richard Henry Dana, the Boston patrician who spent *Two Years Before the Mast* (1840), rarely paused to describe the sea, though we hear about cliffs and icebergs, and occasionally his *feelings* about the ocean.

Even in "Typhoon," Conrad's most striking description is of the heavens, not the sea. The tempest approaches "like another night seen through the starry night of the earth - the starless night of the immensities beyond the created universe, revealed in its appalling stillness through a low fissure in the glittering sphere of which the earth is a kernel" (Conrad 1947b, 217): a glimpse of the Chaos before God let there be light.

On another plane entirely are the sedentary writers. Robert Bridges's "Wintry Delights" (1903) is a eulogy to science wherein the poet (who had medical training) argues that even if we lacked art, beauty, and love, life would be justified by the pleasure of satisfying our curiosity about nature. Geology fascinates us with "vestiges of the Creation," astronomy by mapping "the utter wilderness of unlimited space" (R. Bridges ll. 102, 116). In a world without sensuous appeal, contemplating the Great would still furnish the intellect with sufficient food.

An author as "indoor" as Henry James may seem out of place here, but "The Beast in the Jungle" (1903) shows how the Great could be used as literary metaphor. John Marcher, a passionless, self-centred bore, shuns emotional attachment because he is convinced that a terrible destiny (the beast) awaits him. He turns away from the love of a good woman, May, rather than involve her in his fate. But as he waits for Something to happen, Nothing happens (R. Adams 100). Years go by: the past seems "mere barren speculation"; his *idée fixe* "had lost itself in the desert" (H. James 568). Marcher lives in the existential void of French Symbolists (based on the spatial void of Renaissance cosmography) and in deserts. He sounds "blank" even to himself, and looks upon a "bare horizon" (578, 589). His "Jungle had been threshed to vacancy" - the title-metaphor destroyed - and the resulting plain reveals no sign of a beast (589).

After May dies Marcher goes abroad, but India and Egypt "were nothing to him," or rather painful to one who "in wandering over the earth had wandered … from the circumference to the centre of his desert" (H. James 592). A London tombstone is where he wants to be, and there he finally realizes that "he had been the man of his time, *the* man, to whom nothing on earth was to have happened" (596). There *had* been a beast, then, but one who dwelt in the desert he made, not in the jungle, and who came not with a spring but a whimper.

The desert attracted more creative writers than any other area. James Elroy Flecker (1884-1915) was already considered a poet of some promise when he died in a Swiss sanatorium. His orientalism derived both from an interest in French poets such as Baudelaire and from two years with the consular service in Beirut. The chief poetic product of this affinity was "The Golden Journey to Samarkand" (1913), whose impulse of evocation resembles that underlying Borodin's *Steppes of Central Asia*. In the romantic epilogue, a Pilgrim sings that it is "Sweet to ride forth" in the evening when the shadows are "gigantic on the sand, / And softly through the silence beat the bells / Along the Golden Road to Samarkand" (Flecker 149). A merchant adds, "We travel not for trafficking alone," but for "lust of knowing what should not be known, / We make the Golden Journey to Samarkand"; resonant names, as much as landscape, charmed Flecker. (His play *Hassan* ends with another version of that epilogue.)

Charles Doughty's verse is weightier. After the long struggle to publish *Travels in Arabia Deserta* (1888; ch. 1), he turned to poems about ethnic origins. *Adam Cast Forth* (1908), a mythopoeic analogue of his prose epic, is based on an Arab legend in which Adam and Hawwa (Eve), separated following their expulsion from the Garden, are reunited a century later near Mecca. Three decades after Doughty's own journey, the memories of it seem as vivid as ever. Adam and "Adama" meet on a mountain in Harisuth (Hebrew, "desolation"), the "Land of the Lord's curse," whose "burning stones," "sun-beat and most desolate wilderness," without "any green thing" have moral significance (Doughty 1908, 33-5). The idea of travel as test, implicit in the book, is made overt as a Voice announces a new trial of obedience: to cross a lifeless "High Field" (like the volcanic *harras*), a "vast Wasteness burned of the LORD'S WRATH: / That rent, of old time, from heaven-climbing rocks" (46).

Adam (a larger version of *Arabia Deserta*'s narrator Khalil) and Adama first see this waste at a distance, "shining, as a flint!" Steering by a distant peak across its "illimitable desolation," they "tread on glowing rocks" through stunning heat, day after day (Doughty 1908, 49-50). A storm of contending angels and devils sweeps over them; on the fourth day both fall in the blazing sun, but find water. Adam, bleeding, has to carry Adama at the last, but on the fifth day they make it across, staggering to safety and salvation like Doughty entering Jidda. John Middleton Murry calls *Adam Cast Forth* a "sublime simplification" of a world where Doughty "had become as the first man" (1931, 110). The poem illuminates *Arabia Deserta*, making manifest the spiritual interpretation of Khalil's travails that we infer from the book.

The most extensive and explicit use of the Great in the Edwardian novel is *The Garden of Allah* (1904) by Robert Hichens, who also wrote travel books on Egypt and Palestine. His heroine Domini ("of God"), having undergone a spiritual crisis, is searching for "freedom, a wide horizon, ... the terrible spaces"; in southern Algeria she hopes to come "face to face with an immensity of which she had often dreamed" (Hichens 6, 10). What she wants is what French writers on the Sahara from Fromentin in the 1850s to Eberhardt and Foucauld wanted: liberty, lonely space, spiritual bareness. On the train to the interior, Domini wonders "if God were putting forth His hand to withdraw gradually all things of His creation" and "meant to leave it empty and utterly naked" (17). Later, though, she hears the saying, "The desert is the garden of Allah" (82). The desolation seems absolute, outside of Creation, yet Domini revels in its purity and calls the region "strange and glorious" (18, 24).

Hichens's multivalent desert is also a "garden of oblivion" where one can start over (21). Domini has visions there: a man's face appears in the sun; another time a sunspot looks like "humanity, God's mistake" (31). Amid the "pettiness of modern, civilised life" she had felt "infinitely small," but the desert "suggested eternal things" (29, 34). Eternity is one of the book's motifs; the Sahara extends south "as Eternity stretches from the edge of time" (75). The desert and the steppe, Count Anteoni remarks, share "the wonder of the eternal flats" (194). He tells Domini that "the desert always hints at peace," which is what she seeks (69). Yet it is the murderer's refuge as well as a place where one hears the "still, small voice": hence Domini feels both "terror" and attraction (336, 124). Her main task, it turns out, is to reclaim an errant Trappist for his monastery, while Hichens's is to present a romantic, highly-coloured vision of the desert - not minimal, but rich and varied.

Thus there are several kinds of desert in the fiction and verse of the decades after *The Return of the Native*, as well as varied mountains, polar wastes, and oceans. All areas of the Great might serve the artist in search of natural analogues or contexts for human experience, and serve in different ways. Nor was this entirely a "western" phenomenon. The speaker in *The Book of Khalid* (1911) by Amin Rihani, an Arab poet, intones, "I, Khalid, a Bedouin in the desert of life" (190). And perhaps the most important oriental writer on the Great, the seventeenth-century Japanese poet Basho, was first translated into English in 1902, introducing the *haiku* and Zen sensibility to a western public. Evidently what Hulme felt on the Canadian prairies was part of a broader connection between landscape and art.

Interchapter: Two Sideshows

> ... one who moved and was alone up there
> To loom before the chaos and the glare
> As if he were the last god going home ....

Edwin A. Robinson,
"The Man Against the Sky" (1916)

Most historians agree that World War I did terrible damage to the collective psyche of western civilization. As A.J.P. Taylor put it in his history of the conflict, "The First World War cut deep into the consciousness of modern man" ([11]). It affected my subject along with other cultural phenomena: the war that reshaped Europe's and the Middle East's political order also disrupted global patterns of travel and plans for exploration, impeding efforts to know more of Great landscapes. In two notable instances, however, the war actually shaped or fostered adventures that were then memorably reported. Ernest Shackleton's last book and T.E. Lawrence's first are (in different senses) war literature, as well as important contributions to the annals of human encounters with "chastened sublimity."

A GLORIOUS FAILURE

Ernest Shackleton was obsessed by Antarctica; he could not give it up. Undeterred by two failed attempts to reach the South Pole (the first involving scurvy and differences with Scott, the second an about-face only 97 miles from his goal), and even by Amundsen's success, Shackleton proposed a two-prong expedition to traverse the continent from sea to sea via the Pole. An effective lecturer, he raised the necessary funds, picked a crew from a flood of volunteers, and was about to sail when the war broke out. Shackleton at once put his men and equipment at the service of the government, but was told to carry on: the war would soon be over. So his two ships sailed, separately, into bad weather and heavy ice. Judged by results, the effort was a disaster: Shackleton lost his own ship, the *Endurance*, in the ice and never even landed on Antarctica. On the far side, the *Aurora* was icebound for many months before limping back to New Zealand; its shore party laid depots as planned, but lost three men in the process. The expedition became an exercise in survival and rescue: another of Shackleton's splendid defeats.

But in *South* (1919), Shackleton the author[1] again transmutes an unsuccessful expedition into an epic of human endurance *vis à vis* wild nature: the idea of the voyage that has now entered popular culture through films and books. He dedicated *South* to "comrades who fell in the white warfare of the south [the three men from the *Aurora*] and on the red fields of France and Flanders," linking their voyage to the war whose first half they missed (though its second half claimed some survivors of the Antarctic debacle). Francis Spufford sees the *Endurance* as a sort of time machine, preserving a "bubble" of pre-war culture into 1916 (252), but Shackleton stresses *parallels* with the fighting, not disjunction from it. The white/red image recurs in his preface, and the narrative shows that he and his men felt as "helpless" amid "absolute chaos" as soldiers in the trenches, although their antagonist was "grim elementary forces," not human beings (Shackleton 1999, 80, 88).

Besides being a great adventure-and-survival book, *South* is a record of aesthetic responses to high latitudes. The first glimpse of glacial ice reminds Shackleton that a "great Arctic ice sheet once pressed over Northern Europe" (1999, 31). This sense (born of geology and glaciology) of being able to revisit the Ice Age was then one of the leading attractions of polar regions and high mountains. But meditations on earth history belong to the early part of the voyage, before the *Endurance* was trapped; in the icepack the song changes. In *Heart of the Antarctic*, Shackleton showed that Antarctica was as weird as it was vast and grand, and *South* develops the point. Icebergs float upside down in the sky or pose as islands, land looks like cloud and vice versa, and open water over the horizon is refracted in the sky, so that "Everything wears an aspect of unreality" (37). This was not a wholly negative quality: the idea of

---

[1]   Again assisted by Edward Saunders (Alexander 191).

entering "another world" than their own excited many visitors to
the Great. But when "All normal standards of perspective vanish"
and an explorer finds himself "drifting helplessly in a strange world
of unreality," he is in trouble (39, 47).

Shackleton's deepest response to his trials is religious; he has
a sort of rough-and-ready spirituality not uncommon among
explorers. Beset by the ice, he takes what measures he can, since
"Human effort is not futile," but acts "in a spirit of humility" and
with "a sense of dependence on the higher Power" (Shackleton
1999, 88). When they must abandon the ship, he brings along a page
of Job with the verse, "Out of whose womb came the ice?" As a rule,
though, Shackleton does not preach, especially after the "unreal"
world of the icepack gives way to the "stern realities" of sailing
small boats in the Roaring Fifties (135). That the 22-foot *James Caird*
is "a tiny speck in the vast vista of the sea" on the epic 800-mile
voyage to South Georgia does not even elicit a Biblical quotation
(191). Only near the end, when they have crossed the island and
are within reach of the whaling station, does "the Boss" let go: "We
had pierced the veneer of outside things. We had 'suffered, starved,
and triumphed, groveled down yet grasped at glory, grown bigger
in the bigness of the whole.' We had seen God in his splendors,
heard the text that Nature renders. We had reached the naked soul
of man" (226).

Given the journey they had made, these sentences do not
seem overwrought. They are an interesting mixture of language
drawn from hymns and devotional literature - "glory" is certainly
religious here - with a claim that they had "pierced the veneer"
of appearance and custom to a deeper reality, called "the naked
soul of man." The passage fuses the two principal themes of the
book: spirituality, and the movement from a world of deception to
a world of truth. Shackleton had "no doubt that Providence guided
us," and notes that all three hikers felt the presence of a fourth as
they were crossing the island (230).[2]

One of the three was Frank Worsley, the *Endurance*'s captain,
who navigated the *James Caird* to South Georgia. His book *The
Great Antarctic Rescue* repeats the story of the "fourth climber"
and generally supports and supplements Shackleton's narrative. It

---

[2]   T.S. Eliot's note to l. 360 of Book V of *The Waste Land* ("Who is the
third?") says that "The following lines were stimulated by the account
of one of the Antarctic expeditions (I forget which, but I think one of
Shackleton's) ...." See chapter 8, n. 2.

appears that *South*, far from being hyperbolic, is rather restrained. Worsley, a tough mariner, is much more apt than Shackleton to apply words such as "magnificent" and "majestic" to the icepack, Elephant Island, and South Georgia (1977, 44, 104, 195). He is also readier to acknowledge beauty and purity in icebergs, and to feel "awe at the force of Nature and the insignificance of man" (188). It is Worsley who evokes the scope and power of the seas they sailed: storm waves fifty feet high, swells up to a mile apart in good weather and a thousand miles long, rolling "almost unchecked around this end of the world" (116). Nothing in Worsley's book undermines Shackleton or diminishes their shared adventure.

THE WARRIOR AS MINIMALIST

Halfway around the globe, in a warmer, more arid regime, a bright young archeologist was drawn deep into the desert as he helped foment and organize an Arab revolt against the Ottoman Turks. T.E. Lawrence, arguably the most popular warrior to emerge from the Great War, was also the most famous European desert traveller to that time and well beyond. Under the arclights of publicity he could be flamboyant, and as his life was scrutinized, doubts were raised about both his war record and his private life. Hero-worship turned to iconoclasm, of which Lawrence James's *The Golden Warrior* (1990) is a good example. With the controversies over Lawrence's sexuality, integrity, and accuracy as an historian, however, we have as little to do as with the Cook-Peary battles. Our concern is with his aesthetic response to the desert, and in this regard he is less the Byronic "Lawrence of Arabia," dashing but dark, of Lowell Thomas's lectures, than a man maintaining a tradition. For Lawrence was a disciple of Doughty and Hardy, championing *Travels in Arabia Deserta* and paying reverent calls on "TH" after the war.

Like them, Lawrence was drawn to bareness: the quality of life and of land most often honoured in *Seven Pillars of Wisdom* (1926), which begins by telling how they lived "in the naked desert" (1938, 29). This nakedness is cultural as well as topographic; for Lawrence, "all the Semitic creeds ... preach bareness," and the Bedu, for whom "nakedness of the mind" is sensuous, prefer the wind of the desert to any perfume (39-41). By the end, he has come to share Sheikh Auda's feeling that the "plant-richness" of an oasis or garden is "vulgar, in its fecundity": an "indecency of exhibition" (233, 616). Lawrence made the physical-psychic connection, and declared his preference, most clearly in a 1918 letter explaining the appeal of Arab culture. "The doctrine of bareness in materials is a good one," he wrote V.W. Richards, "and it involves apparently a sort of moral bareness too" (T. Lawrence 1941, 109). Like other desert travellers before and since, he found that minimalism and the desert went hand in hand.

Bareness may take the form of emptiness, again both natural and human. The nomads have "air and winds, sun and light, open spaces and a great emptiness" in their lives, says Lawrence, deliberately leaving the last term ambiguous (1938, 40). So Auda decamps from an oasis at 2 AM to seek "an empty view" (233). This is partly a matter of his religion, which says the world is empty and God is full; thus the richness of an oasis belongs to heaven. But Lawrence - who also grew up in a "Semitic creed" - comes to feel the same way, and *he* can explain it to us: "The abstraction of the desert landscape cleansed me, and rendered my mind vacant with its superfluous greatness: a greatness achieved not by the addition of thought to its emptiness, but by its subtraction. In the weakness of earth's life was mirrored the strength of heaven, so vast, so beautiful, so strong" (512). To some western readers this passage sounds "oriental," perhaps Buddhist, but Semitic religion also has a mystical tradition, traces of which exist in Doughty.

Vastness is another motif of *Seven Pillars*. In the passage above it belongs to heaven, but Lawrence (recapitulating pioneers such as Thomas Burnet) finds it on earth too, especially in Wadi Rumm, a great dry valley in the marches of Jordan and Arabia. Of the horizontal vastness of the desert he speaks only seldom and generally, recalling "the sweep of the open places, the taste of wide winds" (T. Lawrence 1941, 80). But the verticality of Rumm, whose thousand-foot-high sandstone parapets line the valley on both sides for miles, forming a mighty avenue, impresses him as a different kind of power, akin to the archetypes felt in childhood dreams. Lawrence calls Wadi Rumm "a processional way greater than imagination. The Arab armies would have been lost in the length and breadth of it, and within the walls a squadron of aeroplanes could have wheeled in formation. Our little caravan grew self-conscious, and fell dead quiet, afraid and ashamed to flaunt its smallness in the presence of the stupendous hills" (1938, 351). Doughty, too, revered this desert-and-mountain topography.

Actually, Wadi Rumm is a locus of several motifs. It is so superb that "unsentimental" Howeitat tribesmen, not known for appreciating landscape, tell him of it and seem moved there (T. Lawrence 1938, 350). He also sees beauty in "heaven," and a stony desert may have "the monstrous beauty of sterile desolation," but there is no oxymoron or qualification with regard to Rumm - except "in truth I liked Rumm too much" (271, 352). Lawrence has serious work to do; he cannot allow himself to fall into aestheticism. And perhaps there is another problem, arising from the combination of vastness and beauty. John Stuart Mill had warned that contemplation of the Great might teach observers that they were petty, and their good works vain. Lawrence, like other desert travellers, felt this mood at times. In *Seven Pillars* he says that he and the Arabs were "shamed into pettiness by the innumerable silences of stars" (29). Wadi Rumm's "whelming greatness dwarfed" them, so that they felt insignificant (375). In addition, several lesser themes, including the desert as a "mind-landscape," are exclusive to Rumm (375).

Some of Lawrence's ideas remain puzzling. When he writes of "challenging" a *khamsin* wind, for example, is this masochism, asceticism (both can be found in *Seven Pillars* and his letters), or a nod to the macho ghost of Richard Burton? It is also hard to say how far he participates in the purity and spirituality that he attributes to the nomads. Two points are clear, though. One is that the psychic portrait derived from an analysis of his aesthetics can survive close scrutiny. Even a debunking biographer like James depicts a recognizable Lawrence, an ascetic minimalist dedicated to abstinence, simplicity, and the primitive. The second point is that his years in Arabia were the apex of Lawrence's abbreviated career; once the war and the peace were concluded, and his story told, life had nothing else to offer. He assumed various identities and worked at military bases, often tinkering with engines, but "I'm all smash, inside," he wrote Bernard Shaw in 1928 (T. Lawrence 1941, 290). The fatal motorcycle accident of 1935 was redundant. Perhaps, like Robinson's Man Against the Sky, "He may have seen with his mechanic eyes / A world without a meaning."

The 1914-18 conflict is sometimes called a "war without heroes." This was not strictly true - even in Europe there were soldiers of distinction - but the remark is generally valid. The old idea (based on the classics and chivalry) of warfare as a theatre in which stars played roles of noble valor gave way to grim campaigns in which superannuated generals sent ignorant young men to death by technology: artillery, machine guns, aerial bombing. Heroes existed mainly at the margins. The Red Baron belonged to the new knighthood of the skies, as did Billy Bishop, who, like Audie Murphy, came from the new world. "Lawrence of Arabia," with his Scots-Irish blood, illegitimacy, childhood in Wales and Scotland, orientalism, and mediaevalism, was very much of the margins and even of *l'ancien régime*. His campaign in the vast deserts of the Mideast alongside "exotic" nomads, far from the trenches, was the last gasp of chivalry in modern warfare. Ernest Shackleton (also Irish) was excused from war duty and sent to enact his *agon* in the cold purity of Antarctic seas. Their stories, once they became known, were received as blessings by a public sick of Gallipoli and the Somme.

Part Two:
Reassembling the World
1920-1940

The gap that separated the 1918 Armistice from the resumption of hostilities two decades later was an entr'acte between Wagnerian upheavals. In retrospect its hopeful activities seem poignant, its doomsayers deadly accurate, but that is our dramatic irony. For many travellers and explorers at the time, "the going was good"; an air of relief at the lifting of burdens and the resumption of useful life permeates their books. Others, stunned by what the Great War had revealed about their civilization and human nature, brooded darkly on the breakdown of old verities. The age was enigmatic, schizophrenic: were waste lands opportunities, or symbols of our own desert places? Had Hardy's picture of gloomy moderns seeking barren places been prescient, or overdrawn? Was this *Götterdämmerung* or "twilight of the gods" a dawn or a dusk? Shackleton, Gertrude Bell (a suicide in Baghdad in 1926), and Lawrence joined Scott in making early exits, though Nansen and Amundsen soldiered on for a while.

Important aspects of the modern world-view fell into place during this period: the age of the earth, for example, a point of contention between geologists and Biblical fundamentalists in the nineteenth century. The technique of radiometric dating, which promised greater accuracy, was accepted by the Anglo-American scientific community in the early 1920s, leading the US National Academy of Sciences to set the age of the earth at around 1500 million years in 1931. Recent estimates are vastly older, but even the 1931 figure was much greater than scriptural literalists were prepared to admit (Albritton 211-13). Though the religious establishment no longer rushed to refute such numbers, as in Darwin's time, grassroots opposition to the strictly empirical study of the earth and to the geologists' conclusions continued, as it does today. George Meredith remarked in 1893 that the Victorians had moved from religion "through science to despair" (Dean 131). After the war some chose not to take that trip, or found different destinations. Geology was more than ever the science of choice for adventurers and explorers, and a powerful influence on their attitudes.

A second point has to do with the nature of the cosmos. Developments in astronomy in the first decades of the twentieth century probably had more effect on perceptions of space than at any time since the seventeenth century, when the telescope nurtured the "aesthetics of the infinite." Sir James Jeans presented the updated view of the heavens to general readers in *The Mysterious Universe* (1930), whose first chapter is called "The Dying Sun." A "vast multitude of stars," he writes, as numerous as the grains of sand on the world's beaches, yet mostly large enough to contain thousands of earths, wander through space, rarely coming within a million miles of each other; "Such is the littleness of our home in space" (Jeans 1). The puniness of man that sometimes struck polar explorers is put on a cosmic scale. Nor does Jeans shrink from the affective content of this knowledge: "We find the universe terrifying because of its vast meaningless distances … its inconceivably long vistas of time, … because of our extreme loneliness …. But above all … because it appears to be indifferent [or] actively hostile" (3).

Life and its enabling conditions are a rare accident, Jeans argues; most space and matter are either too cold or too hot for us. His conclusion recalls the statements that shocked Victorian readers of *Essays and Reviews* in 1859: "it seems incredible that the universe can have been designed primarily to produce life like our own," since it is so inefficient at doing so (Jeans 5). Christians, Jews, or Muslims wondering where this line of thought is going do not have long to wait. The "utter insignificance of life" undercuts the idea that it is a "special interest" of the Creator; rather we have stumbled into a universe "clearly not designed for life" (10, 13). And whither humanity? Jeans thinks that we are "probably destined to die of cold" as we move away from a cooling sun, an idea familiar to Nansen and H.G. Wells (12). For the learned astronomer, then, traditional religious teachings that flatter our sense of self-importance are contrary to fact: life is a freak, we have always been on our own, and our exit would make no difference to the universe.

Culturally, the postwar scene soon began to look "modern." Grandiose gestures had become suspect, and in some cases impossible, resources being limited. Igor Stravinsky turned from rich orchestral scores for the lavish Diaghilev ballets of 1910-13 (*L'Oiseau de feu*, *Petrouchka*, *Le Sacre du printemps*) to small works for such ensembles as could be mustered in postwar Europe: *L'Histoire du soldat* (1918), *Octet for Wind Instruments* (1923). English poetry became markedly more spare and astringent, shifting its aesthetic centre from Housman through the Trench Poets towards Eliot. Some commentators maintain that minimalism as a style and philosophy of art began in these years. Richard Wollheim in 1965 presented "Minimal Art" as a fifty-year-old phenomenon; Warren Motte traces its recognition by critics to the 1920s.

The cumbersome machinery of travel into the Great began to move again, creaking a bit. With the quests for the North and South Poles concluded - as far as anyone could tell - the emphasis shifted to scaling the world's highest mountain (sometimes called "the third pole"), and closer study of deserts and polar regions.

5

Empty Quarters:
Accepting the Desert

The War temporarily shifted the emphasis from deserts as fields of travel to deserts as battlegrounds. Lawrence, the prime exemplar, retained his interest: *Seven Pillars of Wisdom* was privately printed (1926), then published (1935), books were written about him, and his letters appeared posthumously (1938). Old modes and routes of travel had been damaged, and for a decade it looked as if heroic undertakings might be a thing of the past. The important events in deserts were political, administrative - as when the Grand Canyon became a National Park (1919) - or mechanical: the Sahara was crossed by air (1920) and by automobile (1922).

ARID STUDIES

The first desert books of the 1920s were scientific. Isaiah Bowman, the director of the American Geographical Society, wrote *Desert Trails of the Atacama* (1924) for the AGS, mostly confining himself to the geography, geology, economy, and demography of one of the world's driest deserts (in Chile). His descriptions are detailed but objective, with few feelings or reactions. As chapters on rainfall, mining, and livestock succeed one another, we may ask why the Atacama "more strongly attracted [him] than any other part of South America" (Bowman v). Because the shepherds there retain the "old ways" in a "pure form"? (247) Because it has less than one person per square mile? Or because the desert, like the sea, fosters the poetic and religious instincts? (168) *Why* are deserts "the most interesting" of all the places explorers go? (5) The motives he mentions - science and adventure - could be satisfied elsewhere. Bowman himself wonders why desert-dwellers "seek so severe an environment" (5). He is one of those writers in whom the attraction is stated, but the cause is left for us to infer.

French scientists followed their explorers, priests, soldiers and eccentrics into Africa's deserts. *Sahara* (1923), by the savant Émile Gautier, rests on a foundation of geography, anthropology, geology, and belief in the *mission civilizatrice*. Gautier, more subjective and forthcoming than Bowman, takes pains to assert the Sahara's kinship with other areas of the Great. It is "as strange ... as ... the polar zone," parts in fact being less known than Antarctica; its mountains are like the Alps, or an archipelago; its long level plains give a horizon as regular as the ocean, or suggest the "vast sterile stretches" of interstellar space (Gautier 34, 109). Its extent is formidable, the occasional oasis providing some relief from the "endless dead immensities" around it (110). Gautier also emphasizes the "great antiquity" of the Sahara, whose "very ancient primary rocks" lie "just as they were laid down" (53, 30): a note often heard in Lyell and Darwin, who were always impressed by traces of the primordial earth. Gautier, however, does not shrink from calling the Sahara "senescent" (105).

He never tries to gloss over the desert's dark side. The Sahara's "dreadful solitudes" are not only ancient but dangerous (Gautier 195). It is "a world apart," a place that visitors find "disconcerting" and "unfamiliar" (34, 103). Its dryness is placed in a larger context that increases the Sahara's importance: "the planet itself has undergone a tremendous change of climate in the direction of aridity since the Quaternary age," so desert scholars may be studying our future (94). Gautier's is a balanced portrait. If the Sahara is desolate and empty, its air is pure and healthy; if it is hazardous, it equally demands the traveller's best, challenging our wits and powers of endurance. He tries to take the desert on its own terms, to see it steadily and see it whole. Gautier was influential: an American translation of his 2nd edition (1928) appeared in 1935.

ADVENTURERS AND EXPLORERS

Scientists did not have the deserts to themselves for long, however. In the early 1920s, a Major R.E. Cheesman made two camel journeys in southern Arabia and wrote accounts of them. Eldon Rutter (an

English Muslim who later recanted) went on the pilgrimage to Mecca and Medina in 1925, despite the recent civil war. He described his camel rides and those cities in *Holy Cities of Arabia* (1928), praised by T.E. Lawrence. Rutter has no great love for the desert: he is appalled by a "ghastly" plain of black stones, and the plateau above is an "arid terrible world," though its geology interests him (92, 100). The mountains near Mecca do possess "beauty" and "grandeur"; Jebel Kara's "grim and monstrous majesty" is unequalled in the Alps (352, 355). The route to Medina, however, traverses a "mighty desolation" and "terrible valleys" (360, 487). Avoiding "biblical" phrasing, keeping his sentences short and simple, Rutter sounds more like Hemingway than like Doughty, whose sonorous cadences influenced Lawrence and other desert writers for two generations.

In the United States, an ethnography student read of a huge unexplored mesa in a remote part of Utah and decided that he must see it. On their third try Clyde Kluckhohn and friends managed to ascend Wild Horse Mesa and spent a month on top (1928). In *Beyond the Rainbow* he is candid about the appeal of that time: it was "strange and precious ... partly because no other human beings were near" (quoted Roberts 256). The mesa he thought "perfect, so absolute a thing in itself": the philosophers' *Ding an sich*. A "Gothic Cathedral fifty miles long and four thousand feet high," it possessed great spiritual power (257). Kluckhohn wondered what should become of the place. A National Park, perhaps? Its vistas were as magnificent as Mesa Verde's, he thought; its sublimity exceeded the Grand Canyon's. But National Parks attract hordes of tourists and developers, so better turn it into "a national preserve denied to settlement": no roads, trails, landing strips, or machines - which destroy the conditions that created the national character (259). Kluckhohn attended the University of Wisconsin, which had already given the conservation movement John Muir, and was about to give it Aldo Leopold.

By the late 1920s a resurgence of desert adventurers was visible. French aviators (including Antoine de Saint-Exupéry) were flying over the African desert - with unscheduled stops - and across the Atlantic to South America. A young Frenchman gave his life to reach a ruined city in the Spanish Sahara. Two Englishmen were probing south Arabian deserts. And the veteran Swedish explorer Sven Hedin, a living legend who had been criss-crossing Asia since the 1890s, had received royal support by the turn of the century, and had already published a memoir, *My Life as an Explorer* (1925), which one might have thought valedictory, the author then being 60 - that same Sven Hedin went to China to lead an expedition across the Gobi Desert (1927-28). This time he had international backing and plenty of younger help.

Hedin's reactions to the Gobi are of interest because throughout his travels it had been mountains, not plains, that elicited lyrical tributes (chs. 1 and 2). Yet the author of *Across the Gobi Desert* had felt the power of long flat horizons. Upon first sighting the Gobi, Hedin remarks - hesitating over the adjective - that "there is something imposing, impressive, in these endless expanses" (1931, 114). Later he specifies that the desert is "impressive in its majestic grandeur and solitude" (325). These qualities - solitude, grandeur, vastness - are common in other desert books, but his most frequent reaction is the familiar analogy with the sea: an oasis is like an atoll in the ocean. This illusion of an "open sea" gives him "positive pleasure" and an "impression of mighty Asia" (123). The desert's power is reiterated, while other traits - beauty, desolation, silence, gloom - are noted in passing. Hedin, like Scott, was a man who preferred wild, empty land to comfort at home.

The early 1930s saw a series of ventures into Asian and African deserts. The young French intellectual Michel Vieuchange managed to reach the desert city of Smara in the Spanish Sahara (where French airmail pilots tried not to land), but died of dysentery on the way back in 1930. His journals were published under the title *Smara: the Forbidden City* (1933). It was a mysterious place, known from legends and tales, long inaccessible due to unreliable maps, forbidding terrain, hostile tribesmen, and political uncertainty. Vieuchange's effort (called "a raid") to find Smara at a time of French-Spanish tension over the area was eccentric, to say the least. Having rejected almost everything about France and modern life, he found some meaning in a quest so perilous that he could not travel openly, but had to dress as a Berber woman and latterly be hidden in a basket: the antithesis of the freedom that many sought in the desert. Paul Claudel's breathless introduction treats Vieuchange as a martyr. But to what?

His diary is as minimal as the desert (eight years without rain) in which he travelled. He had to observe through a veil, then from under burlap sacks, and, like Doughty, write covertly. Yet, labouring among rocks and through ravines in fear of attack, he finds "grandeur" in a bare mountainside rising above "arid *bled*" [land] (Vieuchange 57). As his guides are extorting more money, he lies in a dry wash looking at the sky and writes, "it was possible to understand de Foucauld, seeking a God at all costs" (106).[1] Vieuchange caught a fever from bad water, and his foot was infected, so they turned back; despite the suffering, he felt joyful and purified. His second try gave him "a deeper impression of the desert where life is impossible," as he soon proved (178). Smara turned out to be an empty stone city on a stony plain. Still, "it was impressive, that terrible bareness," wrote Vieuchange, nearing his end. As we saw in chapter 1, Yi-Fu Tuan notes that ascetic temperaments prefer stark environments, adding that the desert can be an "austere stage for epiphany" (1974, 51). But most of whatever Vieuchange saw beyond his veil died with him.

THE EMPTY QUARTER

At almost the same time, two servants of the British Empire were probing Arabia's *Rub' al Khali*, the Empty Quarter, each hoping to be the first westerner to cross (Doughty never met anyone who had been there or knew anything about it). Beduin rarely ventured into its vast, arid, sandy interior. They might use waterholes or pasturage near its edge in their sector, or raid other nomads there, but to traverse it meant braving both physical challenges and tribal feuds. One had to travel with an escort for safety - and not the same one all the way over. The first to succeed was Bertram Thomas, who crossed from south to north in the winter of 1930-31. He called his book *Arabia Felix* (1932): the ancient geographers' term for the whole peninsula. "Happy" is an odd epithet for the Empty Quarter, he admits, though it does suit Dhufar, the mountainous province from which he started. Both Thomas and T.E. Lawrence, who wrote a foreword, call the Quarter "virgin": "the last considerable *terra incognita*" (Thomas, viii, xii, xiii).

Initially Thomas sounds like a romantic: knowing "the mind of authority," he avoids "the pitfall of seeking permission" for his trip, hates the idea of machines violating "virgin silences," and uses Walter de la Mare's poem "Arabia" as an epigraph (xiv, xv). Yet he is a competent traveller, well versed in local dialects and customs, inured to camel-riding and hard living. Why are you doing this?

---

[1] Wallace Stegner wrote that vast deserts are "close to whatever God you want to see in them." Quoted in Krutch 1969, p. [4].

ask the Bedu. They sound like Cook's Inuit companions on the trip
to the Big Nail, puzzled as to the point of the project. Thomas says
he likes to travel and wants to serve science (no mention of being
the first non-Arab to cross). Moreover, he often enjoys the country.
The "glorious" Qara Mountains in Dhufar command "magnificent
views" over "much grandeur" (48, 78, 100). Over a pass and inland
are bleak hills, then "a vast waste of red rolling country" (120, 121).
This is not yet the *Rub' al Khali*, but he feels "joy" to be at large in the
"wide clean spaces," on a "vast expanse of featureless wilderness"
that takes two days to cross (124, 135). Finally, out on a broad plain,
Thomas is shown a strip of yellow on the horizon: "the sands of my
desire" (149).

The party head into the high dune country over "rose red
mountains of sand" (Thomas 170). "Mountains" is his first attempt
to convey the *Rub' al Khali*, but it needs more than one Great parallel.
The Empty Quarter is "a vast ocean of billowing sands" that rise
in tiers "like a mighty mountain system" (170). Neither image is
expendable as the terrain changes. Their labours are rewarded
with "moments ... of sublime grandeur" and "an exquisite purity
of colour" reminiscent of a winter's day in Switzerland (171, 174-5).
Farther on, though, they find a "barren ocean" (a Homeric phrase
popular with educated Englishmen then) and "an ocean calm" as
dune country gives way to plain (210, 236). This analogy, Thomas's
favourite way of representing the desert, makes new sense when
he explains that much of it was Eocene seabed: an area of cleavage
between the African and Persian formations. At last, the *Rub' al
Khali* behind him, he stands on a hill and accepts the "waste of low
sands" stretching east and west as "a glorious panorama" - the
adjective he had applied to the mountains of happy Dhufar (293).

In his foreword to *Arabia Felix*, T.E. Lawrence called Thomas "the
last" of those who "walked the inviolate earth," and his journey "the
finest thing in Arabian exploration" (Thomas viii-ix). As he wrote,
however, H. St John Philby, another old imperial hand and once
Thomas's chief, was making an even more demanding traverse of
the Empty Quarter that would make *him* "the last of the great British
explorers of Arabia" (Simmons 372). Born on Ceylon, educated in
England, where he studied oriental languages at Cambridge, Philby
began his career in India. In 1915 he went to Mesopotamia, where
he met Bell and Lawrence, and in 1917 to Arabia, the "threshold
of my destiny" (Philby 1948, 143). He became a friend of King Ibn
Sa'ud, returned as a businessman after leaving the Civil Service,

accepted Islam, and wrote over a dozen books about the country. Philby dated his obsession with the *Rub' al Khali* (the "largest blank space on the map outside the polar regions") from 1918, when he met the archeologist David Hogarth, Lawrence's mentor (Simmons 131).

In *The Empty Quarter* (1933), he recounts his journey and concedes Thomas's priority, but cannot hide irritation at his former subordinate crossing first. "As the Arab poet sang of old," writes Philby, "'Twas I that learn'd him in the archer's art; / At me, his hand grown strong, he launched his dart": as if Thomas's trip were a personal attack (1933, xvii). This is his worst moment; subsequently he is more respectful. But Philby's irascibility and egotism cost him: he wrangled with his nomad escort, who mutinied and turned back. Determined to cross the desert on its broad axis, he cajoled them into making a second attempt, though his guide had never made the trip or heard of anyone doing it. "We are surely the first," he assured Philby, "this is the Empty Quarter; no one comes here, never" (304). His route was much longer and more tortuous than Thomas's, so he did see more of the *Rub' al Khali*. In retrospect, at least, Philby's ten weeks of "pains and pleasures" in the desert were "the greatest and pleasantest experience of all my life" (9).

Occasionally there is a hint of a spiritual dimension to the journey in his biblical-Miltonic phrasing: "And the morning and the evening were the first day" (Philby 1933, 17). This seems not to be the real Philby, however, who is a geographer and natural scientist: sighting stars, making maps and geological notes, collecting flora and fauna for the British Museum. His wish to "throw back the veil of time" and show earth as it was at first, which sounds like Doughty, comes down to compiling data for the "professors" (61). Philby's dry, almost technical style cannot achieve the visionary. And his paean to a vista over a "magnificent, far-flung, desolate scene" near the beginning proves atypical (52). We hear no more of scenic magnificence, though a good deal about desolation. Barrenness and bareness are, unsurprisingly, his dominant perceptions, yet not all observers responded to these qualities in the same way; Doughty could exclaim eloquently over "nightmare soil!"

Most of Philby's epithets for the Empty Quarter are negative. He writes of a gravel plain's "appalling nakedness," and of an "abomination of desolation" where camels cannot graze (Philby 1933, 67, 118). When not appalled, he is apt to deliver verdicts ranging from "dull, monotonous and dreary" to "impressive monotony" in the plain of Abu Bahr, the "father of the sea" (182, 335). Like Thomas, Philby often compares the Empty Quarter to another area of the Great, usually the ocean; "dunes like the breakers of a reef-strewn sea" rest on the ancient beds of rivers, lakes, or ocean bays (152). Once Philby reaches poleward for his analogy, calling Shanna plain the "*Ultima Thule* of our southward wanderings" (223). Shanna is a silent, gloomy land whose lifelessness depresses him. One might expect Philby to welcome the advent of western technology to such a place, yet he (like Thomas) thinks "with a shudder" of the possibility that automobiles might come here (325). We may not understand, but cannot forget, that he remembered crossing the Empty Quarter as "the greatest and pleasantest experience of all my life."

LITERARY TRAVELLERS

A good explorer, Philby was a dull writer. Travellers of a more literary bent arrived after the scientists and explorers. Novelists such as Robert Hichens and André Gide who used the Sahara as a setting attracted other writers, some of whom produced (ostensibly) non-fiction travel narratives, as Pierre Loti, William Morris, and Hichens himself had done.

Of these, perhaps the least likely was Vita Sackville-West, whose *Passenger to Teheran* was published by the Woolfs' Hogarth Press (1926). After Anne Blunt, Gertrude Bell, Mary Austin, and Isabelle Eberhardt, a woman writing on desert travel comes as no surprise, but *Bloomsbury* women rarely confronted barren landscape (though Virginia Woolf's father was the famous Alpinist Leslie Stephen). Sackville-West was only a tourist, of course, a "passenger" in motor transport, as her title acknowledges, and for many garrulous pages she seems to have taken the wrong trip. Egypt's Valley of the Kings is frightening, Aden detestable, Iraq hideous. A reader could be forgiven for abandoning ship in these early chapters. In Baghdad she stays with Gertrude Bell - who may have enlarged her outlook - and then takes the railroad east towards Persia.

When the line ends after a hundred miles, she boards a car of the Trans-Desert Mail and, atop a pass near the border, has an epiphany. Sackville-West admits that she was not psychologically prepared for what she saw: Persia's plains, mountains, space, and serenity seem pre-human (68-70). From a second pass, she looks back on an "immense prospect" of "savage, desolating country! but one that filled me with extraordinary elation. I had never seen anything that pleased me so well as these Persian uplands, with their enormous views, clear light, and rocky grandeur" (71). Discovering the Great for herself, she seems to feel the attraction of which Addison and Hardy wrote. The triviality is gone; she remembers the horizon, not the details, nor does subsequent travel dull the pleasure. Between Teheran and Isfahan she finds "loneliness" as it must have been before humanity, and breathes air of "incomparable purity" in "vast high solitudes" (113, 117). Pure, empty, and spacious, Persia thrills her. Leaving it via a verdant valley down to the Caspian Sea, she remains grateful for that approach over the high plains.

Many kinds of people sought the desert in those years. Clare Frewen, a cousin of Winston Churchill, grew up in several countries and went to school in France until she was 16. There followed heady years of spiritualism, a London debut, wintering in Stockholm as a princess's guest, friendship with Henry James, and marriage to Wilfrid Sheridan, a descendant of the playwright. After he was killed in the war, she left their children with relatives and became a sculptor and a journalist, in which capacity she met Mussolini. He told her chillingly that to succeed, she must make her heart a desert, like his. Not long afterwards, disliking postwar Europe, she retreated to Algeria, having always wanted "to live on the edge of the desert, in the places described by Robert Hichens" (Sheridan 255). In an oasis facing the Sahara's "infinite space" she wrote her memoirs, in which she exclaims, "Mussolini, I have taken your advice and made my heart a desert!" (377, 382). Clare Sheridan seems a classic example of the wanderer drawn to the desert because it mirrors or soothes her inner state.

D.H. Lawrence's strong feelings for desert lands apparently developed during his and Frieda's wanderings through Australia and Mexico, and residence in Taos, New Mexico. These emotions can be glimpsed in *The Spirit of Place* (1935) and *Phoenix* (1936), collections of scattered passages about wild nature. Besides his evocations of Great landscape in fiction (see ch. 8), there are essays that attest more directly to the power such scenes possessed for him. In "New Mexico" (1931), he calls the "magnificence" of morning in the desert his "greatest experience" of the outside world (D.H. Lawrence 1972, 142). "What splendour!" exclaims Lawrence; to him, such "vast ... magnificence" transcends aesthetics (143). That, of course, is why Addison coined "the Great." His long "Study of

Thomas Hardy" (1932) calls Egdon Heath the "great tragic power" of *The Return of the Native* and the root of its characters (415). Hardy's natural settings seemed to Lawrence more important than his people, who move upon the land "almost insignificantly" (480), like explorers in Antarctica.[2]

Karen Blixen, the Danish aristocrat better known by her pen-name Isak Dinesen, had a farm in Kenya from 1913 to 1931. Her memoirs, *Out of Africa* (1937) and *Shadows on the Grass* (1960), which always had their admirers, have gained wider popularity from the film *Out of Africa*. Everything she writes about, the land no less than the people, is transfigured by the fineness of her feeling and style. The aspect of nature to which Blixen responded most keenly - it may have held her longer in East Africa - was spaciousness. Her dreams provided a "quality of infinite space. I move in mighty landscapes …. Long perspectives stretch before me, distance is the password of the scenery" (Dinesen 334). In waking life this longing was met both by the "divine, clean, barren marine greatness" of the Indian Ocean's shoreline, and by "vast stretches" of plain, which "always have a maritime air, the open horizon recalls the sea and the long sea-sands" (243, 200). When her lover Denys Finch-Hatton died in a plane crash, she had him buried in the hills at a place they had chosen with "an infinitely great view": north to Mt. Kenya, and south to Mt. Kilimanjaro (248).

Blixen loved three-dimensional space as astronomers and mountaineers do. To explain the "overwhelming feeling of joy" an earthquake aroused, she compares it to what Kepler may have felt when he deduced the laws of planetary motion (Dinesen 208). But flying with Finch-Hatton in his Gypsy Moth gave "the greatest, the most transporting pleasure" of her African years (167). To describe the "tremendous views" of light, rainbows, clouds, however, is difficult, since "The language is short of words for the experiences of flying, and will have to invent new words with time. When you have flown over the Rift Valley and the volcanoes … you have travelled far and have been to the lands on the other side of the moon." Belonging to the first generation of writers faced with trying to convey the novel sensations of flying, she insists that "the joy and glory of the flyer is the flight itself." Up in the air, in "the full freedom of the three dimensions … the homesick heart throws

---

[2]   Frieda Lawrence evidently shared his feelings. In *Not I, But the Wind* she tells how much she loved seeing the beautiful "Sahara *Wüste*" (D.H. Lawrence 1944, 134).

itself into the arms of space" (167). It is as if the Great had added a new region: the lower sky beneath the astronomical heavens.

The indispensable writer on the sensations of flying is Antoine de Saint-Exupéry; a pioneer aviator before he was an author, he knew first-hand the mail route from the Pyrenees across the Sahara and South Atlantic to the Andes. Besides his novels on this subject (see ch. 8), he treated flight over desert and ocean in *Du vent, des sables des étoiles* (1939, translated as *Wind, Sand and Stars*; revised as *Terre des hommes*). The English and French texts diverge little in their attitudes toward the Great, which, except for the vertical perspective, is presented in familiar terms. Saint-Exupéry "succumbed to the desert as soon as [he] saw it"; "the vast sandy void ... thrilled" him, and he came to love its "golden emptiness" (1965, 83, 139). He asserts that his comrades shared these feelings: "we knew joys we could not possibly have known elsewhere. I shall never be able to express clearly whence comes this pleasure men take from aridity, but always and everywhere I have seen men attach themselves more stubbornly to barren lands than to any other" (82).[3]

Saint-Exupéry's hallmark is verticality. He makes the usual comparison between the desert and the sea, but pilots, like astronomers, deal in "celestial mechanics," and so, on a remote Saharan mesa, meteorite fragments, one per acre, are a "miserly rain from the stars" (Saint-Exupéry 1965, 130, 68). Amid the barrenness of glaciated, volcanic Patagonia, with here and there "the decent loam of ... earth" covering "the surface of the star," he can *feel* that we live on one (64).[4] Saint-Exupéry's urgent message, his *idée fixe*, is that flight "has unveiled for us the true face of the earth" (62). It shows us that "Roads avoid the barren lands," connecting oases, heading for the human, distorting our sense of the planet. The airplane sheds a "cruel light" on "indulgent fictions" about a "merciful and fruitful" world by revealing "the essential foundation, the fundament of rock and sand and salt" with the odd bit of life (62-3). Saint-Exupéry makes this a general proposition, though it is especially true of flight over the Great.

At Punta Arenas, "the most southerly habitation of the world, a town born of the chance presence of a little mud between the

---

3   The corresponding passage in *Terre des hommes* differs in expression, but not in feeling: "... nous avons aimé le désert"; "Dès mon premier voyage, j'ai connu le goût du désert" ([1939], 97, 99).

4   The same point is made in *Terre des hommes*: "la bonne pâte de la terre s'est enfin déposée sur l'astre" (1939, 70).

timeless lava and the austral ice," Saint-Exupéry spent "a single day blessed among days" (1965, 64-5). Why "blessed"? One reason is that Patagonia (and the Sahara) tell us a fundamental truth about the earth; they do not mislead. Another is the (minimalist) view that "perfection" is attained "when a body has been stripped down to its nakedness" (40-1). Saint-Exupéry, like others before and since, believes that "in the desert a man is always free," and that its privations intensify our awareness of the moment and our love of life (101). Even when dying of thirst in the desert, he felt peace and a camaraderie with his fellow-sufferers. As well, the "feeling of eternity" that comes upon us in the wilderness, and the airplane, which brings us "face to face with the eternal ["vieux" in the French] problems," meet a deep need: our "passion for eternity" (70, xi, 66).

The sea also moved Saint-Exupéry; his account of what Mermoz saw during his first crossing of the South Atlantic is as vivid as any scene in the book. In the "Black Hole" off Africa, a region where "tornadoes" are tailing to the sea, Mermoz drops beneath the clouds, after dark, into a "fantastic kingdom."[5] Huge waterspouts, seemingly immobile, join the ocean to the overcast "comme les piliers noirs d'un temple," 'like the dark pillars of a temple' (Saint-Exupéry 1939, 26). But moonlight coming through rifts in the clouds makes diagonal shafts among columns of rising water, and for hours Mermoz explores these "uninhabited ruins," angling from one opening to the next, flying down "corridors of moonlight" between the waterspouts "toward the exit from the temple" (Saint-Exupéry 1965, 13). Like some climbers, Mermoz has found a church in which he can believe. The scene almost defines Great aesthetics, using its least-described area.

The differences between *Wind, Sand and Stars* and *Terre des hommes* are notable but elusive. Material is rearranged and chapters are retitled; "Prisoner of the Sand" becomes "Au Centre du désert." Sometimes the French text seems more "philosophical," or at least more metaphorical: "le désert n'est point fait de sable .... Le Sahara, c'est en nous qu'il se montre."[6] But the world can be a desert in either version, and often the changes are rhetorical rather than conceptual. In trouble after crashing in the Sahara, the English

---

5   "un royaume fantastique." The French and English versions are very
     close. Compare 1965, 13; and 1939, 25-6.
6   "the desert is not simply made of sand .... The Sahara manifests itself
     within us." *Terre des hommes*, 1939, 98.

"I" says, "I felt no sorrow. I was the desert" (Saint-Exupéry 1965, 165). The French persona prefers the immediacy of the present, using a very Gallic idiom: "je n'ai plus de chagrin .... Le désert, c'est moi" (Saint-Exupéry 1939, 203). This identification appears in both languages, alongside tributes to the power of the Great, and a desire to use flying as "a means of getting away from towns and their book-keeping and coming to grips with reality" (1965, 162).

In Freya Stark, the English tradition of eastern travel writers found a successor to Gertrude Bell: an observant traveller (and imperialist) with the literary gifts to recreate her experiences for readers. Born in good walking country (Dartmoor) to parents who hiked and climbed, Stark was first taken to the Alps as a baby. She visited the Near East in 1926 and soon found her métier, travelling throughout the region and writing a series of books about her journeys. Stark wrote on other subjects too, but "she has never written better than under the inspiration of the desert" (Fedden 39). In 1963 Murray published a selection of her writings called *Journey's Echo*, with a foreword by Lawrence Durrell noting that her books, like Doughty's and Lawrence's, always present two journeys: the outer and the inner. In 1980, a journalist found her horse-packing in the Himalayas at the age of 87.

Each of her works has its admirers. Robin Fedden liked the "delightful, highly conscious and sensitive" *Southern Gates of Arabia* (1936), which elevates "the travel book to something more than an account of travel" (39). The amount of journey narrative is modest in most of her works; Stark likes to pause and discourse on the meaning of what she sees, generalizing from particulars. Like Bell, she cares more for people than for landscape, though she can describe that with feeling, as in *The Valleys of the Assassins* (1934), a tale of adventures in the Iran-Iraq borderlands. She rides to Sar-i Kashti with a guide, across a plain where only mud walls give shelter from a dust storm; then into arid hills: "an inhospitable land" whose "feeling of remoteness" and wildness are nevertheless attractive (Stark 1934, 76, 90). Even a river valley can be "indescribably desolate" (186). Yet the "empty Persian plains" she pronounces a "beautiful world," and barren valleys offer a "pleasant loneliness" (202, 206).

Stark's reverence for "lonely and majestic" landscapes - i.e. grand, empty country that she sees alone - is quasi-religious. An "intruder desecrates [her] communion," and the observer *must* be "disinterested": with "poor motives," it becomes "a spiritual form of prostitution" (Stark 1934, 231). We may wonder whether her belief that the British Empire benefited its subjects does not constitute a "poor motive," but what she has in mind is "cheap advertisement or flashy journalism."

Stark's devotion was not to plain desert, but to the kind of desert-and-mountain wilderness that attracted Doughty and Sven Hedin. What impresses her about it varies with the occasion; it is not always barren beauty or pleasing solitude. Peter Bietenholz observes that European writers' images of the desert "corroborate our general knowledge of trends in European civilization" (14), and Stark's *A Winter in Arabia* (1940), finished as the Second World War began, bears him out. We hear for the first time in her work that

It is one of the greatest allurements of Asia that its nakedness is so clothed with the shreds of departed splendour, like a face lined with age, its joys and its sorrows are furrowed upon it, not so much in human ruins as in the very structure of the continent itself. Its vestiges of fertility, irrevocably lost, make it a world not only dead, but ruined. This must be so, of course, everywhere in some degree; but here the time is vaster, the contrast greater, and the drama of nature more obviously identical with the tragedy of man. (Stark 1940, 7)

An interest in bare land - either for its geological clarity or because it seemed "earth's body" - had been part of the aesthetics of the Great from the first, but this sounds more like Hardy than anyone since *The Return of the Native*. What Stark sees, with the lights going out all over Europe, is that these "ruined" lands can be a metaphor for her ruined civilization and "the tragedy of man." The cool but sympathetic and generally optimistic narrator of her earlier books did not speak this way. Barren country still has charms for her - a bare plain may seem "a stripped athlete" - and she can see a dry, "severe" gulch as "lovely," or appreciate the "silent peace" of the wilderness, but the tragic context provided at the beginning of the book is never cancelled or forgotten (Stark 1940, 11, 78, 170).

TERRIBLE BEAUTY

Wallace Stegner's *Mormon Country* appeared in 1942, as his country began its fighting. He does not mention the war, but his description of the "Plateau Province" - "as terrible and beautiful a wasteland as the world can show" - worked on two levels by that time (Stegner 1942, 45). "Terrible beauty," the phrase that W.B. Yeats applied to the Irish Rebellion in "Easter 1916," had become associated with war in general. And Stegner makes a familiar point - that humans dwindle to insignificance on the scale of the Great - in a uniquely forceful way: "Man is an interloper" in the Southwest, where "everything he sees is a prophecy of his inconsequent destiny" (45). This refers to eventual species extinction, but the global slaughter of the early 1940s made that "destiny" seem less remote. Stegner is a powerful writer on the Great partly because of the deft way he weaves "primary" experience into "secondary" material, and partly because his study of John Wesley Powell showed him the harsh realities of America's desert west.

It is not only "the immensity and the loneliness and the emptiness of the land that bothers a man caught alone in it," he writes, but having "nothing human in sight" for 50 or 75 miles (Stegner 1942, 45-6). There are only "large things," only the "windworn beauty of absolute wasteland. And the beauty is death" (46). One could hardly find a better statement of a "modern" response to Great nature: barren lands, possessed of "terrible beauty," teaching that joy and grief and fear derive from that very oxymoron. For Keats's "Beauty that must die," read "Beauty that can kill." Stegner sees in such "naked" lands the "transitoriness of human habitation"; history is dwarfed by geology. In a passage reminiscent of the scene in Hardy's *A Pair of Blue Eyes* (1873) where a geologist clings desperately to a steep cliff, facing a trilobite fossil, Stegner places the reader in a canyon "face to face with two or three petrified minutes of eternity." Here you can "read the rocks," from "your own place in the ladder of an inhuman immortality" back to the "Age of Nothing at All,"

from Basket-Maker to Trilobite in a few thousand feet of rock. ... Here is your true Ozymandias. Look on my works, Ye Mighty, and despair! Your destiny, as man, is to be a fossiliferous stratum in the crust of earth; the land where Time is everything .... (47)

That is, the ruined royal monument in the Egyptian desert of Percy Shelley's famous sonnet (1818) teaches only a superficial lesson compared to what we can learn from a canyon wall. Looking at it again, he sees that land shifts and erosion make even this sort of "petrified immortality" precarious: yet more transience! Stegner wonders whether it is appropriate, or ironic, that the Plateau Province, with "its contempt of man and his history and his theological immortality," is Mormon country (1942, 51). He cannot decide: "In the teeth of that - perhaps because of that - it may have seemed close to God." Many writers on Asian and African deserts (Melville, Flaubert, Doughty, Hichens, and others) have asserted that closeness. The Plateau Province seems to be another of these godly wastes.

Stegner devotes several chapters to men who have been attracted and held by southwestern deserts. "The Terrible River" treats John Wesley Powell and the Colorado, a subject that Stegner would develop in *Beyond the Hundredth Meridian*. "Notes on a Life Spent Pecking at a Sandstone Cliff" traces the career of Earl Douglas, a geologist and zoologist with the Carnegie Institute who "itched for the badlands" and excavated Dinosaur National Monument (Stegner 1942, 305). Fifteen years was enough for the Carnegie, but Douglas stayed on in "the desert he loved" (314). And "Artist in Residence" introduces Everett Ruess, a poet and painter who was starting to sound like a John Muir of the Southwest when he set off into the canyon country and disappeared in 1934 at the age of 20, possibly as a result of his passion for a Mormon girl (Flores 124, 126).

After the war, Stegner would reappear as an historian of the West, a recorder of his childhood years on the Saskatchewan prairie, a novelist, and an eloquent spokesman for conservation of the wilderness on which he built his career. The idea that the desert was fragile - implicit in Thomas and Philby - came to dominate postwar discussions of its value and allure.

6

"Because It Is There":
Great Heights, 1920-41

Among the cultural phenomena of postwar Europe was a resurgence of mountaineering, both in and outside Europe. The excitement of Victorian climbing - Tyndall, Stephen, Wills, Whymper, the Alpine Club's books and expeditions - was revived in a series of assaults on Mt. Everest (Chomolungma), the highest point on earth. As soon as the British obtained permission from Tibet to approach the mountain, expeditions began to sally forth: 1921, '22, '24, '33, '34, '35, '36, '38. Mallory's famous reply to the question why he wanted to climb Everest - "Because it is there" - did not satisfy many. The intense, risky ascents of the 1920s and 1930s were sometimes viewed (by climbers and others) as a reaction to or substitute for armed conflict: perhaps the "moral equivalent of war" of which William James had written in 1910.[1] In any case the level of interest among well-educated and even literary people was high. W.H. Auden, Stephen Spender, and Graham Greene all had brothers who went on Himalayan expeditions (Wollaston 5). Many of the climbers were themselves cultured men.

The flowering of mountain literature at this time is almost as remarkable as the climbs themselves. Besides the many ascent narratives, mountaineers became more analytical and scholarly about their craft. Douglas Freshfield, an important Victorian climber (ch. 2), completed a project suggested to him by John Ruskin: a biography of the eighteenth-century natural scientist from Geneva

---

[1]   W. James 355-9. Claire Engel notes the appearance of bold new techniques and "danger-for-danger's-sake" climbing in the Alps at the time of the Great War (1971, 207).

whose passion for Mont Blanc led to its conquest. But *The Life of Horace-Bénédict de Saussure* (1920) is more than a "life." Covering some of the same ground as Leslie Stephen in *The Playground of Europe* (1871), Freshfield spends the first few dozen pages on a history of European taste in mountains, showing how feelings of repugnance developed into interest, admiration, and awe: a useful source, foreshadowing Marjorie Hope Nicolson's *Mountain Gloom and Mountain Glory* (1959). Only then does he turn to de Saussure's offer of a prize for the first ascent, his climbs (including Mont Blanc), and his extensive exploration of and writings on the Alps.

Freshfield's introductory material was treated at book length by Sir Gavin De Beer, an evolutionary scientist who also wrote on Darwin. *Early Travellers in the Alps* (1930) examines the motives of those who went there in the sixteenth to eighteenth centuries, ending with de Saussure, "the greatest" of them (169-70). De Beer focuses on the history of science here; his *Alps and Men* (1932) and *The First Ascent of Mont Blanc* (1957) are more general. Frank Smythe, himself an active mountaineer, produced a warts-and-all biography of the great Victorian climber Edward Whymper in 1940. Scholarly interest in mountain literature also manifested itself across the Channel; Claire Engel chronicled *Byron et Shelley en Suisse et en Savoie* (1930) and surveyed *La Littérature alpestre en France et en Angleterre aux XVIIIe et XIXe siècles* (1931).

Alongside the historical impulse was a political one, perhaps rooted in criticism of mountaineers as careless risk-takers after the 1865 Matterhorn disaster: to explain the sport to the public. Geoffrey Winthrop Young, a climber whose prose and verse about mountaineering had attracted a number of people to the sport over the years, edited *Mountain Craft* in 1914, but the war delayed publication until 1920. Young wrote the preface and seven chapters, focusing on motives and rewards. Mountains force us back on our "elemental selves," he writes; they give us independence, beauty, and "mystical moments," especially when we climb alone - a risky practice discouraged by most responsible aficionados (Young 1920, x, 151). This approach is unlikely to have assuaged public concerns about climbing.

The twelve chapters by other hands are more specific, even technical: Arnold Lunn on skiing, W.M. Conway on Spitsbergen, Claude Elliot on the Pyrenees, and so on. Conway, an art professor, is unusual in mentioning "beautiful phenomena" as an attraction (Young 1920, 504). Elliot is nearer the norm in listing solitude, wildness, and "freedom from the works of man" as the Pyrenees' charms (556). In 1871 Leslie Stephen had hailed the *Alps* as a refuge from London's throngs, but they seemed less so by the end of the century. *Mountain Craft* reflects a turning from the Alps - too developed and populous - toward ranges less travelled by: a feeling somewhere between misanthropy and Ruskin's antipathy to civilization. Elliot, Conway, and Stephen could feel the pressure of population, and understood (as Wordsworth had in regard to the Lake District) that a surfeit of humanity was inimical to the value of wilderness.

THE GODDESS-MOTHER OF THE EARTH

Mountaineering history and craft appealed to a limited audience, but public interest in attempts to scale the world's highest peak rivalled that in polar expeditions before the war. The idea of Europe's finest young men marching off, not to kill each other, but to meet the greatest physical challenge on the globe, was irresistible. Bulletins wired from India were devoured, books eagerly awaited. It was the eighteenth-century saga of the first ascent of Mont Blanc relived and heightened.

The volume *Everest Reconnaissance* (1991) includes Charles Howard-Bury's diary of his efforts to find the best approach to Everest in 1920, his narrative of the 1921 expedition, and George Leigh-Mallory's report on the climbing. Howard-Bury, a soldier, diplomat, and one of the first westerners in the region, employs a breathless though limited vocabulary. Tibet is above all a country of grandeur (traditionally the central response of Great aesthetics), but almost as often the scene is "lovely." He does not make the old distinction between beauty and sublimity; Everest (sometimes called by its native name Chomolungma, "Goddess-Mother of the Earth") can be both "beautiful" and "magnificent" (Keaney 78, 107). The Himalayas in general are usually "wonderful" or "glorious." When Howard-Bury attempts to analyze the "great charm and fascination" of Tibet, high on his list of reasons is "landscapes so free from all restraint" (152). This is just how Addison originally described the Great - "a spacious horizon is an image of liberty" - though he had not seen horizons two hundred miles distant.

For his contemporaries, Leigh-Mallory seemed the highest type of English youth. Well-schooled, handsome, sensitive, he survived the war, taught at Charterhouse and Cambridge, and was considered England's premier climber as attempts on Everest began. Mallory's flair for style is apparent in his account of the 1921 effort, "The Reconnaissance of the Mountain." Everest first seen is "a prodigious white fang excrescent from the jaw of the world" (Keaney 164): the Earth's Body trope, in which the Great reveals the anatomy of the planet beneath its usual covering of flesh/earth. Haze adds "a touch of mystery and grandeur": like Howard-Bury, Mallory usually felt the mountain as grand. A closer view is described slowly and lovingly, reliving his "sheer astonishment" at the sudden revelation of the ten-thousand foot wall at the head of the Rongbuk Valley; Everest "has to make but a single gesture of magnificence to be lord of all, vast in unchallenged and isolated supremacy" (171). And it is a spiritual lordship: the "amazing simplicity" of the northwest arete reminds him of Winchester Cathedral.

The section on climbing the "enchanted" Rongbuk Glacier focuses on problems of survival and is less aesthetic - until the clouds open to reveal the barrier range on the Nepali border, a sight both "full of wonder" and "terrible" (Keaney 176, 187). In clear weather the surrounding peaks look "splendid" and "beautiful," though Mallory is glad to exchange these "visions of sublime snow-beauty" for some time at base camp (190, 195). As in Muir, Burke's *distinction* between sublime and beautiful is replaced by a spectrum on which beauty *may* graduate to sublimity. In the Kama valley, overlooked by three of the world's five highest summits, we do not hear of beauty, only of "magnificence and splendour"; Makalu, especially, with its "terrific awe-inspiring sweep" of cliffs, possesses "grandeur" in abundance (199, 200). Still, Mallory writes, "the most magnificent and sublime" mountain scenes "can be made lovelier" by flowery pastures at your feet (200).

Later, Mallory has a view of Chomolungma rising above mists on a clear night: "immanent, vast, incalculable," and "diffusing ... an exalted radiance" that reminds him of Keats's star, "in lone splendour hung aloft the night" (Keaney 201). Mallory would have appreciated Mircea Eliade's treatise on sacred mountains as cosmic pillars in *The Sacred and the Profane* (1957). This spiritual view of the peak posed problems for him, however. After leading a team to the 8000-metre level (an altitude never before achieved), Mallory discovered that mountaineering lessens one's reverence for mountains. Even *hearing* about others' ascents could be harmful.

Alpine clubs should "suppress the propagation of a gospel already too familiar" and shelter us from overexposure: "the less we know the better ... too little remains to be discovered. The story of a new ascent should now be regarded as a corrupting communication." Though he had presumably done his best to reach the summit, Mallory could not "help rejoicing in the yet undimmed splendour, ... the unconquered supremacy of Mount Everest" (quoted Ullman 375-8).

Mallory's contribution to *The Assault on Mount Everest: 1922* is more concerned with expedition problems than with aesthetic response, making his point about familiarity; it was the new men who exclaimed and wondered. For Capt. John Noel, a photographer, the Rongbuk Valley was a "hall of grandeur" leading to the peak, providing a "spectacle of astounding beauty and strangeness" (quoted Ullman 82). Fascinated by monks who had chosen to live as hermits amid the solitude and majesty of this "lifted hidden world," he noted the locals' belief that "the spirits of Everest" would repel them from the summit and "punish us severely for our impiety," since it was a sacred mountain (83, 85). But Noel saw his party as "pilgrims ... of adventure" whose "business was to fight the mountain, not to worship it" (86). This is a problematical image (fighting pilgrims?), like "assaulting" the Goddess Mother of the Earth. They did climb to 27,000 feet, where T. Howard Somervell, a physician, was "enthralled by the magnificence of the view," but no higher, and the deaths of seven porters in an avalanche ended the expedition, so that "after events," Noel admitted, "seemed to bear out" the Tibetan view of the project (105, 85).

Though Mallory had had enough of Everest, patriotism demanded another try in 1924, which ended when he and Andrew Irvine disappeared in the clouds on their summit attempt. This loss - mountaineering's equivalent of Scott's Antarctic disaster - gave the sport its most enduring tragic mystery. The last glimpse and the survivors' long vigil have since been replayed endlessly in articles, adventure stories, lectures, and films. Books by Mallory's friends naturally tend to hagiography. John Noel extols his "great heart," "great imagination and ideals": "He was lofty as the peaks he loved" (quoted Ullman 180-1). R.L.G. Irving, once his teacher at Winchester, writes that Mallory (a "Galahad of mountaineering" with an "extraordinary likeness to a Botticelli madonna") was "as fitted to understand [Everest's] majesty as to accept its challenge" (184-6). The finding of Mallory's body in 1999 gave the story fresh life, and raised anew the question whether he and Irvine reached the top before dying.

The rescue effort of Noel Odell, the nearest man to the lost climbers, has received relatively little attention, but David Roberts believes that his "deeds in support of his friends, as he lingered for eleven days above the North Col, climbing twice to Camp VI in a vain search for an explanation of the tragedy, are virtually without parallel in Himalayan history" (162). Odell's chapter in *The Fight for Everest: 1924* is remarkable for its quality of feeling and expression. Being alone on the windy North Col overnight "certainly enhanced the impressiveness of the scene": the "savagely wild jumble of peaks" above the Rongbuk Glacier and the bare cliffs of Everest's north face, which had for a geologist the "interest of their past primeval history" (quoted Ullman 190). Odell dwells on the geological structure of the mountain, but he could "behold with more than single eye," and that evening remains "an ineffable transcendent experience that can never fade from memory" (190).

As days pass, however, and the climbers do not return, Everest shows a "cruel face" or "cold indifference" to "mere puny man," and Odell wonders if they are indeed being punished for profaning Chomolungma, the "Goddess Mother of the Mountain Snows" (quoted Ullman 199-201). Had they not approached with "due reverence"? But even as he thinks so, another mood, with "something alluring," comes over her, or into him, and "I was almost fascinated" (201). Is this what happened, he wonders: that despite Mallory's talk of preserving a margin of safety, he became obsessed with reaching his goal, "that most sacred and highest place of all," and went on, "oblivious of all obstacles"? At any rate they were gone, and no expedition would attempt the mountain for years.

OTHER HEIGHTS

The deaths on Everest raised anew the issue of whether high climbing was inherently too dangerous to be justified. Were such ascents worth the risk? But the mountain world was much wider than Himalayan expeditions. In the United States, parks and laws and wardens were now required to protect mountains from an admiring public. As "the juggernaut of tourism rolled on," Aldo Leopold and Bob Marshall helped found the wilderness movement and enunciated the seminal principle of the "land ethic" (Huth 203-5). Canadian "Group of Seven" painters such as Lawren Harris and Frank Varley discovered spirituality, vastness, and power in their mountain west; they developed a "wilderness ethos" that was almost "a return to the eighteenth-century sublime" (Tippett and Cole 86-9). Vito Cianci observed in 1928 that (for artists) British Columbia's true character lay not in placid pools and gardens, "but in the boundless sweep of sky and country away from man's depressing influence" (quoted Tippett and Cole 122).[2]

Mountaineering and its literature took many forms. The Alpine writings of Abate Achille Ratti, who became Pope Pius XI (ch. 2), reached English readers in *Ascensions* (1922) and *Climbs on Alpine Peaks* (1923). The latter has a foreword by Douglas Freshfield, giving a short history of climbing in the Alps from their days of evil repute through the pioneering ascents of the eighteenth century to the Victorian heyday of the Alpine Club; some of the same material appears in his biography of H.B. de Saussure (above and ch. 2). Freshfield notes that churchmen were among the first climbers, avers that "spiritual vision" is one of the appeals of the sport, and suggests that the Alps were the pope's "former cathedral" (Ratti xxvi, xiii).

Sven Hedin's work was reaching ever-wider audiences in translation (chs. 2 and 5), though it was of particular interest to mountaineers, because he brought huge, little-known ranges in Central Asia to their attention. His autobiography, *My Life as an Explorer*, was published in New York in 1925; *A Conquest of Tibet*, recounting his early travels, appeared in England in 1934 and the United States in 1941. In all his books, Hedin's enthusiasm for discovering what was actually in the white spaces on the map, and for the magnificence of vast empty ranges, is palpable; he can look at a "desolate wilderness" in Tibet and see its "grandeur" (1941, 28).

Mountain books filled a broad spectrum from ornate to prosaic. At the former end was G.W. Young's poetic treatment of mountain climbing, *On High Hills. Memories of the Alps* (1927). Very much the artist, a stylist and an aesthete, Young can come across as thoughtful and sensitive, a keen observer, or as precious and verbose, an overwriter; it depends on the passage and the reader. But no one can miss his deep devotion to mountain climbing: he was most "at

---

[2] Yi-Fu Tuan notes that in China, as in Europe, attitudes towards Great nature were shifting from religious or emotional to aesthetic, though he does not specify the period (1990, 70-1).

home," most intensely alive, above eight thousand feet (Young 1947, 82). A great peak can give us "rare moments of living which we borrow from the golden age" (299). Young sounds religious when he identifies with Moses on the mount and has revelations, Platonic when he proclaims the snowy Alpine highlands "the true surface of dignified earth," with the inhabited valley below a "less real world" (94). He offers recollections of Mallory, and a good deal of his own verse. "There is great easing of the heart, / and cumulance of comfort on high hills" might stand as an epigraph for the whole volume (325). The high hills are not quite all Alpine: in Greece and Turkey he finds that "the desert shares the fascination of the sea and the mountains" (134). Returning to the Alps in 1921, Young rejected any correlation between war and mountain climbing, calling them diametrically opposed enterprises.

At the other end of the stylistic spectrum stands G.M. Dyott's plain tale of his Andean travels, *On the Trail of the Unknown* (1926). Dyott had a sort of revelation while standing alone high on the remote Sangay volcano in Ecuador. He could "hardly summon words" to describe the vision; his "mind flashed back millions of years" to the formation of the land. Struck by the "unreality" of the place, he turned back short of the top (Dyott 66-7). The summit of another volcano, Tungurahua, was weird and "awe-inspiring," especially when it erupted on his second ascent. Not surprisingly, all present were filled with "awe and wonder" (87, 96). Dyott was glad to leave the "loneliness and emptiness" of the uplands and the "icy splendour" of the Andes for the Amazon basin, whence he could still enjoy occasional views of "superb" Sangay at a distance (116, 137).

Mountaineering was a highly international sport. Teams from many countries ranged over the Alps, Himalayas, and other chains, the various nations mixing readily at high altitudes. The 1929 "Munich expedition" to Kangchenjunga in Nepal, one of the world's highest mountains, turned back in storms at 24,000 feet, barely escaping with their lives. The next year a German-Austrian-Swiss-British group came for another try. One of its members was Frank Smythe, who would become the most conspicuous British climber-writer of the 1930s, with a bibliography almost as long as his list of ascents; a series of books stretches through the '30s and '40s (by 1941, Hodder and Stoughton was advertising eight of his mountain books in a ninth). Smythe comes across as both a practical climber, alive to the problems and possibilities of this mountain and this day, and a thoughtful man, recollecting in tranquillity, mindful of the history and philosophy of mountaineering.

Kangchenjunga Adventure (1930) has the tributes to mountain grandeur and the acknowledgments of their beauty, spirituality, and dangers (in about equal quantities) usual in Smythe's books. Presenting the expedition as "primarily an adventure," he recalls that even as a boy he had a passion for mountains; Whymper, Scott, and Shackleton were his "gods" (Smythe 1930, 9, 14). Smythe views adventure, even at the risk of life, as a deep human need, and cites Scott, Mallory, Irvine, and Young as examples. In no hurry to narrate, he devotes a chapter to the "nature and history" of Kangchenjunga and its early explorers, including Douglas Freshfield, his model both as a wandering climber and as a writer interested in the past.

Once on the trail, Smythe finds that the Himalayan *foothills* have the scale of "the main range of the Alps," without their "taint" of civilization and "commercialism": a note of alienation owing less to Rousseau than to Stephen and Freshfield (1930, 79). He learns that Kangchenjunga, whose "magnificent" form is visible from Darjeeling, has for the natives the "grandeur and mystery" of a god's throne (18-19, 21-2). Great mountains, Smythe notes, generally give people a sense of their own "insignificance" (82-3), and within days the vast scale of the country produces "almost a feeling of impotence" in him (111): the effect that John Stuart Mill warned the Great could have. Tibetan music (the "epitome" of the Himalayas) helps by suggesting the "infinity" of space; it seems to go to the "heart of this mystic mountain land, where time and space are limitless" (87, 122).

Smythe knew how subjective aesthetic response is. From afar Kangchenjunga looks beautiful; up close, it becomes "terrible" (Smythe 1930, 102). Of course the mountaineer must be alone "to contemplate mountains as they should be contemplated," and solitude is a rare commodity on expeditions (165). Also, as Mallory said, the climber's own analytical mind and technical knowledge work against the "simple adoration" and "half wild yearning" that first brought him to the hills (172) - a point developed in Smythe's later books. He thinks Ruskin may have been right: mountains are best appreciated from the valleys, and climbing them for sport hurts this appreciation.[3] His own aesthetic sense is obviously keener at a

---

[3] Similarly, Claire Engel wondered if, in France, "l'alpinisme a tué la montagne" (1930, 250).

distance than when he is trying to reach a summit. *Kangchenjunga Adventure* is a long book with a complex aesthetic, blending vast, unreal, "elemental and savage masses," serenity, and intimations of infinity (188).

CHOMOLUNGMA AGAIN

In 1933 a British team went to Everest for the first time in nine years: a strong group that included Smythe and young Eric Shipton. The leader, Hugh Ruttledge, wrote the official book, with a foreword by Sir Francis Younghusband, who had helped to "open" Tibet and organize expeditions.[4] A deeply religious man, Younghusband had no more doubt about what climbing Everest meant than Dante had about Mount Purgatory. The *successful* climber would have an "invincible spirit - a spirit firm and tenacious and ambitious … yet selfless," for Everest was "a symbol of the loftiest spiritual height of man's imagination" (Ruttledge xvii). The very idea of this quest would "hearten many an aspirant to the heights of the spirit," for if climbers would "suffer and sacrifice and endure merely" to reach a material peak, "how much more readily ought they" strive to attain "the whitest, purest, holiest heights of the spirit?" (xvii). The spiritual reading of mountain-climbing could go no farther. Younghusband, the Himalayan counterpart of Scott's patron Sir Clements Markham, was not a mountaineer and never saw Chomolungma.

Ruttledge viewed the matter differently. Sketching the history of attitudes toward mountains, he contrasts early Swiss superstitions about "unfriendly spirits" in the Alps, and Asian devotion to the Himalayas as "holy ground," with the "spirit of adventure and enquiry" in which the English approached oceans and mountains - though he also says that having "exactly the same feeling" about climbing Everest created a bond between Englishmen and Sherpas (Ruttledge 1-2, 104). Thereafter topics such as bargaining and who contributed what to the expedition occupy most of the leader's attention until the retreat, so it is surprising when he notes that

---

[4]　In 1904, then-Col. Younghusband led a large force of British regulars on a nine-month incursion into Tibet, during which they reportedly killed thousands of poorly-armed monks. It has been called "a brutal massacre" and "an infamous chapter in the history of the British Empire" (Heil, 54).

"One felt reluctant to be leaving" the scene of their exertions, "the ever-changing loveliness of ridge and plain, of rock and ice and snow. What had civilisation to offer instead?" (257-8). He supposed that the long marches, the gales and dust, "the bitter struggle ..., the failure" were forgotten then, but perhaps they were remembered, and even formed a part of the bond, as William James said of war and quasi-war.

In suggesting that a Himalayan mountaineer should be a scientist, a philosopher, or both, Ruttledge may have had in mind Smythe (an engineer by training), who wrote the chapter on his and Shipton's summit attempt. In this account, Smythe focuses on practical problems, not scenery. Even in good weather, he found that altitude and cold made them "unmindful of the beauties and grandeurs about us" (Ruttledge 197). At Camp VI (27,400'), when the clouds part at dusk, calling the scene "wintry and desolate" suffices (199). Trying for the summit, Shipton felt ill and soon dropped out; Smythe went on alone to about 28,000 feet. As he turned back, defeated and bitter, the peak seemed "pitilessly indifferent," "utterly aloof and detached" from the striving humans below (205). During his solo, Smythe admits that, like other "solitary wanderers" on mountains, deserts, and polar wastes, he had the illusion of a friendly companion (209). This kept him from feeling lonely, though "the loneliness of the hills is not to be feared" (213).

Both Shipton and Smythe revisited that climb. In *Upon That Mountain* (1943), Shipton recalls how keenly he anticipated the challenge of Everest's upper reaches, "a real mountaineering proposition which would require some concentration of energy and skill" (quoted Ullman 212). Smythe retold it in *The Adventures of a Mountaineer* (1940). The story of the mysterious extra climber is repeated from his chapter in Ruttledge's book, this time with the Shackleton party on South Georgia adduced as a precedent. Again Smythe states that he and Shipton were "unable to appreciate our extraordinary position" at the time, "but afterwards we remembered the glories of the scene near the summit of the world's highest mountain: ... the final pyramid, etched sharply against a blue-black sky, ... the thousands of mountains far below us, ... and afar off the golden plains of Tibet, tranquil and serene in the morning sunlight" (quoted Ullman 229).

His neurons seem to have stored a lot of data. Smythe could now recall the "profound and awful silence" as he turned and looked out over Tibet: "an experience awe-inspiring and magnificent," though he was *then* "incapable of appreciating anything but my own bodily and mental sickness" (quoted Ullman 233). That night he stayed at Camp VI alone, Shipton having descended. "It was an extraordinary experience spending a night higher than any other human being," writes Smythe, but again, "I scarcely appreciated this at the time" (236). An oxygen deficit evidently slows down aesthetic feeling, among other functions. Before bedding down for the night, Smythe took in the "scene of incredible desolation": "great slabs of rock mortared with snow in their interstices," and far below "a great sea of cloud slowly writhing and twisting." It was a rare calm evening on Everest, "not a sound. No stone-fall or avalanche disturbed the serenity." Instead, "There was silence, … absolute and complete," and "permeating all," a deadly cold, like (he thought) "the coldness that reigns in the abysses of space" (236).

Many of the 1933 climbers returned to Chomolungma. Shipton led a small reconnaissance as far as the North Col in 1935. They found the snow too unstable to proceed higher, but indulged in a "veritable orgy of mountain climbing," wrote Shipton, ascending 26 peaks above 20,000 feet (Astill 1). They also found the body of Maurice Wilson, a lone climber who had died in 1934, and a diary explaining his theory of purification through asceticism (172). In the party were young Tenzing Norgay, Stephen Spender's brother Michael, and H.W. (Bill) Tilman, like Shipton a minimalist by preference; their ability to move quickly and lightly made them more welcome to the government and local folks. The next year Shipton, Smythe, Ruttledge, and other veterans went back, but were stopped by the early arrival of the monsoon, creating avalanche conditions. Smythe and Shipton tried again with a small group in 1938; a dislike of large expeditions colours both men's writings from then on. Led by Tilman, the party included Noel Odell, the lone watcher for Mallory and Irvine in 1924. (Odell and Tilman had climbed Nanda Devi in 1936: then the highest ascent ever made.) The 1938 effort also failed in bad weather and the outbreak of war in 1939 produced a long hiatus in further attempts.

The war also delayed Tilman's account for a decade. By the time *Mount Everest 1938* appeared (1948), it was like a time machine from a vanished world. Once more unto the breach went a small band of literate brothers, reading Cervantes, George Eliot, Ruskin, Dickens, and Montaigne on stormy days. While they achieved little, bogging down in the deep snow of another early monsoon, Tilman waxes eloquent on the motives for mountaineering - chiefly freedom - and the right size for an expedition. In the 1930s, he writes, European parties had a dozen climbers and hundreds of porters, but large groups are expensive, generate publicity and national rivalry, and affect Tibetans adversely. Noting the English preference for small parties, he took seven climbers and needed only one-fifth the money and gear of previous expeditions (he would have preferred fewer and less). Since "mountains, thank heaven, are a sanctuary apart," climbers must respect them, and "smaller expeditions are a step in the right direction" (Tilman 10-12). Mechanical aids such as oxygen should be eschewed, for "if we must move with the times then we must give up mountaineering" (103). In 1948 Tilman sounded old-fashioned, but tastes and values would circle back to him.

CLIMBING IN THE SHADOWS

Mountaineering narratives of the late 1930s have an acerbic poignancy, as climbers begin to realize that political and military shades are closing on their beloved realm. This sense of foreboding is clearly felt in Frank Smythe's books about his pre-war Alpine and Himalayan outings. While his view of nature and mountains is homogeneous, his moods differ from place to place, and evolve. In most of the Himalayan books, the grandeur, dangers, and spirituality of mountains take precedence over civilization and its discontents; great things *are* done when men and mountains meet. In his Alpine narratives, however, Europe's machines, land development, political divisions, and militarism threaten the mountain idyll more overtly each year.

Over Tyrolese Hills (1936), for example, narrates a month-long traverse in 1935, and modern problems keep impinging on natural beauty and spiritual serenity. Smythe flies to Zurich to save time, but worries that the "speed and ease" of our machines will put out "the fire of personal adventure" (1938a, 14). Tourist development in the Alpine valleys is another concern: traditional native buildings harmonized with nature, but alien "commercial interests ... and their mushroom-like growths ... offend against natural beauty" (20). On the heights, "iron hand-holds" have been set into cliff faces, and some climbers use pitons: more "artificial means" (159, 149). Silence and peace are briefly enjoyed on a summit - when Italian gunners are not firing - but the lack of fellow-climbers is ominous. A hut-keeper says, "The huts are empty because the Germans cannot

come," and Smythe wonders why "a great race" would issue, or
accept, such an edict (31). A spacious horizon may be an image of
liberty, but in the Alps, the first European laboratory of this idea,
horizons and liberties were contracting.

Four years later, the threats have grown. In *Mountaineering
Holiday*, Smythe's tributes to the Alps' beauty, grandeur, and
"spiritual balm" alternate with attacks on the evils of civilization
(1940b, 30). For eleven months he longs to escape from the city to a
place of austere sublimity where "man is aware of something greater
than his earthiness," a place that will "promote thought," and then
when he does, he finds cars, tourists, "Industrial centralisation"
(55, 61, 103). Smythe mixes hope and doom like an Alpine Isaiah.
Here is unspoiled nature, "spiritually ... positive," offering "peace
and serenity of spirit"; and over there, urban life, spiritually lower,
concentrating the ills we have wrought: materialism, machines,
Nazis (60, 63). He charges tourism with ruining the wild nature it
fattens on.

Trying to enjoy his holiday, Smythe repeatedly falls into
misanthropy. Near a pass on the French-Italian border, gunfire is
heard on Mussolini's side. "This would be a beautiful world were
it not for the inclusion of man," he snaps; "everything in nature is
appropriate except man ... the invader and destroyer of beauty"
(Smythe 1940b, 115). Why was he even included? A few days later,
admiring the splendid panorama from the Mont Blanc ridge in
perfect weather, he again wonders why "quarrelsome man" was
admitted into "the beneficent scheme of Nature" (152). To Smythe,
it is not nature that is red in tooth and claw, but humanity. This is
in July 1939: war is only days away. Then he turns on urbanization.
"Why live in cities?" It is absurd to allow "progress, civilisation,
religion" to condemn us to brutal environments that breed war-
fever and cut us off from healing nature (153). In this case, contact
with the Great has the effect of showing the visitor how unhappy
he usually is.

By way of contrast, *The Valley of Flowers* (1938) is a Himalayan
idyll: four months in the lush Bhyundar valley and on adjacent
mountains. Six years after finding the place, Smythe came back to
do something other than climb Everest ("a duty, perhaps a national
duty," like the poles: 1938b, 4). The aesthetic shape of the book is
clear and positive; beauty and grandeur lie all around, evoking
awe and calming the spirit. It is not always the flowers that supply
beauty and the mountains grandeur (as Addison or Burke would

have said). The forms of peaks and snowfields are often beautiful as well as grand: Smythe knew his Ruskin. Only rarely - when news arrives from the outside world - does he complain as he often does in his Alpine books. Reading the English papers on a flowery plateau is like looking down on an anthill gone mad.

In this book it becomes clear that *western* society is the problem. The "exaltation of spirit" that Smythe felt when he "escaped civilisation" refers to emancipation from "slavery to schedule" and other "futile matters" that vex modern industrial nations (1938b, 38). Mountaineering seems, in William Jamesian fashion, an alternative to war, a useful outlet for our need of danger and struggle. He accepts the Tibetan view that "western progress" brings "unhappiness and war" wherever it goes, and does not reject their feeling that they are "superior to Europeans in spiritual culture" (81). Smythe observes how his guides react to the mountains. They seem "outwardly insensible" to them, but he assumes they "must ... love, respect and reverence" this "sublime" country (24). More solidly, his head guide Wangdi hails the view from Base Camp (which Smythe calls "magnificent") as "Ramro," translated as "beautiful" (53).

The war caught Eric Shipton in mid-stride. Born on Ceylon in 1907, he went from early travel in Europe and India to daring ascents on several continents. His first heroes were Humboldt, Nansen, and Darwin: explorers and interpreters of Great nature. When Shipton was 16, a Norwegian schoolmate invited him to spend the summer walking in the mountainous Jotunheim country, whose "rugged desolation" and "breadth of horizon" excited him (1969, 27). Thenceforth drawn to mountains, he read Tyndall, Stephen, and Whymper, climbed in Britain and the Alps. Summit views did not impress him; "aesthetic appreciation," he decided, comes "unbidden ... at unexpected moments" (38-9). Like Smythe, Shipton recoiled from hordes of tourists: Chamonix (the base for some of the first major Alpine climbs in the eighteenth century) seemed "gross with tourism" in 1928 (45). He went to Kenya to work that year, but took time to climb its highest peaks with Wyn Harris and Bill Tilman, later his companions on Everest.

Shipton accepted Smythe's invitation to join an expedition to Mt. Kamet in 1931, and thus began his "Himalayan Heyday," a decade of pioneer travel in Central Asia. Shipton liked the month of exploration better than the actual climbing. Similarly, the "most enjoyable" part of the 1933 Everest attempt was journeying through Tibet; he found the ascent painful and the expedition "cumbersome"

(Shipton 1969, 76). His friends accused him of "asceticism. They may well have been right" (81). Shipton went from solos or small parties to Everest expeditions and back to small groups, and from "peak-bagging" to mountain travel. In 1934, taking minimalists (including T.E. Lawrence) as his model, he, Tilman, and a few Sherpas explored the Nanda Devi basin. The next year he led the reconnaissance to Everest.

In 1937, between Everest assaults, Shipton's survey team (including Michael Spender and W.H. Auden's brother John) explored the Karakorams, a "world of stark grandeur" that few westerners had visited (1969, 104). Reaching base camp in this poorly-charted wilderness of arid mountains, unlike anything he had ever seen, was one of Shipton's "threshold situations" that stayed "fresh in [his] memory" (109). A second Karakoram expedition was cut short when war was declared; Shipton had to be content with the "experience and happiness" of his "nine expeditions to the greatest mountains on earth" (119). During the war he served as British Consul-General in Kashgar, China, in the desert below high mountain ranges: country that he had been longing to see. To reach Kashgar meant a ten-day ride through the "wild, majestic" Pamirs, whose peaks rise to 25,000 feet (123). In Kashgar he began to write his books.

Many others sought the peace (or challenge) of the hills in those years. F. Spencer Chapman, who chronicled his progress from *Helvellyn to Himalaya* (1940; *Memoirs of a Mountaineer*, 1951), is less well-known than Smythe or Shipton, in part because his interests were more diffuse. Growing up by the Lake District, he climbed British peaks early in life. Chapman was among those influenced by G.W. Young, whom he met at Cambridge. In the Alps, Chapman discovered that high mountains' "beauty and aloofness," and the effort of climbing them, "purged and quickened" his senses pleasurably (1951, 22, 20). He skied the Alps, trekked in Iceland, and went on expeditions to Greenland (ch. 7): the happiest times of his life. His first sight of the Himalayas (1936) revealed "another world"; emerging from jungle onto a "bare open fell-side" gave him "a great sense of liberation and joy" (40, 50). Chapman loved long vistas. The Tibetan plateau was also "another world. A world of immense distances" (198). Believing that we *need* the discomforts and challenges of travel, he wondered if we might even need war.

At the end of the era, Smythe offered his "thoughts about the mountains and what they mean to me" (1941, xi). Little in *The*

Mountain Vision would have been new to his readers; it summarizes what he had been saying all along - that mountains confer peace, spirituality, and quiet happiness - giving more aesthetic history. The mountains (like the sea) inspire us, he writes, but we had to evolve, to outgrow "gloom and fear" of them, before we could see their beauty (1). Even today not everyone understands. Ruskin was right: lowly walkers often appreciate Alpine scenery more than technical climbers do. The *true* mountaineer, though, has G.W. Young's (and Byron's) *"feeling* for mountains," loves their "calm" and "order," and realizes the need to "be primitive" and approach them as a pilgrim (17, 27, 7-8). True, the Alps have been tainted by European vice and folly, but perhaps after the "present catastrophe" we will rediscover their joy and serenity (4). Smythe was willing to hope for the best.

7
Mid-Ice:
High Latitudes Between the Wars

Both poles having been reached before the war - or so we believe - one might have expected interest in the Arctic and Antarctic to drop off, but this was only marginally the case. Books about Scott's last expedition, including Edward Evans's *South with Scott* (1921) and Cherry-Garrard's *The Worst Journey in the World* (1922), found a ready audience and burnished the legend. Explorers and their patrons identified new challenges worthy of time and resources, while Arctic ethnographers examined "discovered" lands to find out how people lived there.

Some familiar names from the "Heroic Age" were heard again. Ernest Shackleton, having turned near-catastrophe into triumph during the war, surviving the loss of his ship and an epic small-boat journey to rescue widely-separated parties, did some war-related work in England, lectured in America, and published *South*. Not yet having had enough of the Antarctic, he conceived a new voyage, found a backer, bought a ship (the aging sealer *Quest*), and summoned his mates for a last hurrah. A few stood forth: that the plan was vague and the ship dubious did not matter. The *Quest* crossed the Atlantic in 1921. Shackleton had a mild heart attack in Rio, but refused medical attention and pressed on to South Georgia, where old friends welcomed them. That night he had a massive coronary and died. His wife cabled that he should be interred on South Georgia, so the crew buried him there, among mariners who had hailed his feats. Then they sailed on to within sight of Elephant Island, where some wept to remember their old pain and comradeship in the "white warfare of the south" before turning for home (Alexander 191-4).

With the South Pole and the Northwest Passage behind him, Roald Amundsen drifted the Northeast Passage in *Maud* (1918-21).[1] In his autobiography, *My Life as an Explorer*, Amundsen recalls a September night on that drift when "The sky was perfectly clear, and a glorious moon made the whole landscape glisten with a vivid whiteness" (1927, 91). Polar bears, visible by moonlight and the aurora, prowled over the ice. The nocturnal Great - a category recognized only with regard to stargazing at first - is prominent during the winter dark; men stand on deck "delighted with the beauty of the night" (91): a rare aesthetic indulgence for the usually reserved Amundsen. He kept up with technological developments and nurtured new talent; in 1926, on Spitsbergen, he met a young American naval officer, Richard Byrd, who had (perhaps) just flown over the North Pole, and helped him plan his first Antarctic expedition (Cameron 192-3). Amundsen himself flew over the North Pole that year with Umberto Nobile, but vanished in 1928 during an aerial search for the dirigible *Italia*, in which Nobile had been trying to reach the Pole. In August 2009 two Norwegian ships began examining the sea bottom near Spitsbergen for traces of Amundsen's airplane.

Flying was the period's most important technical advance in travel to and over the Great. The Sahara was overflown in 1920, and British aircraft made a photo-reconnaissance of Mt. Everest in 1933. On Byrd's Antarctic expedition of 1928-30, G.H. Wilkins made the first powered flight above the continent, aerial mapping supplemented surface work, and the leader had himself flown over the Pole. Another American, Lincoln Ellsworth, sponsored and helped make a flight (almost) across Antarctica in 1935; a Russian plane managed to land at the North Pole in 1937. What flight would mean to the aesthetic experience of the Great was not at once clear. Aircraft (as long as they worked properly) often made it easier to approach and examine remote wilderness areas, but some travellers had always maintained that hardship was an integral part of apprehending the Great. Flying has its own aesthetic, similar to but distinguishable from the one we have traced from Addison and Hardy, as Antoine de Saint-Exupery and Karen Blixen were quick to sense (ch. 5).

In sharp contrast to the leading-edge technology represented by aircraft, the British Arctic Expedition of 1925, led by Frank Worsley

---

[1] A Swedish expedition had gone through the Passage in 1878-79.

(the captain of Shackleton's *Endurance*, his navigator on the run to South Georgia, and a veteran of the *Quest*), set off in a fine old sailing ship. Worsley's account, *Under Sail in the Frozen North*, bills the voyage as wind power's last battle with polar ice, fought by "inspired vagabonds" who spurned comfort for hardship (1927, 27). In the spirit of the Luddites and Tennyson's "Ulysses," the crew tacked and pushed through the ice, determined on something ere the end. They reached 80° North, but the expedition was full of misadventures that engines might have prevented, and they were towed the last 600 miles back to Norway. Worsley seems not to notice, claiming to have added to knowledge by correcting the charts (though his "Geological Notes" show that the lack of a motor hampered scientific work), and calls their voyage the "final triumph" of British square-sail seamanship in pack ice (226-7).

Whether or not the voyage made sense, they may have had what they came for. Even more freely than in *The Great Antarctic Rescue*, Worsley displays his feelings for the natural scene. Spitsbergen under the midnight sun is "a beautiful picture of calm, pure grandeur": qualities he notes repeatedly (Worsley 1927, 36). Sunshine and mirages bring out unearthly beauties; cliffs, capes, and fjords are "majestic" or "noble" (114, 222). Worsley was also keen on the history of exploration. They found an airplane wreck and a hut from the 1924 Oxford Arctic Expedition, while Franz Josef Land set off a roll call of illustrious predecessors, from Weyprecht and Payer (1872) through Nansen's wintering and several recent expeditions. At their farthest north, "Headland after headland" of Franz Josef Land stretches to the horizon, "a scene of calm grandeur and cool loveliness that filled us with pride and gratitude at being allowed to draw back the veil and gaze into Nature's purest beauty" (137). For Worsley, such days imparted an exhilarating energy that made life itself seem "more desirable" (164).

TAKING A CLOSER LOOK

The major innovation in the period's polar literature was Arctic ethnography. Vilhjalmur Stefansson, a Canadian of Icelandic descent, had been active before the war; *My Life with the Eskimo* (1913) recounts his travels of 1908-12. He could be a difficult man, but was an impressive explorer and a prolific writer after settling in Greenwich Village. The best known of his many books is *The*

Friendly Arctic (1921), a prolix account of the "Canadian Arctic Expedition" of 1913-18, during which he discovered one of Peary's cartographic errors (Mowat 1973, 241). Stefansson liked to point out the shortcomings of other writers and explorers (his attacks on the suicidal style of the Franklin expedition made him enemies). He was also accused of overstating the benignity of the Arctic; having grown up in Manitoba and North Dakota, he found it relatively easy to adapt to the Inuit way of life.[2] Stefansson's most resonant dictum was that "the North is a greater frontier than the West ever was"; he expected that it, too, would be needed to absorb an expanding population (1922, 74, 574).

Stefansson saw his work as inaugurating the final stage of polar exploration, in which the Arctic would be accepted as "friendly and fruitful," so *The Friendly Arctic* tries to correct common fallacies about the region (6). Chapter 2, "The North That Never Was," attacks myths about perpetual winter in a silent, dark, lifeless waste, as the Arctic was sometimes depicted after the Franklin disaster. His own party's doctor was surprised not to find summer snow. In sooth, says Stefansson, there is little permanent ice, snowfall is moderate, summer does come, and it is warmer than you think. The north is not, then, "barren, dismal and desolate," nor cruel and relentless – unless *you* are "inept" (20, 22). The natives live in the Arctic because they like it there, not perforce. Stefansson debunks the fictive north, point by point; having made the effort to travel as the Inuit do, he would suffer no fools to make a quick tour and report their impressions as gospel. What the Arctic will give you, he says, is a taste for simplicity. He also praises its "beauty, freedom," "isolation and virgin peace" (258, 685).

Even better qualified than Stefansson and a good deal less strident, the Danish Greenlander Knud Rasmussen set up a trading and observation post called "Thule" in north Greenland (1910), whence he launched a series of journeys. From 1921 to 1924 he led a Danish Ethnographical Expedition (one of whose members was Peter Freuchen, later a well-known explorer) to study Arctic Canada, especially the tribes of the Barren Grounds. After the party split up into sub-groups, Rasmussen travelled and lived with the natives, finding to his delight that they understood his Greenlandic Inuktitut dialect.

---

[2] Like Peary, he took an Inuit mistress. See Berton 49, 74-5, 337; and Wiebe 105-7.

In *Across Arctic America* (1927), a narrative of this "Fifth Thule Expedition," he shows more interest in the people than in the land, which mostly serves as a backdrop. It is bare and vast and lonely: at times an icy desert, gloomy and desolate, at others a "wild scene, ... yet not without a beauty of its own" (Rasmussen 157). All that goes without saying most of the time. Only in the Introduction does Rasmussen linger over a natural scene: the end of his trip on East Cape, Siberia, overlooking Bering Strait. It is a vista of "calm grandeur"; the Cape's height and "pure air" give him the "wide outlook" that defines the Great, and he feels joyful at completing his expedition after three and a half years and 20,000 miles, from the top of Hudson Bay along the southern shore of the Northwest Passage (iii-v). It had been a hard trip, but, as an *angakoq* (wizard) told him, "All true wisdom is only to be learned far from the dwellings of men, out in the great solitudes; and is only to be attained through suffering" (81). The words of this "Inuit Aeschylus" (also quoted in other Arctic books) offer a rationale for travel in the Great, and suggest how much earlier explorers missed.

Capt. Thierry Mallet, an inspector of trading posts in the Canadian north and a close observer of the land, stands somewhat apart from the professional ethnographers. In *Glimpses of the Barren Lands* (1930), humans are "small gray specks" in an immense "chaos of stone," an image used again near the end, where man is a dot in the "utter desolation of that frozen desert" (Mallet 11, 129). He evokes the "appalling monotony" of a "desert of gray moss" before a caribou herd approaches and flows around his party, followed by silence and, again, "utter desolation" (20-3). Unlike Stefansson, Thierry depicts the south as a paradise from which the Inuit feel excluded. Yet he is clearly fascinated by this vast, empty land, which he thinks "all white men" hear a "call" to explore, and understands the cultural pressures on it better than his Inuit friends can: "the day was in sight when there would be no place on this continent untainted by the touch of white men" (24, 33). He comes to prefer solitude to white company, and leaves with regret. Having heard the northern silence with "awe" or fear for months, and then with "love," he now craves that "peace and quiet" with his "whole being" (123).

EXPLORINGS

A remarkable series of polar expeditions began in the late 1920s, as explorers reasserted themselves. Commander Richard E. Byrd, USN, led his first expedition to Antarctica in 1928-30, building "Little America" on the Bay of Whales near the site of Amundsen's *Framheim*. The newly-energized United States deployed more and better technology in the region than earlier parties could; Byrd brought along three airplanes, one of which flew him over the Pole. From above, Antarctica seemed "a pale sleeping princess, sinister and beautiful" (perhaps a nod to Amundsen's image in *The South Pole*), or, more succinctly, "terrible ... beautiful": the familiar oxymoron of early Alpine travel (Cameron 198-203). Radio connections between various parties and with the outside world were equally important. A sensitive observer of himself, his surroundings, and his expedition's intrusion, Byrd said that the radio had ended Antarctica's isolation, but would "destroy all peace of mind, which is half the attraction of the polar regions" (Debenham 104).

The British were focusing on the north. In 1930, a group of (mainly) young Cantabridgians chartered the *Quest* (Shackleton's last ship) for an expedition to Greenland, ostensibly to investigate whether airplanes could safely fly that way to North America. With an average age of 25, they lacked maturity but not talent. The leader, Henry (Gino) Watkins, was already a skilled organizer, fund-raiser, explorer, and pilot. He had led his first expedition to an island off Spitsbergen at the age of 19; his second went to Labrador (1928-29), and he was still an undergraduate. August Courtauld, whose wealthy father had been persuaded to back the venture, had been on two Arctic expeditions as well. F. Spencer Chapman, a mountaineer, skier, and aspiring author (ch. 6), also joined up. He would write the official expedition book, *Northern Lights* (1934).

It is difficult to know what to make of these people. At times they seem legitimate aspirants to the explorer's mantle, or to Hardy's intelligentsia of travel ("the more thinking among mankind"). In his foreword to *Northern Lights*, Byrd hails the "beautiful seriousness of spirit" that the British bring to polar exploration (Chapman 1934, v). At other times they seem feckless collegians, amateurs careless of detail: forgetting the airplane skis, bringing only one boot per dog, building an igloo according to Stefansson's instructions in *The Friendly Arctic*, then leaving the snow shovel outside and getting snowed in. Chapman sees freshly on his first Arctic venture and occasionally notes scenic beauty; Capt. Lemon calls the coast barren but beautiful during the open-boat journey south. Watkins's breathless introduction says that it was all about science and practical applications but Chapman will have to explain because he himself has no time, being off to Greenland again next week. There he disappeared while kayaking alone. He is said to have remarked (presciently, it turned out) that a man should live as though his life would be over at the age of 25.

Courtauld's life seemed symbolic or symptomatic enough to elicit a biography, Nicholas Wollaston's *The Man on the Ice Cap* (1980). He was the scion of a prominent family, the Art-Institute Courtaulds, but for a man born to ease and privilege as Augustine IX, he showed a remarkable affinity for some of the roughest, wildest places on the planet: seas, deserts, Greenland. Courtauld (b. 1904) came to consciousness during the Great War. His public school, Charterhouse (where Mallory taught), lost 700 alumni in the fighting; his Cambridge college, Trinity, 600 (Wollaston 24-33). He spent his young manhood in the shadow of the war, searching for his place in a scarred world. What were those who had missed the fighting to do with their lives? Courtauld liked to walk, sail, and explore. In 1925 he and a cousin went to Finland and made their way up to North Cape, a Great venue where Carlyle sets a crucial scene in *Sartor Resartus*. But Courtauld was not much of a writer: even Wollaston complains of his bored, "Dismissive little sentences" (38).

In his last year at Cambridge, Courtauld discovered one of Shackleton's Elephant Island survivors, James Wordie, in rooms nearby. Much taken with the Scots geologist, he decided to join his expedition to Greenland that summer (1926), and found in the ice-pack "a new world, infinite and alluring" (Wollaston 45). He learned how to survey, vented his disgust at garbage left by previous visitors, and explored inland, climbing mountains, alone or accompanied. In 1927, Courtauld went to the Sahara with two adventurous brothers. They made a tough summer camel trip into the sandstone country of the Tuaregs, exiting via Timbuktu. Courtauld surveyed, mapped, and climbed. The next year he tried his hand on the Stock Exchange (the family felt that he should work a bit), but sailing and learning to fly were more to his taste. In 1929 he went to Greenland again with Wordie (as did Vivian Fuchs, who would lead the first crossing of Antarctica). Wordie took Courtauld and others up Petermann Peak.

That fall he met Gino Watkins. Their 1930-31 expedition made sledge journeys and did experiments, but what captured public attention was Courtauld's five-month solo at an isolated weather station up on the icecap. Why he chose this duty is not clear. His slight chapter in *Northern Lights* says almost nothing about motives or feelings. Possibly the answers are as simple as he makes them sound. By the time his party reached Ice Cap Station after a nightmarish journey, there was not enough food left to maintain two men throughout the winter: it was either one man or none (none would mean abandoning planned weather observations). Courtauld, who had come to think the expedition a "poor show," and was "tired of the company" and of the coast's "jagged, zig-zag, see-saw jumble of rock and ice," volunteered (Wollaston 114, 124, 112). Chapman says that Courtauld was "very keen to stay," despite opposition (1934, 118). And stay he did, whatever his reasons. At first he dug himself out, up to six times a day, but gradually the blizzards wore him down, blocked his tunnels, denied him a spacious or any horizon, and entombed him for the last two months before rescue.

Bishop Fleming later wrote that Courtauld's solitary vigil was "evidently a spiritual experience as if he had been an ascetic meditating in the desert" (Wollaston 197). "Evidently"? We do not know his authority for this view. Wollaston suggests desires for solitude, silence, simplicity, peace, and purity as possible motives, also without documenting them. Courtauld gave him little help, having more questions than answers. "Why is it that men come to these places?" he asks his diary. "What do we gain?" The closest he comes to answering is another query, whether in fleeing from "the worries of the world" to the "grand and awful" we "come nearer to reality" (quoted Wollaston 148-9). Nowhere in Courtauld can we find support for the spiritual interpretation, unless we lean hard on the mention of Greenland's "ascetic nakedness" in his introduction to *Watkins' Last Expedition* (Wollaston 203).

In any case outsiders continued to come to these places, from various motives. A European expedition led by Prof. Alfred Wegener (proponent of the "continental drift" theory that preceded plate techtonics) wintered in West Greenland that year and maintained an outpost in the interior. In 1931 there were three traverses of the island: two by the British and Hoygaard's, plus von Gronau's aerial crossing. Watkins returned in 1932, fatally, and even Courtauld, who had vowed that he was finished with Greenland, came back in 1935 to climb in the "Watkins Mountains." (Thereafter he concentrated on sailing, including trans-Atlantic voyages, wrote his memoirs, and edited an anthology of adventure travel, *From the Ends of the Earth* [1958], published a year before his death.)

The Wegener party also had a man on the icecap: Dr Johannes Georgi, the "hermit of the inland ice," a scientist who took both solo and shared turns at Mid-Ice station (Georgi 56, 81). More outgoing than Courtauld, he wrote a book about the expedition, *Mid-Ice* (English translation, 1935). For all his professionalism and emphasis on science, it has an aesthetic dimension that acknowledges "magnificent lights and colours and views over the wild coast mountains" during the journey to the station (29). Dr Ernest Sorge, coming to join him, found the vistas of sky and snow "overpoweringly beautiful" and the mirages "wonderful" (quoted Georgi 79-80). Georgi knows exactly why he came: to gain experience for further adventures, and because "a man needs to achieve something uncommon" to strengthen him for the rest of his life (62). He found that taking weather observations at -60° gave him "a clean, quite peculiar feeling of enjoyment" (97). But, Georgi notes, the inland ice, while always impressive, is "both evil and good"; "the boundless wastes" dwarf one's "tiny little scrap of individuality," and whole parties are "tiny intruders" to whom nature is indifferent (29, 52, 124).

The Germans were better organized but less lucky than the British: Wegener and Greenlander Rasmus Willumsen perished while sledging back to the coast. "I am all to pieces, absolutely smashed up," Georgi writes; "I see ghosts, cannot bear the dark" (184). It sounds like a nervous breakdown: left alone, he stops working and sits crying, recalling his premonitions and feeling colder than ever before. He then admits that he and other winterers felt "the terror of the 'white sphinx'" (184) - not explained, but presumably the psychic trauma of living at Mid-Ice, as well as blizzards. And now we first hear of barrenness, real and metaphorical: "It is desolate and empty here, both within and around me" (185). The icecap was "magnificent" on the way in; the perceiver has changed. Yet at the end, after listing some of the rubs of the expedition, Georgi adds (in a footnote) that "the memory of these daily unpleasantnesses has faded, and the longing for the great space of the inland ice, common to all who have been to Greenland, has alone remained" (229).

Now-Admiral Byrd wrote the foreword to *Northern Lights* before going back to Antarctica, so he knew about Courtauld's solo, if not Georgi's. His second expedition (1933-35) was another high-tech effort - this time he had a helicopter as well as airplanes and tractors - but there was still some of the minimalist and mystic in him. Even in *Discovery*, the official account, Byrd admits "the intangible attraction of the white continent itself ... unspoiled, spacious and austere," alongside scientific motives; enthuses over the "unreal" beauty of icebergs like huge cathedrals; and regrets breaking the "isolation of the Last Continent of Silence" with his radio (1935, 1, 36-7, 52, 98). He certainly had a keen eye: an ice shower is like "an ocean of rainbows" or "a pillar of cascading platinum" (326). Byrd's most controversial action was to spend the winter night alone at Advance Weather Base, over 100 miles south of Little America II. Frank Debenham (Scott's geologist) calls this a "curious" and "unhappy" action for a leader (104); Byrd effectively abandoned the expedition for months, becoming ill and inert from the fumes of his generator.

Later he wrote a book about this solo. *Alone* is Byrd's "account of personal experience ... in considerable part subjective," omitted from *Discovery* to avoid any "unseemly show" of his sufferings in the *official* narrative (1938, vii). Like Courtauld, he volunteered rather than leave a station unmanned - but Courtauld was not the expedition leader. Byrd is more open than even Georgi about his motives. Part primitivist (life on the Barrier would be "Pleistocene"), part Outward Bound guru, he seeks to live off his "intellectual resources" (7, 17). Above all he "wanted to go for the experience's sake": call it "one man's desire to know that kind of experience to the full, to be by himself for a while and to taste peace and quiet and solitude long enough to find out how good they really are" (3-4). The psychological drift of this program might not reassure Debenham or the Navy, but Byrd felt that "people beset by the complexities of modern life" would understand his action "instinctively," for a stranger on Fifth Avenue may be "as lonely as a traveler wandering in the desert" (4, 6). Finally, he went in search of a "more replenishing philosophy" and "a more rigorous existence" than navy life had provided (7).

At first there was ample food for the imagination; the interest of Byrd is his mixture of Caesar and Hamlet. Flying over the Barrier shows him "the spaciousness of the desert [a common analogy among polar explorers] ... of the raw materials of creation" (Byrd

1938, 36). At Advance Base, a mere "pinprick in infinity," night work on the excavation brings to mind "that terrible frozen pit" at the bottom of Dante's *Inferno* (36, 39-40). Once the others leave, "the things of the world shrank to nothing" (51); like Georgi, he becomes a hermit of the snows. As the sun disappears for the winter, Byrd imagines that "This is the way the world will look to the last man as it dies," and feels like "the last survivor of an Ice Age" (74, 77). Nansen had said as much. The Barrier, a deceptive world, cheats perception with mirages and parhelia, yet "nothing is lovelier," especially at twilight (84-5). In between storms he has a sense of peace, harmony, divine purpose, and "cosmos": the orderly relation of parts to the whole (85-6). Then he begins to asphyxiate himself, and *Alone* becomes a confused fight for survival.

The second International Polar Year (1932-33) attracted both explorers and nations. Norway, Germany, and the United States sent expeditions to claim sectors of Antarctica in the 1930s. The British, claimants of old, maintained a party (led by John Rymill of the Watkins Greenland expedition) for three seasons there. The Oxford Ellesmere Land Expedition (1934-35) went off in the other direction. Like Watkins's effort, it was almost a children's crusade, with an average age of 23. One of its members bore the potent name of Shackleton: Ernest's son Edward, who told their story in *Arctic Journeys* (1936). The expedition had limited success, and Edward was a less interesting writer than his father. While it is good to know that the interior of Greenland is a "huge ice desert" and that "the cliffs of these Arctic deserts resemble very closely the cliffs which border on the deserts of Arabia and Egypt," the son does not make us *feel* those deserts (Edward Shackleton 1936, 44, 59). Perhaps he too should have employed a collaborator.

Read without comparisons, however, *Arctic Journeys* has value, especially in Shackleton's concluding thoughts on the motives of polar explorers - a topic that may have troubled his youth. Scientific knowledge is only an alibi, he has decided. The real motive is personal, something "more subjective and less sentimental" than plain old "Adventure" (Edward Shackleton 1936, 315). Most human endeavour springs from an urge to soothe our restlessness or discontent; we find relief in "dimming or replacing that instinctive urge for 'something,' for 'higher things'" (316). Perhaps no explorer had come closer to saying that his activities were a substitute for religion. Expeditions also satisfy by "ordering one's life" and providing opportunities for achievement. Shackleton is particularly a theorist of misery. In the field, discomfort is "a matter of course": only back home does it seem "hardship" (316). For that matter, he argues, "there is a certain comfort in 'reasonable hardship'"; even the war had its moments (317). Among the explorer's rewards, along with mental stimulation and camaraderie, is the "intense sense of comfort" after long suffering (317-18).

It is odd that, with all his psychologizing and philosophizing about exploration, Shackleton does not take this moment to discuss its aesthetic dimension, occasionally visible in his text. From a hill in northwest Greenland, for example, the main ice field is "a grim sight" under autumn twilight; the "limitless" pack stretches far into Kane Basin, and the cold wind is redolent of the Arctic winter night "soon to close down ... on a dying world," so they head for camp with a mixture of "awe and relief" (Edward Shackleton 83). One might have expected such moments to figure somehow in Shackleton's summary and his analysis of explorers' motives. He actually has less to say about the aesthetic side of travel in high latitudes than does the ultimate 1930s polar "organization man," Adm. Byrd, who embarked on his third Antarctic expedition in 1939 as Europe went to war, and stayed until 1941, when his country did. There would necessarily be a hiatus in polar expeditions - which was all Antarctic and most Arctic travel - until the nations had once again sorted out their differences.

8
Desert Spaces:
Arts and the Great, 1917-1939

Much as Samuel Coleridge depicted polar voyages more vividly in "The Rime of the Ancient Mariner" than those actually with Capt. Cook had been able to do, so some creative artists of the inter-war period limned the aesthetic-emotional landscape of the Great with a resonance that most travel writing lacked. They could bring the Great home - using metaphors drawn from exploration to uncover veiled aspects of ordinary life - or take us there, showing how it looked and felt, or what it meant, to have extraordinarily spacious horizons: fictional equivalents of rough travel. Explorers (sometimes influenced by literature) provided the raw material; artists refined, analyzed, and tried to give durable expression. This symbiosis is clearly visible in the postwar work of several English and American poets. Their verse, which often had pre-war roots but was coloured by the war, shared details and themes with accounts of the Great, and sometimes reproduced the darkness of Hardy's Egdon Heath.

T.S. Eliot's *Prufrock and Other Observations* (1917) - dedicated to a friend who died in the war - gave early hints of the dominant tone of the new verse. "The Love Song of J. Alfred Prufrock" (drafted under the influence of French Symbolists before the war) portrays empty lives in a grim cityscape where the few touches of nature connote illness or menace. Evening lies "spread out against the sky / Like a patient etherised upon a table" (Eliot 3). In "Preludes," a soul is "stretched tight across the skies / That fade behind a city block" (13): the heavens - first source of Great aesthetics - provide only a damaged sublimity now. Prufrock, timid and inarticulate, may walk the shore and see mermaids, but doubts they will sing to *him*. Emptiness, which some explorers found and feared in vast nature, is an existential fact of urban life here, in "Portrait of a Lady," and in the vacant lots of "Preludes."

Eliot's early verse is full of images of aridity. In *Poems* (1920), Gerontion, "an old man in a dry month, / ... waiting for rain" upon "windy spaces," is "a dry brain in a dry season" (Eliot 21, 23). The epigraph to "Sweeney Erect" calls for a grove of "dry and leafless" trees, "and behind me / Make all a desolation" (25). "The Waste Land" (1922) is a desert, while "The Hollow Men" (1925) depicts dry, empty people in a dead land. Yet on the margins of all of these poems is water, remembered or awaited. Gerontion once sailed before the ocean tradewinds, Sweeney's poem is set on "a cavernous waste shore" of the Cyclades, "The Waste Land" is resolved by a thunderstorm, and even the Hollow Men entertain the possibility that something could make the "Multifoliate rose" of Christian salvation bloom in their wasteland (23, 25, 58). Eliot's deserts are not the real thing, but they function like them.

Of course all of these poems are more complex than this use suggests, yet the extent to which Eliot makes barren landscape symbolic of modern spiritual sickness is remarkable. Though "The Waste Land" is indebted to mediaeval legends, Eliot's deserts are not the dark forests of French romance, but Biblical wastes or Salvador Dali paintings. Amid "stony rubbish" reminiscent of the Book of Ezekiel, the speaker seeks shelter in the shadow of "red rock" (Eliot 38, ll. 20-6): a reference to Hugh Miller's work of pious geology, *The Old Red Sandstone* (1841).[1] The "hooded hordes swarming / Over endless plains, stumbling in cracked earth / Ringed by the flat horizon only" (ll. 369-71) suggests Flaubert's novel *Salammbô*, though Eliot cites a passage in Herman Hesse's *Blick ins Chaos* (1922) in which half of Europe is heading for the abyss. The fisherman of ll. 424-5 (Eliot refers us to Jessie Weston's mediaeval study *From Ritual to Romance*) sits on the shore with an "arid plain" behind him.

Eliot uses Great nature in other ways here. At the outset, in Munich (a centre for climbing), a voice says, "In the mountains, there you feel free": a common sentiment of Alpine tourists (Eliot 37, l. 17). Most mountains in the poem are of the dry desert variety, though, "rock without water" (l. 334). Like Hardy's tourist of the future, drawn to barren beaches, one of Eliot's speakers goes to Margate Sands, though (or since) he "can connect / Nothing with

---

[1]   On Miller, see *The Road to Egdon Heath*, ch. 11.

nothing" there (ll. 301-2). Some wintry moments prefigure the
"Who is the third?" passage, an unknown figure walking "up the
white road" ahead (ll. 360-6). Eliot notes that the idea began in "the
account of one of the Antarctic expeditions"; indeed, it comes from
South, when Shackleton's party is crossing South Georgia. This is
interesting for what it reveals of Eliot's reading. Often the influence
went both ways: from the field to the study and back.[2]

Eliot's "wintriness" - bringing a polar chill to temperate climes
- was not unique. Hardy, who had worked this vein before the war
(*Tess*), did so still in his poems. "A Backward Spring" declares, "The
trees are afraid to put forth buds, / And there is timidity in the
grass" at this traditional season of hope and renewal.[3] *The Return of
the Native*'s dark view of modern life reappears in "At the Entering
of the New Year" (1920), which contrasts the hearty welcome
once given January 1st with the more reluctant "New Style."
Human Shows, Far Phantasies (1925), the last collection published in
Hardy's lifetime, contains several notably wintry poems: "Snow in
the Suburbs," "Music in a Snowy Street," and "A Light Snow-Fall
After Frost," whose hoary-headed man on a white road is another
mysterious extra.

Hardy was not imagining this, of course: England can have long,
hard winters. Yet the persistence with which the founder of Thulean
aesthetics kept selecting as his subject the passage of death's chill
from nature to humanity is striking. No doubt it was partly age - he
was in his 80s now - but also world-view. Like Nansen, Byrd, and
H.G. Wells's time traveller to the future, Hardy felt that he might be
seeing the end of the whole project. His final, posthumous volume,
Winter Words (1928), does not contain much verse *about* winter; that
is rather the poet's season. In "An Unkindly May," winter makes an
"unkind" (unnatural) incursion into late spring, but inner winter is
the real issue. "Yuletide in a Younger World," like his New Year
poem, opines that we have lost our relish for these high occasions,
and our freshness of perception as well. Then, having - to say the

---

[2]   Edward Abbey says "The Waste Land" reminded him of Moab, Utah;
      Laurence Ricou notes the influence of "The Waste Land" on Canadian
      descriptions of the prairie (1973, 120). Eliot's question has been tenta-
      tively answered by Greg Child and other modern mountaineers: it is
      the dissociating self of extreme fatigue, stress, and oxygen depriva-
      tion. "Who is the third?" You.

[3]   Quotations from Hardy's poems follow *The Complete Poetical Works of
      Thomas Hardy*, ed. Samuel Hynes, 3 vols. Oxford: Clarendon, 1982-85.

least - made his point, in his last poem "He Resolves to Say No More."

By that time there were intimations of Thulean wintriness in a number of otherwise disparate American poets. Wallace Stevens's "The Snow Man" (1921) has been called one of "the greatest poems of the twentieth century" (Longenbach 25) but divides critics sharply. It asserts in one remarkable 15-line sentence that "One must have a mind of winter / ... And have been cold a long time" to behold wintry scenes "and not to think / Of any misery in the sound of the wind," which, the speaker tells us, is "the sound of the land" (W. Stevens 8). Paraphrasing Stevens is dangerous, but one might say, it is difficult for mortals (including many writers on the Great discussed here) to avoid pathetic fallacy. The final stanza presents a listener in the snow who, "nothing himself, beholds / Nothing that is not there and the nothing that is." While Langbaum uses this as "an example of the new sense of nature" as "unalterably alien" (104), Stevens himself wrote that the poem shows "the necessity of identifying oneself with reality in order to understand it and enjoy it" (H. Stevens 464).

"The Snow Man" can also be read as a display of Buddhist meditative consciousness.[4] Knowledge of Buddhism had slowly been unfolding among European and North American literati since the British (under Francis Younghusband) marched into Tibet and forcibly "opened" it to the West in the late nineteenth century. It was about to reach a wider public. A scholarly commentary on the seventeenth-century Japanese poet Basho, a Zen Buddhist, appeared in 1902, with translations of some of his haiku; in 1933 his prose began to be published. Stevens (who had been reading about Buddhism at least since 1909) built into poems such as "The Snow Man," "A Clear Day and No Memories," and "Of Mere Being" a number of qualities central to Buddhist teaching and also to many accounts of the Great: ascetic bareness, purity, silence, the void or emptiness ("the nothing that is"), simplicity, eternity, and infinity.

We may wonder how much Stevens, working at a Hartford insurance company, knew of the *physical* Great (in "The American

---

[4] See William W. Bevis 1988 (full disclosure: my brother).

Sublime" he says that the sublime comes down to "The empty spirit / In vacant space"), but some American poets actively sought out natural grandeur. *White Buildings* (1926) shows Hart Crane as a lyric poet of the sea - into which he would leap in 1933 - and the sky: its complement and sometimes (as in myth) its lover. In "North Labrador," a "land of leaning ice" embraced by the sky "Flings itself silently / Into eternity" (Crane 15). Labrador seems a place of negation, without spring or life, "no time nor sun," yet Crane hails it as "Darkly Bright." His fascination with ocean's depth and scale resurfaces in "At Melville's Tomb," where glances from the "Frosted eyes" of drowned men "lifted altars" to the skies, "And silent answers crept across the stars" (33). "Voyages," a love poem on two levels, calls the sea a "great wink of eternity" whose "vast belly moonward bends," yearning for space, creating tides (35). Crane's sense of the Great is vivid and intense.

Robinson Jeffers left the east to settle in California in 1914. Building a stone house and tower above Carmel Bay - one of the grandest landscapes American artists have found - he wrote poems hailing the power, size, and antiquity of nature, while minimizing or denigrating human contributions. "Continent's End" is representative of the verse in *Roan Stallion and Other Poems* (1924): the poet stands on a cliff, waves pounding the granite beneath him, and bathes in an aura of space and time. He feels the breadth of the continent behind him, feels (as Conrad did) how the ocean links all points of the compass. Far bigger than humanity, it begot us, yet we both "flow from the older fountain," the "tides of fire" (Jeffers 1935, 272). "Night" salutes the moon as eternal (the sun will die). Vast and primal, Night is alpha and omega; to Her, stars are merely the sparks of "a lost fire dying in the desert," the coals of departed nomads (85). Light and life long to return to her.

In "Credo" (1927) and elsewhere, Jeffers fleshes out his philosophy.[5] No idea-lism for him; the mind's reality is just that: "the ocean in the bone vault is only / The bone vault's ocean: out there is the ocean's." And he believes that "the heart-breaking beauty / Will remain when there is no heart to break for it" (Jeffers 1935, 295). While we are transitory, the "fierce and solitary beauty" of Point Joe and the "nihilist simplicity" of the ocean will endure (250, 253). Later poems draw consolation from this idea while

---

[5]   Oelschlaeger calls it "Inhumanism," a love of the "transhuman" (246, 252).

indicting humanity. "The Broken Balance" (in *Dear Judas*, 1929) is "the hopeless prostration of the earth / Under men's hands and their minds." As in Wordsworth, we choke our natures, sell ourselves, and live insanely, turning the world upside down; "it is time to perish," since "now nothing is good." Dwelling in the Great, Jeffers was as grim as Hardy, though hopeful that the "immortal / Splendor" would resume after we go (1929, 117-18).[6]

Several of these themes also appear in the work of Robert Frost, for many readers *the* nature poet of the period. Taking the struggle for existence "north of Boston" as his field, moving from natural scene to homely profundity, he considers what it means to mend walls, swing birches, and not take a road. Like Stevens, he is less concerned with outer than with "inner weather" ("Tree at My Window"). This is clearest in "Desert Places" (1934), which begins with snow falling on a field at dusk, imagines the "blanker whiteness of benighted snow" to come; then leaps outward but lands inside: "They cannot scare me with their empty spaces / Between stars," because I "scare myself with my own desert places" (Frost 386). Langbaum calls this his "darkest nature poem" (108), yet "Design" - which questions whether providential "design govern in a thing so small" as predation - seems at least as dark. Frost is more balanced and cheerful than the other poets discussed here, although in "Once By the Pacific" he sounds as apocalyptic as Jeffers.

For every Frost or Jeffers there are hundreds of "minor" or "regional" poets. Some of the latter, exploring a particular area in detail, are relevant here. By the 1930s the deserts and mountains of the American Southwest, especially around Taos, New Mexico, apprehended as a spiritual landscape, had attracted an array of writers, artists, and intellectuals, including Mary Austin, D.H. Lawrence, Willa Cather, Robinson Jeffers, Carl Jung, Georgia O'Keeffe, and the painter John Marin, who wrote (1928), "the true artist must perforce go from time to time to the elemental big forms - Sky, Sea, Mountain, Plain - ... to sort of re-true himself up, to recharge the battery. For these big forms have everything" (468). One of the region's poets, Phillips Kloss, expressed his feelings for the land in *Arid* (1932), a volume faithful to the central conception of Powell and Austin, that this was above all "a land of little rain."

---

6   Yet as early as 1963 I could not follow his natural directions to "Tor House" ("If you should look for this place after a handful of life-times...").

Most of *Arid*'s poems treat of desiccation. In "Desert Mystery," the speaker exclaims over a "heart drifting from barren place to place" (Kloss 3); the narrative of "Loco" begins and ends with aridity. Some poems try to explain this obsession. "A Conjecture" notes that "things endure for thousands of years / In the clean climate of this country" (9); preservation is a theme of some of the earliest accounts of deserts, glaciers, and polar regions. "It is the altitude and the aridity, preserving," says Kloss, that suspend the usual course of nature and give a kind of immortality. He does not seem depressed by the desert, nor does he see it as a wasteland. Musicians like to express the ocean, Kloss thinks, whereas artists prefer to paint the desert ("Musician and Artist"). In "Platitudes of Want," he observes that, unlike all *human* conditions, the desert is self-sufficient and "wants nothing. It is integrity" (84). Kloss identifies with the desert's life forms. "My roots are in the dry soil," he writes, like the juniper's.

NOTHING BUT LAND: THE NOVEL

Elaborate descriptions of deserts, often heavy with feeling, also appear in inter-war novels. The French African empire, which gave writers as well as soldiers and priests access to the Sahara, produced *L'Atlantide* (1919), Pierre Benoit's tale of Antinea (a descendant of the Atlantids in Plato's *Critias*), who lives in the Hoggar Mountains and lures French officers to their deaths. This remarkable plot in fact lured a number of Frenchmen to the Sahara, including Henri Lhote, who described the Tassili rock-paintings. Benoit's portrait of the desert is intense, fanciful, and at times as lurid as a Hollywood film, with large doses of mystique and oxymoron. As Lt Ferrières, bored with life, prepares to ride into the desert, he can 'feel struggling inside him the sacred horror of mystery and its attraction ... I desire what I fear,' and stares at 'the desert that is about to swallow him.'[7] Then he meets Capt. de Saint-Avit and all ennui ends.

Saint-Avit, a desert mystic who delights in moonlight rides, resembles the Sahara, open yet mysterious; his mind is 'as unknown as these solitudes' (Benoit 35). He prizes the desert as a refuge from civilization, ridiculing Eugène Fromentin for thinking he was in

---

[7]   "Je sens lutter en moi l'horreur sacrée du mystère et son attrait ... je souhaite ce que je redoute"; "le désert qui va l'engloutir": Benoit 11, 13. My translations are enclosed in single quotation marks.

the Sahara when he was only at its edge.[8] Saint-Avit narrates the rest of *L'Atlantide*. On one trip he was joined by Capt. Morhange, seeking early Christian relics. In a cave, they find the inscription "Antinea," and a Touareg who says there are more such in the Hoggar region, which he calls "the country of fear" (113). All three travel there. The first mountains seem both "sinistre et beau" (111). The Touareg guides them over a 'gigantic chaos of black rocks in a lunar landscape' - volcanic country - to the Mont des Génies (Mount of Spirits), an 'enormous dark bastion' like a feudal dungeon, and shows them a grotto where Antinea's name is again inscribed (116-18).

Here the *capitaines* are arrested (their guide is really Cegheir ben Cheikh, murderer of French officers!) and held in a cave overlooking a 'terrestrial paradise' so beautiful that Saint-Avit bursts into tears: a lush grove encircled by snowy peaks; far off can be seen 'the immense red desert' (Benoit 135, 206). They learn that they are in the power of Antinea, i.e. "the new Atlantid," queen of the Hoggar; she avenges the wronged queens of antiquity by ensnaring young explorers, who die of love. The chaste-seeming Antinea tries to seduce Morhange, and when he rejects her she turns to Saint-Avit. The next morning he realizes that he has killed Morhange. He attempts to kill Antinea but fails, and escapes with a slave girl across the desert. Only Saint-Avit survives. At the end, he and Ferrières set off to look for Antinea, with ben Cheikh as guide! Always in Benoit's background or foreground is desert scenery, the Sahara serving as a kind of Wild West where anything is possible.

André Gide's use of the Sahara in *L'Immoraliste* (1921) is comparatively restrained, though the desert again proves a source of unsettling ideas. Michel, the "immoralist," tells his story to old friends summoned from France at his house near "Sidi B.M.," Algeria, over one night, much as Saint-Avit or Conrad's Marlow might have done. His terrace overlooks a "plain ... like the desert ... the view stretched away into infinity" (Gide 5). A few years earlier Michel had been very ill and tried a Swiss cure, but got "utterly sick" of the mountains - perhaps a bad sign - which now haunt him (126). So he convalesced at Biskra, Algeria (where the Gides honeymooned), and found that he loved the desert, a "land of mortal glory and intolerable splendor" (139). Michel lost his "stability of thought" there, however, for which he blames the

---

8   Fromentin is discussed in ch. 14 of *The Road to Egdon Heath*.

climate, the sky's "persistent azure" (146). He has come to like boys (exit Marlow, tiptoeing). Freedom is one of the oldest attractions of the desert, but Michel's "objectless liberty is a burden," and his "will is broken" (145-6).

North American novelists used long horizons differently, partly because the powerful prairie vistas are not exactly desertic. In Willa Cather's *My Antonia* (1918), Jim Burden remembers being taken west as a child and waking up to a new scene: "There was nothing but land. ... I had the feeling that the world was left behind, that we had got over the edge of it" (Cather 1949, 8-9). Now he knows that it was the land's "scarcity of detail" that "made details so precious" (22). The "pale, cold light of the winter sunset" on the prairie seemed "the light of truth," he recalls, and its cold wind said, "This is reality" (116). He retains this feeling after moving to town: during one sunset especially, when a plow is magnified like "picture writing on the sun" (159). At the end, Burden returns to enjoy tilled fields and houses, but also a bit of old, unbroken prairie that by then represents the priceless and irrecoverable past.

O.E. Rölvaag's *Giants in the Earth* (1924), a Norwegian-language novel that became an American classic, contains two distinct views of the Great Plains. For patriarch Per Hansa, the open prairie symbolizes opportunity in a new land. To his wife Beret, it is fearful, even terrible. The lack of shelter frightens her: there is "no place to hide" (Rölvaag 101). The marvels that Per Hansa sees - beauty, vastness, even infinity - do not exist for Beret, who knows only a desolate, silent wilderness and other solitary souls. At first it is a place where the "evil in human nature" comes out; later nature itself seems monstrous (153, 330, 348). Hers has been called the classic reaction to the plains (Lowenthal 1968, 64-5), but without some Per Hansas, Europeans would not have settled there. His garden, her desert. Per Hansa and the narrator are excited by the idea of "prairie schooners" sailing across oceanic plains and anchoring by sod houses; for Beret it is an ocean with "no heart" and "no soul" (314, 37). Rölvaag's picture is admirably balanced.

Some Commonwealth novelists attempted to appraise Great space. Frederick Philip Grove (aka Felix Paul Greve, a German who left his family behind and lied about his past in Canada) has attracted some critical attention, not all favourable (Abley 54-5). He seems devoted to the land, but his novels are cold and remote (Mitcham 66; McCourt 66). Grove might have agreed. In *Over Prairie*

Trails (1922) he remarks, "I love Nature more than Man" (Grove 1957, 14). This preference serves him well in vignettes of horse-and-buggy rides through "backwoods bushland" that he calls "God's own earth," or over snowy prairies that remind him of "Homer's Pontos atrygetos - the barren sea" (37, 125). Grove notes that as he ages, he seeks out flatter, "more elemental" views, though most of his drives took place in darkness or fog, so there is actually little of the Great (90).

And when Grove tries to write a novel, his predilection hampers him. At the beginning of *Settlers in the Marsh* (1925), Lars and Niels walk into the Manitoba bush, a "wild, sandy land" along the Big Marsh (which Ellen, who wants "wide, open, level spaces," dislikes for its lack of horizon); then into "a sheer waste of heath-like country" (Grove 1925, 11-12, 141). Niels finds freedom in this region, although "the vastness of the spaces" makes human actions seem "inconsequential and irrelevant" (43). The author seems to share Niels's view. Grove admired Hardy, and his setting does suggest Egdon Heath (Wood 198; Ricou 48). But Hardy cares about his characters, and Grove really does not. Few novels treat human relations as thinly as *Settlers in the Marsh*, whose laconic dialogue seems to satirize Swedish reticence. The book shows that Hardy's approach can be taken to a literary dead end.

Martha Ostenso's *Wild Geese* (1925), which treats pioneer life in the same area, has articulate characters and balanced responses, as in Rölvaag.[9] There is a potent sense of the dark prairie stretching to the horizon, "spare as an empty platter" under a "tremendous" sky (Ostenso 13, 161). "Fear of this harsh land" seems natural, and Caleb Gare, "harsh, demanding, tyrannical," is "a spiritual counterpart of this land" (34-6). Yet he sees it only as a commodity, while his daughter Judith loves it. Lind and Mark, who speak of the unity of the "nature of man and earth" out there, which would have interested Hardy (101), are different. Mark is awed by the scale of the north - "eternal sky ... endless plains" - and the "austerity of nature" (105). Lind, oppressed by the prairie's monotony, finds life up north "barren," but the feeling that "this place is sinister" arises mainly from Caleb's deeds (106, 246). Ostenso finally sends a prairie fire to kill him and resolve the plot.

---

[9] For Rees she is one of those who created a Canada of the imagination by fidelity to the land (160-4).

One might expect a novel titled *Ultima Thule* (1929) to be set in Greenland, but "Henry Richardson" (i.e. Australian writer Ethel Florence L. Richardson) used the term figuratively in her grimly realistic tale of an Irish doctor's slide into failure, madness, and death in rural Australia. Theodore Dreiser would have admired it; Sinclair Lewis did. On one level, Thule is the bush town where Richard Mahoney begins to fall apart, or the seaside resort where he has a stroke, or the outback station where he dies. On another, it is his surrender to madness, or his death. Mahoney is paralyzed by the Great space that inspired larger spirits: riding a train across the bush, he is "staggered by its vastness. - And emptiness" (Richardson 52). Yet there is something he wants and needs out there. One night near the end he is found standing at the front door, beyond which lay "space, freedom, peace," and the sea (271). Mahoney is buried in bare, rolling country outside of town, within earshot of his beloved sea, breaking "eternally on the barren shore." Nothing hinders the wind or eye there; "the vast earth meets an infinitely vaster sky" (345). Mahoney is finally subsumed into the Great.

Deserts or prairies were the favoured terrain of the period's nature novels, though there are exceptions: the American pulp writer H.P. Lovecraft's novelette *At the Mountains of Madness* (1931), a concoction about Antarctica combining Poe with Admiral Byrd; Hemingway's *Green Hills of Africa* (1935) and several stories, including "The Snows of Kilimanjaro" (1936), in which the volcano represents death or heaven; and Saint-Exupéry's *Vol de nuit*, where lost aviators, low on fuel and trapped above the clouds, wander the night sky over the Andes, sole inhabitants of a starry world, 'infinitely rich, but doomed' (1931, 142). Most writers did not limit themselves to one area of the Great, but used what they needed, as Saint-Exupéry did with the desert and the sea in *Terre des hommes* (ch. 5).

Such a writer is D.H. Lawrence, whose portraits of physical nature in fiction and essays were so vivid and pervasive that Richard Aldington made an anthology of them, *The Spirit of Place* (1935). It reminds us how often the Great appears in Lawrence's work: the "talk of Canada, ... where the plains are wide" in *The White Peacock*; the Lincolnshire fens in *Sons and Lovers*, showing Paul "the sweeping relentlessness of life"; the Alpine scenes of *Women in Love*; the fearfully "vacant spaces" of Australia in *Kangaroo* (1944, 6, 54, 142). In *Sea and Sardinia* (1921), the sea has the feel of "freedom," especially the freedom to escape other people (D.H. Lawrence 1956,

26). A placid morning breeds the wish to "sail for ever ... through the spaces of this lovely world," a "world empty of man" (45-6). *The Plumed Serpent* (1926) gives a fearsome depiction of Mexican terrain, its mountains looming "terribly" over human "specks," its history "another kind of vastness" (1950, 55, 170, 457). *Phoenix*, Lawrence's posthumous papers, adds to this list New Mexico, Caribbean waters ("The Flying Fish"), and a long "Study of Thomas Hardy" (1932) arguing that he writes better about land than about people, who move "almost insignificantly" upon Egdon Heath (1972, 480).

CROWDED DESERTS:

BRITISH POETRY AND DRAMA

W.H. Auden provides good examples of the extensive use that British poets and playwrights made of the Great in the 1930s. "As I Walked Out One Evening" deals mainly with the ravages of time, but some of the images come from wild nature ("Into many a green valley / Drifts the appalling snow"), which has a disturbing tendency to follow one home: "The glacier knocks in the cupboard, / The desert sighs in the bed" (Auden 1991, 133-4). Metaphorical deserts were popular between the wars: Eliot's wasteland, Frost's desert places, François Mauriac's *Le Désert de l'amour* (1925), Auden's own "deserts of the heart" ("In Memory of W.B. Yeats"). Auden uses other areas of the Great as well. "Western culture" sails pompously "Over the barren plains of a sea" ("A Voyage"), there are mountains of fear and mountains of love in "Two Climbs," and the formidable terrain of "Journey to Iceland" emits "a glitter / Of glacier, sterile immature mountains intense" (174, 149-50). Though "North means to all *Reject*," one may still "feel pure in its deserts."

Auden collaborated with Louis MacNeice on *Letters from Iceland* (1937), an assortment of prose and verse showing that more than an interest in Icelandic literature drew them there. MacNeice tries to explain the appeal in a poetic epistle to friends: "I like it if only because this nation / Enjoys a scarcity of population" (Auden 1969, 30). Misanthropy? MacNeice insists that he and Auden were just gathering facts. Every creature, he says, casts about "Looking for itself, its nature, its final pattern" (32). Their trip to Iceland, then, like most travel, is actually introspection, self-discovery; "the North begins inside" (251). Then why bother travelling to this raw island? Chants MacNeice, "Better were the northern skies / Than this desert [Hampstead] in disguise" (253). Evidently they wanted what Hardy said modern men would seek: a real, open, admitted "desert," answering to something in themselves, not *suburbia deserta*.

Auden's and Christopher Isherwood's *The Ascent of F.6* (1937), "a tragedy in two acts" full of literary allusions and archetypal symbolism, shows how politicians, the public, even friends and family pervert the desire of young men for heroic challenge, with fatal results. In the race between two nations to be the first to climb a "terrifying fang of rock and ice" on the frontier between British and Ostnian Sudoland, Ostnia is Germany; F.6 (also called "Chormopuloda") is Everest and K-2 (Auden 1958, 27). England's leading climber, Michael Random, at various times echoes or parallels T.E. Lawrence, Scott, Mallory (who saw Everest as a "fang"), Hamlet, and King Lear. In the first scene, he sits atop a hill reading Dante on Ulysses: another heroic model. The play struggles to present a "tragic hero" in antiheroic times; dark passages redolent of Matthew Arnold, T.S. Eliot, and postwar *Angst* recur in Random's speeches and in those of Mr and Mrs A, the living-dead suburbanites. Random aligns himself with classic mountaineering literature before he dies on top, however: "F 6 has shown me what I am" (94).

Random's brother and mother appear on F.6. Auden's own brother John (to whom the play is dedicated) was a Himalayan traveller who in 1937 was surveying the Karakorams with Eric Shipton and Michael Spender, the poet's brother, among others. Stephen Spender used images of Mt. Everest in "The Uncreating Chaos," but his imagination was drawn chiefly to the north, where several British expeditions went in the 1930s. "Polar Exploration" treats the Arctic as a metaphor - of what is uncertain. Time and space lose meaning in that "total whiteness"; a sceptical veteran will only say, "To snow we added footprints" (Spender 55). Back in the city, he wonders whether the Arctic ice was "anger transformed," like the frozen lake at the bottom of hell where Dante's Satan lies (56). And there are other possibilities. "The raw, the motionless / Skies, were these the spirit's hunger?" Were their marches really "the will's evasion"? Is the North perhaps "a palpable real madness ...?"[10] The poet would rather ask questions than assert anything.

---

[10]   Spender made minor revisions for the version in his *Collected Poems*, used here.

T.S. Eliot also participated in the 1930s revival of verse drama. In *The Family Reunion* (1939), the peripatetic, tormented peer Harry tries to express his view of life in images reminiscent of *The Waste Land*. Haunted by the "sudden solitude in a crowded desert," he has learned that even violence is no escape; "one is still alone / In an over-crowded desert" (Eliot 235). Later, Harry recalls how he moved from the "endless drift / Of shrieking forms in a circular desert" to being "Under the single eye above the desert" (277), as in Hichens's *The Garden of Allah* and the Arab saying, "In the desert there is only He." This movement, similar to Eliot's own (and *The Waste Land*), makes Harry's denouement predictable. He casts off his English ties for "the worship in the desert," discomfort and deprivation, "A stony sanctuary and a primitive altar" (281). This rings a bell, and Eliot later confirmed that Harry would emulate the career of Charles de Foucauld (Hamilton 243). Like MacNeice, Harry prefers a real desert to a metaphorical one, and will "follow the bright angels" there (Eliot 281).

In sharp contrast, Hugh MacDiarmid's "On a Raised Beach" (in *Stony Limits*, 1934) strongly affirms the geological basis of life. "All is lithogenesis": history, religion, poetry (MacDiarmid 1:422). "I must begin with these stones as the world began," he says; we come from and return to stone, the stellar material, so it is foolish to make metaphors "Instead of just accepting the stones" (1:424-5). What does that mean? Our ideas and religions do not bring us nearer to God and are "irrelevant" to the "intense vibration in the stones" (1:426). "This is no heap of broken images" throws down the gauntlet to the born-again Eliot; we need to "find the faith that builds mountains" before we "seek the faith that moves them." MacDiarmid will not bate the thrust of his argument: "These stones go through Man, straight to God, if there is one" (1:427). They alone of all creation can confront Him, as Job tried to do. For the poet, stones are "kindred" to "Alpha and Omega" (1:428-9).

Place is vital in the poem. The beach shows MacDiarmid how important it is to find leaders who are as essential and self-sufficient as stones, but it is not the only site that moves him. "I am enamoured of the desert at last," he writes; "The abode of supreme serenity is necessarily a desert" (MacDiarmid 1:431). This is a keen, not a passive serenity. "I will have nothing interposed / Between my sensitiveness and the barren but beautiful reality," he insists. This "seeing of a hungry man" (a quote from Doughty's *Arabia Deserta*) will have a "deadly clarity," whose menace he is willing to risk. MacDiarmid rejects the "escapist" label: he is running not from but towards life. Seeing that "We have not built on rock," it is fitting and (again) necessary that "These bare stones bring me straight back to reality" (1:432). For MacDiarmid, the stony raised beach and desert hold the meaning of life, death, and sublimity.

CORRESPONDENCES IN NATURE:

THE FINE ARTS

Finally we ought to note some utilizations of the Great in non-verbal arts, for its gradual acceptance was (as Hardy foresaw) a phenomenon of general culture. In Canada, the "Group of Seven" painters who ventured west in the '20s found landscapes that were "empty and silent," and came to prize their "solemnity and solitude" (ch. 6; Tippett and Cole, 86-9). For Lawren Harris and Frank Varley the Rocky Mountains and the Coast Range were numinous entities; Jock MacDonald, Varley's student, added eastern philosophy to nature worship in the 1930s.

As North American painters worked to free themselves from Old World influences and develop their own styles, some European artists were altering their own inheritance radically. The Catalan painter Salvador Dali produced conventional landscapes as late as 1923, but by 1926 his backgrounds had opened out into the long empty vistas that became his trademark. The plain and distant mountains of "Girl with Curls" also appear in "Apparatus and Mountains" (1927) and "Shades of Night Descending" (1931), where they are vaster and notably barren. How Dali acquired this penchant - travel, reading, other paintings - is not clear, but for a decade it was a prominent feature of his work; "The Average Bureaucrat" (1930), "Myself at the Age of Ten" (1933), and "Sugar Sphinx" (1933) all set their subjects in front of deserts and mountains. In a number of later canvases, including "Telephone in a Dish" (1939) and "The Last Supper" (1955), however, barren backgrounds are less conspicuous, as if what was once a signature flourish had been absorbed - a development that might repay further study.

Several composers tried to evoke Great nature by acoustic "painting," using dynamic and tonal contrasts to suggest vastness, as Borodin had. Gustav Holst's orchestral suite *The Planets* (1921), composed during the war, is an obvious case. He was more interested in astrology than in astronomy: Jupiter is "jovial," the Bringer of

Jollity, rather than the greatest of planets; Uranus a magician fond of dances rather than an incredibly distant object; and Saturn the Bringer of Old Age, not the beautiful ring-bearer. But sometimes the different systems support each other: Mars is loudly martial, with discords, pounding timpani, and a marshalling of orchestral forces leading to a *ffff* finish. Then Venus, our twilight star, brings peace and love slowly on quiet flutes, celeste, rising celli, and harps playing harmonics. Mercury, with its short year, is fast and flickering, full of runs, *glissandi*, and sixteenth notes. Neptune, "The Mystic," accords best with the feelings of the stargazer. Played mostly *andante* and *pp*, its slight theme is sparsely scored; Holst requests a "dead tone." At the end, a distant female choir vocalizes wordlessly, repeating the last bar "until the sound is lost in the distance," imitating Borodin's *In the Steppes of Central Asia*.

Holst was also interested in Buddhism and Thomas Hardy. His tone poem *Egdon Heath* (1928) bears the subtitle "Homage to Thomas Hardy" and an epigraph from chapter one of *The Return of the Native* ("a place perfectly accordant with man's nature"). Holst's approach is austere; the score calls for half as many winds as in *The Planets* (almost a third of which "may be dispensed with") and no percussion, but "a large body of Strings." The brass are directed "not to accent any notes," and the whole orchestra to observe the "difference between *p* and *pp*": the levels at which much of the piece is played. With its generally low volume, low registers, and slow tempi - mostly *adagio* and *andante maestoso* - *Egdon Heath* can disappear into the woodwork; it picks up where "Neptune" left off, with distant, inhuman, nearly inaudible sonorities and intimations of immensity. Despite some lyric passages, audiences have never liked it as well as Holst said he did. Perhaps they sense a Buddhist detachment and feel excluded or insignificant. Of course minimalism that attracts large numbers of people risks self-contradiction.

Anton von Webern, a minimalist composer whose lifetime output of quiet, short pieces can be performed in about three hours, learned to love wild nature early in his native Austria. He often went to the Tyrolean Alps: gathering flowers with his future wife, using the climbing huts, joining Alpine Clubs, and making many ascents. The Moldenhauer biography documents rambles and working holidays in the Tyrol from 1905 until his death in 1945, interrupted only by the wars. After his friend and fellow serial composer Alban Berg praised Thoreau's *Walden*, Webern read it with pleasure; he also had Emerson's *Society and Solitude* (Moldenhauers 352).

Webern was an avid correspondent who often expressed his need for nature. In a letter to Berg in 1912, he wrote, "For me, this is a spiritual matter. From time to time, I must breathe this ... rarefied air of the heights. ... Transparent, clear, pure .... All this must mean something. I have to seek these regions periodically" (158).

What did "all this" mean for his work? Webern used the Alps as an escape from the city, finding that he did his best composing in a mountain cabin during the summer. His play *Tot* (*Dead*, 1913), set in the Alps, is full of nature worship (Moldenhauers 199-203). Webern wrote Berg that mountaineering was "a search for the highest, a discovery of correspondences in nature for everything that serves me as a model ... for all that I would like to have within myself"; and years later he added, "I have struggled all my life to reproduce in music what I perceive there" (231, 316-17). Sometimes this meant direct imitation - *Im Sommerwind* (1904), or the Quartet Opus 22 (1928-29), whose program notes refer to the Alps - but usually the connection is more general. He taught that mountains demonstrate "the creative idea and its organic development": evolution was basic to his conceptions of life, art, and nature (507, 512). Webern's use of Goethe's sentence about the colour of the mountain sky as a motto, and his love of Gregorian chant for its purity of line, were at one with his love of the Alps.

Across the ocean and at the other end of the spectrum of accessibility, Ferde Grofé's *Grand Canyon Suite* was premiered in 1931 by Paul Whiteman's orchestra, which had introduced George Gershwin's *Rhapsody in Blue* (orchestrated by Grofé) in 1924. Grofé, a New Yorker, wrote a series of suites about great natural features of his country: the Hudson River, the Mississippi, Death Valley, and everyone's favourite example of the American Great, the Grand Canyon. The *Grand Canyon Suite* carries the programmatic impulse about as far as it can go - thunder, wind, bird calls, raucous braying - but mixes it with jazzy moments *à la* Gershwin, and more general mood music, as in Holst.

Grofé's notes in the Robbins edition of the Suite (1943) suggest how descriptive it is. "Sunrise" begins with clarinets climbing the space between low timpani and high violins. Muted trumpets and piccolo lead to a horn theme: dawn. Gradually the instruments assemble and the volume builds, through flutes and bells, to a violin motif, then *crescendo* and *accelerando* to the blare of full day. "The Painted Desert" is, by contrast, slow, quiet, and mysterious, like Holst's *Egdon Heath*. "On the Trail," too catchy for the good of Grofé's reputation, became an advertising jingle, but "Sunset" is meditative, with horns answered by muted horns, like a distant echo. Finally, "Cloudburst" is overtly pictorial: wind machines and thundering timpani. Markings in the score trace the storm's arrival and departure, whereupon "Nature again rejoices in all her grandeur." If much in Grofé now seems obvious and trite, it is because he helped develop the idioms that became our film music.

Grofé, Webern, and Dali remind us how variously Great nature can affect and be expressed by artists of that or any era. From novelists' direct descriptions, and the impressionistic or metaphorical uses in poetry and painting, to a simple harmonization of qualities between the Great and a product of the musical imagination, the types of possible connections are manifold. A minimalist work such as Nathalie Sarraute's *Tropismes* (1939), with its "emptiness" of matter and simplicity of style (Motte 27), reproduces qualities that explorers admired in deserts and polar regions, that Stevens found in Buddhism and winter, and that Webern sensed in the mountains.

Interchapter II: There Was Light

> And these cliffs are absolutely enchanted ...
> like the dream cliffs of a child or
> the place where resides the
> soul of Wagner's music ....

Jack Kerouac, Greenland, 1942

These lines - which I first saw reproduced as poetry by a Beat enthusiast - come from the (prose) diary Kerouac kept while serving in the US Navy. His ship was supplying a construction site in Greenland, where the 20-year-old apprentice dharma bum could hear the north wind's "message of barren desolation," warning "I am ruthless and indifferent, like the sea," and no friend to man (Kerouac 135). Yet the fjord near Godthaab seemed enchanted, and he took pleasure in climbing a four-thousand-foot mountain of black rocks under a "high free sky" (139).

The Second World War, like the first, inhibited exploration of the Great and many kinds of literature, but it also created new travellers - military seamen, desert warriors, an American fighter pilot who flew over the summit of Everest - and left us some powerful commentaries. The most striking difference between the two war literatures is the near-total absence of substantial figures remotely comparable to Shackleton or Lawrence of Arabia in the second. The most likely candidate was Admiral Byrd, but his 1939-41 Antarctic expedition produced only reports. Most travel writers not caught up in the fighting settled for a separate peace, or pre-war memories.

While his compatriot Jean-Paul Sartre stayed home and wrote under Nazi occupation, Saint-John Perse (Alexis Saint-Léger) took refuge on Long Beach Island, New Jersey. In "Exil" (1941), his sadness and alienation see the nearby sand dunes as a Sahara, then as a void. On the beach, he watches the world 'like a horseman ... at the edge of the desert.'[1] His walks and his soul are "Numidian" (Saharan), and the sky is also desertic (Perse 16, 36, 24). In no mood to enjoy freedom or seek oases, he chose a place 'as null as the ossuary of the seasons' because he wants 'the barest space' in which to create 'a poem born and made of nothing.'[2] Perhaps here, living "le thème du néant," Perse can somehow honour his exile (16). *Le néant*, the void, has a special place in French literature, chronicled by Robert Adams in *Nil* (1966). Before Sartre's *L'Etre et le néant* (1943; *Being and Nothingness*), Baudelaire used the void of space as an image of nullity. For Perse, a snow-covered Atlantic beach performs the same function. In "Neiges" (1944), he is surrounded by 'an ocean of snow,' which becomes the human condition: "Ainsi l'homme mi-nu sur l'Océan des neiges."[3] Perse's sorrow, unsated by a desert, projects a polar ocean as well.

Another French exile, Antoine de Saint-Exupéry, produced a classic during the war. *Le Petit prince* (1943) is a dark children's book in the tradition of Swift, and it works equally well for adults. The Little Prince leaves his asteroid to wander through the cosmos, meeting various types who are gently satirized. Finally coming to Earth, he lands in the Sahara and meets the narrator, who is trying to repair his airplane, as the author had done. "Le désert est beau," remarks the Little Prince; the narrator reflects, "Et c'était vrai. J'ai toujours aimé le désert."[4] After climbing the Sahara's mountains, the prince pronounces the earth a dry, pointy sort of planet. He also meets a serpent. "One is rather alone in the desert," says the prince politely. "One is also alone among men," returns the serpent, who knows all about metaphorical deserts (Saint-Exupéry 1999, 2:286). The war is felt in the theme of exile and in the denouement. The prince wants to go home but cannot lift his body there, so he asks the serpent to bite him, after which "he falls as gently as a star," and

---

1   "Comme le Cavalier ... à l'entrée du désert" (Perse 12). My translations are enclosed in single quotation marks.

2   "nul comme l'ossuaire des saisons"; "l'aire le plus nue pour assembler aux syrtes de l'exil un grand poème né de rien, un grand poème fait de rien" (Perse 10, 12).

3   'Thus [is] man half-naked on the ocean of snow' (Perse 90). Perse's Danish translator, Thorkild Hansen, also wrote a life of Carsten Niebuhr, the eighteenth-century Arabian traveller.

4   'The desert is beautiful.' 'And it was true. I have always loved the desert.' Saint-Exupéry 1999, 2:303.

the narrator's coda proclaims the desert "the loveliest and saddest landscape in the world."[5] A year later, flying for the allies, Saint-Exupéry disappeared on a reconnaissance mission over occupied France.

The literature of wartime exile included laments for the loss of favourite playgrounds. Arnold Lunn was a prolific author who began climbing and skiing the Alps in the 1890s and writing about them before the first war (ch. 2). Unable to reach the Alps during the second war, he relived the good old days in *Mountain Jubilee* (1943). Like Frank Smythe in *The Mountain Vision*, Lunn blends nostalgia for climbs and climbers past with meditations on the appeal and value of climbing, which he compares to seafaring as spiritual exercise. He quotes an Everest veteran: "the best find their way to the mountains or to the sea ... the hard sports ... breed men" (Lunn 1943, 23). Lunn's attitude is complex. Mountains have a spiritual influence on their devotees - God made "mountains for our discipline and our delight" - and serve some as a substitute for religion (62). Mountaineering is an ascetic activity, a frank exchange of present pain for eventual happiness and even exaltation.

In this connection, high mountains can be said to furnish a "moral substitute" for war (William James is cited) by providing dangers that focus our thoughts and test us (Lunn 1943, 47). Even more emphatically than Smythe, Lunn says that the Nazis perverted this function, making climbing a *rehearsal* for war. The true mountaineer does not think of "conquering" a peak; it is rather "self-conquest" that climbers strive for, the subordination of the body's desire for ease and comfort to the higher purposes of the will (57). All this lofty-minded rigour does not blind Lunn to the rewards more commonly derived from mountains: the "vestal loveliness" of the high places, their air of magical mystery, their serenity (29). Lunn is a Shelleyan Neo-Platonist who sees in the great ranges "broken reflections" of eternal beauty (252). He mildly corrects Leslie Stephen *en passant*: mountains were made great not to dwarf us, but to lead us higher. Also an historian of attitudes towards mountains, Lunn prints a 1647 tribute to the beauty of the Andes by the Jesuit Alonso Ovalle (267).

Another nostalgic exile, R.V.C. Bodley, a veteran British officer, wrote *Wind in the Sahara* (1944) in America during the war. He had become disillusioned with military life, and at the Paris Peace

---

[5] " ... le plus beau et le plus triste paysage du monde" (2:321).

Conference (1919) T.E. Lawrence and Gertrude Bell interested him in the Sahara. Bodley recalls his first glimpse of the desert: its "immensity" and "infinite horizon," its quality of being "empty" yet "attractive," more majestic than the ocean, more awe-inspiring than the Himalayas (where he had served), the Grand Canyon, or the Arctic (Bodley 13). Majesty is mentioned often, along with silence, and his health and happiness as a nomad sheep-raiser. There are literary influences, too. Bodley calls the Sahara "the Garden of Allah," as Robert Hichens had, and the Berber woman with whom he became involved is "Antinea," from Benoit's *L'Atlantide* (ch. 8; Bodley xvii, 122, 123-6). He hopes desperately, and rather pathetically, to find the "golden wildernesses" unchanged after the war (x). Simple, pure, and spiritual ("I could not be a complete agnostic in the desert"), the Sahara remains his Land of Heart's Desire (42).

Most wartime literature naturally tended toward sombreness. Canada produced some particularly dark work set in the dwarfing Great. In Sinclair Ross's *As For Me and My House* (1941), a relentlessly bleak novel, characters are specks oppressed by the hostile environment of the prairies. The town of Horizon cowers from the wind under the "immense ... high cold night" (Ross 5). Philip Bentley, a closet artist doing time as a preacher, sketches "a landscape like a desert. Almost a lunar desert, ... distorted, barren" (80). Mrs Bentley, the narrator, believes that the prairie is disturbing because "we dare not admit an indifferent wilderness, where we may have no meaning at all" (99-100). Among ancient hills, Paul Kirby explains how many millions of years old they are, and goes farther back still, tracing them to "dust and nebula" until the sense of eternity overwhelms her - a scene indebted to Fontenelle's *Entretiens sur la pluralité des mondes* (1686) and Hardy's *Two on a Tower* (1882). This conversation enlarges her vision: looking across the prairie henceforth gives her a "queer, lost sensation" of "being hung aloft in space" (150). Near the end she takes a night walk in the "dark, deep wind," flooding north "like a great blind tide" in which the earth is "a solitary rock" (159).

Ross's novel might have been much the same without the war, but not Earle Birney's "Vancouver Lights" in *David and Other Poems* (1942). Looking down on the city at night from the North Shore mountains, the speaker feels "a troubling delight" that is partly a fear "of nothing pulsing down from beyond and between / the fragile planets": of *le néant* (Birney 36). As the lights go out all over

Europe, he realizes that "We are a spark beleaguered / by darkness."
Impelled to speak at this critical juncture, he notifies the universe
that "there was light" - the past tense acquiring new significance.
Nor were we victims of a natural disaster: "we contrived the power
the blast that snuffed us." Other landscape-conscious poems in
the volume include "Reverse on the Coast Range," "October in
Utah," and the title-poem. In "David," two young men go climbing
in the Rockies on a day off from their summer jobs. David, the
more experienced, leads, but on The Finger he has a bad fall that
paralyzes him. Unable to face life as a cripple, he begs to be finished
off. The speaker pushes the broken body over the cliff, under one
more "wide indifferent sky" (Birney 9).

Also in 1942, a remarkable drama was unfolding on the other
side of the world. When the Germans occupied Norway, Wilfred
Skrede and three friends decided to flee to a country where they
could train to fight. England was impossible, so they went east,
hoping to reach Canada through Asia. The steppes of Turkestan
seem "naked," unending, and "melancholy" to Skrede, but his
feelings change as he grows accustomed to barrenness; Sinkiang's
"sterile, sandy desert and naked rock" are "wonderfully beautiful"
though "desolate" (11, 13, 117). The men have to take any ride they
can get, and Skrede's back is broken in a truck accident. He remains
buoyant, sending his friends on while he convalesces. Eventually
he reaches Kashgar, where Eric Shipton was then the British
Consul. Quite taken with Skrede, Shipton finds him a doctor and
sends him on to Bam-Dunjah, "the Roof of the World" - Skrede's
title.[6] Left on the Indian border by his escort, he is picked up by
a party from the other side and taken to a hospital. Skrede writes
of feeling "insignificant" in the mountains, but it is hard to think
that his courage does not signify. Eventually he reached Canada,
qualified as a pilot, and flew missions against Germany before the
end of the war.

The publication of R.H. Blyth's *Zen in English Literature and
Oriental Classics* in Tokyo attracted little notice in 1942, but it was
prophetic. The Pacific war brought more westerners than ever into
contact with Buddhism, and among the results was the Beat poets'
interest in Zen, which Blyth calls Asia's "most precious possession"
and "the strongest power in the world" (vii). He spreads a wide
net, finding aspects of Zen in Jesus, Shakespeare, Don Quixote,

---

[6] Shipton mentions the episode in his autobiography: 1969, 132.

Bach, Wordsworth, R.L. Stevenson, and others. Blyth sees in Zen qualities often attributed to the Great: it calls for "asceticism," prizes simplicity and bareness, and seeks realism, "the thing as it is" (31, 427). He derives some of the most exalted concepts of religion from Great nature, as eighteenth-century deists did. Without "rolling waters," the "depths of the sky and vast horizons," he asks, how could we conceive of eternity and infinity? (34) After the war, a growing number of scholars, writers such as Gary Snyder and Jack Kerouac, and ordinary people would decide that Buddhism helped to make sense of the world as they found it.

Part Three:
The Post-War World
The Fragile Great

One of the most influential world-views in western culture just before and after the Second World War was existentialism. Born from the failure of received philosophy and religion to make sense of the modern world for many, existentialism holds that truth and meaning must be generated from one's own existence. Some trace it from Dostoevski, but its French proponents, Jean-Paul Sartre and Albert Camus, gave the idea forms suited to European experience in the 1930s and 1940s. The protagonist of Sartre's novel *La Nausée* (1937) is periodically nauseated by his society, a response elucidated in the treatise *Being and Nothingness* (*L'Etre et le néant*, 1943). Man is "the being by whom Nothingness comes into the world"; *le néant* (though it reveals Being to consciousness) "lies coiled in the heart of being like a worm" (Sartre 1956, xvi, xviii-xx, 21). In his play *The Flies* (*Les Mouches*), Sartre pronounces the desert sinister, with its two *néants*, sand and sky, facing each other (1947, 190).[1] A character in *No Exit* (*Huis clos*, 1944) gives *le néant* and *la nausée* their characteristic shape when he asserts, "Hell is other people" ("L'enfer, c'est les Autres": 1947, 92).

Similar feelings have driven some explorers to the Great. Two Victorian adventurers, Richard Burton and Leslie Stephen, wrote that their motives for crossing deserts and climbing mountains included a wish to elude swarms of their fellow beings. Travellers rarely exhibit pure misanthropy - hatred of humanity - but rather

---

[1] Camus, whose Algerian origins provided the settings for *L'Étranger* (1942) and other works, called the desert "a land of useless and irreplaceable beauty" (quoted Woodrow 1979).

detest crowds. This note, audible in the nineteenth century, was heard *crescendo* in the twentieth. The anthropologist Claude Lévi-Strauss realized on a postwar trip to Brazil that humanity was sick from an excess of itself; "our world has suddenly found itself to be too small for the people who live in it" (23-4). *Tristes tropiques* (1955, translated as *A World on the Wane*) is an honest and pessimistic book, full of Montaignesque doubts about the value of western civilization and science, a travel book that finally rejects travel: "Farewell to savages, then, farewell to journeying," he writes (398). It is not wholly negative, however; besides his cats and his garden, Lévi-Strauss finds himself drawn to Buddhism, as a number of intellectually curious or peripatetic moderns have been.

The United States was generating its own problems and proposing its own solutions. It had long since become a "developed" nation, still richly endowed with wilderness, but in danger of losing it to mining, forestry, grazing, and other commercial or utilitarian pressures, functions of its growing population. In the nineteenth century formidable spirits had written in defence of conservation: Thoreau, Muir, and George P. Marsh, who called for a more enlightened and ethical stewardship of nature in *Man and Nature* (1864). Of their twentieth-century successors, the most important was Aldo Leopold, who began to develop his ideas as a Forest Service officer in the 1920s; his essay "Conservation Esthetic" (1933) warned of the motorized tourist: "Antlike he swarms the continents" (281). But his status as the Moses of environmentalism is based mainly on *A Sand County Almanac* (1949), which introduced his (at first limited) audience to the chief concepts of ecology.

The main principles of Leopold's work relevant here are in the foreword of *A Sand County Almanac* and two essays. Few passages in nature writing have had the impact of that foreword, which identifies "our Abrahamic concept of land" as the central obstacle to a responsible stewardship. "We abuse land because we regard it as a commodity belonging to us" (as when God gave Abraham the Promised Land in Genesis 12), writes Leopold, initiating a debate that still continues. Instead, he says, we must recover the Hellenic idea of the *polis*: "When we see land as a community to which we belong, we may begin to use it with love and respect," and thus become ecologists (A. Leopold xviii-xix). Leopold tried to weld various concepts of land into a single vision. "The Round River" uses Paul Bunyan's fable of "a river that flowed into itself ... in a never-ending circuit" as an image of "the biotic continuum" (188-9);

"The Land Ethic" develops the idea of *homo sapiens* as community member rather than conqueror.[2]

Leopold soon had eloquent seconders. Wallace Stegner (ch. 5), who had already written about Utah's *Mormon Country* (1942), went on to a study of John Wesley Powell, *Beyond the Hundredth Meridian* (1954), and helped spread the ecological message in books and essays. His submission to the Outdoor Recreation Resources Review Commission, "Wilderness as Idea" (1967), was read as a speech by the US Secretary of the Interior, Stewart Udall, and reprinted by the Sierra Club. Stegner's paper is both historical meditation and call to action. We are a wild species that needs the wild, he argues. His list of what must be protected includes mountains and forests; the prairie (remembered from his Saskatchewan boyhood), "as lonely and grand and simple in its forms as the sea"; and "great reaches of our western deserts, ... close to whatever God you want to see in them, ... lovely and terrible wilderness, such ... as Christ and the prophets went out into; harshly and beautifully colored, broken and worn until its bones are exposed" (Stegner 1967, 12-13).

Joseph Wood Krutch, an Ivy League professor whose life changed when he saw the Arizona desert, also endorsed the land ethic. A quotation from *Sand County Almanac* prefaces his anthology of *Great American Nature Writing* (1950), and he quotes Leopold on the threat of roads and cars in *Baja California and the Geography of Hope* (1969). Krutch is happy that Mexico kept Baja in 1848; thus it has not been "marred" by "progress," of which he, too, is sceptical (1969, 8). Perhaps mindful of Leopold's warning about "Abrahamic" land use, Krutch wonders if Genesis has it wrong, and it was after the fifth, not the sixth day - before, not after man - that God pronounced the world good. And Lynn White, Jr, told the American Academy for the Advancement of Science in 1967 that the "Historical Roots of Our Ecological Crisis" lie in "Christian arrogance towards nature," which insists "that it is God's will that man exploit nature" (126). White foresaw "a worsening ecologic

---

[2]   For Oelschlaeger, the land ethic is Leopold's greatest contribution (205). He argues that science and conservation (or ecology, economy, and ethics) are brought together in his writings (210-13).

crisis until we reject the Christian axiom that nature has no reason for existence save to serve man" (127).[3]

Leopold's stature has continued to grow. Roderick Nash's *Wilderness and the American Mind* (1967, rev. 1982) includes a chapter on "Aldo Leopold: Prophet"; Nash's *The Rights of Nature* (1989) finds Leopold seminal for ecological thought. Arne Naess incorporated Leopold's ideas into "deep ecology" from 1973 on.[4] Literary historians have also taken note. Glen Love holds up Leopold as a model in "Revaluing Nature: Toward an Ecological Criticism" (1990); Lawrence Buell stresses the importance of Leopold to the development of *The Environmental Imagination* (1995). Further affirmation of the Leopold-Stegner-Krutch line of thought appears in creative work such as Gretel Ehrlich's *The Solace of Open Spaces* (1985) and Belden Lane's *The Solace of Fierce Landscapes* (1998).

Simon Schama argues, in *Landscape and Memory* (1995), that humans create the idea of wilderness by modifying every ecosystem, and proceeds to *celebrate* this impact (7-9). But surely some distinctions are necessary, some awareness of the problems that human greed, ignorance, and numbers have posed and still pose for wilderness. In asserting that human culture has "always made room for the sacredness of nature," he ignores some of his own data (e.g. Gutzon Borglum carving Manifest Destiny on Mt. Rushmore, sacred to the Sioux), and differs from most recent environmentalists and travellers (18). The science writer Jonathan Weiner is much more representative of the mainstream when he looks at the Galapagos Islands ("ecosystems ... stripped to the bare bones") and sees "a diagram of limits" on life: the same diagram that Powell and his successors saw in American deserts (Weiner 58, 14). *The Beak of the Finch* (1994) ends with a vision of earth's population, "crowded, restless and anadromous, looking up at the stars" (302) - a perception that at least reflects the hard-earned wisdom of our time.

---

[3] For an attempt to answer White, see Harold Oliver, "The Neglect and Recovery of Nature in Twentieth-Century Protestant Thought" (*Journal of the American Academy of Religion*, LX/3 [1992], 379-404). Oliver points out plenty of "neglect," but the "recovery" is only his proposal for a new theology.

[4] See Naess and David Rothenberg, *Ecology, Community and Lifestyle* (Cambridge, 1989), esp. pp. 27-32, arguing that humans need to limit their numbers and their interference in the non-human world. See also Oelschlaeger 317.

Besides environmental crises and fears about overpopulation, the exponential growth of worldwide adventure travel has affected modern attitudes towards the Great, and created some problems for it. The increasing postwar prosperity of a larger, almost global middle class; the spread of relatively cheap air travel; a revolution in outdoor equipment that enables people of average means and constitutions to endure remote, hostile environments; and the desire of many to escape crowded cities or bland suburbs (as in Auden and Isherwood) have all contributed to this phenomenon. You can now, for some thousands of dollars, purchase a guided trip to places that explorers once only dreamt of - the Sahara, the poles, Mt. Everest - and be fairly sure of surviving to write a book, if not succeeding. This movement has two branches: one for comfort-seekers, the other for those who welcome challenge and even some pain. The second attitude helps explain how the Outward Bound Schools could grow from a wartime survival course for the British merchant marine to an international chain that gives clients regulated exposure to harsh (and in some cases Great) landscapes to teach competence and self-reliance: one index of our appetite for wild nature.

9
Arid:
Understanding Modern Deserts

It has a stark beauty all its own. It's like much of the
high desert of the United States.

Neil Armstrong on the moon, 1969

The Second World War, like the first, created a gap in travel to
and non-fiction writing about deserts, which in the late 1940s were
of more interest to novelists (ch. 12). Once travellers returned,
however, their output rivalled mountain literature in bulk. The
number of modern desert books, in fact, is such that coverage must
become more selective than ever.

Early in the period there appeared a writer who would greatly
influence American attitudes towards wilderness, an avatar of
Hardy's thinking modern drawn to barren lands. Joseph Wood
Krutch taught English at Columbia, wrote on eighteenth-century
English stage comedy, and held no brief for nature when a visit
to the Southwest in the late 1930s revealed "a new, undreamed
of world" to him (1963, 5). He became interested in Thoreau and
Aldo Leopold, whom he helped popularize (Nash 1989, 74-6). His
anthology *Great American Nature Writing* includes selections from
Austin's *Land of Little Rain* and his own *The Twelve Seasons*, which
credits deserts with a "spiritual quality" and sublimity (Krutch
1950, 373). But *The Desert Year* (1951), reflecting on a sabbatical
spent in Arizona, reached a broader public. Krutch tries to
explain in general terms why he went there, and what the appeal
of such a place is. For him, the attractions included a different
kind of beauty, a feeling that he "had known and loved it in some

previous existence," and a sense of kinship with landforms that are austere, joyous, spiritual, and aesthetically pleasing (Krutch 1963, 7).

Krutch undertakes to explain to developers, exploiters, and others "What the Desert Is Good For." For him, one of its "uses" is to make us contrast its relatively few and scattered life forms with our problems of crowding. Biochemists say they can feed billions more people with a "protein food" made in yeast vats, but where will they all live? "Will every square foot of soil ultimately be not only owned but occupied? Will every other living thing be exterminated to make way for one vast anthill of yeast-eating men?" (Krutch 1963, 89). Recalling that Thoreau wondered whether seeing New York's "herds of men" every day might lessen one's respect for humanity, Krutch compares the desert, which limits the means of living, to the jungle, which provides means but not space and lets the population fight it out (91). He prefers the desert way, and finds it ominous that we have created "a sort of artificial, technological jungle" - cities - in which we struggle with each other, not with nature (95). Looking down on "arid emptiness" from a peak, he realizes that "Loneliness is essential" for all of us, and wonders if God should have rested after the fifth day (123-4).

Krutch does admit some limitations to his vision. Total desert overwhelms most people (Gertrude Bell noted this); hence most residents use well water to make oases around their houses. Yes, we might say, they want shade and windbreaks, but for him the principal reason is aesthetic: the desert has "the grandeur of something powerfully alien, indifferent, and enduring," or again "a kind of beauty ... fundamentally alien" to us (Krutch 1963, 245, 250). More comfortable when the earth wears vegetable clothing, we feel "something like terror" with this "beauty bare" (251-2). Krutch himself moved to Arizona and spoke out for preservation of arid lands in his books and essays. *The Voice of the Desert* (1954) offers "A Naturalist's Interpretation" of it. "The Mystique of the Desert" - often invoked but seldom defined - consists of transcending the rational, offering a glimpse of something larger, called Nature or God. "Conservative" and "contemplative" or sublime and "awful," deserts have the power to mold character (Krutch 1955, 221-2).

THE MOST BEAUTIFUL DESERT IN THE WORLD

Louis Carl and Joseph Petit's *Tefedest* (1953) signalled the return of Saharan travel books by Europeans. The young Parisians' "Journey to the Heart of the Sahara" involved a camel trek from Tamanrasset to Tefedest in the Hoggar to study rock-paintings in 1949. They did that, but most of their book describes the land and the natives. Carl and Petit come across as fresh, excitable, independent witnesses who tell what they saw and felt, not what they have read (the exception being a weakness for "Antinea, the black force of the desert" in Benoit's *L'Atlantide*: Carl and Petit 61). Their groping for the desert's meaning in the foreword is awkward, but the main text, focussing on their responses to the "enchantment of Saharan twilights, a symphony in red and blue," the customs of their Tuareg guides, and the "lunar landscape" of the Hoggar, does better (30, 111). There is no monotony: sunsets may seem peaceful or eschatological, the desert a "tragic backdrop," or actively hostile, a veritable "*Dies Irae*," or "irrational, obsessive" (158, 207, 210). The landscape's power is a constant theme, bringing out their essential selves; in the end they feel nostalgic for it.

Another Frenchman saw the Sahara as *Le Plus beau désert du monde* (1955). But Philippe Diolé, an associate of Jacques Cousteau, has a complex mixture of responses, his *idée fixe* being that desert and ocean are "much alike" (15).[1] He elaborates on this commonplace: both have "unbounded empty distances," seem virginal yet are "harsh" and "melancholy," stand apart from society and "above time and space," offer solitude and "instants of eternity," and represent "Promised Lands of the mind and spirit" (15-20). The "*beau désert*" is profoundly empty, he says, sometimes calling it a "void." But emptiness has positive connotations for Diolé - a vast plain possesses "empty majesty" - and his explanation has a distinctly modern ring (87). The "emptiness and desolation" once considered the Sahara's curse are exactly what give it the appeal of every "vacant and unexploited" place in the twentieth century, when hordes of young travellers are searching for "land without cities" (177, 75-6).

Diolé believes that the Sahara's assets, "aeration" and "lightness," derive from its being "so sweeping, so empty" (179).

---

[1]   The book caught the psychoanalyzing attention of Gaston Bachelard in *The Poetics of Space* ([1958] 1964, 204-8).

Its rewards, by-products of vacancy, are a Doughtian awareness of "spiritual confrontation" and "spiritual gain" (21, 18); solitude; bareness, the "stripping away of nonessentials" (29-30); and a feeling of being "outside time," in a primeval, edenic world (94). Nearly as important to him are several qualities often cited by desert travellers: vastness, silence, and superiority (in some respects) to western society - the reaction that often causes desert lovers to be dismissed as misfits or misanthropes. Diolé believes that human "passions poison the inhabited earth ... the desert is a refuge" (30). The Sahara has kept what we have lost, especially space for thought. His guides ask, "If there is no Sahara in [France], where can a man walk on endlessly, freely ... under a boundless sky?" (88). A sense of freedom (however defined) has of course been one of the desert's prime attractions since Addison. Diolé speculates that while his contemporaries still take comfort in verdure, "Perhaps one day" doctors will "prescribe mountain cures": just rock without greenery (121). Hardy had predicted as much.

The guru of this generation of *saharistes*, Henri Lhote, was still active. In *The Search for the Tassili Frescoes* (1958) he writes that although his motives were always scientific, his more than 25 years of Saharan travel have also been "enthralling" and "exciting" (Lhote 16). The Tassili region, "as wildly beautiful as the Hoggar" and "more grandiose," has a "strange" and "lunar" aspect, making it "a world apart" from ours (27): a common reaction of visitors to the Great. Much of the book is Saharan history, archeology, and ethnography, with a sprinkling of Lhote's own impressions. Life there was and is hard, he says, but it affords "the superb feeling of freedom that is induced by vast horizons" and "pure air" (94). At the end, moved by anticipatory nostalgia for the rocks and stars, he is sad to leave.

STUDYING DESERTS

During the 1950s, research on deserts became a significant sub-genre of writing about the Great. Georg Gerster's *Sahara* (1959) describes the then-French Sahara (up to "where the edible dates begin"), including history, proverbs and etymologies, desert lore, travellers' biographies, and modern trends (ix). His main interest is Europeans who have fallen under the spell of the Sahara, such as Gen. Laperrine (and other French officers), "hopelessly in love with the desert"; and Lhote, a man of "monastic austerity" who devoured Benoit's novel and showed that the central Sahara was once populated and civilized (16, 17). He also gives sketches of Isabelle Eberhardt, Charles de Foucauld, and Frances Wakefield, an English doctor whom Gerster styles the "T.E. Lawrence of the Sahara" (140). She translated the Bible into the local dialect and became a "mystic of the desert," which "cast its spell on her" (140). (Her brother was a member of the 1922 Everest expedition.)

Like Saint-Exupéry, Gerster was fascinated by aerial views of the desert. From above, the Tassili mountains seemed islands in a sea of sand, forming a "magnificent, melancholy landscape" (Gerster 28). The melancholy is in part historical perspective: knowing that "the desert was green" as recently as 3000 BC, he sees it as "the corpse of a once well-watered landscape" (30, 56). Nor are its prospects cheering. Gerster discusses recent development of the Sahara at length, noting that old hands, those who have felt the desert's pull, condemn the deceptions of its exploiters. He also remarks that the Hoggar "possesses the secret of eternal youth" (135), but how this secret is to be protected from the exploiters is not explained.

Gerster's themes - the Sahara's fascination, memorable travellers, and vulnerability - are heard again and again, with variations, over the next decades. In *The Great Sahara* (1965), James Wellard professes scorn for the "vast literature of romantic rubbish" about the "timeless" desert; "It is really all hard geological fact," he insists: facts by then well known to the oil companies that were drilling there (15). So "we can't talk of beauty, or romance" in the Sahara - despite "a silence ... never heard outside the real desert," "a sense of timelessness," and glimpses of the "primeval ... mystery" that attracted the early hermits (15-16). Fighting off his own romantic demons, Wellard narrates the history of Saharan exploration, with occasional lapses, as when Jebel Zenkekra reveals "the strangeness and fascination of the true desert" (32). He suggests that the Sahara baked the nonsense out of French officers, leading them through asceticism to spirituality.

Accepting just the emotions Wellard meant to exclude, Uwe George supplements the history and science of *In the Deserts of This Earth* (1976) with personal impressions. He walks over the horizon from camp in order to feel the "sense of loneliness and forsakenness" at the "center of a vast empty disk," the loss of "inner standards" of place where no "visible standards of measurement" exist, and an "oversensitivity" and silence in which breathing and blood circulation are audible (George 4-5). But those "incomprehensible expanses" also give "a sense of boundless freedom," and the self-reliance that deserts demand of us enables a "recapture" of identity wherein we transcend "production-oriented society" and "return to the dreams of childhood" (5). Wellard's "romantic rubbish" is George's hard fact: "the desert is a landscape in which the human spirit can exult, a landscape that can satisfy man's deepest craving, which is for spiritual freedom" (5-6). It would be hard to find a stronger endorsement of the liberty many have felt in the desert. At night, George senses the "vast void" and the oneness of all life (175-6).

But the desert's "cruel, merciless side," which has meant hardship and death for some, is also part of the story; despite their vulnerability to human exploitation, and our efforts to contain them, deserts are spreading (George 6). Someday all the causes of desert formation could unite to turn earth into a "dry, uninhabitable wasteland" (15). Rebutting those who foresee an icy end, George estimates that over a third of all continental land is now "desert or desertlike," and envisions "earth's future fate as the desert planet" (92, 56). In his view, "the desert represents an advanced stage of [the] cosmic impulse towards the more probable state: disorder"; i.e. the Sahara foreshadows the final anarchy (73). Chapter 3, "Parching Continents," presses the argument home. "As our planet slowly becomes a desert" and the deserts consume oxygen, we will die off (190). In places, earth is already moving into the last of three phases: primal desert, biophase, final desert - where Mars already is.

A corroborative witness, Jane W. Watson acknowledges the "stark, bare grandeur" of deserts and their growing populations' need for water, but in *Deserts of the World* (1981) she too warns of spreading desertification (17). Watson agrees that one-third of the earth's surface is arid or semi-arid, and estimates that deserts are expanding by about 15 million acres a year; the Sahara advanced 50 miles south between 1930 and 1980. For her as for Uwe George, then, deserts are coming to us, and the question is how to respond to the challenge.

The conclusions that scholars reach, however, depend on which desert they are discussing. A. Starker Leopold (Aldo's son) judges the great North American desert issue of his time to be large-scale human intrusion on previous realms of "privacy and solitude," lowering the water table (171). "Barren wastes" for him are fragile, not threatening. Like Stegner and Krutch, he expounds the doctrines of ecology, urging us to plan carefully and husband the desert, preserving some untouched, for "There are no longer any 'waste' spaces on the earth" (172). Growing population pressures must somehow be relieved; "there are too many of us now," and "on a crowded, used-up earth, [deserts] may make all the difference" (172). Along with these large issues, he admits a personal attraction. The desert is "endlessly alluring to men of science ... a likably lonely place" for its "provocative challenges," no longer available in well-travelled regions (113). A note of nostalgia, tinged with dread, is unmistakable.

Gary Nabhan and Mark Reisner sound a good deal like the Leopolds as they consider the American West a generation later. Nabhan, an ethnobiologist, joined the growing chorus of ecological concern in *The Desert Smells Like Rain* (1982). "Bless the desert," he prays, requesting divine intervention; despite the title, and descriptions of native rain dances, the book's theme is aridity (Nabhan 1982, x). "We" - the immigrant hordes - are exhausting the Southwest's aquifers at a hundred times the rate of replenishment, and generally ignoring the natural laws that govern deserts' health. He repeated the indictment in *Gathering the Desert* (1985): water is "overallocated" in Southern California, meaning that the place is not sustainable (quoted Gilbar 229). Along with Stegner, Krutch, and others, Nabhan echoes Powell's nineteenth-century warning that most of the West is desertic and must be treated as such.

Reisner's *Cadillac Desert* (1986, rev. 1993) is also about *The American West and Its Disappearing Water*. Like Powell, he says that the West cannot support a large population. We should have listened to pioneers like Lewis, Clark, and Pike, who were "appalled" by the "arid waste," but a series of greedy, corrupt, ambitious, or ignorant men built cities in it, drawing down the aquifers and diverting water from elsewhere (Reisner 18-19). The Dust Bowl of the 1930s, when drought, plowing, and overgrazing made parts of the West desertic, was a warning, yet the pace of development and immigration has quickened since. Flying over the emptiness of Utah, Reisner looks down on the Salt Lake City area, "the most ambitious desert civilization" in world history, and wonders: at what price? (2) The modern American West, he concludes, is unsustainable without huge amounts of Canadian water, which must be procured at any cost, or the West as we know it will cease to exist. His book deserves to be better known; perhaps it is too frightening to be faced.

The diversity of French interest in deserts is apparent in a special issue of *Traverses* magazine, "Le Désert" (1980), which includes geographers, demographers, historians, film buffs, and cultural critics. Italo Calvino can see (after an hour at the edge of the Sahara) how monotheism arose from its aura of infinity ("Le Désert" 1980, 2). Jean Baudrillard gives a semiotic reading of American wastelands: deserts (a sort of *"éternité suspendue"*) have in their vastness "the power of pure extent," while western cities and California culture are somehow desertic (54-7). Several of these ideas - infinity, religion, the desert as metaphor - are themes of the issue, along with other familiar motifs of desert literature: deserts as oceans, the fear of void and solitude, human threats.

Gilles Lipovetsky is the most provocative of these savants. With *le néant* assuming global dimensions, he suggests, deserts are our modern substitute for metaphysical speculation on the void. Everyone now asks to be left alone, solitude and solipsism are facts of life, and the desert neither begins nor ends; metaphorical deserts resonate through western culture, even as it invades real ones. "Le Désert" does not mention desertification: instead, like the Americans, writer after writer reports that overpopulation, development, and tourism are damaging deserts. For Jean Dresch ("Fin du nomadisme pastoral?"), the question is not *if* but *when*; the modern world has no place for nomads. Nadia Tadzi's "Explorations sahariennes" is elegiac: "explorers" are now prospectors and oil men, the Tuareg are being *"sedentarisés,"* and *"il n'y a plus de caravanes"* (148). The pressures of human needs and exploitation dominate the volume.

In a class of his own, Sven Lindqvist was "drawn" to study the desert at the age of 33 when he realized, "This is my landscape" (2, 4). *Desert Divers* (1990) interweaves his experiences in the Sahara with "dreams" of others who have "dived" there, though they were not actual well-divers. Imagining Darwin reading Lyell, Lindqvist "dreams" of geological time and vast slow changes over five hundred million years until the Sahara is understood as just an episode between ice ages; dreams too of Saint-Exupéry, Michel Vieuchange, André Gide, and Eugène Fromentin, finding the Sahara early and romanticizing it. His longest dream is of another romantic, Pierre Loti, and of Isabelle Eberhardt's fascination with him and the Sahara. Though he criticizes the romanticizers, Lindqvist seems to share their feelings, saying that he would love to live in a lush oasis in the silence of the desert.

TRAVERSING DESERTS

Of the few old-style wanderers who tried to stay clear of technology, only one deserves comparison with Doughty (though not as a writer), Bertram Thomas, and Philby. Wilfred Thesiger's travels began in the Sudan and Ethiopia (where he was born) in the 1930s and eventually covered vast tracts in Africa and Asia. He recounted them in *Arabian Sands* (1959), describing two crossings of Arabia's Rub al-Khali (Empty Quarter) in the 1940s, *The Marsh Arabs* (1964), and *The Last Nomad* (1980), a look back at his career: Thesiger was always writing elegies. A reporter found him camped on "a bleak volcanic desert" in Kenya in 1981, planning a trip to India (Winn 3). When some young Canadians visited him at home in England before they attempted the Empty Quarter in 1999, Thesiger (then 89) told them that "curiosity about what was on the other side" had spurred him on, and that he had found "peace there" (Clarke). The editor of *Points Unknown. A Century of Great Exploration*, calls Thesiger "the finest Western explorer of the desert who ever lived" (Roberts 93).

While not aesthetically inclined, Thesiger had strong feelings about the land he laboured across, and understood the labour as integral to the feeling: travel as travail. In the prologue to *Arabian Sands* he observes that the "empty wastes" of that "bitter, desiccated land" impose hardship and privation on its denizens, yet "this cruel land can cast a spell which no temperate clime can match" (Thesiger 1964, [15]). This "spell" is his favourite topic. He has already told us of what it consists: emptiness and hardships enchant him. Thesiger is another ascetic minimalist, drawn to Lawrence's story of "the empty wind of the desert" being the best scent at the perfumed castle (83). He sets his reactions in a context of particular interest here: "it was the very hardness of life in the desert which drew me back there ... the same pull which takes men back to the polar ice, to high mountains, and to the sea" (18). He believes that Capt. Scott and Everest climbers shared his goal of inner peace through hardship, and did try other Great landscapes - the Karakoram and Hindu Kush, chiefly - yet "[n]one of these places ... moved me as did the deserts of Arabia" (12).

Thesiger identified several motives for what he did: the chance to "win distinction as a traveller," the "peace that comes with solitude" (but also comradeship), the taste of freedom, and "the attraction of the unknown" (1964, 18, 22-3). One aspect of deserts missing from this list but prominent in his books is bareness. In the Libyan desert he tops a rise and catches his breath at the "stark emptiness" of the landscape, which goes on day after day as his wonder grows (32). Riding to Tibesti in 1938 through "the real desert," Thesiger sees (as Lawrence had) that the nakedness of the land induces inner bareness: socioeconomic differences "are stripped away and basic truths emerge" (36). This whole complex of lived qualities - freedom, peace, hardship, camaraderie, bareness - made the wastes of Africa and Asia irresistible to Thesiger; he was sorry to finish his great crossing, and back in England felt homesick for the desert. In the Rub al-Khali, he wrote, "I had found all that I asked" (329).

But everything he valued there was vanishing. Thesiger sounds like a mediaeval cleric on the transience of life, a Luddite on machines, and Thoreau on the futility of pilgrimages to Walden Pond. "If anyone goes there now looking for the life I led they will not find it," he writes, "for technicians have been there since, prospecting for oil" (Thesiger 1964, 11). The agents of destruction are almost always western things and practices. "Today the desert where I travelled is scarred with the tracks of lorries and littered with discarded junk imported from Europe and America," though that is less important than the "demoralization" of the Bedu (11-12). Driven off the desert, the nomads of Arabia are degraded and "doomed" (329). In the Sudan, Thesiger had "no faith in the changes we were bringing about"; loving the past, he "dreaded the future" (34).

The Marsh Arabs exhibits a similar pattern. In the 1950s the marshes of southern Iraq had "the stillness of a world that never knew an engine," reedbeds "stretched to the world's end," life had not changed in five thousand years, and there was "the same feeling of freedom" as in the desert: "the same endless empty space" with "only the bare necessities of life" (Thesiger 1967, 23, 57, 210). Yet already guns were eradicating the birds, the marshes would probably be drained soon, and that way of life, too, would be gone. The elegiac note recurs in *The Last Nomad* and in interviews; Thesiger stayed on message. Once upon a time he could find serenity, freedom, a certain intensity of living - "on the edge," we would say - and a sense of cutting through pretenses to "basic truths" in the wild places, but machinery and tourism drove him out as inexorably as they expelled the nomads (Winn 5).

Other candidates for "the last nomad" have appeared, lacking Thesiger's credentials as travellers, certainly, yet not without courage and vision. Geoffrey Moorhouse, an English journalist, set out to cross the Sahara from west to east in 1972: a journey not only long (3600 miles) but unnatural, cutting athwart the traditional trade routes familiar to guides, and bureaucratically difficult, crossing more national frontiers than a north-south traverse. Though Moorhouse made many errors, failed to reach his goal (abandoning the attempt in Algeria, halfway across), and lacks eloquence, his effort, and the honesty with which he chronicles his reactions to the worst the Sahara could offer, earn our respect.

Highly responsive to desert landscape, Moorhouse weaves a dense aesthetic tapestry. *The Fearful Void* (1974) is well titled: fear is his most frequent reaction, "void" his dominant image of the Sahara, and the two are closely connected. It is clear from the first that Moorhouse is afraid of how he will respond to emptiness, and that a strong motive in travelling is to confront this fear. Thesiger had told him that he himself would be crushed by the desert if he were in it alone (Moorhouse was not "alone," of course: he needed guides). And indeed, once there, Moorhouse feels a "deep primeval fear of the void around": the "blank anonymity of the endless dunes," the "eternal nothingness" in which he is as insignificant as a caterpillar, as terrified of *le néant* as a Symbolist poet (106). Yet the beauty of the Sahara and the powerful life of the spirit there are also frequently attested, and serve as defences against the fearful void.

Near the Hoggar Mountains in southern Algeria, many components of his experience finally coalesce for Moorhouse. On a cold, clear dawn, "a new world lay endlessly ahead" of him and his guide, "an eternal plain." In this "towering and barren universe," they are mere "insects" who may never succeed in crossing the "pure and unbounded space" to arrive anywhere. "It was appalling, but, at the same time, it was exciting," and Moorhouse, who in three months had felt little of the Sahara's "magnetism," says that "now, in its utmost desolation, I began at last to understand its attraction. It was the awful scale of the thing," together with its purity and beauty (227). All of the classic writers on desert travel - Burton, Fromentin, Doughty, Thesiger - have similar passages. In the end, having reached Tamanrasset and Charles de Foucauld's monastery at Assekrem, he can look around and say, "This *was* a holy place, and would have been even if no man had ever trodden it" (253).

Another Englishman, Michael Asher, took up the torch in 1986, starting from Mauritania with camels, guide, and his Italian wife of five days. Treating the Africa traverse as a honeymoon was unprecedented, perhaps hubristic, but both had worked in Africa and spoke Arabic; Asher had ridden camels with Sudanese nomads. His book, oddly titled *Impossible Journey* (1988), recounts their successful crossing, even longer than Moorhouse's plan: 4500 miles, clear to the Nile. What strikes Asher most often is the Sahara's vastness, and close behind is his fear of that space. At the outset, his guide wants to have "nothing before [him] but the emptiness"; Asher, surveying the "vast ocean of nothing," is not so sure (27, 30). His story is one of newlyweds coming to terms with a "dreadful void," a "desolation, and infinite emptiness," in such a way that it became a "part of us" (162, 102, 104). As this happens, he begins to see other, more uplifting infinities, and to feel the "spell" of which Thesiger writes (128). At last, on the banks of the Nile, there is "sadness and nostalgia for the beauty we had seen," but their marriage seems to be working (288).

Like many desert travellers, Asher compares it to an ocean. In 1990 the British adventurer Tim Severin, who had made his name by recreating notable ocean voyages in small boats, set out to ride horseback across Mongolia *In Search of Genghis Khan*. Genghis' title, he writes, meant "Oceanic Ruler," and Mongol herdsmen still "use images more suited to the sea" (Severin 1992, 21). Metaphors aside, Mongolia is a "cold desert. Bleak, harsh and empty" above all: "a vast emptiness" from the air, "complete emptiness" on the ground (17, 28, 51). In the Gobi as in the Sahara, life is "stripped to the bone"; at Hangay, Severin finds the "sense of isolation and emptiness overwhelming" (22, 150). Yet his portrait also includes many expansive and spiritual touches. A nomad chieftain's tomb overlooks a "sweep of ... open valley": a "timeless setting," like their camping place "on the broad sweep of a magnificent grassy slope" (63, 143). Noting that the ascent of a Holy Mountain is a "pilgrimage" for his native companions, Severin recalls that Mongolian shamans typically retreat to a mountain for three days, and that William of Rubruck gave Europe its first substantial description of Buddhism after a trip to Mongolia in the thirteenth century (80).

WALKING THROUGH TIME

The American desert narrative blends curiosity and adventure with tourism and development. The attraction of the Grand Canyon - a litmus test of public attitudes since Pres. Roosevelt urged its preservation in 1903 - increased steadily. Almost every year brought more tourists, first by railroad, then by bus and car. Some descended the mile from rim to river, on burros or on foot. After the war, growing numbers wanted to float down the Colorado on rubber rafts and see what Major Powell had seen; in 1966, over a thousand people did so. Touring companies, which supplied rafts and guides, mushroomed, increasing the demand. In 1968 the figure was three thousand; in 1970, nine thousand. The National Park Service became concerned for the canyon, and when the number of floaters reached 16,432 in 1972, decided to cap it there (Nash 1982, 331): a classic example of adventure tourism choking on its own success. One can hardly imagine Powell's reaction.

As this frenzy was beginning, Colin Fletcher - a Welshman who had been a commando during the war and laboured in the Empire from Kenya to Canada before settling in California - found the Canyon. Constitutionally opposed to collective or technological approaches to nature, he liked to walk and write about walking: hence *The Winds of Mara* (Kenya), *The Thousand-Mile Summer* (from Mexico to Oregon), *The Complete Walker*, and *The New Complete Walker*. Fletcher admits to being "what might be called a compulsive walker" drawn to any large blank on a map (6n.). In 1963 he became the first person to walk the length of Grand Canyon National Park, a two-month perambulation described in *The Man Who Walked Through Time* (1967).

Fletcher is tough but sensitive to shifting moods, natural and human. He prizes above all the "pleasure of open vision" gained from moving through "a country of space and light" (C. Fletcher 54). Conversely, when deep in the canyon, beneath the "impenetrable blanks" of the Redwall cliffs, feeling their "weight and power" and "the utter insignificance of all mankind," he understands the sense of "oppression" in Powell's journal (32-3). But on the open desert above, the Esplanade is "space engraved into the land," and "the master pattern" is light, depth, space, and silence (65, 5). As summer comes on he emulates the animals and walks "naked, in space and silence and solitude," his own bareness and simplicity mirroring the land's (145). These are precisely the qualities that technological society menaces, he warns, though during his walk, Fletcher feels that he has "broken free" from that world (86). Once a friend joins him for a stretch, but the experiment is a failure; friend leaves early, and the author finds his wonted silence and solitude all the sweeter after the interruption.

Fletcher's journey is also spiritual: he compares himself to a pilgrim-knight. Beforehand, he suspected this might be "a pilgrimage," and on the Esplanade finds "moments [that] held the promise of ... progress in my pilgrimage" (C. Fletcher 10, 74). *Pilgrim's Progress!* Fletcher does not preach Christian doctrine, however; he is more of a reverent free lance. A preliminary reconnaissance raises his hopes of finding "whatever uncertain grail I was going down into the Canyon to look for," though he realizes that he "must face, sooner or later, a trial of the spirit" (29, 33). In fact there are almost daily tests of his will, judgement, and composure, but he does eventually find a chalice of sorts. William Bass, a wanderer with tuberculosis, came to the Canyon for its healthy air in his 20s. It worked: he retired from guiding tourists at 76 and died at 83. His ashes were strewn on "Holy Grail Temple," ironically described as "an imposing minaret of a butte" (113). And Fletcher continues a long tradition of reading eroded cliffs as analogues of religious architecture when he sees the nocturnal Canyon as "a long, cool, dimly lit cathedral" (190).

Along with such moments of grace, however, go fear (which Fletcher believes underlies every challenge) and doubt; he would understand Moorhouse's feelings in the Sahara. Emotional ambivalence is central to his project: before he started, the "apparently waterless waste of rock" loomed "mysterious and terrible - and beckoning," and deep in the Canyon at night he feels a "terrible blackness" (C. Fletcher 6, 34). But this mood does not last, and later he writes of overcoming his fear of "the huge and horrifying vaults of time" before humans: a more cerebral problem (211). There remains, though, a belief that we are ruining wild nature. Initially he "hopes [to] escape from civilization," but the trouble turns out to lie deeper, in man, "the noisy animal"; as time passes, Fletcher feels more and more "affinity" with the ages before the coming of homo sapiens (28, 99, 157-8). The book ends with an attack on developers and dam-builders, who cannot erase "The story of the earth" (a translation of "geology" used by Doughty), but *can* spoil the "space and solitude and silence" that are the Canyon's essence (231).

INTERPRETING DESERTS

Few have the will, the stamina, and the gifts - or hear a call - to be explorers, but since the war a number of writers have offered explanations of what brought them to (or back to) deserts or held them there. Arabia and the Sahara made new converts, who found a growing market for their stories. Peter Iseman reported to *Harper's* that sunrise in Arabia's Hejaz mountains "lets the mind soar, out of time, in an ecstasy of desolation," while the Empty Quarter offers the "primal allure of emptiness ... that elsewhere might only be experienced on open seas, high mountains, or polar ice" - i.e. in the Great (46). Alain Woodrow wrote for *Le Monde* on his "Expérience de solitude au Sahara," a five-day walk arranged by Terres d'Aventure of Paris, one of the new adventure tourism companies. He claimed that even on a short tour he could feel the Sahara's deep spiritual appeal, and understand its fascination for Camus and Charles de Foucauld.

Many of these explicators have been North Americans who share Thesiger's alarm at how developers, vandals, tourists, and settlers are abusing vulnerable "wastelands." They include impressionable souls from the Canadian prairies. The novelist Gabrielle Roy grew up in Manitoba, "entre les horizons si nouveaux et si vastes qu'ils étaient, comme les horizons de la mer, d'un attrait irrésistible."[2] Ukrainian songs tried to convey the oceanic immensity of the plains, and the wide arch of sky made her wonder what was over the horizon. The adult Roy wants to recover how that space made her feel: the joy that is the soul moving into accord with the infinite ("semble s'accorder à l'infini": 22). Another child of the prairies, Mark Abley, left at 20 but returned years later to find out why "images of Saskatchewan would rise unbidden" in his mind (2). *Beyond Forget* (a French town on the "everlasting plain") is the story of that return (34). Apart from vastness, solitude, and pure air, Abley does not build up his themes; he simply mentions familiar reactions to flat lands - infinite, eternal, empty, liberating - and moves on, pausing to warn that the prairie is becoming a "wasteland" as residents leave (198).

Warmer southern deserts, however, were beginning to fill with escapees from elsewhere. Ann Woodin's *Home Is the Desert* (1964)

---

[2]   'Between horizons so new and vast that they had, like ocean horizons, an irresistible allure.' From "Souvenirs du Manitoba" (1954), Roy 13.

describes her family's life in Arizona, enjoying its flora, fauna, and rocks, though wondering how many more people like themselves would be arriving. Her themes are familiar: love of the desert and fear of its exploiters. Love develops slowly in the "lean and frugal" Southwest, "a hard-mind place" composed of "severity and reserve," but comes all the more deeply in the end because of the austerity (Woodin 1, 6-7). The fear arises when she sees graffiti on a cliff in Glen Canyon and realizes that dam-builders and yahoos threaten what she loves. For the moment she can still enjoy the dry mountains, sea-like desert, and the "enormous windy solitude" of Pinacate, "a sea of lava, a bleak biblical wilderness," a place of "awful splendor" where you meet - yourself (205). The final chapter, "Survival," passionately asserts the value, and fragility, of deserts, warning about overpopulation and over-development. Woodin was a protégé of Joseph Wood Krutch, who wrote the introduction and is quoted on the joys to be found outside civilization.

Deserts have called diverse Americans in various ways. The poet/pilgrim Thomas Merton translated some sayings of the fourth-century Desert Fathers as *The Wisdom of the Desert* (1960). His introduction suggests that hermits such as St Anthony were seeking a kind of "purity" that would produce tranquillity and a "sublime Nothing" - rather like Zen Buddhists, he believed, which was his own inclination (Merton 1960, 8-9). The Fathers knew that silence was holy, and could be found in the desert. Merton argues that they were not misanthropes, but searchers for a "kind of simplicity" desperately needed today (11).

A man of a different stripe - though not so different as he first appears - is Edward Abbey, one of the most forceful of modern desert writers, who found his calling during two summers as a park ranger in Arches National Monument near Moab, Utah, in the 1950s. He "liked the work and the canyon country" and "would have returned ... each year thereafter," writes Abbey, "but unfortunately for me the Arches, a primitive place when I first went there, was developed and improved so well that I had to leave" (1970, xi).

A maverick *provocateur*, Abbey sets the introduction to *Desert Solitaire* (1968) in a bar in Hoboken, *hopes* that "serious associate professors of English" will dislike his book, and warns readers away from Arches because "most of what I write about in this book is already gone or going under fast. This is not a travel guide but an elegy" (1970, xii, xiv). He is part Thesiger, an angry desert-lover who hates the roads, tourists, dams, and tract housing that are despoiling it. But Abbey has another side, and his contrasted themes work in counterpoint: the spirituality of the desert, the desecrating materialism of society. Chapter titles ("The First Morning," "The Serpents of Paradise") allude to Genesis, with the idea of a Fall fully realized in "Polemic: Industrial Tourism and the National Parks." Moving through the "red wasteland" ("God's navel") asserting that "forests and mountains and desert canyons are holier than our churches," Abbey sounds like Muir *redivivus* (4, 52). Mirages are "Palestinian miracles," and a desert canyon is *"locus Dei,"* a place of God (135, 176).

But he will not be categorized, or cozy up to anyone. When Honoré de Balzac drops by the bar to assert that "In the desert there is all and there is nothing. God is there and man is not," Abbey snorts, "God? ... who the hell is *He*? There is nothing here ... but me and the desert. ... I am not an atheist but an earthiest" (1970, 184). Abbey can talk about a godly desert, but let no one else presume. He and Merton might get along, sharing a love for "the bare bones of existence" in a "grand desolation," for the inhuman transcendental (wilderness is "something beyond us and without limit"), and even for nothing, *le néant* (6, 132, 167). Though Merton's Catholicism is useless, or worse, to Abbey, his later Buddhism might have struck a chord. The Grand Canyon is "like a section of eternity" where "man is a dream, thought an illusion," and "the fables of theology and the myths of classical antiquity dissolve like mist" in a hot sun (194). And "It means nothing," he insists, "The desert says nothing" (194, 240). Or does it say, Nothing? The finality with which Abbey declares traditional belief systems irrelevant rules out everything but an existential or Buddhist approach to the void.

When not shouting, Abbey endorses much of what had been written about deserts for a century. He is a minimalist, loving arid land because it is elementary, empty, and silent - until the noisy animal arrives. He is also an adventurer - "the desert is stimulating, exciting, exacting" - and a philosopher, finding *"Claritas, integritas, veritas"* (lucidity, wholeness, truth) in the desert (Abbey 1970, 135). It is a Higher Reality: eternal, vast, mysterious. Twice he uses the earliest defining term for the Great, "sublime." But Abbey is an ecologist, too, insisting that "There is no shortage of water in the desert but exactly the right amount ... unless you try to establish a city where no city should be" (126). And he is a cultured barfly: Eliot's *The Waste Land* evokes the country around Moab, which reminds him of twelve-tone music. Like "the apartness, the otherness, the strangeness" that we feel in the works of Berg, Schoenberg, Webern, and Krenek, "the desert is ... a-tonal, cruel, clear, inhuman, neither romantic nor classical" (255). Schoenberg and Krenek, he notes, spent time in the Southwest.

In trying to explain why he is a "desert rat," Abbey invokes the "something about the desert" that drew Doughty, Lawrence, Austin, and Krutch before him (1970, 239). Query: if mountains, oceans, and deserts all have "grandeur, ... spaciousness, the power of the ancient and elemental," why is the desert more "alluring" than the others? (239-40) He answers that whereas mountains and seas send clear messages, the desert is silent. Opaque, passive, austere, it just lies there and "lures a man on and on ... in a futile but fascinating quest" (242). Yet the parallels between the regions of the Great are deeper and more fundamental than the differences; Abbey is just stating his own preference. In *The Journey Home* (1977), he struggles with his responses to Death Valley, which is "ugly" at one time, "lovely" at another, then the "most beautiful" of "all deathly places" (quoted Gilbar 202-3, 209). His old prophetic rhythm is heard: the Funeral Mountains, a "primeval chaos," advertise that "God was here," yet all around one sees the folly of excessive water use in the desiccated Southwest (205).

We can only glance at some of the numerous North American desert writers who have emerged since Abbey. Barry Lopez, for example, writes in *Desert Notes* (1976) that one enters minimal, arid environments by "a series of strippings," and feels there "the impact of nothing" (1981, xii, 77). He shares impressions rather than information in this early work, but *Crossing Open Ground* (1988) transcends self-absorption to give an ecological perspective on the pressures that tourists, settlers, and developers put on places like Glen Canyon and the Kaibab Plateau, with its "soft and subtle beauty" (Lopez 1989, 179). Lopez too warns that Americans are draining the Southwest, perpetuating a culture that "devours the earth" instead of maintaining a "filial relationship" with it (198, 204).

The most profound, intense, and in some ways traditional desert book of the 1980s, Gretel Ehrlich's *The Solace of Open Spaces* (1985), is both objective and creative: emotion based on fact. The title piece is set in the badlands of Wyoming, where mountains give the "vastness a sheltering look" (Ehrlich 1). Her themes are the land's emptiness, spirituality, and vulnerability. Herding sheep in the mountains ("Empty sky ... Empty heart"), you can see for a hundred miles in every direction (59-60). Convinced that "Space has a spiritual equivalent" and the West a "paradisical beauty," Ehrlich accepts Seamus Heaney's idea that "landscape is sacramental" (14, 52, 71). She also talks of grandeur, solitude, purity, but a shadow falls on the solace of the title. The "dark side" of Wyoming's grandeur is the "small-mindedness" of its settlers; Americans "build *against* space," for all its intimations of spirit and sanity (13, 15). Barbed wire is not a symbol of freedom. Already the wilderness is gone, though some wildness remains. Thus Ehrlich tries to maintain a balance between solace and depression.

With the 'nineties came an abundance of fresh material on deserts. Californian John Daniel explains in *The Trail Home* (1992) that he finds silence and religion in the desert, while his friend, a Vedic monk, feels closer to the mystery of Being there. *National Geographic* published several accounts of desert exploration. George B. Schaller's "In a High and Sacred Realm" evokes the "harsh ... grandeur," "infinite horizons," and "stark beauty" of Tibet's Chang Tang desert (68, 76). In this land of bare rock, where history is laid out as in a geology text, one seems to step back in time. Like Doughty, Schaller finds that "both body and mind can travel" (77). The Québec periodical *Moebius* emulated *Traverses* by devoting an issue to "Le Désert" (#45, 1990); it includes both short stories about metaphorical or inner deserts ("Un désert dans ma tête") and reports on travel.

The aesthetics of chastened sublimity and the Great never required true desert; a heath or plain will do. Sharon Butala's *The Perfection of the Morning* (1994) recounts her "Apprenticeship in Nature" on a high treeless plateau with shortgrass prairie in Saskatchewan. At her new husband's ranch she endures a period of adjustment, but then is "freed into the elements" of "the one true landscape" (Butala xiv). She can be in "awe at the beauty and openness of the landscape," and yet at the same time feel it as a home (xv). Butala knows that most people would find this prairie "sparse and uneventful," but watching "that magnificent spread of pure light across the grassy miles," she cannot agree (62, 13). To her the plains are beautiful and terrible, ancient and elemental; she approaches them with "reverence," as if to a "church" (xvi, 101, 144). Two writers make more sense to her there than elsewhere: Wallace Stegner and Hardy, especially (with farms failing all around) *Tess of the D'Urbervilles*.

Western America's landscape was the subject of much of
the decade's desert writing. The idea of loss pervades Jonathan
Raban's *Bad Land* (1996), an historical and personal excursus across
the Montana and Dakota prairies that immigrants settled. From
England himself, Raban identifies with their trials, and with those
who described "boundless" grasslands that went on "interminably":
words that seventeenth-century cosmographers applied to the
universe when the Great and "the aesthetics of the infinite" were
forming (56, 48, 51). Some of those visitors, he notes, were taken
aback by the "oceanic" vistas. Robert Louis Stevenson's eye
quailed before the vastness of the plains; painter John Noble found
their loneliness "appalling"; and Albert Bierstadt discovered the
"agreeable horror" of Burke's *Essay on the Sublime and the Beautiful*
out there (56, 59). With a car and hotels available, Raban's reaction
is different: it is "dangerously elating to be able to see so very far
under a sky so very clear" (109). "Romantic Sublime" paintings look
"cheesy," yet he himself thinks of the plains' "sheer bald exposure"
as lying open and vulnerable to God's eye (290, 207).

Whereas Raban discusses *historical* land abuse, contemporary
environmental dilemmas dominate *A Society to Match the Scenery*
(1991), the proceedings of a conference. Wallace Stegner rose like
the ghost of Powell to insist that the great fact of the West, its aridity,
must be respected. Another speaker warned that the solitude and
"spiritual recharging" that national parks once gave are now
buried under regulations (Holthaus 1991, 116). Gary Holthaus, who
edited the volume, also wrote *Wide Skies: Finding a Home in the West*
(1997). Real or mythical, harsh and beautiful, the West connects us
with "something vast," he affirms (Holthaus 1997, xii). A former
pastor, Holthaus (like Abbey) alternates between hailing the land's
"magnificent vistas" and urging westerners not to "further foul"
their "increasingly crowded" nest (107, 19). Already the mountains
are scarred by logging, and "computer commuters" are on the way
(13). Will they be a problem, or part of the solution? Quoting poet
Gary Snyder, Holthaus heads for the desert, whose "indifference"
is powerful but liberating, to "take stock of my life" (162-3, 157).

Belden Lane's *The Solace of Fierce Landscapes. Exploring Desert
and Mountain Spirituality* (1998) resembles Gretel Ehrlich's title, but
solaces differ, and Lane's is religion: he is a Presbyterian minister
who teaches at a Catholic university. His book updates Merton's
Wisdom of the Desert by including *modern* writers on barren lands.
Lane's "acute, personal longing for fierce terrain" (such as that of

New Mexico and the Sinai Peninsula) and for the silence and austerity one finds there is the dominant motif (17). He values the impact of deserts on the "spiritual imagination," paradoxically producing both a sense of self-discovery and a loss of self-consciousness - a forgetting or emptying of the self, as in Zen Buddhism (6). Lane places himself in the apophatic tradition, which rejects icons and verbal analogies of God, instead using mountain and desert images for divinity. God may be sensed, he believes, in the majesty and simplicity of harsh, empty landscapes. But Lane also writes in the centuries-old tradition of the spiritual Great, begun by the early deists, who found God in the Book of Nature.

Obviously the motives that have impelled people to spend time in deserts are more diverse than Hardy foresaw. But whether his prophecy that people would someday seek out the barren is best illustrated by a religious writer such as Lane, a crusader such as Abbey, a settler such as Woodin, or an adventurer such as Colin Fletcher or Beth Wald no longer matters; monks, activists, housewives, and travellers are all in the picture. Wald told the Banff Festival of Mountain Books and Films in 1999 that she loves to go to the plains of Patagonia, which she (like Darwin and W.H. Hudson) finds incredibly beautiful and unforgettable. "Patagonia is about wind and space," she said, and ultimately about freedom. A spacious horizon is an image of liberty.

10
The World-Roof:
Over the Top

The postwar sense of mountains grew from epic struggles to scale the highest peaks on earth: the *Bam-Dunjah* or "roof of the world," as the Khirgiz call the Himalayas. Then, with less fanfare, climbers tried other routes and lower peaks, or the same ones with fewer resources, or looked for high-altitude spiritual enlightenment. Now we are regularly told that adventure tourism is desecrating what was once considered the purest, most inaccessible part of the planet.

Before Everest took over, some old hands resurfaced. Frank Smythe had time for two more books before his early death in 1949. *Again Switzerland* (1947) is a prolonged sigh of relief and gratitude at being able to return to his first love. "Again I knew youth," he exults, "the jump of the heart and the catch of the throat" at the pure majestic beauty of the Alps (Smythe 1947, 96). Once more he hails solitude and silence, feels joy amidst vast, enduring forms, attacks development and tourism, affirms that comfort sharpens his sense of beauty. Postwar, he insists that outdoor recreation *can* meet the human need for struggle and risk: William James's idea. Smythe also contrasts the restless dissatisfaction of westerners with Buddhists' "serene contentment" (79). The veteran mountaineer could not rest himself: his final illness caught him at Darjeeling. In his last book, *Climbs in the Canadian Rockies* (1950), Smythe gave thanks that it was still "possible to escape to a land ... safe ... from civilisation," where he could feel his "spirit lofting to the wide horizons" (224, 53). He died at 49.

Another familiar voice, Arnold Lunn, who had published a book on the Alps before the First World War, brought out an Alpine memoir after the Second. *Mountains of Memory* (1948) blends history, aesthetics, and recollection. Lunn lived in Switzerland whenever possible, and saluted his return there in 1945 as "Paradise regained" (1948, 120). His tributes to the beauty of the Alps and his laments that they are being ruined by developers accord with Smythe's, but Lunn has his own accent, distinctively Platonic. On a moonlit night, the Alps seem immaterial and one accepts the idea-lism of Plato and Berkeley; the great peaks are "heavenly archetypes" of "eternal loveliness," worshipped by early devotees as a "secret shrine" of "clean beauty and austere loneliness" (122, 63). Lunn also insists on the "close connection between the ascetic and the aesthetic," for "the reward of beauty is associated with the discipline of toil" (77). Down with ski lifts! Hardy might have seen him as one of the "more thinking among mankind," yet Lunn's views were dated. Mountains made sense to him only in a "theocentric" framework; Ruskin was more convincing than Leslie Stephen, let alone Darwin (233).

His Alpine focus itself was obsolete; mountaineers' interests were more global than ever. In *Mountains of Tartary* (1950), Eric Shipton accounts for his spare time while serving as British Consul at Kashgar, China, in the 1940s. When he admits to having "lost a good deal of my interest in climbing mountains," he means in expeditions to scale high peaks, not in mountain exploration (Shipton 1950, 36). The horseback ride from India through Hunza to Kashgar traversed "the most spectacular country I have ever seen," which seemed "the ultimate manifestation of mountain grandeur" (14, 222). Shipton stresses the need to move slowly through Great landscapes: the weeks of riding, requiring "long absorption in those wide horizons," produced "complete receptivity" and allowed him to get to know Ladakh, whose Buddhism also impressed him (60). Highly sensitive to vastness, he particularly likes a "wide horizon" edged by mountains, for its "splendid sense of space and distance" (134, 156). Shipton did eventually climb in a remote district with his old Kenya and Everest friend Bill Tilman, finding on Chakragil the beauty, magnificence, and power that he prized.

Many non-mountaineers were also drawn to the hills in some fashion. A striking example is Lucas Bridges's memoir of growing up in Tierra del Fuego: the *Uttermost Part of the Earth*, as his title has it (1948). Born there to missionary parents in 1874, he was raised among Fuegian and Ona natives, learning their languages. Bridges loved the fjords, glaciers, and forested slopes - described by Darwin in *The Voyage of the Beagle* - around them. As a child, he was "obsessed by a passionate longing to explore those ranges of mountains that hemmed us in" (E.L. Bridges 66). His father would take him sailing in a small boat westward along Beagle Channel to where the scenery became "more and more wild and desolate," and, as glaciers appeared, "grand in the extreme" (124). The book is *inter alia* a requiem for the dwindling Ona people, doomed by white incursions and diseases. With his "passion for wandering among the mountains," Bridges shares their love of what he and they call *Yak haruin*: "My country" (459, 336).

In 1949 the British government sent a South African, Laurens van der Post, to explore two massifs in Nyasaland, Central Africa, hoping he would find arable lands that would help feed the Empire. He did not, but his account of this *Venture to the Interior* (1951) became a classic travel book. Flying over the barrens of the Sudan and Ethiopia, van der Post visualizes Africa as "a natural argument based on a logic of desolation" (75-6). His surface journey, though, is through verdant hills. The epigraph to "Encounter With the Mountain" is Hopkins's "O the mind, mind has mountains; cliffs of fall / Frightful," which sets the tone for his reconnaissance of Mount Mlanje's "lost world," a frightening place dominated by primordial powers that kill his companion (109). Balancing the hell of Mlanje, his weeks on the Nyika plateau are an almost pre-lapsarian paradise. He never thinks of reaching a peak; like Eric Shipton, his interest is exploration. Apropos of David Livingstone, Van der Post remarks that "a search for [the land, waters, and sky of Africa] could easily be identified with a search for God" (191).

Histories and memoirs both reflected and fed public interest in mountaineering after the war. James R. Ullman's *Kingdom of Adventure* (1947) - a chronicle of attempts on Everest from the beginning to a fighter pilot's overflight in 1942, quoting first-hand descriptions, with an inquiry into how and why it would be climbed - whetted appetites for the coming assaults. Claire Engel gave similar treatment to Europe in her historical survey of *Mountaineering in the Alps* (1950). Wilfred Noyce took a broader view in *The Scholar Mountaineers* (1950); his "fathers of our modern movement of mountaineering" include Dante, Petrarch, Rousseau, and Romantic poets as well as climbers from H.B. de Saussure to Shipton (9). A chapter on Capt. Scott sees him as having been engaged in a similar enterprise, and Noyce wishes he had room to discuss the Buddhist worship of mountains. F. Spencer Chapman's

Memoirs of a Mountaineer (1951), comprising *Helvellyn to Himalaya* and *Lhasa, the Holy City*, traces his adventures from Wales to Tibet before the war.

In 1950, a French team caught worldwide attention by climbing Annapurna (the first ascent of an 8000-metre peak). The expedition united some legendary Alpinists: Lionel Terray, Gaston Rebuffat, and Maurice Herzog, the leader, who wrote *Annapurna* (1952), soon translated into English, with an introduction by Eric Shipton. While the book strikes many familiar notes - grandeur, "awe and aesthetic pleasure," "vistas of chaos" and a "peculiar exhilaration" deriving from "this barrenness" - it has a distinctly French flavour (Herzog 33, 36). In the preface, Lucien Devies of the organizing committee praises Herzog as leader, climber, and reader of Mallarmé and Pascal. Herzog's foreword ("dictated at the American Hospital at Neuilly where I am still having a rather difficult time" recovering from amputations required by frostbite) says that "in touching the extreme boundaries of man's world, we have come to know something of its true splendor. In my worst moments of anguish, I seemed to discover the deep significance of existence" (12). He finds "justification for an *acte gratuit*" - their climb - in an existential freedom achieved through intense and protracted suffering (12).

Yet when, at the end, Herzog returns to the question of what the climb signified, existentialism is not the only answer. Yes, they found freedom and beauty "on the frontiers of life and death," but they also "adored [the mountains] with a child's simplicity and revered them with a monk's veneration of the divine" (Herzog 311). For Buddhists (whose religion is praised as wise and beautiful), of course, the Himalayan summits *are* quasi-deities. There is also something of the questing knight in Herzog's calling Annapurna "an ideal that had been realized," an abiding treasure for the climbers (311). Secure in that victory, the engineer, the tailor, the photographer, the doctor, the diplomat, and the Chamonix guides will move on into new lives. Finally, sounding more like Thoreau than like Camus, Herzog writes, "There are other Annapurnas in the lives of men" (311). The physical mountain, receding, takes its place in a series of ideals to be sought and challenges to be met.

CHOMOLUNGMA REVISITED

After Annapurna, it was widely believed that Everest must soon yield to fresh recruits and modern technology, though the Chinese conquest of Tibet forced western climbers to seek a new route via Nepal (which had opened its borders to them in 1947). A British reconnaissance led by Shipton found the approach in 1951, but the Swiss received the only climbing permit for 1952. Aided by Tenzing Norgay, who had worked with the British in the 1930s and become the foremost Sherpa climber, they almost succeeded. The British received the 1953 permit and, with France due to try in 1954, felt that this was their last chance. An organizing committee raised money, tested equipment, assembled supplies, and chose the leader. The obvious choice, Shipton, was known to dislike large expeditions and declined to accept a co-leader, so Col. John Hunt was chosen. He picked the team, developed the plan that (as the world knows) put two men, Edmund Hillary and Tenzing, on the summit, and wrote the expedition book.

The Ascent of Everest (1953) demonstrates the logistical skill with which Hunt made units of his large team leapfrog up the mountain in a series of advances and strategic withdrawals, while supplies flowed steadily uphill. The days of the unified party were over; only radio calls and adherence to the master plan gave the discrete elements coherence. It worked: when the first assault pair turned back, the next was in position to make the summit - but this is not our brief, any more than aesthetics is Hunt's. The colonel rarely ventures into realms of emotional response, although he does address the question of motivation. Asked the point of climbing Everest, he vetoes "material reward," science, and "a passion for climbing." What remains, then? "We climb mountains because we like it," he writes, "to solve a problem" of long standing, and to meet the challenge of "entering the unknown" (Hunt 19-20).

When he does notice "beauty and grandeur," Hunt makes some interesting distinctions (247). Base Camp, enclosed by cliffs, is "lifeless without ... grandeur" and "not ... beautiful," whereas the lower rest camp, with its flowing spring, flowers, animals, and birds, allows weary climbers to see "the high peaks as things of beauty" again (130-2). Similarly, the south summit and ridge look "beautiful," but the col below them is a windy waste, "dreary and desolate" (191). Hunt is impressed by the scale and "vast expanse" of the Lhotse face - once; he does not mention it again (137). Reviewing the expedition at the end, he remembers scenery, comradeship, and spirit-quickening adventure. Many challenges remain - climbing it without oxygen, other routes, other summits, the moon! - and so he welcomes a project to found a school in Darjeeling where Sherpas will teach boys to climb. Such a plan, thinks Hunt, would be "analogous to the Outward Bound Schools" and "worthy of the highest praise" (248-9).

He asked Hillary to write the Summit chapter. The New Zealand beekeeper narrates the ascent flatly, almost without feeling. Returning to teammates at Camp IV, "we greeted them all, perhaps a little emotionally" (Hunt 225). Hillary's article for the London *Times* and *LIFE* magazine is similar, although he admits that dawn of their summit day was "indescribably beautiful" (Hillary 1953, 132). Nor do his later accounts add much: it was given to Hillary to climb Everest, not to render the experience in words. The chapter "High Adventure" in his book of the same title (the former included among the narratives he edited as *Challenge of the Unknown*, 1958) offers graphic details of the ascent and some emotion, but little of that is aesthetic. In a book on Nepal by Hillary and Desmond Doig, *High In the Thin Cold Air* (1962), it is Doig who expatiates on the "magic" of the country; Hillary simply acknowledges an "uplift of spirit" when he looks at the mountains (21, 237).

One would like to know more about the reactions of Tenzing Norgay on his eighth try, but this is problematical. Interviews show that Tenzing spoke a pidgin English in 1953; *Tiger of the Snows* (1955), his "autobiography," was ghostwritten by James R. Ullman (see above). Allowing for paraphrases and verbal slippage, and cross-checking with other sources, however, we can see that the ascent had a strong spiritual dimension for Tenzing. He dedicates the book to Chomolungma, remarking that God is like a great mountain, to be approached with love. Ullman comments that, for Tenzing, "the peaks are a place of pilgrimage" (Tenzing xvi). Although he found the south col "wild and lonely," Tenzing felt a "closeness to God" on the summit, where the view was "wonderful and terrible" (180, 249). While we may query the adjectives, Hillary reports that Tenzing placed an offering of chocolate, biscuits, and candy at the top: "a token gift to the gods that all devout Buddhists believe have their home on this lofty summit" (Hunt 222). He himself left a crucifix there.

The saga of Chomolungma would waver between maximal and minimal efforts as the various goals Hunt enumerated were reached.

The Chinese ascended via the Northeast Ridge, Americans used the West Ridge to traverse the summit, and so on. Many nations and groups sent teams: Yugoslavia, Japan, Poland, the USSR, Russia, Australia, Canada, women, Sherpas. Given their prevalence, tales of Everest can hardly be avoided, though they tend to obscure the breadth of interest in mountains.

ELSEWHERE: SELECTED PERIPATETICS

The hunger for space and wilderness as populations thickened did not require Himalayan expeditions; many found a separate peace. R.M. Patterson left his bank job in England to explore the Nahanni basin in northwest Canada during the late 1920s and built a cabin there: experiences memorably recalled in *The Dangerous River* (1954). Whenever possible, Patterson climbed a mountain in order to view the "immense country" (1966, 116). Vastness is his chief memory of it, and "wild, chaotic beauty" (74). His sense of having found Eden is expressed through Biblical allusions, and David Finch's biography shows that a spiritual love of mountains dated from his childhood. Patterson sometimes felt like the first or last man in an empty land. At Last Man Camp, he and his partner are "pygmies" there on "sufferance"; the "place was meant for loneliness and not for men" (124). If solitude was the price he would pay it, exploring alone for weeks, isolated but not unhappy. From a high plateau Patterson sees that "a man could go on for ever over that great, green upland country" (127). In his final toast and in a foreword he recalls the freedom of those "last days of the old North," for even in 1929 outsiders were beginning to push into the Nahanni country (8).

In the preface to Eric Newby's *A Short Walk in the Hindu Kush* (1958), Evelyn Waugh recognizes the "longing, romantic, reasonless, which lies deep in the hearts of most Englishmen, ... to set their feet where few civilized feet have trod" (Newby 1998, 10). Newby had already worked on a blue-water sailing ship and been a prisoner of war in Italy - he wrote books about both - when he left his job in London's fashion business to travel with a friend in Afghanistan in 1956. What impressed him in the Hindu Kush was its silent vastness: long plains, remote villages, mountains that "seemed like the bones of the world" (Newby 250). Despite occasional feelings of insignificance and fear, he enjoyed the solitude and freedom.

Desolate Nuristan struck him as "impressive and beautiful," even, momentarily, a "paradise" (146, 100). Towards the end they come across Wilfrid Thesiger and camp together. As Newby and his friend blow up their air mattresses to place on the stony ground, Thesiger, "as hard as nails," snorts, "God, you must be a couple of pansies" (253, 255).

After his Everest contretemps, Eric Shipton ran an Outward Bound School, revisited the Karakorams, and then turned to the Americas. Reading Darwin interested him in Patagonia, so he funded a trip there with science projects and saw enough to want more. As recounted in his autobiography, *That Untravelled World* (1969), Shipton went to the southern Andes in 1959-60 to locate a volcano in a glacier, enduring terrible weather, and again the next summer to cross the icecap with friends. Though high in the Andes, it was like polar travel: man-hauling sledges and making landfalls among "an archipelago of rock peaks" (Shipton 1969, 229). A month on the plateau, mostly in storms, produced occasional "exultation" and the reward of intimacy with one of earth's "wildest regions" (231). His trip to the Cordillera Darwin is narrated in *Tierra del Fuego* (1973), along with some regional history (including the Bridges family, whom Shipton sees as kindred spirits). His small party made several ascents, finding at times "gentle beauty," at others "Arctic grandeur" and "Alpine beauty" (Shipton 1973, 14, 119). At the end he felt "utterly content" (1969, 241). Shipton went on to climb in Ecuador and Alaska, and to explore the Galapagos.

Wilfrid Noyce, a veteran of Everest 1953, also disliked big expeditions and preferred "untravelled worlds." Everest failed on both counts: a large, unwieldy party and a route littered by previous efforts. Planning his own climb a few years later, he chose five friends and a peak in the Karakoram so obscure that the Surveyor General of Pakistan had not heard of it. *To the Unknown Mountain* (1962) is both an account of the ascent of Trivor and a meditation on the nature of mountaineering, by then established on a "universally wide basis" and less concerned with beauty (Noyce 1962, 3, 93). The title, alluding to Paul's sermon at the altar "To the Unknown God," is the first of a series of religious references. Noyce says that "some who frequent high places substitute 'Mountain' for 'God'," notes a "valley of dry bones" on the approach, and claims that climbers are "seeking their Grail" up there (1, 4, 38). Having reached his summit/grail, Noyce understands that the quest was more important than the victory, which dovetails with the book's secular theme, that "we are challenged inevitably by the immense and hostile" (6). Finally the mountain remains unknown, he admits, but it has helped the climbers know themselves better.

The journalist Paddy Sherman, another British emigrant to Canada, goes mountaineering with a few friends whenever he can. In *Cloud Walkers* (1965), he recalls several of those climbs. Mt. Slesse (where he helped recover bodies from an airplane crash) is a place of "deep quiet" and "stark grandeur" where Sherman "would gladly lie" himself (1965, 91). Alaska's Mt. Fairweather seems to justify locals' "superstitious fear" of mountains' "supernatural power"; his party climbs one peak "almost too beautiful to desecrate," and the subsequent earthquake feels like divine anger (145-7). *Expeditions to Nowhere* (1981) ranges farther afield, to Africa and South America. The Andes inspire awe; Illimani in Bolivia has a mighty ridge "that sets the spirit free" and a "world primeval" on its summit (Sherman 1981, 213, 216). In sharp contrast, Mt. McKinley (Denali) in Alaska is a mob scene. When Sherman went there in 1978, some 439 climbers had registered to attempt the ascent that season.

THE BUDDHISTS ARRIVE

The West's knowledge of Buddhism and other Asian religions had grown in the nineteenth century with scholarly translations and travellers' reports (abetted by British imperialism); after the war this awareness spread from small groups to a wider public. The interest of literary figures from Thoreau and Emerson through Yeats to Wallace Stevens and the Beats suggests that Anglo-American culture was looking for alternatives to Judaeo-Christian religion, and that Buddhism - non-theistic, human-centred, psychological - was well qualified to provide such an alternative (the 1893 congress on world religions hesitated about inviting Buddhists, who did not seem to have a god). European mountaineers such as Smythe, Shipton, and Maurice Herzog contributed to this process by reporting favourably on the Buddhists they met in the Himalayas. Later came foreigners who not only roamed Tibet and Nepal but to some degree accepted Buddhism and wrote as Buddhists.[1]

---

[1]   My account of this cross-cultural phenomenon is indebted to a conversation with Norman Fischer of San Francisco (10 May 2002); and to William W. Bevis, *Mind of Winter* (1988), as well as to standard sources such as Christmas Humphreys, *Buddhism*.

The pioneer of these last, Lama Anagarika Govinda, describes his pilgrimage into Tibet in *The Way of the White Clouds* (1966).[2] For Govinda, travel is an allegory of the soul's journey to enlightenment, à la Dante's *Purgatorio*; the true pilgrim welcomes the discomforts of the road as part of the Way. The latter point operates on three levels. Historically, the "harshness of life" in Tibet and the struggle for existence there built the spiritual strength of its people (Govinda xii). More broadly, the converse is true: "often where nature is kind and gentle, man is not" (206). And for the individual, danger and hardship are the price of access to the "divine presence on the most sacred spot on earth": Mt. Kailas (201). It is not clear to what extent other peaks share the sanctity of Kailas, the centre of the world, but there is no doubt that a "sacred mountain" is "a vessel of cosmic power"; only an egotist would try to climb or "conquer" it (197). No mountaineer, Govinda counsels us to keep our distance, to circumambulate reverently.

While any journey may enlighten, that from the "low plains of our daily existence," where we slumber in complacency, up to the "way of the white clouds" is especially efficacious (Govinda 198). The mountain path to Tibet is "like a journey through different world-planes into the Far Beyond" (41). The reward of that trip is a sense of freedom as the trammels of civilization give way to the "purity of [Tibet's] mountain forms" (61). Learning from these mountains in a landscape that seems "the organic expression of primeval forces," Govinda approximates the spirit in which mountaineers approached the peaks, though he would not follow them there (61). He calls attention to Tibetan sacred music, in which the higher tones arise from a deep bass "like the forms of sentient life from the elementary forces of nature - which are nowhere more apparent than in the gigantic mountain ranges and in the vast, lonely highlands of Tibet" (30). Though his base at this time was Ceylon, Govinda's preparation for Tibet included time spent in the Andes (of which he still dreamt) and in the Sahara.

The Catholic monk who wrote *Wisdom of the Desert* (ch. 9), Thomas Merton, became interested in Asian religion in his later years. He studied Zen in the 1950s and corresponded with Buddhists, curious to know what their faith might contribute to his. By the time Merton first went to Asia in 1968, he had read so much about Buddhism

---

2   In much the same way, the seventeenth-century Buddhist poet Basho recorded his walks through Japan as a spiritual progress.

that the trip felt like "going home" (1973, 5). From the air he sights the "awesome" Himalayas - the word not yet spoiled - and later walks in the "majestic mountain silence" of their foothills (54, 79). Seeing the great summits, he senses that he "needs" them, and later dreams of Kanchenjunga (135). Merton's readings in Rudolph Otto and Marco Pallis (an English Buddhist and mountaineer) prepared him to see mountains as holy, and several of the qualities he sought for himself - liberation, solitude, silence, a "pure" and "infinite" state - crop up repeatedly in climbers' writings (96). Tibetan Buddhists reminded him of the Desert Fathers he had studied. Their music had "the sound of emptiness": even, at its best, that of *dzogchen*, the "ultimate perfect emptiness" (69, 143). The boundary between natural and existential void is often uncertain in mountain literature; for Buddhists, it does not exist.

Peter Matthiessen, a naturalist and popular writer of fiction and non-fiction, combines Buddhism with mountain travel in *The Snow Leopard* (1978, dedicated to three Zen masters), telling of his walk across the Himalayas to the Crystal Monastery in 1973. The title is ironic - he never sees the leopard - but Matthiessen, like Noyce, finally realizes that the journey is its own reward: the quest *is* the grail. He presents his autumnal trek through a "wild and desolate" land as an affair of the spirit, "a true pilgrimage," in which mountains are holy and serve as metaphors (Matthiessen 191, 4). There are particular holy mountains, such as Machhapuchare, but wilderness summits in general further "spiritual pursuits" (210). Thus the Himalayas are "a higher kingdom" both topographically and spiritually: the centre of the world for Hindus and Buddhists (6). He has an epiphany while there, a vision of "eternity" and "ringing splendor," yet the "Emptiness" of the Himalayas is still "terrifying" as well as "exalting" (233, 179).

Matthiessen and his companion, biologist George Schaller (who *did* see a leopard), agree about Asian culture, the emptiness around them, and what the Himalayas have to offer. Schaller writes a *haiku* that ends, "Suddenly nothing" (Matthiessen 251). Though both men seek unpeopled space, the Sartrean phrases "The fewer people, the better" and "sick of *people*" are ascribed to Schaller; Matthiessen prefers to stay positive, looking for a sense of Oneness in the "vast space and silence" (28, 165, 238). Silence is one of his favourite qualities, along with the "white light" characteristic of both the Himalayas and mystical experience (67, 241). One reviewer, Jim Harrison of *The Nation*, called the book "a kind of lunar paradigm and map of the sacred" (in those years of missions to the moon, Matthiessen describes the landscape of "mountain desert, sere and bare," through which they move as "lunar": 272). The people he values besides Schaller and his head Sherpa, Tukten, are the authors he quotes: other Buddhist travellers (Basho, Govinda), explorers (Sven Hedin), novelists (Malcolm Lowry), and "mystic" poets (Blake, Thomas Traherne) - people who might understand what he found in lieu of a snow leopard.

Though he grew up in India, Andrew Harvey did not discover Buddhism until his Oxford years, and adopted it still later. *A Journey to Ladakh* (1983) tells of his search for true Buddhism in a land that received it from India three centuries before Christ. Attracted by Ladakh's reputation for bareness, Harvey was stunned by the majesty, silence, and "purity" of its mountains; his mind felt as "empty" and "as large as the landscape" (13-15). These qualities dominate his account. The journey from India through the Karakoram into Ladakh is both "an education in wilderness" and "a progress into a bareness" central to Buddhist teaching (23). Again and again he notes the mind-expanding powers of the country's space and light, and how natural emptiness promotes the mental emptiness, *Sunyata*, which is the goal of Buddhism. Learning to "see through the word to the thing," he feels freed, purified; the void, isolation, and silence of *Sunyata* take over from the world (92). At the end Harvey goes to the highest monastery in Ladakh to seek more peace and enlightenment in less of everything.

Parts of Alan Hammond's *To Climb a Sacred Mountain* (1979) might appear in an anthology of Buddhist texts, though his interests are broader. He reverently climbs mountains sacred to any religion, hoping for a "glimpse of the infinite" and "self-illumination" (Hammond 3). Buddhist lore shares space with accounts of Mt. Lassen in California, Mt. Athos (Greece), and Mt. Sinai. Published by the Illuminated Way Press, the book is a California period piece - climbing as sex, self-discovery, and spiritual exercise - as if mountains really do mirror what cultures bring to them. Yet we also hear many of the classic responses of nineteenth-century Alpinists: peace, glory, solitude, majesty, freedom, eternity, and more awe than in many a decade, perhaps because the author is a throwback to early amateur climbers and usually goes alone. Hammond notes that Buddha was called The Golden Mountain, and that Nirvana is said to resemble a mountain peak.

Again, what is striking about this cultural development is how many desiderata Buddhism shares with the Great. Christmas Humphreys, who founded the Buddhist Society of London (1924) and wrote the Penguin volume *Buddhism* (1951), which introduced many readers to the subject, identified twelve principles common to the various schools of Buddhism. Among them are ideas and goals that climbers had been articulating since the eighteenth century: purification through detachment, acceptance of the mutability of nature (as in evolutionary geology), the attainment of inner peace. Humphreys uses mountain imagery to describe Zen: scriptures are "foothills of ... understanding," and "he climbs best who carries the lightest load" (104, 179-80). Zen's first principle, "Vast Emptiness," also describes many mountain ranges and deserts (181). Other writers identify asceticism, physical discipline, and spirituality (all discussed by travellers to the Great) as basic to Buddhism.

EVEREST: THE NEXT GENERATION

Chomolungma became a theatre of competing styles and attitudes to mountains. While large national expeditions continued (the 1963 US effort used 900 porters to carry 27 tons of supplies), resistance to them increased. Woodrow Wilson Sayre and three friends set out in 1962 to rediscover the core emotions of mountaineering, which he analyzed in *Four Against Everest* (1964).[3] Sayre, an English professor, found most mountain reportage too external, so he tried to tell the "story of the inner life of men under stress" (11). He does that, but his last chapter, "Why Men Climb," is of special interest. Trying to go beyond Mallory's famous answer, Sayre lists his own motives, principally beauty, solitude, camaraderie, relaxation, self-reliance, adventure, and challenge (he also notes that the world is too crowded, adding a misanthropic touch). His reading has shown him that all of these except relaxation and self-reliance are shared by most climbers. (Their "sense of communion with God" [218] is conspicuously absent from his personal list.) Sayre concludes that "Men climb mountains because they are not satisfied to exist, they want to live" (219).

---

[3] In *Dark Summit*, Nick Heil describes how they entered Tibet illegally and attempted the North Face.

The 1975 British assault on Chomolungma's southwest face was exactly what Shipton and Sayre disliked. Chris Bonington, its leader and the author of *Everest the Hard Way* (1976), accepted in principle that "one should use the minimum force ... necessary" (1977, 36). On an earlier, smaller attempt, he remembers, "loneliness" made the mountains "even more beautiful" (21). Yet a minimal approach to the Southwest Face was, he thought, out of the question. It required Hunt's kind of expedition: large force, siege tactics, serial assaults. Bonington chose 18 European climbers, raised £.100,000, struck a Management Committee, hired drivers, accepted five journalists, employed countless porters for the march in (the expedition was so large that it had to travel in two distinct parties) and 81 Sherpas from Base Camp up. On the mountain, he would walk away from camp at night in search of beauty and peace.

Everest the Hard Way is a study in what had happened to Himalayan adventuring by the 1970s. Bonington feels called upon to discuss the economics of expeditions, the ethics of technology, the rubbish and deforestation left by touring trekkers as well as by climbers. Losing a Sherpa makes him and others wonder if it is all worth it. Bonington also quotes from teammates' diaries: an innovation that highlights problems and relationships. We hear grumbling, second-guessing, and embryonic political correctness - or cultural sensitivity - in a climber's guilt about exploitation of Sherpas, but there are few aesthetic remarks in any of the journals. It is mainly the summit climbers, Dougal Haston and Doug Scott, who attest to the "strange beauty" of the "Savage, wonderful country" near the top, which "held us in awe" (Bonington 176, 181-2). A spell of bad weather and the death of a climber remind Bonington how "puny and fragile" even a large expedition can be (200). He recalls "moments of ... wonder at the beauty and scale of the mountain," but ends the book with 142 pages of appendices on logistics, equipment, food, etc. (205).

Compromising between Sayre and Bonington, the Austrian Everest Expedition (1978) cost £.65,000 and used 20 Sherpas. It is best known for its stars, Peter Habeler and Reinhold Messner, having reached the summit without oxygen: a first, the dream of many climbers since the 1920s. Habeler's book *Everest: Impossible Victory* (1978) stresses the spirituality of the climb, from the Sherpas' reverence for Himalayan peaks to mountaineers' "hallucinations" (the Extra Man theme) and his own "metaphysical" relationship with Messner, marked by long silent conversations (1979, 3, 7).

High on Everest, Habeler believes, "the veil which hides the great beyond is particularly thin"; near the top "I seemed to step outside myself" in ecstasy - likely a sign of oxygen deprivation - and "prayed uninterruptedly" to the power that was guiding them (103, 111-12). Both climbers are devotees of the "old traditions ... from the pre-technical age," and ascetics (or masochists) who delight in pushing the body to its limit, where only a "second wind ... from the innermost soul" makes further ascent possible (7, 30). Habeler is well-read, comparing the Khumbu icefall to Dante's Hell, and using Mallory's word-portraits of Chomolungma.

Habeler quotes Messner as saying that he climbs to "find himself," up "where one is reduced to what is fundamental and quite elementary. Only then am I at one with myself" (119). The same idea recurs in the piece Messner wrote for *National Geographic* after climbing Everest again in 1980. He came in from Tibet (re-opened to westerners that year), whose "endless space" and "barren landscape" he found "captivating" (Messner 1981, 556); and again ascended without oxygen, this time alone from about 21,000 feet. Asked why, Messner replied, "I want to experience the mountain as it is, and truly understand how my own body and psyche relate to its natural forces" (560). His goal, then, was to know the deepest reality, about himself and about Chomolungma. He felt fear, of course, as during "all [his] thirty years of climbing mountains" (564). Messner again had the delusion of a companion while climbing alone, and declared the tripod that a Chinese expedition had placed on the summit a desecration. Whether he and Habeler, and others who have spent time in the "death zone" above 24,000 feet without oxygen, have suffered brain damage only time will tell.

UNTO THE HILLS

Again, Everest was only a small part of the story. Mountaineers went everywhere; Europe, Asia, the Americas, Africa, even Antarctica had their remote and difficult peaks climbed and described. Several journals existed to publish accounts of daring efforts (in many cases a sketch for a book). And behind the leading-edge daredevils came legions of walkers and watchers, eager to record their devotion to the heights.

Hamish Brown, for example, hiked Britain's entire chain of "Munro" summits. *Hamish's Mountain Walk* (1978) reveals a man well read in early climbs of those hills, including a poet in 1618, a party of ladies who brought along a piper so that they could dance on a peak in 1813, John Keats, and Queen Victoria. Near the end of his book, Brown reviews the motives that have brought people to the Munros. His own incentives include the solitude of "Lonely, brooding mountains," and the "peculiar joy" of such places (Brown 324, 213). The aesthetic appeal of barren hills possessing the "wide sweeping beauty of 'desert'" places (like the "wonderfully empty desolation" near Ben Nevis), and the spiritual rewards of being on a pilgrimage, a "ladder ... to Heaven," are also important (304-5, 146, 334, 329). Brown says that he likes to escape from normal life - not misanthropically, but from the conviction that nature is more godly than man. He found an active kind of peace in the hills: passing tests, meeting challenges.

In sharp contrast, Bruce Barcott's *The Measure of a Mountain. Beauty and Terror on Mount Rainier* (1997) concentrates on one peak. Besides its geological history, he discusses the various ways in which people have responded to the volcano, beginning with the oxymoron of his subtitle. Spiritual responses predominate in all periods. Rainier "inspires in us a feeling akin to spiritual awe," writes Barcott: "reverence, adoration, humility"; we look at it and see "the vastness of God" (2). Nor is this peculiar to Rainier: many religions attest the "spiritual significance" of mountains, and native peoples often revere high places (19-20). Yet when he finally reaches the top and recalls an 1870 description of it as "sublimely awful," he admits, "I felt nothing sublime or awful" (244; cp. p. 2). This is the old complaint - dating at least from Leslie Stephen - that the strains of climbing often hamper the aesthetic response we feel at a distance. Barcott also witnesses to Rainier's "power" and "purity" (64).

Other writers re-created early ascents or meditated on mountains. Arnold Lunn looked back over *A Century of Mountaineering* (1957); Walt Unsworth edited a collection of Victorian climbing narratives and re-told the human history of Mont Blanc. John Jerome's *On Mountains* (1978) blends geology, glaciology, mountaineering, and modern developments such as the Alps coming back into fashion with adventurers after being out of favour for decades. Jerome, who had edited *Skiing* magazine, quotes "Gradient is the elixir of youth" from Jerome Wyckoff (xv). Plate tectonics strikes him as the latest example of the theme of mutability running from Galileo through

Lyell to quantum physics: "We aren't the center of anything"; what we need is "a kind of geologic navigation" (59).

A good deal of mountain writing (re)appeared in anthologies published at the millennium's end. *Epic* (1997) is a collection of mountain survival stories from Shackleton to Krakauer and beyond. Steven Gilbar's *Natural State ... California Nature Writing* (1998) sets early work (Joseph Leconte's Yosemite journal, Joaquin Miller's impressions of Mt. Shasta, John Muir) alongside recent accounts in which their "grandeur" and "solitude" acquire problematic contexts (Hildegarde Flanner notes that the vistas of the San Gabriel Mountains she once enjoyed are now effaced by Los Angeles smog). David Roberts's *Points Unknown. A Century of Great Exploration* (2000) includes many writers discussed in this volume. Since his brief is "great empty spaces," he gives us Shackleton and Scott on Antarctica, Thesiger and Abbey on deserts, Shipton and Krakauer on mountains (11). Roberts believes that "adventure is alive and well," though threatened by technology and - ironically - "the proliferation of adventure travel companies" (12, 13). He notes that two million tourists "swarmed over" the Grand Canyon annually in the 1960s - but five million by 2000 (173). Yellowstone, Yosemite, and other large national parks have undergone comparable increases.

CHOMOLUNGMA PROFANED

Messner's achievement might well have rounded off the saga of Everest; he had met the prime challenge in mountaineering, the grail of climbers since Mallory. But there was another chapter, a coda of sorts, in which Chomolungma became an object of commercial interest and was (as many Tibetans had always feared) sullied. More and more trekking companies brought tourists to and (some way) up the mountain, qualified or not. If one man could climb it alone without oxygen, then surely, in a democratic age, anyone could, with some assistance, make a stab at a "conquest." Adventure tours proliferated, prices rose, garbage accumulated; civic-minded outdoor clubs sent expeditions to remove empty oxygen cylinders and equipment boxes (but not corpses) from the main approach routes. Marx famously said that tragedy returns as farce; perhaps heroic epic returns as sordid spectacle.

If the general reader knows one book about modern climbing on Everest it is probably *Into Thin Air* (1997), Jon Krakauer's account of the 1996 disaster. Prior to this, he paid his dues with years of hard ascents and magazine pieces. The best of those appear in *Eiger Dreams* (1990), which exhibits his love of wilderness adventure and his theme: the conflict between strenuous, even heroic efforts to survive in some of the harshest venues of the Great, and society's drive to tame wild nature and make it safe for tourists. The title-piece evokes the "larger-than-life figures" - Rebuffat, Terray, Messner - who have pitted themselves against the North Face of the Eiger (Krakauer 1997a, 2). Yet a climber battling the elements in that harsh world of vertical rock and ice can now open a door in the cliff and enter the tunnel blasted out in 1912 for a cog railway: not far from midway station with its picture windows, but at risk of being crushed by a train. That contrast is Krakauer's subject.

Most of *Eiger Dreams* transpires on mountains. Krakauer began climbing at the age of 8, and at 20 realized that he was happy in a cold wind atop one of Alaska's Arrigetch Peaks, with their "severe, haunting beauty" (1997a, xi). He went on to the Alps, the Himalayas, Denali (Mt. McKinley), the Rockies, Patagonia (where "the wind sweeps the land like the broom of God"), Antarctica, and the new sports of canyoneering and bouldering (42). Krakauer was quite taken with mathematician-Buddhist-boulderer John Gill, who, "overwhelmed by ... the scale, by the wide-open space" of the American West, discovered that solitary climbing produced "exhilaration" (20). A student of Zen, Gill tries to reach "emptiness" and "stand apart from the outer world of climbing" so that his "mind goes blank" (21). Solitude and spaciousness are among Krakauer's themes, along with the "otherness" of big mountains, but they are jostled by his concerns over too many tourists taking scenic flights over Alaska, flying paragliders at Chamonix, the "death sport capital," or riding the *téléphérique* to the Aiguille du Midi; and too many climbers crowding onto Denali (87).

At times Krakauer lets mountains be holy and mountaineers be pilgrims, but it is clear that an excess of new climbers is causing problems. "A Bad Summer on K-2" analyzes why thirteen people died on the Pakistani mountain in 1986: more than had been lost in its entire 84-year climbing history. In the 1970s, Habeler and Messner "upped the ante" by ascending Himalayan peaks without oxygen, support teams, or "siege tactics"; they called this "climbing by fair means" (Krakauer 1997a, 150). All very well for them, but as more climbers with less experience and ability tried to follow suit, the previous Himalayan mortality rate of one death for every thirty attempts became one in five on K-2 that year (161). And there is also a reckless "new modus operandi" that cannot be blamed on Messner and Habeler: "climbers now begin their ascents with the understanding that if things go wrong, the bond between ropemates - a bond that was until recently held to be sacrosanct - may be discarded in favor of a policy of every man for himself" (150). It is against this background of eroding ethics (and margins of safety) in the pursuit of high goals that *Into Thin Air* should be read.

In that book, structured like a Greek tragedy, Krakauer begins by telling us that nine climbers died on Everest in the storm of May 10-11, and three more later that month. He is candid about what they were doing: climbing Everest is "an intrinsically irrational act," whose difficulty and mystique possess a "deep fascination" (quoting Eric Shipton; Krakauer 1997b, xiii, 5). When he writes of vastness, barren beauty, unearthly vistas, and the "almost Calvinistic" devotion of climbers seeking some approximation to "a state of grace," *Into Thin Air* sounds like early ascent narratives, but such passages are overshadowed by those in which he recounts the growing "commercialization of Everest" (136, 23). The number of people wanting to climb the planet's highest summits and the number of companies serving them increased sharply in the 1990s. Krakauer counted 30 expeditions on Everest in May 1996, 10 of them commercial. Fees skyrocketed: the Nepali government, which charged $2300 for an expedition permit in 1991, charged $10,000 *per climber* in 1996; a client might pay a guiding company $65,000 (22-4).

This "selling" of Chomolungma is what *Outside* magazine sent Krakauer to investigate, and he does not shrink from unpleasant details. In the Western Cwm, the body of a Sherpa lies near the track; the next day, he sees a European corpse. Most bodies, he learns, are not brought down from Everest (which is considered impractical), and most climbers pretend not to notice them.[4] Then, with "so many marginally qualified climbers flocking to Everest these days," crowding at campsites and on routes is inevitable (Krakauer 1997b, 271). The night that his group left for the summit, two other teams followed within the hour. They got in each other's way, creating traffic jams (especially at the Hillary Step, a notorious

---

[4]   Conrad Anker, who found Mallory's body in 1999, reports that that was the third corpse he came across that morning.

bottleneck) and slowing progress. Thus more climbers were still high up when the storm struck in the afternoon. Another problem is the need to accommodate rich clients. Krakauer saw a Sherpa "towing" one of them up the summit pyramid, having already tired himself carrying up her satellite phone (167), so he was not available to help others later, and died on the mountain. The client survived.

Krakauer concludes that while Chomolungma has always been dangerous, the "hubris" and "rivalry" of guides from different companies has added to the natural perils (1997b, 272-3). And the disregard for human life that he observed on K-2 reappeared on Everest. Three members of an Indo-Tibetan team died high on the Tibet side in 1996. They were seen, alive, by two Japanese climbers on their way up. No help was given; no words were exchanged. "We didn't know them," one of the climbers told a British journalist later, and his partner added, "Above 8,000 meters is not a place where people can afford morality" (241). Such scenes are clearly not what Thomas Hardy had in mind when he foresaw intellectuals and later tourists choosing mountains over gardens, but rather a gruesome parody of the idea that sensitive moderns will be drawn and attuned to the heights. If there is a Hardeian presence in this book it is Krakauer himself, reporting, with horror, that Chomolungma has become a high-altitude charnel house. By 2002, 175 climbers had died on Everest, but more than that reached the summit in 2001.

In the years since the disastrous season of 1996 on Everest, its "selling" and crowding have continued or increased, morals and manners seem to have deteriorated further, and more climbers have joined the ranks of frozen corpses. Some of the book titles reflect the prevailing mood: *Chomolungma Sings the Blues* (Ed Douglas, 1997); *High Crimes: The Fate of Everest in an Age of Greed* (Michael Kodas, 2008); *Dark Summit: The True Story of Everest's Most Controversial Season* (Nick Heil, 2008). Kodas tells tales of theft and betrayal (even among teammates), of irresponsible guides and unqualified clients, increased drug use on the mountain, the growth of Everest cybermedia, and the rise of the cheaper, even less-regulated north (Chinese) side. Heil, concentrating on the events of 2006 - whose high death toll was second only to that of 1996 - shows what happens when crowds of obsessed but poorly prepared climbers reach the "death zone," where many will ignore the fallen to do their own thing. Together, they paint a scene of chaos, commercialism, corruption, and carnage: part circus, part frontier town. The few bright spots include attempts by some outfitters to bring order to a mostly lawless environment, and a number of selfless acts by western climbers and Sherpas, some of whom have been paid to carry out high-altitude burials.

Sherpas, who it is agreed did much of the hard work involved in reaching the summit of Everest, have recently assumed more control over activities on the mountain. They own hotels and trekking companies, organize climbs that use other native groups as porters, and charge visitors to use fixed ropes installed on difficult portions of the route. Thanks largely to Sir Edmund Hillary, several of their villages now have schools or hospitals. The son and grandson of Tenzing Norgay have become authors and lecturers. In *Touching My Father's Soul* (2001), Jamling Tenzing Norgay takes a Buddhist view of the 20,000 tourists who annually visit the Khumbu valley. One reason people come there, he thinks, is to know the "purity" of the five elements (which are deities) and to exchange the material world for that of "spiritual thought" (Norgay 218). Looking at ocean, sky, or mountains, we realize "There is no real thing there" that one can label, Norgay writes, yet in their "quietness" we come nearer to "understanding ... emptiness" (218). Thus he reminds us of the spirituality that once surrounded mountains, before ambition, greed, and self-actualization took centre stage.

11
High Latitudes:
Modern Thule

The lure remains strong. When the US Navy advertised 260 construction jobs at its new Antarctic base in 1955, four thousand sailors volunteered. In 1979 an Air New Zealand jet on a sightseeing flight to Antarctica crashed into Mt. Erebus; none of its 300 passengers, seeking a glimpse of the white continent, survived. Tourists pay thousands of dollars apiece to sail to the Antarctic or the Arctic on cruise ships, some reaching the North Pole aboard huge icebreakers and stepping gingerly onto the ice. This passion for polar regions has taken the forms of large governmental efforts stressing science, tourist voyages stressing comfort, and small, private attempts to have the experience in a purer form by accepting pioneer conditions. The dialectic between maximal and minimal approaches is even sharper than in Himalayan mountaineering: partly because the poles are more difficult and expensive of access than Tibet or Nepal, and partly because the American presence in Antarctica has become hegemonic, actively discouraging private adventurers.

GOING IN FORCE

For years after World War II, individuals had to operate within the framework of large national expeditions. Formerly such efforts had relied on private patrons, with some government support, but only public resources could fund the more ambitious style of postwar ventures. The United States, emerging from the war as the world's richest and most powerful country, led the way. When Adm.

225

Richard Byrd returned to Antarctica in 1946-47, his six airplanes flew off a US Navy aircraft carrier to land at Little America IV and conduct aerial surveys. France maintained a post in Adélie Land from 1950 to 1952. The mid-1950s was a boom time: eleven nations built over fifty stations to prepare for the International Geophysical Year (IGY, 1957-58), which focused on Antarctica. Dr Vivian Fuchs led the "Commonwealth Trans-Antarctic Expedition," which made the crossing that Shackleton had planned in 1914. The US Navy landed a plane at the South Pole in 1956: the first visit since Scott's, and the beginning of a de facto domination of the Pole.

Rear Admiral George Dufek, who planned Operation Deepfreeze (also the title of his book), was in that plane. He had volunteered for Byrd's 1939 Antarctic expedition on an impulse. In the icepack, Byrd asked what he thought. "It's a hell of a lot of ice, but what good is it?" replied Dufek, who weathered the ensuing chill and "gained more respect for the Antarctic and its potentialities" (Dufek 11). After the war he went to Greenland to build the Thule naval base, to Antarctica again with Byrd, and to another Arctic posting before Deepfreeze. Dufek notes that "recession of the ice," allowing polar explorers to "probe farther," has led to increased competition and expense, hence more government involvement (50). His map of Antarctica shows the wedges claimed by seven nations, not including the United States. Yet at the South Pole ("Bleak and desolate, it was a dead world") and at points along the coast he plants American flags (199-200). After all, his country "lost" the North Pole and north Greenland through lack of vision (172).[1] A complex character, Dufek appreciates the majesty of Erebus, the "great and rare beauty" of storms and glaciers, atmospheric purity, and the environmental costs of his operation (94).

Expedition leaders preoccupied with logistics seldom make good reporters, and the style of "official" accounts is usually bland. *The Crossing of Antarctica* (1958) is the joint production of Fuchs, who led the first crossing of the continent (from the Weddell Sea via the Pole to the Ross Sea), and Edmund Hillary, who headed the Ross Sea Party and laid depots for Fuchs's team. Then, ignoring a directive from the expedition's executive committee asking him to stop, he went on to the Pole, arriving before Fuchs. The aspect of rivalry between two strong egos, the subject of much comment at

---

[1] Since Cook and Peary were both Americans, this must mean that the US failed to *claim ownership* of the North Pole.

the time, is muted in this book, dedicated to the Queen. The sparse aesthetic gleanings from their massive exposure to Antarctica are a by-product of mechanized travel: the noise, smell, and vibration of tracked vehicles with cabs shut off the riders from direct contact with the environment most of the time. Outside their machines, they were more likely to react to the surroundings. In camp, Hillary could appreciate the "magnificent" scene, as did the dog-sledge travellers of the survey parties and the aviators (Fuchs and Hillary, 197). Fuchs, who had been in Greenland with James Wordie and Augustine Courtauld in 1929 and in the Antarctic in 1949, rarely mentions his natural surroundings.

When Hillary recalled the experience later, he was more forthcoming; *No Latitude for Error* (1961) gives a fuller account of motives and responses than does the official book. Meeting Fuchs, Hillary sees him as moved by "love of adventure," and personal and national pride, not just by science, and Hillary concurs: "I have never needed a spate of excuses ... before I considered a job was worth attempting" (1961, 14). He himself was pleased to be going to "vast areas ... where no man had trod before," which was still true of most of the continent (64). Hillary admires the glaciers and peaks of South Georgia and the colours of Antarctica: the absence of any negative reaction, even at first, is notable. Presumably his New Zealand background and Himalayan trips aided his appreciation of "magnificent mountain scenery," the "strangely beautiful scene" of the Ross Ice Shelf at midnight, and the Skelton nevé's "unforgettable beauty" from the air (86, 122, 142). There is more aesthetic sensitivity than in his Everest writings, as if experience (and lower altitude?) had sharpened his responses.

Hillary's portrait gains by its darker tones. From the air, the South Pole station is "a lonely and gripping sight" amidst the "wide spaces" of the plateau, and this emotion is stronger on the ground (Hillary 1961, 88). Although reaching the plateau with his tractor train gives Hillary "a greater sense of achievement" than climbing Everest (!), once the last supply planes leave, he feels the "loneliness and isolation" of the "wide wastes" (171). Most of the time, driving an enclosed tractor keeps such emotions at bay, but when stopped, outside, and alone he realizes the "complete desolation" of his "barren and ominous" surroundings (196). There is "an air of gloom over the landscape," which seems vaguely lunar, and he scrambles back into the cab with "a slight chill around my heart" (197). At last, deeply fatigued and sick of driving as they near the pole, he likens the three tractors to "tiny black ants crawling over the snowfields of eternity" (215). If he had comparable feelings on Everest, he did not disclose them. Their inclusion here enhances his credibility, and brings the reader more fully into the text and the experience.

Some of the best books on polar travel have come from subordinates like Scott's Cherry-Garrard, and beginning with the IGY we also have accounts from visitors, mostly journalists. Noel Barber, an Englishman accredited to Operation Deepfreeze, was sent by a London daily to report on the Trans-Antarctic Expedition. In the first chapter of *The White Desert* (1958), he tackles the question of why Antarctica fascinates many. To the interest of all exploration, he suggests, it adds the enduring "mystical challenges" of mountains and deserts (Barber 9). Here "the desert is white but the emotional appeal of its emptiness is as great as if it were brown" - Barber loves deserts - and "no man who has lived from choice in its utter loneliness … can fail to enjoy it." Mysticism and enjoyment come up repeatedly, as do science and "spiritual rewards," for "all adventure is clothed in the magic of the spirit," and Antarctic explorers especially need "a spiritual quality" (9-10).

Not that Barber romanticizes Antarctica, as formidable in his portrait as in Hillary's: "lonely, dead, cruel, inhospitable and irresistible" (10). It is "a white hell" for those who have "no soul," driving them over the edge (an American at isolated Liv Station loves McMurdo Sound because he can kill seals there), but "a white heaven" for the "visionary" (9). As in the early days of travel in the Great, Barber's Antarctic is litmus paper for the soul: it will test, and it may reward. When he flies to the South Pole and calls its "utter desolation … almost frightening," the adverb seems a bit of bravado, yet within a few days he is "happily walking about, just taking in the fantastic desolate stretch of white" (73, 79). The continent is also a time machine. "Virtually unchanged since the ice age, Antarctica is the last resort of yesterday," and not everyone can handle that temporal shift (9). Applicants were probably not told that the "man who travels to the bottom of the world is also travelling back in time," but Barber finds it so (10).

In that period some attempts were made to express the human meanings of wilderness. The United Nations' International Union for the Protection of Nature (1948) proclaims "natural beauty" an important part of "spiritual life" (Nash 1982, 361-2). The question with any such effort, of course, is whether it is more than a rhetorical flourish. Out of the IGY came the Antarctic Treaty, which sought to maintain the spirit of scientific cooperation and keep the continent clean and peaceful. Signed by participating nations and several others, it was ratified in 1961, and did protect Antarctica against certain forms of exploitation for 30 years. Some nations scaled down their involvement; others stayed to run scientific programs (such as monitoring the hole in the ozone layer), map the continent, and search for valuable minerals. Adm. Dufek, whose country maintained and increased its presence, wondered in *Operation Deepfreeze* whether Antarctica would acquire strategic importance, and whether it would become economical to exploit its mineral wealth (150, 172-3).

A generation after Barber, another journalist flew in: John Langone, the science editor of a Boston newspaper. *Life at the Bottom* (1977) focuses on *The People of Antarctica*, but readers of Scott, Shackleton, or Amundsen will be shocked by what had happened to "the people" in six decades. The educated, literate pioneers have given way to bored mechanics and foul-mouthed military ranks. Polar life in the machine age seems rawer than ever; if travel and survival have been reduced to a system, much else has been reduced, too. Langone records the odd reaction to Antarctica as challenging, deceptive, beautiful (at night), or awe-inspiring. But these are passing touches compared with the hours of tape-recorded ramblings by people at the base (would a transcript of the talk in Scott's hut have been this depressing?) and the details of pollution at McMurdo Sound, a "filthifying" that is accepted as "unavoidable" with "colonization" (Langone 62). Langone's epigraph is from Tennyson's "Ulysses," but his characters are not from that world, and the American scene he records was dominant.

ON THEIR OWN

Barely noticed next to such massive operations by military and scientific establishments, efforts by individuals and small groups to know the polar regions directly, with as little fuss and technology as possible, slowly gathered way: less a counterpart of large expeditions than a protest against what they miss and (later) what they do to the environment. Minimal ventures into the Arctic and Antarctic, however, never easy, became more difficult as means of access and good sites for base camps became government monopolies.

For almost two decades after the war, the private perspective appears only in historical work or the reports of a few isolated travellers. In Canada, Farley Mowat's *Top of the World* trilogy (*Ordeal By Ice*, 1960; *The Polar Passion*, 1967; *Tundra*, 1973) made a considerable contribution to boreal history. In New Zealand, L.B. Quartermain produced *Two Huts in the Antarctic* (1963), focusing on early explorers, and *South From New Zealand* (1964), bringing the story up to the IGY. Most improbably, Frederick Cook emerged from years of prison and obscurity to narrate the story of his *Return From the Pole* in 1908-09 (1953; see ch. 3). Dying before publication, he was spared the new wave of disbelief, but his book reminded its readers of the days when men were forced into heroic roles by the elements if they braved the polar regions at all.

Passersby or tourists might record their impressions of the Arctic fringes. Manitoba novelist Gabrielle Roy described her reactions to Labrador in "Voyage en Ungava" (1961). From the air it had a tragic beauty; the 'bare plateaus, a vast barren extent, a landscape as it were outside the world,' fascinated her.[2] On the ground, the 'terrible rocky land' seems to absorb humans, leaving only 'silence. Total. Infinite,' but it cannot absorb the cast-off fuel drums of the US Air Force: this 'serious' island is now a garbage dump (Roy 104, 106). She wonders what the attraction of this sad, barren region is (other visitors observed that the natives do not consider the land sad or barren).

A young Norwegian, Bjorn Staib, noticing that Nansen's 1888 crossing of Greenland had not been repeated, led the first small sortie into polar regions after the war. *Nanok* (1962; trans. *Across Greenland in Nansen's Track*, 1963) lists his motives as admiration for Nansen, a desire to test himself in "a sporting challenge," and belief in hardship: standard elements in first-hand reports on the Great (Staib [13]). On the mountainous coasts, grandeur dominates: the ice-drift is "a magnificent sight," Umivik has an "aloof majesty," and at the end he and his friends sight the "magnificent" west coast peaks (24, 35, 122). The "vast dome of inland ice" is also "awe-inspiring," but includes sombre tones (34). Umivik seems "cruel" as well as majestic, and when the fog clears on the icecap, the scene is daunting (35). The ice looks "interminable" (as the universe did to seventeenth-century astronomers), an "endless white plain" that

---

[2]   "plateaux dénudés, une immense étendue stérile, un paysage comme hors de ce monde" (Roy 101). My translations are enclosed in single quotation marks.

he twice calls infinite (85-6). Staib's palette has only a few strong colours, but there is no doubt that he had a genuine, powerful, and coherent aesthetic experience.

The 1960s saw a number of private adventures in the north. Staib tried to cross the Arctic Ocean in 1964, but was delayed until warm weather forced him back. An American, Ralph Plaisted, set out towards the Pole with a team of snowmobiles in 1967; he failed then but succeeded the next year. At the same time a "British Trans-Arctic Expedition" led by Wally Herbert undertook to complete the crossing that Staib had begun. Plaisted and Herbert crossed paths during the latter's 1967 "reconnaissance": four months of dog-sledging from Greenland to Resolute Bay in Canada. As Plaisted made his second attempt, Herbert's group left Point Barrow, Alaska, for Spitsbergen, a sixteen-month ordeal (1968-69). In *Across the Top of the World* (1969), Herbert recounts both trips rather hastily, but also supplies some useful background. The roots of his interest reach back to his youth in Egypt and South Africa, "where the wide open spaces had excited and disturbed" him (W. Herbert 28). In 1955 he went to Antarctica as a surveyor, stayed for two and a half years (into the IGY), and met the future companions of his Arctic expedition.

Herbert could not forget the Antarctic. In 1960 he drove up through Norway, sailed to Spitsbergen, then Greenland, bought dogs, and escorted them to the New Zealand base in Antarctica. Herbert spent two years there, dog-sledging over unexplored country and realizing that he was out of tune with his time. Amundsen was his hero, visits to Scott's and Shackleton's huts were acts of piety, driving dogs to the Pole was his passion - but the days of dog-sledging seemed to be over: his hosts wanted to have motorized sledges and aircraft, like the Americans. And soon "there would be nothing left to explore in the Antarctic" (W. Herbert 34). He proposed a dash to reach the Pole on the 50th anniversary of its first attainment, but his superior in New Zealand disapproved. The American commander at McMurdo told him flatly that "times had changed" and rescue would be out of the question (39). Herbert settled for a climb of Mt. Nansen and a sledging trip to within 270 miles of the Pole. On the Axel Heiberg Glacier he admired - and partly retraced - Amundsen's route, despite attempts at official interference on the radio, also known as "our burden" (44).

Giving up on Antarctica but not on huskies and polar travel, Herbert took his plan for a North Pole traverse to Sir Vivian Fuchs

- who had recently traversed the South Pole - and gained a strong backer. He also consulted Peter Freuchen, who had travelled with Knud Rasmussen. It was three years before Herbert's "training run" from Greenland to Canada took place, but finally they were sledging along that historic route. The north end of Axel Heiberg Island, Cook's jumping-off point for the Pole, seemed "uncommonly barren," a "forbidding bleakness of ice and snow" (W. Herbert 82). Landscape description and aesthetic feeling are rare in Herbert, very much the expedition leader, as caught up in plans and logistics as Fuchs or Chris Bonington; one usually has to infer why he went and what he gained. The introductory chapter of *Across the Top of the World* examines the motives of polar explorers, finding them purer (less commercial) than in most fields of endeavour. His own, he says, were scientific, though he also admits to wanderlust and Pole fever. Herbert sees "an analogy to mountaineering," the North Pole being the summit of the world, "a horizontal Everest" (12, 99).

After four years of preparation, Herbert's team finally set off for their Arctic Ocean crossing. But they were not self-contained like his Antarctic heroes, or Rasmussen or Stefansson; only a series of supply drops by British and Canadian planes, arranged via radio, could sustain them. "Our burden" had become our lifeline. Unable to cut the umbilical cord to the outside world of technology, Herbert never really enters the emotional space that Nansen, Amundsen, and Shackleton inhabited. His few references to "beauty" are as apt to refer to the vapour trail left by his dogs as to moonlight falling on broken ice floes, or the "beautiful sight" of Phipps Island at journey's end (W. Herbert 190).

Their success no more ended journeys on the Arctic Ocean and to the North Pole than Hillary and Tenzing kept subsequent climbers off Chomolungma. An Italian expedition drove dog teams to the Pole in 1971. Given the nature of the Arctic Ocean, it would never be the same journey twice.

DRIFTERS

Oceans, which were part of Addison's Great ("a wide expanse of waters"), have figured here chiefly in polar voyages. In more general seafaring literature, such as Richard Henry Dana's *Two Years Before the Mast* (1840), vastness, grandeur, and other themes characteristic of the Great appear as well. But tiny rafts have also been committed to blue water by mariners, despite the warnings of sceptics. Their patron saint is Norwegian anthropologist Thor Heyerdahl, who with five friends drifted a balsa raft from Peru to Polynesia in 1947 to prove that the latter *could* have been peopled in that way, and wrote *Kon-Tiki* (1948), a classic of marine adventure. On the ocean he found "peace and freedom," a great emptiness, and "purity" (Heyerdahl 1963, 95, 129). Heyerdahl later built a boat of papyrus reeds in Africa and sailed it to the Caribbean to show that ancient Egyptians *could* have crossed the Atlantic. It took two tries, recounted in *The Ra Expeditions* (1970), in which, along with talk of finding eternity under the stars, there is a good deal about the polluting of the Atlantic.

The 1970s abounded in sailors who reached their goals with minimal help and technology - Francis Chichester circumnavigated the globe, and Willie de Roos the Americas, solo - but the one most relevant here is Tim Severin, whom we met riding the Mongolian steppe (ch. 9). In 1976 and 1977, he and some friends sailed a *curragh* (leather on an oak frame, a mediaeval design) from Ireland to Canada via the Faroes, Iceland, and Greenland, to demonstrate that St Brendan and other Irish monks of his time (6th century AD) *could* have done so. The publishers and reviewers of *The Brendan Voyage* (1978) compared it to *Kon-Tiki*, though Severin points out that a *curragh* is not a raft, and that sea ice was the great danger on his high-latitude expedition. What gives Severin's narrative its unity and much of its interest is the close match between what the monks were seeking and what the moderns found. The former (who must have been fairly remote in Ireland) sought islands where they could be even more "isolated from the evils of the world"; sailing to those islands, Severin is struck by their abiding "Sense of isolation" - a word whose root is *isola*: "island" (1979, 233, 223).

Drawing on the *Navigatio* or *Voyage of St Brendan* and other early texts, Severin notes Brendan's desire to "inspect the wonders of our Creator" (1979, 221). His own crew, "awed" by the great cliffs of the Faroes, with thousands of seabirds feeding in a tide rip at their base, and later by the waves and ice of the open Atlantic, relive the monks' wonder (111, 114). Near the end, Severin calls such moments of "visual splendor" and danger the most memorable part of the voyage (235). The emotions he reports are strong, primal, and mixed; fear and grandeur go hand in hand, as when storm waves, "grand monuments to the power of Nature," threaten their craft (169). Icebergs have that blend of beauty and danger found in reports by early Alpine travellers, and other feelings reiterated in the text - such as being dwarfed by vast primeval phenomena - are also common in the literature of the Great. Severin compares the Irish monks seeking "a desert in the ocean" to the Desert Fathers, and notes that the Arctic, too, has mirages (77). The sense of peace found amid great emptiness, felt as precious and surreal, has many parallels in mountain and desert books.

The 1977 reprint of Frank Worsley's *The Great Antarctic Rescue: Shackleton's Boat Journey* provided a reminder that the kind of voyage Severin chose to make had been done before, involuntarily, with more distress and no protection.

FROZEN DREAMS AND NIGHTMARES

Antoine de Saint-Exupéry's point about humans living in oases of fertility surrounded by deserts acquired cosmic scale as American satellites moved out through the solar system in the 1970s. *National Geographic*'s report on "What Voyager Saw: Jupiter's Dazzling Realm" (Jan. 1980) depicted worlds both alien and familiar: the moons that Galileo observed. Io, with mountains 30,000 feet high, "a painted desert," and a sea of frozen sulphur, is an "utterly arid" place of black lakes and volcanoes (Gore 23, 25). Europa, rather "like ... the Arctic Ocean" with its "pack ice," is "relentlessly flat," except for craters and ice mounds (25). To travel on Ganymede would be "like crossing a glacier," and Callisto, "a wondrous jumble of icy spikes and jagged protrusions," is also glacier-like (27, 28). The descriptions naturally drew on the moons' nearest earthly counterparts: the oceans, deserts, mountains, and polar wastes of the Great.

The Arctic inspired a number of popular books in the 1980s, including Barry Lopez's *Arctic Dreams* (1986), a blend of history, legend, science, and personal observation. Lopez mentions several times that the Arctic tundra is a "cold, light-poor desert"; arid, barren, and harsh, it reminds him of Thesiger's Arabia (1986, 34). Yet he finds the Arctic beautiful, spiritual, and austere, as did many of the earlier visitors he cites. The undertone to this nuanced treatment is the threat of growing ecological crisis in the North - seen at the time as a function of development and population pressure rather than climate change - which is also prominent in his *Crossing Open Ground* (1988).

By then the boldest private expeditions were heading for the southern polar region. In 1980-81, three Britons drove their "motors" across Antarctica on longitude zero. Two others, Roger Mear and Robert Swan, with a Canadian, Gareth Wood, man-hauled from the Ross Ice Shelf to the South Pole in 1985-86, and the next summer Dr Monica Kristensen, a Norwegian glaciologist, and three companions dog-sledged over 2000 kilometers of the white continent. In 1989-90, two parties crossed Antarctica, one of them including Reinhold Messner.

Mear and Swan titled their book *A Walk to the Pole. To the Heart of Antarctica in the Footsteps of Scott* (1987). Swan, who wrote the introduction and epilogue, was obsessed with Scott, and hoped to "set the record straight on the gallant man's behalf" (Mear xiii). No one questions Scott's gallantry, of course. Swan seems quixotic on this matter, and there are other problems. The idea of walking to the Pole and then being flown out is as much a contrast to as a parallel with Scott, and their decision to accept help from a party of American geologists camped on the Beardmore Glacier brings about a kind of Fall, in which the mystique of their enterprise, its sense of isolation and purpose, evaporates. Moreover, Mear (following Chris Bonington's model) insists on recording in his narrative the petty irritations that plagued them, thereby diminishing the adventurers. Apparently Wood, the silent partner in the book, often had to mediate between his volatile and opinionated companions.

Why did they go, and how did they feel about what they saw? All three had served global apprenticeships in wild places. Swan, who had skied around Iceland's Vatnajökull icecap and bicycled from Cape Town to Cairo, met Mear on the British Antarctic Survey in 1980; Mear and Wood met while climbing on the hills of Britain. In the book, what chiefly moves Swan and Mear is the ambivalent beauty of Antarctica: "surreal" for Mear; a "wild loveliness," dangerous and "daunting," for Swan (98, 267, xiii). References to its huge scale and timeless, "primeval" aspect are also frequent. To Mear, Antarctica's "vast, silent landscape" is "a scene ... lost in time" (243, 53). Compared to the rest of the world, it seemed an extra-ordinary place where "normal rules did not apply"; standing on Mt. Erebus, he was "viewing the world like a dream" (103, 91). Both authors found the blankness of Antarctica's "white void" formidable, and were in awe of its dangers (159). Mear often mentions the barrenness, and his sense of insignificance amidst seemingly infinite space.

They had to reach their goal in a land where "science and adventure have moved steadily apart" since the IGY, science being the only motive acceptable to the ruling power (Mear 17). Both authors criticize the American regime as uncooperative and hostile. Mear in the chapters "A Question of Access" and "A Matter of Principle," and Swan in his epilogue, document how US authorities opposed their "walk" and pressured New Zealand to do likewise. A US official told them that "it was not American policy to assist private expeditions ... signatories to the Antarctic Treaty had agreed not to encourage such ventures"; they "had no place in the Antarctic" and would be "unwelcome" (24, 29). An officer at McMurdo said bluntly, "we don't support your endeavour. ... We told you not to come" (249). Mear and Swan print a letter to *The Times*, signed by Edward Shackleton, Vivian Fuchs, John Hunt, and others, protesting against this "aberration" from "normal Antarctic hospitality" (272). The private perspective on nature in the Thulean sector of the Great was becoming increasingly hard to achieve.

As Swan and company walked "in the footsteps of Scott," so Reinhold Messner and Arved Fuchs followed Shackleton's intended track. Messner, having already made a solo ascent of Chomolungma without supplemental oxygen (recounted in *The Crystal Horizon*, 1989), told their story in *Antarktis - Himmel und Hölle zugleich* (1990; trans. *Antarctica. Both Heaven and Hell*, 1991). He greatly admires Shackleton, and respects Swan and Mear, but ridicules Fuchs's use of mechanical transport. Maintaining that the "Shackleton traverse" has thus not yet been done, Messner endorses Michael Parfit's assertion: "what technological civilization does on the ice continent, becomes a caricature of this civilization" (1991, 60). With Messner, environmental concerns take centre stage in the Antarctic; we hear much about the World Park Antarctica proposed by Greenpeace, whose ship helped remove traces of the Footsteps of Scott expedition from McMurdo Sound. Putting "feeling for the landscape" at the top of his agenda, Messner walked across Antarctica (without seeking permission from anyone, a protest against national claims) because of "the quality of its wildness" (17, 37).

Only two topics come up in his book more often than the environment: wonder at the vastness of the land, and a belief that it has spiritual meanings. Messner, a thoughtful man, a Zen gardener who describes himself as "a pupil of St Augustine," likes to quote Dante (1991, 14). The "heaven and hell" of his subtitle, in fact, refers to the *Divine Comedy*, whose images he saw reproduced throughout the "white desert" (32). Antarctica convinced Messner that the earth was once the paradise described by Dante in the *Paradiso*. Howling storms and the high-tech American South Pole base ("an inversion" of natural order) are hellish, though once embarked on the second half of the trip across the polar plateau, Messner feels restored to a time and "state when nature alone was 'God'" (217). "I could not imagine anything more beautiful," he says; "This silence, this vastness, this peace! This was heaven" (223). But in addition to Dante, Nietzsche is also heard from time to time, suggesting that there is really no right or wrong, no ethics, in Antarctica. It is pure nature and experience, beyond good and evil.

Messner's fascination with white - obviously the dominant sense perception in Antarctica - rivals Melville's. It tends to occur in compounds such as "white desert," "white wilderness," and "white infinity," one of his favourite qualities (1991, 12, 101, 291). What he loves about this vast blankness is that, by being pure, "unendingly beautiful," and even sublime, it brings him peace and joy (338). Antarctica feels like a different planet: weird, grave, and empty, speaking to Messner's misanthropic side. He detests central Europe's banality and deadness; *his* heaven would be quiet and "devoid of people" (77). *L'enfer, c'est les autres*, especially during the New Year's Eve party at the South Pole station, which sickens him. Ironically, Messner had written in his diary, the "knowledge that there is nobody anywhere gives to the whole an elevated mood" (303). The man who soloed Chomolungma then writes, "This journey is the trip of a lifetime" (308). Messner is a devotee of the vastness that produces awe and defines the Great, whether in mountains or white polar deserts.

Everest climbers seem drawn to Antarctica. Seven months after the disaster that inspired *Into Thin Air*, Jon Krakauer described a six-man expedition to Queen Maud Land in *National Geographic*. He and his companions, says Krakauer, were "seeking a blank spot on the map" at a time when few places retain the "bracing aura of terra incognita," and Queen Maud Land (though examined by Norwegians in 1993-94) still qualified (1998, 48). Seen from the Razor, a vertical rock pillar, "huge, jagged peaks" jut from the icecap, "stark, barren," beautiful, and never climbed; all is "immensity and austerity"; a "desolate beauty" extends in every direction (47, 69). Antarctica, Krakauer writes, has "thousands of magnificent peaks, including some of the comeliest and most formidable mountains on the planet" (54). Every serious climber in the world would be there were it not for "staggering logistic and financial hurdles," placed there or heightened by the opposition of the National Science Foundation, which runs the American scientific programs (56). After Mear, Swan, and Messner, it is interesting to hear an American make this point.

ARCTIC SOLITUDES

In the Arctic, a tough, determined individual with limited resources could still experience the Great first-hand and alone. Robert Perkins, a Bostonian, flew to the source of the Back River in Canada's Northwest Territories in 1987 and paddled his canoe through the Barrens *Into the Great Solitude* (1991). In defense of going alone, he cites Knud Rasmussen (quoting an Inuit sage): "True wisdom is only found far away from people, and ... only through suffering" (see ch. 7; Perkins xv). He knows himself a mere tourist compared to explorers such as George Back (Franklin's artist) and Rasmussen, but becomes a student of the land as he moves north. One day he climbs an esker like "a blond whale" that has surfaced "for a thousand-year moment out of the tundra sea" (25). Generally we are afraid of "wide-open space," Perkins believes, yet in time he perceives the tundra's "loving indifference" and the way in which "everything remarks the whole" (167, 181). He begins to resent any traces of humanity, and as he comes to feel more integrated with the ecological web, the natural cosmos, he can hear it saying, "If you love us ... don't come back" (218). And Perkins finally accepts this anti-human argument: the fewer of us there, the better.

A comparable though more extreme figure is Don Starkell, a Canadian who in 1980 left Winnipeg with his two sons to paddle canoes 12,000 miles to Brazil (one son gave up). Ten years later he headed north from Churchill, Manitoba, in a kayak to traverse Hudson Bay and the Northwest Passage. *Paddle to the Arctic* (1995) tells how, over the next three summers, with companions or alone, he struggled to within 30 miles of Tuktoyaktut on the Beaufort Sea before the September freeze-up forced the RCMP to evacuate him. That travel companions dropped out on both trips is understandable; clearly he could be a difficult man: driven, stubborn, at times clumsy. Not surprisingly, his most frequent epithet for the Arctic is "lonely," but his courage, determination, and desire for large doses of contact with the wild are beyond reasonable doubt.

The loneliness he projects onto the environment exists in layers. There is the general sense of travelling in a "large and lonely land," feeling insignificant and "humbled" by a North seen as "great, lonely, and clean" (Starkell 257, 218). Within this frame, some places stand out as heightened versions of the prevalent solitude. Cape Bathurst, the most northerly point on the Canadian mainland, looks "dismal, depressing, and lonely" (255). Southampton Island at the top of Hudson Bay evokes several of Starkell's most frequent responses. A "lonely, wild, deserted place" of high winds, hungry bears, "stark shores," and "desolate moonscape" interior, it feels "barren and cruel" to him, although Victoria, his paddling partner for a time, enjoys its "stark beauty" (90-2). ("Stark beauty" was Neil Armstrong's reaction to the lunar surface in 1969.) Those two qualities, separate or conjoined, appear almost as often as loneliness, from the fearful beauty of Hudson Bay's icebergs to a tiny island near the end, "a frozen desert ... icy, cold, and stark" (268). Starkell also admires the purity of water so clear that the bottom can be seen distinctly thirty feet below. Seventeenth-century Arctic mariners had marvelled at just this clarity.

By the 1990s a growing number of amateurs were heading north to walk across tracts of Baffin or Devon or Ellesmere Island, with an adventure travel company or on their own. John Moss, a Canadian academic, describes his Baffin Island trek in *Enduring Dreams* (1994). He, too, quotes Rasmussen's *angakoq* on wisdom born of lonely suffering: Aeschylus, with a pinch more of misanthropy and masochism. Hauling a boat across the sea ice of Cumberland Sound gives "pleasures that [Moss] can't articulate," but which are remembered as "exhilarating" (47). He is not surprised that so many people are drawn to the "infinite silence" of the North, for in its "austere climate," "apparent emptiness," and "absolute stillness of time," we may discover aspects of ourselves and "intimations of our continuity" with nature (91, 125). Knowing that some consider ecotourism imperialistic (a label he applies to Farley Mowat), Moss brings an occasional native voice into his text. The shaman Uvavnuk (as translated by Rasmussen and Freuchen) sings, "The great sea moves me!" and "The vault of heaven / Moves me!" (156).

Books of this kind are proliferating at an impressive rate. Almost every real or virtual trip to a library discloses new accounts of polar travel, whose numbers now rival those of mountain and desert books. Every conference on exploration and "extreme" travel introduces adventurers with jaw-dropping credentials. At the Banff Mountain Film and Book Festival in 2003, for example, Norwegian Børge Ousland, the first man to reach both Poles unassisted, talked about his new book *Alone Across Antarctica*; he outdid Messner by walking the "Shackleton traverse" *solo*, and then crossed the Patagonia IceCap. One could also hear Hillary's friend George Lowe of the 1953 Everest expedition, Peter Matthiessen, Tashi Tenzing (the grandson of Tenzing Norgay), and others describe their ventures into Great landscapes. There was no doubt in the minds of participants that the interest and the travel will continue to increase. Panelists discussing "The Next Great Projects" mentioned the usual suspects - ascents in Greenland, kayaking around Cape Horn - but two of the five specified mind, imagination, dreams, and spirituality as territory needing to be explored further. All agreed that one should take risks in a "pure" style, and that adventure is far from dying out.

12
Badlands:
Great Space in the Postwar Arts

As first-hand knowledge of "spacious horizons" spread from explorers to the public, verbal and pictorial images of the Great became more common in the arts consumed by a general audience. Powerful narratives and striking pictures can produce both wonder and a strong desire to see for oneself. Books of high-quality photographs, television documentaries, and even "desktop" images on computer screens have brought majestic natural beauty to the global village, and more visitors to parks and wilderness areas. Literature, cinema, and music have taken Great venues as theme or background; scholars discuss their meanings and uses. Thomas Hardy predicted that intellectuals and then tourists would head for areas of "chastened sublimity," which has happened, but representations of those places have also been brought home, one way or another, to many more people. In films such as Australia's *Picnic at Hanging Rock* and England's *Lawrence of Arabia*, powerful landforms are central characters, much as they are in *The Return of the Native*.

Nowhere is there more extensive deployment of Great landscape than in the novel, the preferred literary form of most readers today. In the United States, the free-ranging "western" is a part of the national myth, but quite different cultures have their own "big sky" novels. Haldór Laxness, winner of the 1955 Nobel Prize for Literature, set *Independent People* (*Sjalfstaett fólk*, 1946) on the heaths of his native Iceland in the early twentieth century, though the life depicted seems nearly mediaeval. No later novelist is closer to the spirit of Hardy; characters are shaped by the mighty forms of that cleft rock in the North Atlantic and defined by their responses to it.

241

When the Mistress of Myri, a florid poet, calls its mountains "grand and inspiring," she sounds vacuous (Laxness 24). No one else talks about the mountains, which are just a backdrop to life on the moors where sheep may safely graze and existence is possible. It is "the high heath" that has value for the shepherd Bjartur, and not just practical value: "It was his spiritual mother, his church, ... as the ocean must inevitably be to the seafarer" (86). But he doesn't *gush* over it, though the narrator may.

Bjartur is also a poet, and while he walks over the empty moor "as if ... through infinity," enjoying "true freedom," nothing distracts him from composing verse (Laxness 86). For this purpose "The silence of the moors was perfect," and he feels "perfect ... harmony" there (87). In fact, Bjartur has much better relations with the heath than with any human being, including his daughter Asta Sollilja. When the two make a journey down to the coast, we see the moors through her eyes for the first time. To Asta, they seem wonderfully spacious and "free" at first, though later a bare, windswept plateau, "lonely and grey," has a "chill isolation" (195). Beyond its "dreary monotony," however, appears the ocean, and she is "overwhelmed by the prospect of such infinity" (196). Rain and mist make the return journey a "monotonous eternity": a quality with which "the moors stand in indissoluble communion" (210, 347). Laxness's vision is large and symbolic; autumn rain falls like "everlasting waterfalls between the planets," and the last scene transpires on what are finally admitted to be "the moors of life" (236, 480).

In Search of Myself (1946), the autobiography of German-Canadian novelist Frederick Grove (ch. 8), testifies that oceans and plains wrought powerfully on his imagination. As a boy he lived in Sweden, by the sea, to which he felt drawn. An uncle took him on a trip to northern Russia when he was 18, and what impressed him most was the "vast Kirghiz steppe" (Grove 1946, 149). "The effect of that landscape on me was enormous and enduring ... the steppe changed my whole way of life" (150). After seeing the Sahara and sailing to Canada (whose prairies reminded him of Siberia), he decided that "the sea and the plains" were his only homes (156). The consensus now is that Grove made up his pre-Canada past (Abley 54; Wood 199), but for our purposes it makes little difference. Call it a novel instead of a memoir: Grove still exhibits an affinity for vast barrens, desolate beauty, and the "pure and simple" life to be lived there (1946, 150).

THE DESERT WITHIN: PAUL BOWLES

No one considers Paul Bowles a "representative" postwar American novelist. An expatriate, a link to the Lost Generation (at 21, he called on Gertrude Stein in Paris) and their 1940s counterpart, he wrote "easterns," not westerns, and was a serious composer whose friends included Aaron Copland and Virgil Thompson as well as Gore Vidal and Christopher Isherwood. He was also - in his novel *The Sheltering Sky* (1949) and in stories and poems - an important commentator on the Great. Much has been written about him, ranging from Theodore Solotaroff's essay "The Desert Within" to critical monographs and biographies. It is likely that Bowles's interest in the desert was related to certain aridities of his youth. In his autobiography *Without Stopping* (1972), he describes an intensely lonely and unhappy childhood. Gena Caponi shows how the "barren" Long Island tract-housing developments that supplanted the marshes and meadows he had known affected Bowles's development (15). Gertrude Stein read him at once as a horrible product of the new American suburbs, "a manufactured savage" (Bowles 1972, 119).

Bowles broke away as soon as he could: intellectually via theosophy (a blend of Eastern religions), story-writing, music, and surrealist literature in the Paris journal *transition*; then physically. An ecstatic introduction to the Alps on his first trip to Europe made a wanderer of Bowles, although he placated his parents by doing a year of college, and studied musical composition with Copland. He soon returned to Europe, met Stein, and introduced her to Copland. She suggested that they might find Tangier a congenial place to work. Bowles never forgot his first sight of Africa: the Algerian coast from at sea. Happy and excited, he felt that this was a "magic place" (such as he had always believed he would find) where Nature communicated directly with human consciousness, bypassing the mind (Bowles 1972, 125). The two men rented a cliff-top house in Tangier from which on clear days they could see across to Spain. Bowles travelled in Morocco and Europe, stopping occasionally to compose. In 1932 he wrote a chamber piece based on St John Perse's poem *Anabase* (1924), narrating a journey across the Gobi desert.

He went to North Africa and the Sahara for the winter, travelling by camel for almost a month between oases. This first desert journey was seminal for his literary work later, though he still saw himself as a composer. Bowles returned to America, settling in New York, but distracted by memories of North Africa. (It was Massachusetts, not Algeria, that he described to Gertrude Stein as "desolate country": Caponi 67.) Mexico, he found, offered some horizons comparable to the Sahara's. Bowles was delighted with the "savage landscapes" south of Monterrey, and the "impassable wilderness" of Tehuantepec was "unforgettable" (1972, 198, 201). On a later trip to Mexico, though, he would sit staring at a volcano from his house. "The vastness of the landscape had a paralyzing effect on me," he recalled; as Thomas Mann said, "a great natural spectacle impedes the desire to create" (226). He did compose in an adobe hut that "faced the nothingness to the south," however, and relaxed in a hammock on the veranda, "hanging there in space" (236).

After the war, Bowles began to turn his experiences into stories. (*Without Stopping* relates this development to meeting Jean-Paul Sartre; Bowles obtained the US translation rights to *Huis clos*, taking the title *No Exit* from a sign in the New York subway.) In "Under the Sky" (1946), the "huge high sky" in which lightning flashes dominates sordid doings in a dusty Mexican town; in "Pages from Cold Point" (1947), the "powerful drug" of ocean and sky gives a "feeling of space"; in "The Delicate Prey" (1948), a murderer is buried alive in the Sahara's "infinite wasteland" (Bowles 1979, 77, 91, 171). The story that most closely foreshadows *The Sheltering Sky* is "A Distant Episode" (1947), in which a linguistics professor is taken by nomads, who cut off his tongue and sell him into slavery. At the end he escapes and runs off into the setting sun. In his introduction to the *Collected Stories* (1979), Gore Vidal writes that Bowles saw "the horrors which lie beneath [civilization], as fragile, in its way, as the sky that shelters us from a devouring vastness," and that he "glimpsed what lies back of our sheltering sky ... an endless flux of stars," a "terrible infinity" (8, 9).

Bowles planned *The Sheltering Sky* (its title suggested by a popular song, "Down Among the Sheltering Palms") on a Fifth Avenue bus, but wrote it in North Africa. In the book, three deracinated Americans, Port and Kit Moresby, along with Tunner, go to the Sahara, which seems preferable to a Tangier hotel, with its "visible proof of isolation" (Bowles 1978, 58). They might be refugees from Hemingway's *The Sun Also Rises*, or people Bowles knew in Tangier, but they have the bad luck of the professor in "A Distant Episode." Everything goes wrong: Kit sleeps with Tunner, the Moresbys leave him, Port dies of typhoid fever, Kit runs off with a caravan, becomes a harem wife, is found and returned to Algiers, mad. There she disappears. Robert Nye comments that the desert here "is of the heart; these American wanderers are not confronting any 'primitive' reality not already in their mental luggage" (22). As early as Book One, where "tea in the Sahara" turns out to mean death, we realize that the sky provides as much shelter as a palm tree in a hurricane.

Bowles is said to use words "as if they were notes," deploying phrases "in accord with the principles [of] musical composition" (Nye 22). The theme of his tone poem is ways of seeing nature. At the Moresbys' first vista of the Sahara, Port believes that "the very silences and emptinesses that touched his soul terrified" Kit, and tells her that the sky is "a solid thing up there, protecting us from what's behind" (Bowles 1978, 100-01). Which is "Nothing," he says (101).[1] Imprisoned, Kit finds the sky an "immaculate, vast clarity," but "pitiless"; later she remembers Port's remark, and stares "Unblinking" at the sky's "solid emptiness" (282, 312). Often the problem seems inner, not cosmic. Looking out a window at the desert, Port feels divided from it; rocks and sky are "ready to absolve him," but "in the act of passing into his consciousness, they became impure" (168). As he dies, the sky seems to split open. Eventually Tunner comes to hate the desert as "too powerful," while Kit, travelling with the caravan, sees it as "dead" and "cruel" (251, 275-6).

The Sheltering Sky has been called the classic statement of Bowles's existentialism, making Camus and Sartre look "vague" (Solotaroff 30), but Bowles sustained his interest in the Great as a metaphor of the human condition long past that novel. *Next to Nothing. Collected Poems, 1926-1977* and *Collected Stories, 1939-1976* show that deserts fascinated him for over half a century. Among the poems is an "Elegy" dated 1927, saying farewell to civilization; Bowles was 17. "We are all too late / Everything is finished" sounds conventional, but "We are all unsuited to dwell here in this plain" - years before he first saw the Sahara - does not (Bowles 1981, 10). "Taedium Vitae" (1929) is set in a windy waste with mountains on the horizon: a Dali landscape. "Poem" (1929) pictures negation

---

[1] Compare Jean-Paul Sartre: "Il n'est ni triste ni gai, le désert, l'innombrable néant des sables sous le néant lucide du ciel: il est sinistre" ('The desert is neither sad nor cheerful, the innumerable void of the sands under the clear void of the sky: it is sinister'). *Les Mouches* (*The Flies*), 1947, 190. My translations are enclosed in single quotation marks.

as a desert with "No / Blade of grass" (31). Such images continue through his French poems of the 1930s into the arid mountains of the 1970s: "mountains of the mind" with "blind ravines" in "Etiquette," empty valleys and "Roads of nothing but / sharp pebbles and stones" in "Next to Nothing" (64, 68).

Bowles's shorter prose pieces also use barren wastes as symbols and settings. We have glanced at some early stories, and in "Istikhara, Anaya, Medagan and the Medaganat" (1975), a tale of warfare in the Sahara, "the air, the light, even the sky suggest some as yet unvisited planet" (Bowles 1979, 401). *Their Heads Are Green and Their Hands Are Blue* (1963) is a collection of travel pieces from the 1950s. In a foreword, Bowles writes that "landscape alone" is generally "of insufficient interest to warrant the effort it takes to see it"; human interest is central (1963, vii). Yet he evidently saw more literary potential in some locales than in others. "Africa Minor" (1959) propounds that North Africa "is conducive to reflections upon the nature of the infinite," for "In the arid landscape the sky is the final arbiter" (21-2). No wonder (as Melville liked to point out) the great monotheistic creeds sprang from the desert. Bowles insists on the spiritual power of lonely, austere desolations; "the spell of the vast, luminous, silent country" makes other places seem weak ("Baptism of Solitude," 157-8).

Paul Bowles is an extreme case of the artist drawn back repeatedly to the desert because of some inner quality to which it corresponds or speaks. Several writers on Bowles have explored this issue, drawing on his fiction, poems, and autobiography. *Without Stopping* is a rapid parade of people and places, with few hints of how Bowles regarded them, and an odd disconnect between incident and response. A bohemian freedom is implied, yet he says almost nothing about his love or sex life. There are repetitions and gaps. Haste is pervasive, in the life and in the writing, but whither away? The book is so elliptical, omitting attitudes as well as dates, that one wonders what the sensibility behind it was holding back. For all the movement, the authorial persona of *Without Stopping* seems as bare and arid as a gravel plain.

BIG SKIES

"Western novels" are a diverse lot, culturally and generically. The postwar type was launched in 1947 by two quite different books:

A.B. Guthrie, Jr's *The Big Sky*, an American bestseller, and W.O. Mitchell's *Who Has Seen the Wind*, a success in Canada. Guthrie's book is a well-researched historical novel about the West in the 1830s and '40s, Mitchell's a partly autobiographical story of growing up on the Saskatchewan prairie a century later, but they have in common the central role of Great landscape in the protagonist's development. As in Hardy, vast tracts of empty land are important. In *The Big Sky*, Boone Caudill runs away from a violent, drunken father in Kentucky and goes up the Missouri River on a trading boat. Put ashore to hunt game, he "could see forever" from a hilltop because "It was open country ... without an end. It spread away, ... rolling, going on clear to the sky." Boone is the strong, silent type, yet "It made the heart come up. It made a man little and still big ... this was the way a bird must feel, free and loose" (Guthrie 121). The land and a Blackfeet girl are his emotional constants. Back east he feels "cramped" and smothered; the "West is better" (403, 411, 423).

Who Has Seen the Wind's sensitive young protagonist sees the big sky earlier. Brian is 4 when he first ventures out onto the prairie alone and hears the wind "sighing through great emptiness" (Mitchell 11). The narrator (quoting Psalm 103) tells us that some consider the wind a symbol of God; by the end it stands for life and time as well. Brian does not know all this yet, but he knows that a dead baby pigeon should be buried on the prairie, not among houses, and that the joy of spring is "most exquisite upon the prairie" or when the wind blows (123). Later he notices that the song of the meadowlark makes the prairie seem "suddenly vaster" (103). Huge and empty, "the prairie was forever," like God, and its silence "stretched from everlasting to everlasting" (246-7). Critics have praised Mitchell for his style, ecological consciousness, and willingness to tackle major philosophical questions; what matters here is his choice of a setting that provides "the skeleton requirements, simply, of land and sky," which Mitchell calls "the least common denominator of nature" (3).[2]

These books offer more, of course: the magic of Mitchell's prairie, the pathos of Guthrie's elegies. His old mountain men lament that the "virgin" country of their youth has been ruined by settlers and railroads, though to young Jim it seems as fresh as "the beginning of the world" (Guthrie 74, 251). Neither writer

[2]   McCourt; New 127-8; Ricou 95-6.

was allowed to define the Western, however; each decade brought fresh approaches. William Eastlake, a New Yorker who became a New Mexico rancher, sets *Portrait of an Artist With Twenty-Six Horses* (1958) in the Sangre de Christo range and tries to address the Navajo dilemma: tradition or modernity? The artist is drawn to the city; his mother runs a café in Coyote; his father Twenty-Six Horses lives in a hogan. All wonder whether the old feeling for the land in which they themselves were steeped can last, whether they will still talk to the ground and go up on a mountain to die under the "awful ... and infinite" sky (Eastlake 75). "The earth understands," says the father (24). Once, Eastlake's camera pulls back to show just three men on the "aged invincible earth" (84). Even a white man knows that "in the loneliness of the beautiful land, we were all in love" - with the land (211).

"Deserts of love" came to us from mediaeval European literature, but the American-Canadian novelist Jane Rule's *Desert of the Heart* (1964) is located in Nevada, where the two main characters' responses to desert help define them. Evelyn, who has come from California to Reno to await her divorce, feels "a Catholic desolation" when she first sees the waste, while her young friend Ann, a local, regards "the desolation ... as her inheritance, and love[s] life" (Rule 49, 83). Ann prefers Eliot and Auden to Dylan Thomas or Frost, whose "landscapes suffered in this particular out-of-doors" (117). For her, arid land is "the simple truth about the world," now that "The earth's given out" (118). Evelyn demurs, but admits, "I live in the desert of the heart," and takes to admiring Ann's beauty to distract her from the real desert's "terrors" (124-5). Out of the 23rd Psalm, Dante, and Yeats she constructs a "hollow woman prayer"; its refrain is "unless I can dwell in the desert forever" (128-9). The mood is Bowlesian, with less sky. As Evelyn moves toward Ann, she adopts her view of the desert, which she (fondly) imagines man's "genius for destruction" will not alter (229).

Edward Abbey's *The Monkey Wrench Gang* (1975), an energetic novel with an activist agenda, shows the extent of Evelyn's naïveté. Abbey, who had made his anti-development position clear in *Desert Solitaire* (ch. 9), sends four ecological guerrillas to blow up bridges and tracks, knock out power lines, and sabotage other industrial works that are ruining their beloved desert. It is a witty, playful book - unless you are a contractor or construction worker - but beneath the antic vandalism is a deep feeling for the desert in its natural state and against all possible "improvements." Abbey's

"Lawrence of Arizona" fantasy is optimistic about these activities: the gang is quite successful until they are caught, and at the end people whom they do not know have begun to imitate their tactics elsewhere (since the novel was published, a number of ecological militants have in fact attacked developments on natural sites). In Annie Proulx's *Close Range. Wyoming Stories* (1999), one character calls himself "a monkey-wrencher, a hard man who would hammer a spike into a tree without hesitation" (224). He does so because "They've wrecked the west, they're wrecking the world," and force is all they understand. Abbey's gang agree.

Robert Kroetsch's novel *Badlands* (1975) presents a symbolic landscape that Eliot, Bowles, and Rule would recognize. It narrates two journeys into the Alberta badlands: archaeologist William Dawe's hunt for dinosaur bones in 1916, and his daughter Anna's search for her past in 1972. The whole book, then, is a quest for the past, in country like a "vast, empty grave," under "the blank prairie sky" (Kroetsch 40, 49). *Badlands* is a highly land-conscious novel, some characters having a strong sense of place and little other sense at all. Most members of Dawe's expedition are chthonic, earth-dwelling: McBride emerging from the river mud like a reptile; the coal miner who just stays down; the old Chinaman arising as if "a chunk of the earth itself stood up"; Tune; and Dawe, whose humped back is "like a butte, the land itself ... come hunching down to the shore" (120, 56). Whatever the land is, for good or ill, these people are. Temperance is a "virtue, parched as the desert and pure," yet a prison has been built in the badlands on the theory that "hell should be constructed in hell" (69, 76).

Much in the text supports the latter image. The blank sky of the expedition's start becomes a "failed sky" with a "broken sun" (Kroetsch 133). Anna Dawe remarks that "the sun shines in hell too," and thinks that Dawe lost his humanity in the badlands (263). The men come to resemble the objects of their quest, dinosaurs, "bones bleaching in this blaze of sun" - especially Dawe, his injured leg encased in plaster after a fall into Cretaceous earth (189). Yet there is more to the badlands than this: moments of beauty, a sense of encountering great power, even a transcendent reality, generating a dreamlike quality. "A man could get hurt here," as Web says, but in and beyond the pain there is learning (40). Like Doughty in Arabia, Dawe's "desert agony" is a struggle with something bigger than life and more important than suffering (152). At the end the two Annas walk to the river's source - glacial lakes in the Rocky Mountains -

and there finally lay down the burden of the past. Kroetsch's work as a whole has been called "one of the most forceful expressions of human solitude" in Canadian prairie novels, solitude being what seekers of the Great often find.[3]

"Big-sky novels" by popular authors - Tony Hillerman, Larry McMurtry, Cormac McCarthy - have become a staple of American fiction. They seldom devote much time to scenery, which is simply a context for action. In Hillerman's *Coyote Waits* (1990), sacred rocks are crucial to the plot and several characters are sensitive to the desert. The Ship Rock country lifts Jim Chee's spirits at sunset: "Beautiful," he thinks (Hillerman 102). Joe Leaphorn tells a professor that "an immensity" of grasslands and mountain ranges is "The heartland of the Navajos," their "Holy Land" (202-3). Both then watch the vast landscape in reverent silence. Similarly, McCarthy's *All the Pretty Horses* (1992) emits a strong sense of Texan and Mexican land as great and old, dwarfing the characters - 50 miles of plain, 100 miles of cordillera - but most responses are felt or implied rather than stated. The night sky is the most moving natural phenomenon for the characters, as for the first admirers of the sublime. Grady and Rawlins lie on a road watching "stars falling down the long black slope of the firmament" as they talk of other things (McCarthy 26). At the end, Grady rides across a plain into a "bloodred sunset" like a movie hero (302).

Great tracts of empty land and wide skies also dominate humans and their works, setting limits to action, in Annie Proulx's stories of Wyoming, *Close Range* (1999). The "great harsh sweep of wind" over wild and "indifferent" country "provokes a spiritual shudder" and often seems sad or desolate (Proulx 99). Yet many of her characters find it addictive, like Jimmy, who went away to California for a few years but "missed Wyoming, its hardness imprinted on him," and came back, "maybe suffering some perverse need for animosity" ("A Lonely Coast," 190). Driving over the mountains and into Casper at night is like coming down to "a lonely coast" with wind instead of water - though "the water was here once" (203). As in the eighteenth century, the sublime is often nocturnal. In "Pair a Spurs," Batts remembers lying outside at night to watch a comet: "Beautiful. Terrible" (163). Proulx contributed an appreciative note to the paperback reissue of Laxness's *Independent People*.

---

[3]   Ricou 135. Dorothy Seaton (1991) argues that Kroetsch's badlands represent the fragmentation of discourse.

LONELY BUT FREE: POETIC VOYAGES

The Great was also a subject or a tool in verse, with Hardy's "chastened sublimity" often the mood. Some pre-war poets returned to the subject afterwards. In the 1930s W.H. Auden had written of mountains, metaphorical deserts, and Iceland; in 1949 he gave the lectures that became *The Enchaféd Flood. The Romantic Iconography of the Sea* (1950), exploring the origins of some important metaphors. "The Sea and the Desert" (taking its epigraph from Doughty's *Adam Cast Forth*) surveys what those two areas have symbolized. Both are wildernesses where a solitary can be free, like the cowboy in "Tumbling Tumbleweeds": "Lonely but free I'll be found."[4] There are, however, significant differences between them. The sea is "primitive potential power," the Alpha of life; the desert is Omega, and "an image of modern civilisation," the "desert of the average" (Auden 1950, 20, 26). As in Auden's poems, cities are "mechanised deserts" (29). *The Enchaféd Flood* is one of several postwar attempts to make critical sense of the Great, including Mircea Eliade's *The Sacred and the Profane* (1957) and Marjorie Hope Nicolson's *Mountain Gloom and Mountain Glory* (1959).

Auden's history-of-ideas poem "Mountains" (1954) runs the gamut of feelings about heights. The ancients did not (and serious people do not) rejoice in mountains, it says, for climbers, though "Spiritual," serve a dubious god (Auden 1991, 560). Yet the speaker considers their world "a fine refuge ... / ... Where the nearest person who could have me hung is / Some ridges away" (561). Up there, in the right conditions, he could be happy for five minutes - although "Five minutes on even the nicest mountain / Are awfully long" (562). Here Auden sounds like Leslie Stephen: playful, misanthropic, elusive.

Another work by a major poet of the pre-war era published that year takes a different kind of unworldliness farther. "A Clear Day and No Memories," one of Wallace Stevens's last poems, is an exercise in absolute subtraction. Since "the air is clear" we should have distant horizons, but the speaker keeps telling us what is *not* to be seen or known: there are "No soldiers in the scenery," we have "No thoughts of people now dead," and the air "has no knowledge except of nothingness" (W. Stevens 475). Minimalist or

---

4   The famous Sons of the Pioneers song was written by Canadian-born Bob Nolan about 1934 and sung in several films.

Buddhist, the poem wants to see through the "shallow spectacle" around us to the Void beyond, which seems to be less the terrifying nullity of Pascal and Baudelaire, the *néant* of the Symbolists and existentialists, than the whole Truth and nothing but the Truth. There is a venerable tradition of reading the Great as a higher, transcendant reality (see "Reality" in the Lexicon).

Most modern poems that use the Great in some way - Archibald MacLeish's "Voyage to the Moon" (1969), for instance, or Gwendolyn MacEwen's "Terror and Erebus" (1987), on the search for the Franklin Expedition - feel slight alongside Nikos Kazantzakis' *The Odyssey. A Modern Sequel*, composed before the war and translated into English in 1958. Kazantzakis, best known outside Europe for *Zorba the Greek*, worked on his epic for a dozen years, bringing in much non-Homeric material, such as later treatments of Odysseus, and real-life travel. Like Dante's and Tennyson's, his hero is the archetypal wanderer. Dissatisfied with his long-sought home, Ithaka, he sets off again, to Sparta, Crete, Egypt. After serving a prison term for rebellion, Odysseus, who is evolving from savagery to spirituality, travels to the source of the Nile, founds an ideal city, and becomes a famous ascetic. Death "knocks him down" (for the first time) as he travels south in Book 19, after which the action becomes increasingly allegorical.

Allowed by Death to continue, Odysseus reaches the ocean, builds a coffin-skiff, and sails south. Passing the rocks of Yes and No (a nod to Thomas Carlyle?), he climbs an island mountain and sees before him "an endless, mastless, sterile sea" (Kazantzakis Book 22: line 308). Despite a storm, he yells with joy, "for now he knew he liked much better than all joys, / than even the act of love, to roam at the world's end" (22: 337-8). Laughing, crying farewell to the world, and calling God "a labyrinthine quest deep in our heads" and in our hearts' "wide waterways," Odysseus sails into the Antarctic Ocean (22: 414, 419). When his skiff is wrecked on an iceberg, he swims to a land which, despite icy rocks and "the inhuman silence of the snows," has a hot spring and birds: a reprise of the quaint theory of warm polar regions used by Poe (22: 501). As the sun sets for the winter, he finds a native igloo village such as occurs in the Arctic. There is no joy here, only survival, but Kazantzakis revels in the scenery: stars like icicles above desolate snowfields, hunters looking for seals in a green sea.

In the spring an earthquake smashes the ice and all perish except Odysseus. He does not hope to escape Death; rather, like Scott's Titus

Oates, he seeks the right time and place to die. Paddling towards icebergs, Odysseus expires in a "vast solitude" of "icy wastes," but so gradually, over hundreds of lines, that it is not clear when (Kazantzakis 23: 187, 312). He contrasts the "white wretched bitterness" around him with Mediterranean warmth and his old life there, communes with the elements, and says his goodbyes (23: 358). In the pale light of a lingering dawn he finally dies, "and ancient Mother Silence spread her brooding wings / on the world's wastes as she had done before Life arose" (23: 1143-4). Odysseus merges into a scene all white and crystal, snow and ice. In Book 24, his mind becomes a vast landscape upon which many people he has known recapitulate his life and help him on his final voyage aboard an icy death ship: Kazantzakis maintaining his polar iconography to the end.

MON PAYS, C'EST L'HIVER: MUSIC

Wintriness and other aspects of the Great have also figured in the work of a number of modern composers. The most distinguished of them, Ralph Vaughan Williams, showed an early interest in representing the ocean musically, though *A Sea Symphony* (1910) focuses on Walt Whitman's poetry rather than the sea itself, being an oratorio, not a tone poem like Debussy's *La Mer*. Commissioned to write the score for the film *Scott of the Antarctic* in 1947, Williams read Cherry-Garrard and other polar books; again his stimulus was literature. Though appalled by evidence of Scott's poor organization and dubious decisions, he was fascinated by the acoustic potential of the scenery, and wrote most of the music even before seeing the script. Less than half of it was used in the 1948 film, however: what Williams saw as tragic the director wanted to make heroic. Sombre sections (e.g. "Doom" and "The Deaths of Evans and Oates") were either shortened or omitted. What the studio liked were playful or determined movements like "Penguin Dance" and "Pony March," and the Elgar-like pomp of the "End Titles" music.

Williams reworked the score as the basis of his 7th symphony (*Sinfonia Antartica*, 1953), drawing on written accounts, expedition photographs, cinema images, and literary allusions.[5] The brooding

---

[5] My account of the two works is indebted to Michael Kennedy's liner notes for the Angel recording of the 7th Symphony (S-36763, n.d.), and for the Chandos recording of *The Film Music of Ralph Vaughan Williams* (CHAN 10007, 2002).

Prelude (whose epigraph is from Shelley's *Prometheus Unbound*) introduces a portentous rising theme, a wordless women's chorus, and a wind machine - shades of Holst and Grofé - all of which return in the Epilogue. As in every movement, something tries to rise from the depths in ominous passages, usually for the lower strings and winds. The Scherzo is quite different: a jolly, bustling piece representing the voyage to Antarctica, though even here the heaving of the deep is heard, and violins imitate the wind. An epigraph from Coleridge's "Hymn Before Sunrise in the Vale of Chamouni" prefaces Landscape, a slow movement by turns quiet and strident, beautiful and foreboding. Williams spreads the instruments across several octaves to suggest vastness; then brings on a ponderous walking bass as the pole party slogs on. Distant trumpets segue into a quiet, lyric Intermezzo.

The Epilogue (its epigraph from Scott's last journal entry) is a march that begins with a fanfare, but is shot through with uneasiness. The music keeps building and falling; efforts to get something started fragment; nothing lasts long. Deep bass again warns of trouble on the way. The march and hero-theme (from the Prelude) finally give way to a wind machine and wordless voices, dying away to *niente*, nothing, as at the end of Holst's "Neptune" in *The Planets*. Williams and Antarctica, unencumbered by directors and studios, have their way.

Growing up in New England, American composer Alan Hovhaness hiked in the White Mountains, and one of his earliest scores (Op. 2, 1931) tries to represent a "Storm on Mount Wildcat" with drums and brass. After a trip to explore his Armenian roots, he called his Symphony #2 "Mysterious Mountain" (1955). Later symphonies have more explicit titles: #7 is "Nanga Parvat" (now usually rendered Nanga Parbat: one of the first big challenges of Himalayan mountaineering); and #14, "Ararat" in Armenia, traditionally Noah's first landfall. Settling in the Pacific Northwest, he named symphonies for "Mount St Helens" (1984) and "Glacier Peak" (1991). His draft program notes for the former show an interest in geology: "Ever since 1966 ... I have loved the Cascade and Olympic Mountains. ... in my childhood I climbed many times the mountains of New Hampshire, and I loved those ancient worn-down mountains .... Now I live between the young volcanic

Cascade Mountains and the oceanic Olympic Mountains ... and I find inspiration from [their] tremendous energy."[6]

The musical treatment of these subjects varies over time. The printed score of "Nanga Parvat" describes the "Kashmir Mountain of 26,000 feet" as "serene, majestic, aloof, terrible in storm, forever frozen in treeless snow. The name means 'Without Trees.' It is one of the world's most dangerous and difficult mountains to climb."[7] The first movement represents the "Tiger-like ferocity of Himalayan Mountains," and the third, the "Grandeur of mountains at sunset." In the early "Mysterious Mountain," the first movement features slow, homophonic progressions of block chords in the strings or horns over a plucked bass. The winds sometimes sound "mysterious," but the middle movement, a double fugue, and the final movement, with its slow chordal passages, have no obvious connection to mountains outside of the composer's mind. Certainly there is no word- or scene-painting as in Borodin, Strauss, or Grofé.

The later symphonies are more representational. "Mount St Helens" is a kind of "Surprise Symphony." The first two movements again offer string or wind chords moving over a plucked bass, with the odd solo. They have a soporific sameness, giving a sense that not much is happening. Then, after some broad, concordant gestures in the "Volcano" movement, a bash on the kettledrum, a roll of timpani, and crashing cymbals announce the great eruption of May 1980. Blaring horns and kettledrum solos lead to loud, sustained cacophony, but, in time, hymnlike chords and pealing bells conquer the drums. Peace and order allow new life to begin. "Hymn to Glacier Peak," his most successful "program" piece, is more subtle. Open, rather grand chords for strings, horns, or both support the idea of a "hymn," while the orchestral fugue of the last movement, with its "peaking" shape - overlapping rises and falls - probably comes as near as music can to depicting the skyline of a long mountain range.

Canada's 'few acres of snow' (Voltaire) have entered its music in various forms. In 1964 the Québec poet/singer Gilles Vigneault published a popular song that begins "Mon pays, ce n'est pas un pays, c'est l'hiver."[8] It soon became almost a Québec hymn. The

---

6   Quoted from the booklet accompanying Telarc CD-80604.

7   *Symphony #7 for Wind Orchestra*. New York: Peters, 1960.

8   In *Avec les vieux mots*, 1964: 'My country is not a country, it is winter.'

human is subsumed by the natural: the singer's 'path is not a path / It is snow'; his father built a house 'In the white ceremony / Where the snow marries the wind.' Even his garden is a plain, a "grand pays solitaire" where Vigneault, full of the widespread political anguish of the '60s, cries that his country is the wrong way around.

Another product of 1960s Canada, R. Murray Schafer says that he conceived the idea for his symphony *North/White* while flying over the "spectacular and terrifying" Arctic, but he is usually less concerned with snow than with wilderness in general (Mulhallen 134). For him, Canadian music ought to have a natural dimension. The string quartet *Waves* takes the interval between wave crests as its unit of time. "Environmental music" such as *Music for Wilderness Lake*, nursing its "vital spark of space and land," is to be performed at specified locations, usually outside, not in concert halls (147, 135). Schafer tries to blur the art/nature boundaries: in *And Wolf Shall Inherit the Moon*, also known as "the Wolf Project" and the Epilogue of the *Patria* cycle, participants - who are creators, actors, audience, and everything else - camp out for eight days (Schafer 271).

THE SOLACE OF OPEN SPACES

Prose fiction, whose great scope and power to create and maintain images over an expanse of time have given it broad appeal, remained the major literary purveyor of Great landscape, in such volume that only a few titles in English can be considered here. Australia, with its border of arable country around a huge desert outback, has produced many relevant works. Several of Patrick White's novels explore the "possibility of a relationship with a landscape" too formidable for comfort (1978, 3). A person may be drawn to a desolate place "by something solitary and arid, akin to his own nature" (Austin in *A Fringe of Leaves*), or simply dropped there to struggle with external nature (1978, 188). In *The Tree of Man* (1955), White suggests a correlation between empty land, empty sky, and the inner "void" or "nothing" of Amy and Ray: another *néant* (1975, 338, 397). His people view simplicity as both inner and outer, the surrounding wilderness as metaphorical. Perhaps, they think, life is a passage through "the great deserts of human and divine injustice" to the "desert of progress" (1975, 50, 417). Some characters merge with the land as place names or "grow from the landscape with the trees," sharing a "communion of soul and scene" (1975, 490, 420).

In *Voss* (1957), based on journals of Australian exploration, desert metaphors take over.[9] There is a "desert of mortification and reward" outside decent society (both part of "the desert of earthly experience"), and there are "deserts of conscience" (White 1981, 74, 423, 440). For Laura, Voss *is* a desert, "vast and ugly," which is "why you are fascinated by the prospect of desert places," she tells him, "in which you will find your own situation taken for granted, or ... exalted" (87-8). He wanders through an objective correlative of his own nature, then, but the phenomenon is larger. The Bonner house is a desert during Laura's illness; the friendship of Laura and Belle is "an umbrella in the middle of the desert" of society (437). The lure of real deserts for men such as Voss has only a minor role here. Brendan Boyle sees that "the apparent poverty of one's surroundings ... proves in the end to be the attraction," and that desert travel is a metaphor: "to explore the depths of one's own repulsive nature is more than irresistible - it is necessary" (167). For Voss, deserts are places where one can "discard the inessential and ... attempt the infinite" (35). The core emotion of contact with the Great is this existential winnowing.

Set in northern Australia and also based on travel books, Randolph Stow's *To the Islands* (1958) begins with old Heriot heading out into the bush, thinking that he has killed a man. He has not, but his flight shows what effect this land has on different people. When Dixon goes to a hilltop looking for Heriot, "the country filled his eyes, beauty struck at him, and in a strange stillness of mind he recognized it" (Stow 99). The searchers traverse "a strange country of austerity and luxuriance" (141). Heriot himself wakes up among aboriginals, remembers walking past cliffs and boulders, "the debris of vast and ancient landslides," and feels "simple" and "bare" (131). Near the end of his purgative journey he loves "nothing but the constant sky" (189). At last Heriot wanders onto cliffs above the western sea, called the "Ultimate" (203). There are no islands in sight ("to the islands" means "to die"), so he settles down in a cave to wait. Throughout, the wilderness serves as arbiter and observer of an old man's struggle with the meaning of his life.

Deserts are the alpha and omega of Bruce Chatwin's impressionistic tale of Australia. *The Songlines* (1987) is presented

---

9   The King Penguin edition (1981) says that Voss is a version of Lud-wig Leichhardt. Geoff Dutton, in *The Hero as Murderer* (1967), instead nominates Simon Eyre, the subject of Francis Webb's poem "Eyre All Alone," in *Socrates* (1961).

as a travel book, but given how freely (we are told) Chatwin treated his experiences, it belongs here with the fiction. "Songlines" are aboriginal "dreaming-tracks": walkabout narratives and mental maps from the old (dream) time. As a young man, Chatwin had eye trouble for which "long horizons" were prescribed, so he went to the Sudan, where his immediate "sense of homecoming" launched him upon a career as a wanderer (17-18). The scholarly mediaeval traveller Ibn Khaldun and sojourns in "dry places" taught him that our species' youth was spent in deserts, where "the great monotheisms" were born (19). We may have been at our best and happiest there, "closer to the First State"; perhaps "greener pastures pall on us" because we were designed for desert walking (196, 162). But the flat, treeless waste of central Australia *should* have been settled by "people who could cope with wide horizons," not by islanders "afraid of space," says Arkady, his guru, who insists that the world "has an ascetic future" - if any (128, 133).

Elsewhere, the British-Canadian writer Malcolm Lowry turned his experiences of Canada, Mexico, and the sea into the stories of *Hear Us O Lord From Heaven Thy Dwelling-Place* (1961). In "The Bravest Boat," about a toy canoe that floats on the Pacific for twelve years, the narrator is fascinated by the idea of its "absolute loneliness amid those wastes, those wildernesses, of rough rainy seas ... the whole vast moon-driven expanse like the pastures and valleys and snow-capped ranges of a Sierra Madre in delirium"; and of its sailing past "giant pinnacles, images of barrenness and desolation, upon which the heart is impaled eternally!" (Lowry 22). The last phrase recurs in "Through the Panama" as Sigbjørn Wilderness - Lowry's alter ego - describes "the inconceivable loneliness and desolate beauty of the interminable Mexican coast" (35). Wilderness is obsessed with inner-outer correspondences: "hangover within and without," negotiating a topographic Passage and an "important spiritual passage," et cetera (74). He reappears in "Present Estate of Pompeii," where life is compared to the "desolation" of "eternally wading through ... *The Waste Land*" (188). For Lowry and his persona, alcoholism was triggered by cultural sterility.

Metaphorical deserts reminiscent of Auden's haunt the early books of John Fowles, the rising star of English novelists in the 1960s. Miranda in *The Collector* describes herself and G.P. as "Two people in a desert, trying to find both themselves and an oasis where they can live together" (Fowles 1973, 205). Nicholas in *The Magus*, deprived of the women he covets, fears an "emotional desert" or "wasteland of days" (1979, 563, 643). In *The French Lieutenant's Woman*, a long evening of being "bored in company" is a desert (1970, 94). So it is not surprising that *Daniel Martin* (1976) has a chapter set at Palmyra, an oasis in Syria's stony desert, where metaphor and reality dovetail. Daniel, "a man driving through nothingness," finds in the scene (a "vast plain" and "endless ruins") a symbol of his relationship with Jane (1977, 587). In the hotel he tells her harshly, "We're sitting surrounded by what you did to us"; he and she have "learnt nothing all these years. Except how to make deserts even more barren" (590). Palmyra's ruins seem to him an "inexorable commentary" on inner ones (606).

The extraterrestrial deserts of Frank Herbert's *Dune* novels have a much different valuation, closer to that of earthly travellers such as Doughty and Thesiger. The books focus on Arrakis (Dune), "the desert planet," and its native Fremen: "free men," Bedu, whose language draws heavily on Arabic (*erg, hajj, jihad, ramadan,* and many other terms in the glossary). The protagonist, Paul Atreides or Muad'dib, combines aspects of a Greek hero, the Prophet Mohammed, a Mahdi (saviour), and Lawrence of Arabia. The films made from the books derive much of their power from desert images. Like other creators of imaginary worlds, Herbert worked out Dune thoroughly - location in the universe, royal houses, language, geography, and so on - but his attention to ecological issues is striking. The first book, *Dune* (1965), has an appendix on "The Ecology of Dune" that articulates a familiar terrestrial truth: "freedom diminishes as numbers increase" (F. Herbert, 493). Dune's "planetologist" observes that an ecological "Law of the Minimum" constrains life and growth (138). But the hardships of Arrakis also promote the life of the spirit: Paul, like Doughty, understands that "hard times" develop the psyche, and the Fremen/Bedu take wisdom from the desert, which teaches them to "waste not" (162, 16).

Of the modern Canadian writers - Margaret Atwood, Rudy Wiebe, Al Purdy[10] - who have brought the Great into their books

---

[10] In Purdy's *North of Summer* (1967), "Northwest Passage" ruminates on Arctic history, especially early explorers such as Frobisher, while "Trees at the Arctic Circle" admires the minimal existence of Baffin Island's dwarf willows. "Tent Rings" presents the Arctic as "the land where nothing changes": the old note of preservation (Purdy 88). There are other relevant poems in *Sex and Death*, *The Stone Bird*, and *Piling Blood*. See also Atwood, "Death By Landscape" in *Wilderness Tips*; and Wiebe, *Playing Dead: A Contemplation Concerning the Arctic*.

in various guises, Farley Mowat has made the most substantial contribution. His wrenching stories of Inuit who live(d) in harmony with nature, and the whites who blindly and arrogantly ruin their lives, make up *The Snow Walker* (1975), a work that has been unduly neglected. Perhaps the motion picture of the same title, which draws on several stories in the volume, will finally bring the book the attention it deserves.

The title story sits in the middle, casting shadows over the whole collection. The Snow Walker is death; a member of a starving band who leaves camp to spare the others, like She Who Walked, is met by the Snow Walker. In the following story, "Walk Well, My Brother" (the focus of the film), an insolent white bush pilot and a tubercular Inuit woman try to survive a forced landing on the tundra. He feels a "chill of dismay" at the "measureless horizon ... more intimidating" than any piloting problem (Mowat 1977, 138). Charlie is modern mechanical man, alienated from the land though moved by it; Konala, initially despised as a "Husky," teaches him the skills he needs to survive before she dies. "The Blinding of André Maloche" is another survival story, in which Inuit save a white from dying on the tundra, though later twists move it beyond the adventure category. In his introductory essay, "Snow," Mowat notes that all the northern circumpolar peoples treat snow as an ally, but know that when conditions become too harsh, some - starting with the old - have to "walk out" (like Oates) or use the "Noose of Release" (82). Where whites are in charge, their ignorance leads to abuses of power such as the Hudson Bay Company's notorious uprooting of Cape Dorset Inuit in 1934 ("The Dark Odyssey of Soosie").

In that context, the title of Gretel Ehrlich's *The Solace of Open Spaces* (1985; see also ch. 9) sounds ironic, and indeed the book is full of inner tensions. Her Wyoming - like other high plains and desert mountains - is beautiful, silent, arid, and clean, but wildness is going, she says, where wilderness went, a victim of farmers' fences and ranchers' wire. Dim wits such as darken Mowat's Arctic also live here, manners are crude, and drought may be internal as well as external. Seamus Heaney wrote that the richest knowledge of landscape is a marriage of geographical country with "the country of the mind" (132). This seems to work better for Ehrlich than it does for settlers frightened of space and determined to defend against it; the "solace of open spaces" is hers, not theirs (Ehrlich 15). Wyoming can be harsh, indifferent, humbling, yet the whole panoply of the Great is there: deserts, mountains, the heavens, and in winter even an "Arctic seascape" (74). Barrenness and grandeur keep company still.

Even at this length, the literary material is far from exhausted; as in baseball, the lines of play theoretically extend to infinity but are interrupted by pragmatic walls. We could still profitably discuss William Golding's novels; some plays of Harold Pinter, who employs Great space to symbolize the human condition in *Landscape* and *No Man's Land*; the protagonist of Joan Didion's *Play It as It Lays*, who imagines driving out to the desert, "into the hard white empty core of the world" (Didion 161); or several anthologies of recent years, which have revived many half-forgotten works. Steven Gilbar's *Natural State … California Nature Writing* (1998; see ch. 10), for example, contains much relevant material: Henry Miller on his fears that a human invasion will overwhelm the Pacific coast in *Big Sur and the Oranges of Hieronymous Bosch*; Jack Kerouac on mountain-climbing with Gary Snyder, from *The Dharma Bums*; Edward Abbey's and Gary Nabhan's warnings about southern California's insatiable thirst; James Houston's vision of tectonic plates as a fractured human skull in *Continental Drift*; Ken Nunn's attack on greedy developers in *Tapping the Source*, and so on. But every inquiry must stop at some point, once the main lines are clear, and we have now reached that point.

Conclusion:
Too Many of Us?

The first volume of this study examined Thomas Hardy's theory about modern responses to nature. In *The Return of the Native*, he argues that the "chastened sublimity" of Egdon Heath is "perfectly accordant with man's nature" *now*, appealing to a "recently learnt emotion" - perhaps what he later called "the ache of modernism." Hardy hypothesizes a shift in "our" - someone's - aesthetics of nature: "The new Vale of Tempe may be a gaunt waste in Thule"; ancient Greece's lush standard of natural beauty is being replaced by sparser scenes. But is this culture-specific, or global? He mentions that "our race when it was young" disliked "gaunt wastes." Are we to read *species* for "race"? Or *Europeans*? In any case, Hardy predicts that this change, if it has not already occurred, will come soon for "the more thinking among mankind," and that "ultimately ... the commonest tourist" will prefer Iceland, high mountains, and northern beaches to neat spas and green parks.

Investigating the historical part of this idea in *The Road to Egdon Heath* required excursions into religion, philosophy, the history of science, and literature (including travel books). With the help of historians of ideas such as Archibald Geikie, Alexandre Koyré, and Marjorie Hope Nicolson, I derived Hardy's "Thulean" sensibility from Burke's "Sublime," Addison's "Great," and the strain of seventeenth-century science and cosmology that Nicolson called "the aesthetics of the infinite." And there proved to be considerable evidence among poets and travellers in support of the phenomenon to which Hardy pointed.

To evaluate Hardy's prediction about future tastes in landscape, however, I have had to launch out on my own. Few scholars have worked in this area: the subject overflows disciplinary boundaries, and parts of it belong as much to popular culture as to any of the "higher" studies. This is no reason to shy away, though; Hardy addressed his remarks to the general public, and in scholarship a topic must be followed where it leads. This one has exhibited a life of its own, taking directions that would have surprised Hardy, as they have me. I did not originally expect to find myself discussing Buddhism, ecology, overpopulation, or the *fragility* of the Great (once considered far above human reach). Yet it was in those directions that the road *beyond* Egdon Heath has led.

Hardy's predictions were, I think, partly correct. Some at least of "the more thinking among mankind" (e.g. Muir, Doughty, Nansen, Foucauld, Bell, the Lawrences, Stark, Sayre, Messner, Krakauer) *have* sought out "Thule," along with a great many other less extraordinary people. You must now make reservations for the world's more popular trails, climbs, and wilderness excursions, as well as for hotels. "The commonest tourist" *does* roam Iceland and the Alps - and Everest, and the Sahara, and the poles - with enough folks left over to fill the parklands and resorts. Among the developments that Hardy did not foresee in 1878 were the pace of population increase, the spread of prosperity through a growing middle class, the cheapening of a far-flung system of transportation (including air travel), and the rise of private companies that escort clients into the wild. Tastes in nature have not so much shifted their centre as broadened to include the whole spectrum of travel.

In the century and a quarter since Hardy wrote, all kinds of travel - business, science, education, tourism, "ecotourism," adventure - have increased hugely to both Tempe and Thule. Business people go where profits are to be made, in Arabia or the Amazon; scientists study rainforests or Antarctic diatoms. Glossy brochures offer cruises to the Caribbean or Alaska, birding in Costa Rica or Norway, kayaking in Tonga or Greenland, hiking in Venezuela or Tibet. All this would probably have confirmed Hardy in his belief that inherited notions of natural beauty were at least making room for a more austere ideal. The principle may operate incompletely and slowly - he said that it would reach some before others - but it *is* operating. The "exclusive reign" of "orthodox beauty," as he cautiously put it, has ended.

Hardy erred most widely in thinking that people would go to the world's barrens in a spirit of melancholy, seeking the balm of a kindred sombreness for their *Angst*. This was not true of many nineteenth-century travellers (Lyell, Darwin, Fromentin, Tyndall), and it was even less true in the twentieth, during which Gloom fell from 9th place to 17th as a response to Great venues (see Lexicon). Most of those who sojourned in the Great went in a mood of excitement, adventure, and discovery, as did Nansen, Amundsen, Scott, and Shackleton in high latitudes, Thor Heyerdahl and Tim Severin at sea. Joy is a prominent emotion among mountaineers from Conway, Smythe, and Shipton through Herzog, Hillary and Tenzing to Messner and Habeler. When conditions are adverse the mood darkens, of course, but as a rule it recovers as fortunes improve. Among desert travellers one does find some escapism, world-rejection, even misanthropy; parts of Doughty, Bell, and Thesiger can be read in this way. But even of them, that is a narrow interpretation, ignoring their many good times, and it is wholly inadequate to describe Eberhardt, Austin, Krutch, Abbey, and other modern desert travellers.

Clearly we cannot limit ourselves to Hardy's words in deciding whether "orthodox [natural] beauty" is *passé*. Besides what he misconstrued or did not foresee, he speaks about this development so broadly as to suggest that it might be universal. Did he intend it so, or was he thinking only of England? Differences between languages, cultures, and sexes are ignored; nor have I been able to do more than provide a certain amount of data relevant to those questions. There is some material here from Continental Europe (mostly France and Scandinavia), America, and the Commonwealth, but very little by societies farther from Hardy's Anglocentre.[1] Fewer women than men appear in this book, though more than in the first, as attitudes and opportunities broadened somewhat. Exactly how and why their views differ from the men's, I have not presumed to say. Some recent (male) anthropology suggests that men like wide horizons, while women prefer enclosures or refuges (Bourassa 82; Flores 22-4). I am wary of any explanation that smacks of determinism, but socio-biological factors may well be involved here. Systematic comparisons of culture, language, and gender remain "matters for further study."

Setting Hardy aside, then, what has it all meant? At the broadest level, to accept "Thule" is to assimilate, or at least come to terms with, the great barren spaces "where man is not" (Blake); to move "from desolation to splendour," in Tippett and Cole's formulation.

---

[1]   Yi-Fu Tuan writes that China saw the shift from religious to aesthetic attitudes towards nature observable in western culture, and comments that "harsh environments" encourage "perceptual acuity" (1974, 70-1, 77).

In the nineteenth century the Great was a battleground of science and religion, whether one went there looking for God's handiwork, a substitute god, information, or excitement - or just stayed home and thought about it. Interest in and exploration of landscapes defined as "Great" accelerated markedly in the twentieth century; tourist travel to them increased sharply. Many have argued, and many more have agreed, that these "waste lands" should be protected and studied, i.e. that they have something to do with us after all, and are fragile, which has much to do with us. We are still trying to understand and agree on exactly what that connection is, a metaphorical as well as an empirical effort. This is where the aesthetics of particular places becomes important. The most interesting part of this project has been the interplay of ideas, qualities, concerns, and emotions raised by or projected onto Great landscape over three centuries.

In *The Road to Egdon Heath*, responses to the Great are arranged in a "Lexicon" that sets out their affiliations and usages. The subsequent fortunes of these reactions are in some cases telling. It is to be expected that Vastness and Barrenness would be among the most frequent remarks both early and late: these are defining characteristics of the Great. One might say the same of Solitude (since Great landscapes are thinly populated), though its rise from 8th place in early texts to 3rd place probably shows how this quality is noticed or prized in a more crowded world. Beyond that we should take nothing for granted. That these areas are often perceived as possessing Grandeur is in line with Addison's manifesto. Grandeur's fall from 1st (early) to 6th (late) may reflect the kind of modern disillusion that Hardy posited, or fatigue with a word perceived as too ringing, but is less dramatic than the crash of Sublimity from 2nd to 28th. Overused in the nineteenth century, the term became associated with a gushing, thoughtless romanticism. Few serious twentieth-century writers would touch it.

Not that travellers were less sensitive to feelings: the Sublime had simply become a pseudo-response. Other formerly popular reactions that faded are Awe, which ran afoul of the modern sense of "awful" and carried religious overtones; Geology (less a divisive topic than a normal part of modern explorers' mental equipment); and Deism (Natural Theology), which saw God in nature and thus appealed neither to the secular nor to scripture-based Christians. What supplanted them were Spirituality, a vaguer form of reverence, which rose from 5th place to 2nd; and Beauty, up from 7th

266

to 4th. Addison *distinguished* the Great from the Beautiful, but that distinction gradually broke down over the nineteenth century. In the twentieth, vast barren solitudes came to be credited with both Grandeur and Beauty, *pace* Addison and Burke. Other responses that occur significantly more often post-Hardy are Silence and Purity, both much desired and rarely found; sensations of Emptiness (rising from 26th to 7th) and Insignificance in the presence of the Great; and Misanthropy (up from 22nd to 10th).

Misanthropy may not be quite the right word, but an almost Swiftian revulsion against swarming humanity - a desire to escape crowds, fear of our burgeoning numbers, a sort of species-satiety - is a motif in both primary reports and research on the Great after Hardy. As Starker Leopold put it, "There are no longer any 'waste' spaces" on the earth: "there are too many of us now" (172). This vision haunts desert writers appalled by the pressures that rising populations put on scanty supplies of water and vegetation, and they are not alone. Stanford Demars explains the growing pains of Yosemite National Park in terms of its exponential increase in visitors: a thousand in 1869, 100,000 in 1922, a million in 1954, three million in 1987. Roderick Nash acknowledges that the problems caused by tourist mobs in such areas have made misanthropes of some environmentalists, and echoes Starker Leopold: "too many people" are crowding the planet (1982, 381). Daniel Boone, fleeing west from the sound of his nearest neighbour's axe early in American history, seems an increasingly resonant and emblematic figure.

Away from population centres, the Great has often afforded an austerity, a spareness, lacking in society and thus considered desirable. Bareness, the 11th most popular trait before Hardy, ranks 9th after him; Bare plus Barren would be by far the largest category (see Lexicon). Jonathan Weiner describes the ecosystems of the Galapagos as "stripped to the bare bones": that may be why Darwin could see more clearly there than elsewhere (58). Some travellers, especially desert-lovers like Doughty, were proto-minimalists convinced that less is more; most (83%) of the Minimal responses occur after 1878. Minimalism might take the form of an interest in Zen Buddhism, which encourages the shedding of inessentials. Carried to an extreme, the idea of bareness can lead to a fearful sense of Void: the Nothing of Joan Didion's novels, Robert M. Adams's Nil. Struggles with the Void increase somewhat after Hardy, from 25th place to 19th, but were never as common as Bareness itself.

Bareness, however, is a subtle, ambiguous response; it can be internal or external, divine or human, welcomed or feared, in various combinations. Fenimore Cooper's Natty Bumppo, standing on the open prairie, wonders what "the Yankee choppers" will say "when they have cut their path from the eastern to the western waters, and find that a hand, which can lay the 'arth bare at a blow, has been here and swept the country, in very mockery of their wickedness. They will turn on their tracks like a fox that doubles, and then the rank smell of their own footsteps will show them the madness of their waste" (Cooper 76). The human penchant for clear-cutting inconvenient truths and profitable verdure meets its divine match and recoils as from a mirror. "Our spiritual state is a Waste Land," writes Joseph Warren Beach (555). Yet - or thus - we are drawn to bare and barren lands, as Hardy predicted.

The response that Cooper invites ("the madness of their waste") becomes common in the next century. Dozens of reports from the field after 1878 preach conservation, preservation, ecology, or environmentalism, a development reflected in scholarship, where a "green party" inspired by Muir and Aldo Leopold has brought wild nature into philosophy, literature, and history. In *Wilderness and the American Mind* (1967), regularly taught in college courses now, Roderick Nash argues that wilderness (whose popularity constitutes a revolution in intellectual history and threatens its own existence) is the "basic ingredient of American civilization"; relates it to developments overseas; and notes that whereas travellers once went to cities for pleasure, they now go to the country (1982, xi). In *The Rights of Nature* (1989) he broadened his scope to our whole concept of nature, tracing an expansion of concern and "rights" from exploitation to conservation (the efficient use of nature) to ethical environmentalism, built on ecological science, native ideas of sacred space, and feminist "gyn/ecology."

Younger scholars have since worked this vineyard. Allison Mitcham in *The Northern Imagination* (1983) notes how many writers on the North are conservationists. Glen Love (1990) calls for ecological criticism of western American literature, based on a "new ethic and aesthetic embracing the human and the natural" as enunciated by Leopold, Krutch, and Nash (213). Jonathan Bate argues in *Romantic Ecology* (1991) that Wordsworth anticipated modern environmental thought and that important aspects of the Romantic movement were "green" (5, 8-9). Lawrence Buell's *The Environmental Imagination* (1995) traces the "green" strain in American letters from Thoreau and Muir through Austin and Leopold to Abbey, and refutes critical theory sceptical of whether texts can represent the environment. Chris Fitter, working out a new aesthetic of *Poetry, Space, Landscape* (1995), makes the ecological impulse one of his four primary drives or matrices of perception (15). Indeed, it has become difficult to find contemporary writing about the Great *not* informed by an environmental perspective.

The spread of "green" values (a product of knowledge as well as sensibility) both exemplifies and furthers the evolving "rights of nature" that Nash postulates. When enough of the "more thinking among mankind" reached their Egdon Heaths, they interested themselves not only in the "congruity" between landscape and self, but in the threat that our species poses to the purity, solitude, and even the existence of such places. It was only a step to advocating protection, partly on grounds of self-interest. Gretel Ehrlich writes of the solace of open spaces, Belden Lane of the solace of fierce landscapes. If deserts and mountains afford "solace," that is a basis for socio-political as well as personal and spiritual involvement. Maria Tippett and Douglas Cole called their history of artists' attitudes toward western Canada's scenery *From Desolation to Splendour*. When governments support deforestation or oil-drilling amid "splendour," what began as aesthetic perception may lead to political action. But then "aesthetics and politics were never far apart," comments Derek Gregory (47). Ironically, Egdon Heath itself was an imaginative construct from what pieces of moorland remained in southwest England in Hardy's time.

Belief systems that rank nature below humanity also menace the Great. Lynn White, Jr, told a scientific convention in 1967 that "Our Ecological Crisis" is rooted in "Christian arrogance towards nature" (126), a development of Aldo Leopold's idea in *Sand County Almanac* that the "Abrahamic concept of land" as commodity is at fault. Nash discusses several attempts to "green" Christian thought, as well as Christian resistance to "eco-theology" (1989). Since James Watt, Ronald Reagan's Secretary of the Interior, told Congress that "after the last tree is felled, Christ will come back," the fundamentalist rejection of good stewardship in view of an approaching apocalypse has continued. Harold Oliver's "Neglect and Recovery of Nature in Twentieth-Century Protestant Thought" (1992) documents the neglect, while the recovery is merely his ideas for reform.

There are other problems for nature, such as solipsism. By ignoring the threats of development, overpopulation, and pollution, Simon Schama can *celebrate* humanity's impact on the earth; this is reassuring but complacent, leaving us, as Swift said, in "the happy state of being well-deceived." Schama, who sees landscape as "the work of the mind," offers his book as "a contribution to self-knowledge" (7, 18). Similarly, Gaston Bachelard writes that "Immensity is within ourselves" (1964, 184). True, though immensity also surrounds us, and we must take responsibility for our impact on it. Academic and theoretical work needs to take account of the real, "secular" world, as Addison and Hardy do. There are more of us now, and we reach more places, but we also know better how to see their wonder. The earth's age, which some in Darwin's time still believed to be only a few thousand years, is now estimated at around four billion circuits of the sun. Our horizons are still spacious, still liberating, and not unknowable.

CHRONOLOGICAL TABLE:
A selection of relevant dates

1869	J. Muir builds cabin in Yosemite, begins journal D. Freshfield, *Travels in the Central Caucasus...*
1871	R.W. Emerson visits Muir in Yosemite W. Morris visits Iceland (also '73)
1872	Austrian Arctic Expedition (to '74) M. Twain, *Roughing It*
1873	French expedition to Timbuktu (annihilated '74) Muir, "Prayers in Higher Mountain Temples"
1874	Club alpin français formed Wilfrid and Anne Blunt ride in the Sahara W. Whitman, "Winter Day on the Sea-beach"
1875	Nares, Markham explore Arctic Ocean (to '76) J.W. Powell, *Exploration of the Colorado R.* (in '69) J. Ruskin, *Deucalion* (1875-83)
1876	C.M. Doughty begins Arabian travels (to '78)
1877	The Blunts ride in Syria, Mesopotamia (to '78)
1878	Swedish expedition traverses NE Passage (to '79) The Blunts ride in Arabia (to '79) I. Bird, *A Lady's Life in the Rocky Mountains* Powell, *Lands of the Arid Region of the US* T. Hardy, *The Return of the Native*

1879	USS *Jeanette* heads north from Bering Strait
	Muir travels to Alaska (also 1880, 1890, 1899)
	A. Blunt, *Bedouin Tribes of the Euphrates*
	R.L. Stevenson, *Travels on a Donkey*; goes west

1880	A. Borodin, *In the Steppes of Central Asia*
	C. Dutton, *Plateaus of Utah*
	A.C. Swinburne, "By the North Sea"
	Twain, *A Tramp Abroad*

1881	P. Flatters' French Sahara Expedition massacred
	A. Greeley-US Army Arctic Expedition (to '84)
	USS *Jeanette* wrecked north of Siberia
	Muir sails north; *The Cruise of the Corwin*
	A. Blunt, *Pilgrimage to Nejd*

1882	1st International Polar Year
	C. Foucauld explores Morocco (to '84)
	Dutton, *Grand Canyon*
	Whitman, *Specimen Days*

1883	A.E. Nordenskiöld goes 75 mis. onto Greenland icecap
	G. Meredith, *Joy of Earth* poems

1885	British Association forms Antarctica Committee
	A. Daudet, *Tartarin sur les Alpes*
	C.T. Dent, *Above the Snow Line*
	G.M. Hopkins, Sonnet 42 ("mind has mountains")
	W.H. Hudson, *The Purple Land That England Lost*
	A. Tennyson, "Vastness"

1886	R. Peary and Maigaard go 100 mis. onto Greenland icecap
	P. Loti, *Iceland Fisherman*
	F. Nietzsche, *Beyond Good and Evil*

1887	Freshfield's 2nd Caucasus expedition
	G. De Maupassant, *Mont-Oriol*

1888	F. Nansen crosses Greenland east-west
	J. De Mille, *Strange Manuscript...*
	Doughty, *Travels in Arabia Deserta*
	Foucauld, *Reconnaissance au Maroc*
	Meredith, *A Reading of Earth*
1889	A.A. Ratti, "Monte Rosa"
1890	Nansen, *The First Crossing of Greenland*
1891	Peary crosses Greenland west-east (to '92)
	H. Garland, *Main-Travelled Roads*
	Hardy, *Tess of the D'Urbervilles*
	Morris, "Iceland First Seen"
	E. Verhaeren, *Les Apparus dans mes chemins*
1892	Muir founds Sierra Club
	Dent, ed., *Mountaineering*
	Hardy, *The Well-Beloved*
	Stevenson, "Across the Plains"
	E. Whymper, *Travels Amongst the Great Andes*
1893	*Fram* enters Arctic ice (Nansen, O. Sverdrup; to '96)
	S. Hedin begins Asian expedition (to '96)
	Hudson, *Idle Days in Patagonia*
1894	French troops occupy Timbuktu
	G. Bell, *Safar Nameh (Persian Pictures)*
	H. Ibsen, *Little Eyolf*
	M.M. Ippolitov-Ivanov, *Caucasian Sketches*
	Muir, *Mountains of California*
	L. Stephen, "A Substitute for the Alps"
1895	C. Borchgrevinck lands on Antarctica
	W. Conway, *The Alps from End to End*
	Loti, *Le Désert*
	A.F. Mummery, *My Climbs in the Alps and Caucasus*
	Powell, *Canyons of the Colorado*
	Stevenson, *The Amateur Immigrant*
	Verhaeren, "Le Fossoyeur"
	H.G. Wells, *The Time Machine*

1896	Conway et al. cross Spitsbergen Hedin explores Tibet
1897	S. Andrée's attempt to reach N. Pole by balloon fails F. Cook, R. Amundsen to Antarctic on *Belgica* (to '99) Conway, *The First Crossing of Spitsbergen* Hardy, "Zermatt: To the Matterhorn" Nansen, *Farthest North* J. Verne, *Le sphinx des glaces*
1898	Sverdrup begins mapping Arctic Ocean (to '02) Peary expedition to top of Greenland (to '02) British Antarctic Exped. (Borchgrevink; to 1900)
1899	Bell climbs in Alps, travels to Mideast I. Eberhardt's first trip to Sahara Hedin begins new Asian expedition Garland, *Boy Life on the Prairie*
1900	Italian Arctic Expedition (to '01) Cook, *Through the First Antarctic Night* J. Conrad, *Lord Jim* R. Kipling, *Kim*
1901	R.F. Scott's first Antarctic Expedition (to '04) Italians reach 86°34' N.: new record Borchgrevink, *First on the Antarctic Continent* Muir, *Our National Parks*
1902	Three scientific expeditions to Antarctica (to '04) Scott sledges to 82°17'S., makes balloon ascent Muir and T. Roosevelt camp in Sierras Conway, *Aconcagua and Tierra del Fuego*
1903	Amundsen begins Northwest Passage in *Gjöa* (to '06) T. Roosevelt's Grand Canyon address M. Austin, *The Land of Little Rain*

1904	Foucauld travels in Sahara (to '05)
	Conrad, *Nostromo*
	R. Hichens, *The Garden of Allah*
1905	Bell travels in Syrian desert
	Yosemite National Park established
	Scott, *Voyage of the Discovery*
1906	Amundsen completes Northwest Passage
	Peary reaches 87°6'N.: new record
	Hedin travels in Tibet again
1907	Bell, *The Desert and the Sown*
1908	Cook claims to have reached North Pole
	Ernest Shackleton's Antarctic expedition (to '09)
	V. Stefansson's 2nd Arctic expedition (to '12)
	Doughty, *Adam Cast Forth*
	T.E. Hulme, "Lecture on Modern Poetry"
1909	Peary claims North Pole, rejects Cook's claim
	Shackleton to 88°23'S.; Mawson to S. Magnetic Pole
	Peary, *The North Pole*
	Roosevelt, *African Game Trails*
	Shackleton, *Heart of the Antarctic*
1910	Scott's last Antarctic expedition (to '13)
1911	Amundsen party reach South Pole
	Foucauld moves into hermitage at Assekrem
	Bell, *Amurath to Amurath*
	F. Delius, *Song of the High Hills*
	Morris's Iceland journals (1871, 1873) pub.
	Muir, *My First Summer in the Sierra*
	Nansen, *Northern Mists* (Eng. trans.)
1912	Scott party reach South Pole but perish
	K. Rasmussen crosses Greenland (1st Thule Exped.)

Ladies Alpine Club formed in England
Amundsen, *The South Pole*
N. Douglas, *Fountains in the Sand*
M. Henson, *A Negro Explorer at the North Pole*
Muir, *The Yosemite*
H.M. Tomlinson, *The Sea and the Jungle*
A. Webern's mountain letter to A. Berg

1913
First ascent of Denali (Mt. McKinley), Alaska
Koch and Wegener winter on Greenland icecap
Russians discover Severnaya (North) Zemlya
Stefansson's Canadian Arctic Exped. (to '18); *My Life With the Eskimos*
Bell rides in Arabia (to '14)
J.E. Flecker, "The Golden Journey to Samarkand"
A. Lunn, *The Englishman in the Alps*
Scott's Last Expedition (various authors)
A. Weigall, *Travels in the Upper Egyptian Deserts*

1914
Shackleton's Trans-Antarctic Expedition (to '17)
Muir completes Alaska book; dies

1915
Shackleton's ship frozen in Antarctic O.; sinks
Ecological Soc. of America established
W. Cather, *Song of the Lark*
T. Gran's Antarctic diary published (in Norwegian)
Muir, *Travels in Alaska*
R. Strauss, *Eine Alpensinfonie* (1911-15)

1916
Shackleton reaches S. Georgia Is.; rescues men
E.A. Robinson, "Man Against the Sky"

1917
T.S. Eliot, *Poems*

1918
Amundsen begins NE Passage drift in *Maud* (to '21)
Cather, *My Antonia*

1919
Grand Canyon NP established
P. Benoit, *L'Atlantide*
Shackleton, *South*

1920	Sahara first crossed by air
	Permission given to climb Everest (from Tibet)
	Freshfield, *The Life of H.B. de Saussure*
	G.W. Young, ed., *Mountain Craft*

1921	First Everest reconnaisance (G.L.-Mallory, C.H.-Bury)
	Rasmussen, 5th Thule Expedition (to '24)
	Shackleton dies on *Quest* expedition
	E. Evans, *South with Scott*
	A. Gide, *L'Immoraliste*
	G. Holst, *The Planets*
	Stefansson, *The Friendly Arctic*
	W. Stevens, "The Snow Man"

1922	Mallory et al. reach 8000m. on Everest (1st time)
	Sahara first crossed by automobile
	A. Cherry-Garrard, *Worst Journey in the World*
	Eliot, *The Waste Land*
	Ratti (Pope Pius XI), *Ascensions*

1923	É.-F. Gautier, *Le Sahara*
	Ratti, *Climbs on Alpine Peaks*

1924	Mallory and A. Irvine disappear on Everest
	Oxford Arctic Expedition
	I. Bowman, *Desert Trails of Atacama*
	H. Crane, "North Labrador"
	R. Jeffers, *Roan Stallion*
	O.E. Rölvaag, *Giants in the Earth*

1925	British Arctic Expedition
	F.P. Grove, *Settlers of the Marsh*
	Hedin, *My Life as an Explorer*
	M. Ostenso, *Wild Geese*

1926	R. Byrd, Amundsen fly over N. Pole
	Crane, *White Buildings*
	G.M. Dyott, *On the Trail of the Unknown*
	D.H. Lawrence, *The Plumed Serpent*
	T.E. Lawrence, *Seven Pillars of Wisdom* (pvt. prntg.)

V. Sackville-West, *Passenger to Teheran*

1927
Amundsen, *My Life as an Explorer*
Jeffers, "Credo"
Rasmussen, *Across Arctic America*
F.A. Worsley, *Under Sail in the Frozen North*
Young, *On High Hills*

1928
Byrd's first Antarctic expedition (to '30)
G.H. Wilkins makes first flight over Antarctica
Holst, *Egdon Heath*
E. Rutter, *Holy Cities of Arabia*

1929
Byrd flies over South Pole
Jeffers, "Broken Balance"
H.H. Richardson, *Ultima Thule*

1930
G. Watkins and Wegener expeditions winter in Greenland (to '31); A. Courtauld alone on icecap for 5 months
M. Vieuchange dies in Spanish Sahara
C.E. Engel, *La littérature alpestre en France*
T. Mallet, *Barren Lands*
F.S. Smythe, *Kangchenjunga Adventure*

1931
Three parties cross Greenland
B. Thomas crosses Arabia's Empty Quarter
F. Grofé, *Grand Canyon Suite* (performed)
Hedin, *Across the Gobi Desert* (English trans.)
D.H. Lawrence, "New Mexico"
A. de St-Exupéry, *Vol de nuit*

1932
H.St.J. Philby crosses Empty Quarter
P.W. Kloss, *Arid*
Thomas, *Arabia Felix*

1933
Byrd's 2nd Antarctic expedition (to '35)
A. Govinda travels in Tibet
H. Ruttledge leads British Everest expedition
Philby, *The Empty Quarter*
Vieuchange, *Smara*

1934	British Antarctic Expedition (to '37)

1934   British Antarctic Expedition (to '37)
L. Ellsworth crew flies across Antarctica
Oxford Ellesmere Exped. (Edward Shackleton; to '35)
F.S. Chapman, *Northern Lights*
R. Frost, "Desert Places"
Hedin, *Conquest of Tibet* (English trans.)
H. McDiarmid, "On a Raised Beach"
Ruttledge, *Everest 1933*
F. Stark, *Valleys of the Assassins*

1935   J. Georgi stays at mid-ice, Wegener dies, in Greenland
Shipton leads British Everest reconnaissance
Byrd, *Discovery*
T.E. Lawrence, *Seven Pillars* published

1936   E. Hemingway, "The Snows of Kilimanjaro"
D.H. Lawrence, *Phoenix*, "Flying Fish"
Edward Shackleton, *Arctic Journeys*
Smythe, *The Spirit of the Hills*

1937   Russian airplane lands at North Pole
W.H. Auden-C. Isherwood, *Ascent of F.6*
Auden-L. MacNeice, *Letters from Iceland*
K. Blixen/I. Dinesen, *Out of Africa*

1938   H.W. Tilman leads British Everest expedition
T.E. Lawrence dies; letters published
Byrd, *Alone*
Smythe, *Over Tyrolese Hills*; *Valley of Flowers*

1939   Byrd's 3rd Antarctic expedition (to '41)
Eliot, *Family Reunion*
St-Exupéry, *Terre des hommes*

1940   Chapman, *Helvellyn to Himalaya*
Smythe, *Edward Whymper*; *Mountaineering Holiday*
Stark, *Winter in Arabia*

1941	St-John Perse, "Exil"
	S. Ross, *As for Me and My House*
	Smythe, *The Mountain Vision*

1941   St-John Perse, "Exil"
           S. Ross, *As for Me and My House*
           Smythe, *The Mountain Vision*

1942   E. Birney, *David*
           R.H. Blyth, *Zen in English Literature*
           W. Stegner, *Mormon Country*

1943   Lunn, *Mountain Jubilee*
           St-Exupéry, *Le Petit prince*

1944   R.V.C. Bodley, *Wind in the Sahara*
           St-John Perse, "Neiges"

1946   Byrd's 4th Antarctic expedition (to '47)
           Grove, *In Search of Myself*
           H. Laxness, *Independent People*

1947   A.B. Guthrie, *The Big Sky*
           W.O. Mitchell, *Who Has Seen the Wind*
           Smythe, *Again Switzerland*
           J.R. Ullman, *Kingdom of Adventure. Everest*

1948   UN's Int'l Union for the Protection of Nature
           E.L. Bridges, *Uttermost Part of the Earth*
           T. Heyerdahl, *Kon-Tiki* (in Norwegian)
           Lunn, *Mountains of Memory*
           Tilman, *Mount Everest 1938*

1949   Auden, *Enchaféd Flood* lectures
           P. Bowles, *The Sheltering Sky*
           A. Leopold, *Sand County Almanac*

1950   French climb Annapurna (1st 8000-meter summit climbed)
           French Antarctic Expedition (to '52)
           Engel, *History of Mountaineering in the Alps*
           W. Noyce, *The Scholar Mountaineers*
           E. Shipton, *Mountains of Tartary*
           Smythe, *Climbs in the Canadian Rockies*

1951	Chapman, *Memoirs of a Mountaineer*
	J.W. Krutch, *The Desert Year*
	L. van der Post, *Venture to the Interior*

1951   Chapman, *Memoirs of a Mountaineer*
J.W. Krutch, *The Desert Year*
L. van der Post, *Venture to the Interior*

1952   M. Herzog, *Annapurna* (in French)

1953   Chomolungma/Everest climbed: E. Hillary, T. Norgay
Bowles, *Their Heads Are Green* ...
L. Carl and J. Petit, *Tefedest*
Cook, *Return from the Pole*
J. Hunt, *The Ascent of Everest*
R.V. Williams, *Sinfonia Antartica*

1954   Auden, "Mountains"
R.M. Patterson, *The Dangerous River*
W. Skrede, *The Roof of the World* (English trans.)

1955   V. Fuchs builds Antarctic base on ice shelf
P. Diolé, *Le Plus beau désert du monde*
A. Hovhaness, *Mysterious Mountain*
Krutch, *Voice of the Desert*
C. Lévi-Strauss, *Tristes tropiques*
Norgay/Ullman, *Tiger of the Snows*
P. White, *The Tree of Man*

1956   US plane lands at S. Pole: 1st visit since Scott

1957   International Geophysical Year focuses on Antarctica; Fuchs party cross continent (to '58)
G. Dufek, *Operation Deepfreeze*
M. Eliade, *The Sacred and the Profane*
White, *Voss*

1958   N. Barber, *The White Desert*
Fuchs and E. Hillary, *The Crossing of Antarctica*
Hillary, *Challenge of the Unknown*
H. Lhote, *Tassili Frescoes* (in French)
E. Newby, *A Short Walk in the Hindu Kush*
W. Eastlake, *Portrait of an Artist With 26 Horses*

N. Kazantzakis, *The Odyssey: a Modern Sequel* (in Eng.)
R. Stow, *To the Islands*

1959   G. Gerster, *Sahara*
               W. Thesiger, *Arabian Sands*

1960   Blixen/Dinesen, *Shadows on the Grass*
               T. Merton, *Wisdom of the Desert*

1961   Hillary, *No Latitude for Error*
               A.S. Leopold, *The Desert*
               M. Lowry, *Hear Us O Lord*
               G. Roy, "Voyage en Ungava"

1962   Shipton explores Tierra del Fuego
               Hillary and D. Doig, *High in the Thin Cold Air*
               Noyce, *To the Unknown Mountain*
               B. Staib, *Nanok*

1963   C. Fletcher walks the Grand Canyon

1964   US Wilderness Act protects some wild sites
               J. Rule, *Desert of the Heart*
               W.W. Sayre, *Four Against Everest*
               Thesiger, *Marsh Arabs*
               A. Woodin, *Home Is the Desert*

1965   F. Herbert, *Dune*
               P. Sherman, *Cloud Walkers*
               J.H. Wellard, *The Great Sahara*

1966   Over 1000 float Colorado R. through Grand Canyon
               Govinda, *Way of the White Cloud*

1967   C. Fletcher, *The Man Who Walked Through Time*
               Krutch, *Baja California and the Geography of Hope*
               F. Mowat, *The Polar Passion*
               Stegner, "Wilderness as Idea"
               L. White, "Historical Roots of Our Ecological Crisis"

1968	R. Plaisted reaches North Pole via snowmobile
	W. Herbert expedition crosses Arctic O. (to '69)
	Over 3000 float through Grand Canyon
	E. Abbey, *Desert Solitaire*
	The Asian Journals of Thomas Merton
1969	First men walk on the moon
	W. Herbert, *Across the Top of the World*
	Shipton, *That Untravelled World*
	A. MacLeish, "Voyage to the Moon"
1970	Over 9000 float through Grand Canyon
	Heyerdahl, *The Ra Expeditions* (in Norwegian)
1972	16,432 float Grand Canyon; numbers capped there
	Bowles, *Without Stopping*
1973	Shipton, *Tierra del Fuego*
1974	G. Moorhouse, *The Fearful Void*
1975	Abbey, *The Monkey Wrench Gang*
	R. Kroetsch, *Badlands*
	Mowat, *Snow Walker*
1976	C. Bonington, *Everest the Hard Way*
	U. George, *Deserts of This Earth* (in German)
	B. Lopez, *Desert Notes*
	P. White, *Fringe of Leaves*
1977	W. de Roos circumnavigates Americas (to '79)
	J. Fowles, *Daniel Martin*
	J. Langone, *Life at the Bottom*
1978	H. Brown, *Hamish's Mountain Walk*
	P. Habeler, *Everest: Impossible Victory*
	P. Isemann, "The Arabian Ethos"
	P. Matthiessen, *The Snow Leopard*
	T. Severin, *The Brendan Voyage*

1979	Sightseeing plane crashes in Antarctica
	A. Hammond, *To Climb a Sacred Mountain*
	A. Woodrow, "Alone in the Sahara"
1980	R. Messner climbs Everest alone, without oxygen
	British drive across Antarctica (to '81)
	"Le Désert" issue of *Traverses*
	Thesiger, *The Last Nomad*
1981	Messner, "At My Limit"
	Sherman, *Expeditions to Nowhere*
	J. Watson, *Deserts of the World*
1982	G. Nabhan, *The Desert Smells Like Rain*
1983	A. Harvey, *A Journey in Ladakh*
1984	"Footsteps of Scott" Antarctic exped. (to '86)
	Hovhaness, *Mt. St Helens*
1985	G. Ehrlich, *The Solace of Open Spaces*
	J. Krakauer, "Eiger Dreams"
	Nabhan, *Gathering the Desert*
1986	Four dogsledge 2000 kms. in Antarctica (to '87)
	M. Abley, *Beyond Forget*
	Lopez, *Arctic Dreams*
	M. Reisner, *Cadillac Desert*
1987	B. Chatwin, *Songlines*
	Krakauer, "Club Denali," "Bad Summer on K-2"
	G. MacEwen, "Terror and Erebus"
	R. Mear and R. Swan, *Walk to the Pole*
1988	M. Asher, *Impossible Journey*
	Lopez, *Crossing Open Ground*
1989	Two expeditions cross Antarctica (to '90)
	Krakauer, "Flyboys of Talkeetna," "Chamonix"
	R. Wiebe, *Playing Dead ... Concerning the Arctic*

1990	T. Hillerman, *Coyote Waits* Krakauer, *Eiger Dreams*, "Devil's Thumb" S. Lindqvist, *Desert Divers* (in Swedish) "Le Désert" issue of *Moebius*
1991	Messner, *Antarctica: Both Heaven and Hell* R. Perkins, *Into the Great Solitude* Severin, *In Search of Genghis Khan* *A Society to Match the Scenery*, ed. G. Holthaus
1992	Hovhaness, *Glacier Peak* C. McCarthy, *All the Pretty Horses*
1993	G.B. Schaller, "In a High and Sacred Realm"
1994	S. Butala, *The Perfection of the Morning* J. Moss, *Enduring Dreams ... Arctic Landscape* J. Weiner, *Beak of the Finch*
1995	D. Starkell, *Paddle to the Arctic*
1996	Twelve die on Everest J. Raban, *Bad Land*
1997	B. Barcott, *Measure of a Mountain* Holthaus, *Wide Skies* Krakauer, *Into Thin Air*
1998	Krakauer, "Queen Maud Land" B.C. Lane, *The Solace of Fierce Landscapes*
1999	A. Proulx, *Close Range. Wyoming Stories*
2000	D. Roberts, ed., *Points Unknown ...*
2001	J.T. Norgay, *Touching My Father's Soul*
2003	B. Ousland, T. Ulrich cross Patagonia icefield E. Douglas, *Tenzing: Hero of Everest*
2006	Eleven die on Everest

2008   N. Heil, *Dark Summit* (Everest)
        M. Kodas, *High Crimes* (Everest)

LEXICON
From Trees to Forest

The thoughts and feelings that people have had about Great nature are the data at the heart of these volumes. But an abundance of detail in the text may obscure large patterns, so *The Road to Egdon Heath* included a Lexicon or "dictionary and grammar of responses" to clarify and codify the main interests, motives, and reactions of those who have discussed spacious horizons. In making that Lexicon I undertook a two-stage analysis, the first noting what company each response kept in writers' minds. For example, devotees of Astronomy also tend to talk about Eternity, Infinity, Vastness, and Sublimity, which may thus be said to form an "idea-cluster" around Astronomy. Seventy-odd clusters, some of them quite complex, were only a modest advance in clarification, but the affinities they expressed did enable me to resolve all the responses into ten groups. Four of these - Spiritual, Spacious, Minimal, and Temporal - dominate; the others, including Adventure, Science, Metaphorical, and Dark, play supporting roles.

This second Lexicon updates the first with as little repetition as possible. The "dictionary" gives fewer examples, and since the connections between responses change little in the modern period, less is said about "grammar." The groups look familiar, having most of the same members, though there are exceptions, e.g. the addition of ecological thought to the Science Group. What is most interesting about this second installment is how the popularity of various responses and clusters shifts in the later period, though here we move into statistics, which, being highly unstable, must be handled with due caution. The degree of subjectivity is high - what is a "response"? What makes a "group"? - and it is unlikely that any two readers would make exactly the same choices. Does a sensation of Liberty belong in the Spacious or in the Adventure Group? Always? Is Mutability a spiritual or a scientific response? The question becomes crucial with a widely-occurring trait such as Grandeur, which in older texts is usually a spiritual emotion, but in modern ones affiliates with the Spacious Group.

Bearing such pitfalls in mind, I can still hazard a few generalizations. As intellectual history predicts, the Spiritual Group has become less important. Though Spirituality itself - a general sense of reverence, not necessarily "religious" - rises to 2nd place among all reactions, this is offset by the slippages of Awe, of Natural Theology (from 13th place to 42nd), and of Sublimity.[1] On average, responses in this group drop ten places in the modern period. Less predictable is the rise of the Minimal Group, a result of the increased appeal of Bareness, Barrenness, Emptiness, Silence, Simplicity, and Solitude. Minimal qualities are mentioned more frequently than those of any other group after *The Return of the Native* (1878), and they move up on average more than three places in the rankings. Members of the Spacious Group are mentioned less often, but it includes the most popular response, Vastness. If every Grandeur response is placed there, the Spacious ranks ahead of the Spiritual Group, and its members have the highest average rank of any grouping.

All such analyses depend on underlying assumptions, but the make-up of two other groups is clearer. Four of the five responses in the Temporal Group lose ground after Hardy's novel, their average rank slipping six places. The age of the earth was a less divisive issue in the twentieth century, and the fall of the most popular Temporal response, Eternity, from 10th to 15th may reflect the fading taste for metaphysical concepts. The Dark Group is interesting because of Hardy's hypothesis that moderns would turn to landscapes of "chastened sublimity" in a spirit of sombre disillusion. I have argued above that this has not generally been the case, and here are some of the reasons. The responses of Chaos, Gloom, Incomprehension, and Weariness all lose ground, dropping the average rank of group members three places. The only Dark traits that rise in rank are Pain-for-Gain and Misanthropy, the latter born of hostility to some aspects of western civilization and fear of

---

[1]   A comparison of absolute numbers would be misleading because almost two-thirds of the responses come from the post-1878 period. Thus I use rankings, a relative measure, instead.

over-population; it is the Dark response most often mentioned after 1878.

The vicissitudes of individual responses are discussed in the Conclusion and in the alphabetical entries below, which also define the response, give examples of its usage, and relate it to kindred qualities and groups. The cardinal numbers in parentheses indicate the number of *works* in my reading that exhibit that response before and after 1878, not the number of *times* it appears (an enthusiast such as William Morris, who expresses awe nine times in one book, could skew the results). Since the early and late numbers cannot be compared directly (64% of the total responses being post-1878), the ordinals give the *rank* of each response in its period as a rough guide to changes in popularity. So: (number early, rank early; number late, rank late). As in the first Lexicon, I omit the rarest responses - here, those appearing in fewer than ten modern sources. They are, in descending order: Camaraderie, Health, Preservation, Richness, Wintriness (9); Aesthetics/Discomfort (8); Solemnity (6); Profundity, Weariness (5); Mirror, Mutability, Zen (4); Fame (3); Ecstasy, and Morality (2). Lexicon entries are capitalized in the text.

ADVENTURE (4, 37th; 20, 35th): Fewer travellers than one might expect admit that a love of derring-do brought them to the Great, but those who confess this love include some of the greatest: Nansen, Shackleton, Smythe, Hillary, Messner. Smythe, narrating his party's attempt on Kangchenjunga in 1930, explains that their central impulse was towards physical and mental adventure, even unto the risk of life, which he saw as a deep human need. Such writers often mention Liberty and Fear as integral parts of the experience. Other members of Adventure's Group are Challenge, Enjoyment, Intensity, and Self-Knowledge.

ANTIQUITY (25, 20th; 34, 27th): The age and seeming permanency of the Great, one of its strongest attractions for early travellers, remained interesting even after controversy over the geological age of the earth had moderated. Gertrude Bell calls a moonlit night on the desert a scene "as old as the world"; Edward Abbey identifies ancient, elemental power as part of the appeal of deserts, mountains, and oceans. Antiquity belongs to the Temporal Group, along with Elements, Eternity, and Preservation.

ASCETICISM (1, 40th; 12, 42nd): A few modern travellers appreciate the Great for (not despite) its spareness and the discipline that imposes. Arnold Lunn was a great devotee of the spiritual benefits conferred by mountaineering: "self-conquest … is the secret of our strivings," he wrote; the ascetic, knowing that "happiness must be paid for by pain," willingly "sacrifices pleasure to happiness." Some other climbers (e.g. Eric Shipton), desert-lovers, and polar explorers endorse the idea. Such writers tend to make Challenge, Pain-for-Gain, and Simplicity the great virtues. Asceticism belongs to the Minimal Group.

ASTRONOMY (12, 30th; 20, 35th): The heavens excited later adventurers somewhat less than they had those before Hardy, but the night sky still moves desert walkers, polar explorers, and poets with intimations of unimaginable scale. Tennyson's "Vastness" is a vision of earth's history as "a trouble of ants in the gleam of a million million of suns." Both Tryggve Gran (of Scott's last expedition) and Hillary thought that Antarctica had a "lunar" appearance. Astronomy, a member of the Science Group, generally prompts thoughts of Infinity, Eternity, Vastness, and - in earlier references - Sublimity.

AWE (61, 6th; 64, 11th): The quasi-religious blend of reverence and fear known as awe was one of the most frequent reactions of early travellers to the Great. When used by later visitors, the word tends to be more secular, a blend of admiration and wonder, like Messner's amazement in Antarctica. Late nineteenth-century mountaineers such as Muir and Ratti still use the word in its older sense, whereas for Bonington in the 1970s awe is part of his astonishment at the vastness, beauty, and wildness of the upper reaches of Mt. Everest. Awe, belonging to the Spiritual Group, is often evoked by Grandeur and Sublimity, or by transcendental qualities such as Eternity and Infinity.

BARENESS (45, 11th; 67, 9th): Many early travellers to the Great, and even more of the recent ones, remark on its nakedness, austerity, or starkness. Desert writers such as Bell and Abbey often note the landscape's clean, simple lines, but mountaineers and polar explorers also register this response. During the first walk on the moon in 1969, Neil Armstrong said that it has "a stark beauty all its own." For T.E. Lawrence and some imaginative writers (e.g.

Bowles), topographical bareness reflects or symbolizes moral bareness. A member of the Minimal Group, Bareness has a spectrum of connotations ranging from Simplicity, Liberty, and Self-Knowledge to Emptiness, Barrenness, and the Void.

BARRENNESS (82, 4th; 117, 2nd): Post-1878, only Vastness is mentioned more often than desolation as a quality of Great nature. Barrenness can be a straightforward geographical description of a desert, perhaps with a warning that its hostility to life is earth's likely future; a symbol of a yearning for liberty (Hudson); a sign of inner vision (Govinda); or an existential metaphor, as in Eliot's *The Waste Land* or Fowles's *Daniel Martin* - a trope developed from nineteenth-century writers. It remains a multivalent quality, deadly but fascinating. Part of the large and increasingly popular Minimal Group, Barrenness is often associated with desirable qualities such as Simplicity and Reality, as well as with Emptiness and Wintriness.

BEAUTY (58, 7th; 113, 4th): Despite Addison's and Burke's attempts to establish the grand or sublime as distinct from the beautiful, many travellers have seen some kind of beauty in all areas of the Great. This was an even more popular response in the twentieth century, as aesthetic norms loosened and proliferated, than earlier; few qualities are cited more often. Muir and Herzog saw beauty in the mountains, Krutch and T.E. Lawrence in the desert, Nansen and Byrd on polar ice, Jeffers on the Pacific coast. Beauty belongs to the Pleasure Group, and is often mentioned in connection with feelings of Purity, Richness, Cosmos (order), and Natural Theology. In Oxymoron, Beauty is paired with Fear.

BUDDHISM (0, -; 14, 40th): That all references to Buddhism postdate 1878 is not surprising: most westerners knew little or nothing of that religion until the twentieth century. Once they did learn of it, however, a number of travellers saw parallels between the appeal of the Great and Buddhist teaching about emptiness, silence, and simplicity. Some of them were or became Buddhists (Govinda); others added Buddhist practice to their own faith, or were drawn to Buddhist qualities (Merton). Most of the interest came from mountaineers (Shipton) and professional writers (Kerouac, Matthiessen). Although it clearly belongs to the Spiritual Group,

Buddhism's emphasis on Bareness, Emptiness, and Solitude gives it strong ties to the Minimal Group.

CALM (14, 28th; 60, 12th): Relatively few early travellers to the Great mentioned peace or oblivion as reasons to go there, but this has since become a popular category. Sackville-West, struck by the "serenity" of Persia's plains and mountains, and Heyerdahl, finding "peace" on a raft in the middle of the Pacific, are among dozens who report sensations of rest, relief, and seclusion in all areas of the Great. Calm often arises from sensations of Emptiness and Solitude, particularly if the traveller has been feeling Weariness or Misanthropy. After Beauty, it is the most important member of the Pleasure Group.

CHALLENGE (4, 37th; 34, 27th): While few early explorers of the Great said that they went for the challenge, their modern counterparts are more willing to admit that they feel drawn to exacting projects that demand courage and skill. Examples come from all areas, but especially from mountaineering. Hillary called his anthology of adventure travel *The Challenge of the Unknown*; for Messner, climbing Everest alone and without oxygen was "the greatest challenge." Part of the Adventure Group, Challenge can shade from Masochism or Fear to Intensity and Self-Knowledge in its connotations.

CHAOS (7, 34th; 10, 44th): A few early travellers saw the Alps or the Arctic as "chaotic." As the laws governing the natural sciences came to be better understood, such responses became rarer. The term is often applied impressionistically to a scene that the writer feels is somehow beyond nature or prior to the creation, as when Austin describes "hills ... squeezed up out of chaos," or Conway writes, of a Spitsbergen glacier, here "Nature ends." Chaos belongs to the Dark Group; its affect is usually Fear or Gloom, but it can produce Awe as well.

CONSERVATION (0, -; 34, 27th): Nothing better illustrates what has happened to the Great in modern times than this category; references to preservation, environmentalism, or ecology, and attacks on our destruction of wild nature, begin in the mid-nineteenth century. Reports come from every area: Muir in the Sierras, Conway in the Alps, most Everest visitors since the 1970s, Thesiger in Arabia, Messner in Antarctica, Heyerdahl on the Atlantic, et cetera. Smythe wrote in 1947, "The spoliation of beautiful scenery in the interests of commerce is … to be fought whenever possible." Conservation is a Dark-tinged concern, although its ecological wing gives it a Science component as well.

COSMOS (10, 31st; 15, 39th): The obverse of the feeling that the Great is chaotic, Cosmos is a sense of harmony or identification with a larger whole. While Byrd felt a sense of cosmic order on the Antarctic Barrier ice, and Perkins on a solo canoe trip in the Arctic, mountaineers (Muir, Smythe, Shipton) are most likely to have this vision. Science, particularly geology and glaciology, was vital to the development of a sense of Cosmos, yet it is also a spiritual response linked to Natural Theology, and its popularity declines slightly in the modern period, along with most other qualities in the Spiritual Group.

DESERTNESS (5, 36th; 16, 38th): Some travellers and writers have a complex response to desert: it serves them as a symbol, or nexus of connotations, so that the physical fact acquires resonance and evokes added emotion. Uwe George, seeing "earth's future fate" in the Sahara; Krutch, comparing Arizona's desert to New York City's; and Web, in Kroetsch's *Badlands*, calling temperance a "virtue, parched as the desert and pure," all use deserts as a *tabula rasa* upon which to write other concerns. Desertness, whose components come from the Minimal and Dark Groups, belongs to the Metaphorical Group.

DULLNESS (13, 29th; 15, 39th): The proportion of travellers to the Great who found it tedious, dismal, or monotonous shrank in the modern period, but not to zero. Canada's prairie or tundra, Iceland's moors, and hot deserts sometimes elicited this reaction, as did some mountainous areas. Conway pronounced the glacier-scoured *Plaine morte* in the Alps a "dreary desert-basin," and the shore of Spitsbergen a "dreary waste." Hunt applies the same adjective to the South Col of Everest, and Shipton to Tierra del Fuego. Dullness, the most insipid member of the Dark Group, is often accompanied by Barrenness or Gloom.

EARTH'S BODY (15, 27th; 21, 34th): Some early writers on mountains and deserts imagined them as the body or skeleton of the earth (verdure being its clothing). This metaphor survived in the twentieth century among desert writers such as Bell and Diolé, mountaineers, including Muir and Noyce, and creative writers. Auden and MacNiece (echoing Mallory on Everest) call the haunted mountain in *The Ascent of F.6* a "terrifying fang of rock and ice"; a Fremen desert nomad in Frank Herbert's *Dune* chants, "The world is a carcass." A member of the Metaphorical Group, Earth's Body is often mentioned in connection with Bareness, Geology, and Vastness.

ELEMENTS (16, 26th; 38, 26th): Part of the appeal of the Great has always been the idea that it approximates the basic, primordial earth prior to human action. That pleased the eighteenth-century interest in primitivism, but Elements has kept its popularity in the modern period. Abbey describes the Utah desert as "the bare bones of existence, the elemental and fundamental"; Byrd saw the Antarctic Barrier ice as "the raw materials of creation." And Messner has said that he climbs in order to go "where one is reduced to what is fundamental" *in one's self*. Elements belongs to the Temporal Group, but is also associated with Geology (Science Group) and several qualities in the Minimal Group.

EMPTINESS (16, 26th; 79, 7th): Empty space impressed astronomers among others in the seventeenth century, and this emotion was applied to vast, unpeopled earthly spaces in the nineteenth century. These became more popular from Hardy's time on as populations grew, literature took an interest in voids, and Buddhism praised emptiness. Most references come from desert or tundra travel. "What a scene of emptiness!" exclaims Philby in Arabia's Empty Quarter. Some mountaineers, seafarers, and polar explorers mention it as well. Imaginative writers such as Bowles speculate on a connection between empty (or bare) land and spiritual vacancy. Emptiness fits in the Minimal Group, where it is closely associated with Barrenness and Silence.

ENJOYMENT (24, 21st; 55, 15th): The Great can be demanding and harsh. Only a modest number of nineteenth-century writers list happiness or elation among its rewards, but more do so in the modern period, with greater familiarity and better equipment. Evans writes of the joys of winter in Antarctica, Stefansson was often happy in the "friendly Arctic," Muir in the mountains, and Thomas found joy in the Empty Quarter. This category includes a wide range of shadings: Lhote calls the Sahara "exciting" (others mention thrills or exhilaration), while Philby rated crossing the *Rub' al-Khali* as his "pleasantest experience." Enjoyment belongs primarily to the Pleasure Group, but has cousins such as Self-Knowledge in the Adventure Group.

ETERNITY (46, 10th; 55, 15th): Originally the Great was of interest in part because it shadowed forth Infinity and Eternity, transcendental qualities associated with the Creator. Eternity is not mentioned as often in the modern period, when religious responses become rarer. Bell, however, noted that the desert has eternal associations for nomads, Shackleton was awed by the "eternal snows" of Antarctica, and Lunn pays homage to the "eternal loveliness" of the Swiss Alps. Eternity links the Temporal and Spiritual Groups, and has a close connection to Astronomy in the Science Group.

FASCINATION (9, 32nd; 30, 30th): This vague, general term conveys a sense of being attracted for reasons not easy to define, as when Thesiger writes that Arabian sands "cast a spell" on those who venture there. Peary put down his repeated Arctic expeditions to the "lure of the North," while his rival, Cook, found a "fascination in the scenic effects" of summer nights on the Antarctic Ocean. Shipton suggests that the "deep fascination" of climbing is that, despite all our preparation and equipment, "the mountain still holds the master card." Fascination cannot be said to have a grammar: it is a catch-all term, a summation.

FEAR (42, 12th; 59, 13th): Descriptions of the Great as dangerous or terrible are common in both the early and modern periods. One school (including Burke and Nietzsche) held the Great to be by definition fearsome; others disagreed. Colin Fletcher posits some fear at the root of every big challenge, although his account of walking the Grand Canyon balances fear with moments of beauty and peace. Severin gives danger and visual splendour equal billing on his small-boat voyage across the Atlantic. Hillary does not mention fear on Everest, but a lonely moment on an Antarctic plateau produces "a slight chill around my heart." Fear belongs to the Dark Group, but is closely connected to the Adventure Group, to Sublimity, and to Oxymoron.

GEOLOGY (46, 10th; 43, 22nd): Many early writers on the Great paid close attention to geology, especially in the nineteenth century, when its evolutionary message was controversial. Interest fell off somewhat in the twentieth century as the controversy waned, but geology has remained a discipline that serious travellers use to describe the land. Numerous desert writers (Doughty, Loti, Thomas, Krutch) and mountaineers (Muir, Conway, Smythe, Krakauer) make geological observations. Scott had geologists on his team, and Nansen took note of rock formations. Geology belongs to the Science Group, but for its adherents may bring up emotions in the Temporal, Minimal, or Spiritual Groups.

GLOOM (50, 9th; 50, 17th): A fair number of travellers to Great landscapes have always found them melancholy or bleak at times. This is most evident in desert and polar travel; few climbers seem to have felt Ruskin's "mountain gloom" (Conway considered Spitsbergen much gloomier than the Alps). This category covers a range of responses, from remarks on cloudy weather or Thesiger's recognition that the Saharan Tibesti is "a sombre land" to outright depression. Gloom belongs to the Dark Group; Fear, Misanthropy, and Pain-for-Gain are often its companions.

GLORY (14, 28th; 23, 32nd): The connotations of this term run a gamut from religious (mainly early usages) to aesthetic, in which sense it is synonymous with splendour, as when Mallory calls the Himalayas in clear weather "splendid." Many mountaineers use the form "glorious," some with conscious reference to Ruskin's "mountain glory," but there are also examples from polar areas and deserts. Rarely it may allude to desire of fame through heroic endeavour. Glory has links to both the Spiritual and Pleasure Groups; it usually appears with Beauty, Enjoyment, or the Sublime.

GOD IN DESERT (8, 33rd; 19, 36th): A divine presence is sometimes felt in waste lands, despite appearances of abandonment. Not surprising in pious men (Doughty, Foucauld), this response also crops up in agnostics and free-thinkers such as Abbey, who calls Utah's rock desert "God's navel," Austin ("the rawness of the land favors the sense of personal relation to the supernatural"), and Bowles. God in Desert, like Holiness of Mountains, is a special case of Natural Theology, in which God is read from creation. All belong to the Spiritual Group.

GRANDEUR (97, 1st; 97, 6th): The Great was sometimes called the Grand in the eighteenth century, and defined by majesty or magnificence; no attribute is mentioned more often in early discussions of the Great. Although it has fallen a few places, Grandeur is still one of the most frequent reactions in all areas. Cherry-Garrard acknowledged the "wild desolate grandeur" of Antarctica, Moorhouse saw grandeur in the Sahara's Hoggar Mountains, and Hunt remembered Everest's "beauty and grandeur." Grandeur links the Spiritual and Spacious Groups, aspects of the latter such as Vastness or Infinity triggering responses in the former category (Awe, Natural Theology, Sublimity).

HOLINESS OF MOUNTAINS (26, 19th; 40, 24th): The ancient idea that high mountains (especially their summits) are holy altars occurs often among climbers and admirers of mountains from the late eighteenth century to the present. It is slightly less common after 1878 (when most types of spiritual response decline), but Muir, Conway, Lunn, Smythe, and others find more than a sense of achievement on their peaks. Herzog wrote that his party felt "a monk's veneration of the divine" on Annapurna; Tenzing Norgay said that God was like a great mountain, to be revered; and Krakauer describes climbing a glacier as a pilgrimage. Like God in Desert, Holiness of Mountains is a subset of Natural Theology in the Spiritual Group, where most of its kindred are found.

INCOMPREHENSION (4, 37th; 11, 43rd): A few travellers report finding the Great strange or unearthly, usually because it suggests transcendent concepts such as Eternity, Infinity, or Void (Kant defined the sublime/Great as beyond comprehension). Most early uses occur in mountains, most later ones in deserts or polar regions. Dr Cook noted "strange other-world scenic effects" on the Antarctic coast in 1898; both Gautier and Lhote call the Sahara "a world apart." Incomprehension's grammar is complex. Most allied qualities are in the Spiritual or Spacious groups, but it can have a Dark aspect.

INDIFFERENCE OF NATURE (3, 38th; 14, 40th): A few travellers and novelists observe that Great nature dislikes or at least does not care for visitors. Odell found Chomolungma's face "cruel" and wrote of her "cold indifference" to climbers; Tierra del Fuego struck

Shipton as a "hostile land." Writers on the North American West are apt to assert what Ehrlich calls the "absolute indifference" of the land. Part of the Dark Group, Indifference is often accompanied by Weariness, Gloom, or Fear.

INFINITY (33, 15th; 53, 16th): The movement of divine attributes, infinity and eternity, into the physical cosmos ("the aesthetics of the infinite") played an important role in the birth of the Great, and Infinity has remained a common response to it, especially in deserts and polar areas. Even an agnostic such as Abbey describes wilderness as "something beyond us and without limit." Nansen had intimations of infinity on the Arctic Ocean, as Muir did in the Sierras; Byrd called his Advance Base in Antarctica "a pinprick in infinity." Such usages are of course not taken literally. Infinity is associated with Vastness and Grandeur in the Spacious Group, but also has a strong connection to Natural Theology in the Spiritual Group.

INSIGNIFICANCE (29, 16th; 69, 8th): Astronomy and geology taught some early observers to feel dwarfed to insignificance by space, time, or force. This has been an even more frequent response in the modern period: almost universally among desert writers, and often heard from polar regions. Fewer mountaineers admit to it, though Odell felt "puny" on Everest. Sometimes there is a sense that a place was not made for humans (Chatwin in Australia, Conway on Spitsbergen), and that humility is the proper reaction (Ehrlich in Wyoming). Insignificance belongs to the Spacious Group, near sensations of Vastness, Grandeur, and Infinity. It may also have a Spiritual dimension.

INTENSITY (6, 35th; 13, 41st): This response (called Awareness in *The Road to Egdon Heath*) describes the reports of some travellers that they feel more alive and aware in the Great than elsewhere. Chadwick notes that the Alaskan wilderness produces an "awareness of how intensely alive your mind, your body, and the world around you can be." Examples come from all areas, especially the mountains. Intensity is usually associated with Challenge, Enjoyment, and Self-Knowledge in the Adventure Group.

KNOWLEDGE (12, 30th; 31, 29th): A desire for scientific knowledge of the Great has always moved some of its visitors. Mountaineers (e.g.

Herzog), desert travellers (Thomas), and most polar explorers have professed to desire the enlargement of knowledge (sometimes partly an appeal for support). Nansen wrote that Arctic exploration shows the "power of the unknown over the mind of man." Knowledge is the general term of the Science Group, yet also has a quasi-religious sense connected to Natural Theology: the knowledge may be that of God's creation.

LAND/SELF (18, 24th; 20, 35th): The notion of landscape being related to one's mind or body carried over from the early to the modern period, mostly among imaginative writers such as Fowles, whose Syrian desert stands for spiritual dearth in *Daniel Martin*, and Kazantzakis, whose Odysseus is often indistinguishable from the natural scenes through which he voyages. This trope is also used by some travellers; Doughty alludes to the "deserts of his corrupt mind." Land/Self is in the Metaphorical Group, and closely related to Mirror.

LIBERTY (18, 24th; 58, 14th): Addison founded the Great on the premise that "a spacious horizon is an image of liberty." This equation became more popular in the 20th century, at least among desert travellers and mountaineers. The Sahara gave Uwe George "a sense of boundless freedom," and Herzog writes of feeling free on Annapurna. Polar regions are evidently more confining; only Stefansson has felt liberated in the Arctic. Although Liberty originated in the Spacious Group, most of the qualities that writers mention to explain *why* they feel free - Bareness, Emptiness, Solitude - are in the Minimal Group.

LURE OF THE DESERT (10, 31st; 48, 18th): This vague phrase refers to those times (more numerous since Hardy) when writers assert the appeal of the desert without explaining what attracts them. Bell "wonder[s] why one takes pleasure in such a landscape, but the fact remains that one does." Austin describes the desert as "land that once visited must be come back to inevitably." Gerster says that the French in the Sahara service were "hopelessly in love with the desert." Some postwar American writers - Bowles, Krutch, Stegner, Abbey - abound in this feeling. Lure of the Desert comprises a number of other responses, usually unspecified, and belongs to no group.

METAPHORS (33, 15th; 58, 14th): Metaphorical uses of the Great, especially the desert, have remained popular among travellers and writers. Rihani's Khalid describes himself as "a Bedouin in the desert of life"; Stark sees "the drama of nature" in Arabia as "identical with the tragedy of man." Shipton, noting that China's Takla Makan desert is spreading, remarks that scientists and statesmen will probably have made the planet a desert before the basin is completely arid. Metaphors heads its own group, containing responses such as Earth's Body, Land/Self, Mirror, and Wintriness. Several other qualities used metaphorically are found in the Minimal Group: Bareness, Barrenness, and Void.

METAPHYSICS (6, 35th; 17, 37th): Some travellers have always seen the Great as a realm beyond ordinary physical nature, which is what Metaphysics means here. The idea may or may not take a more specific form (Holiness of Mountains, God in Desert, or Natural Theology) where the divine is sensed; and cause Incomprehension. Metaphysics crops up often in mountaineers from Muir to Krakauer, and in polar explorers, notably Nansen and Shackleton. This response also covers the feeling of an invisible presence, the "extra man" sometimes reported in the Himalayas and the Antarctic. Metaphysics is closely related to qualities in both the Spiritual and Metaphorical Groups.

MINIMALISM (4, 37th; 19, 36th): Few texts before or after Hardy assert that "less is more," yet the minimalist impulse is strong, particularly among desert travellers (Doughty) and novelists. Diolé writes that the Sahara offers what we are nostalgic for: "silence, solitude, the stripping away of nonessentials"; Weiner presents an island in the Galapagos as "a diagram of limits" that "speaks of bare necessities." While pure Minimalism has been uncommon, the Minimal Group is the largest in the modern period and comprises some of the Great's most popular qualities: Bareness, Barrenness, Emptiness, Silence, and Solitude.

MISANTHROPY (22, 22nd; 65, 10th): The word may not be strictly accurate: these critics often travelled with friends. We should distinguish between dislike of the species (Sartre's "Hell is other people") and antipathy to (western) civilization or to crowds, but many modern writers on the Great express one or the other. Krutch wonders if God pronounced the world "good" before, not after, creating man. Most examples exult in empty areas, or, more recently, warn of over-population; "there are too many of us now," writes Starker Leopold. Desert writers and Smythe's books are full of such sentiments. Misanthropy belongs to the Dark Group, yet it often accompanies positive and benign responses such as Calm, Liberty, Purity, and Solitude.

MUSIC (4, 37th; 22, 33rd): Certain composers, including Borodin, Richard Strauss, Grofé, and R.V. Williams have tried to render sublime natural scenes musically, often in orchestral tone poems. Some writers have had similar impulses. For Cather's heroine in *Song of the Lark*, the Largo in Dvorak's *New World Symphony* evokes the high plains of Wyoming. Bowles writes that the playing of a lone *qsbah* in a Moroccan wilderness "completely expresses the essence of solitude." Abbey asserts that Schönberg, Webern, and others have composed music consonant with the Utah desert. Music has affiliations with several groups - Pleasure, Spacious, Spiritual - without "belonging" to them. Like novels and poems, it offers a way to articulate feeling for the Great.

MYSTIQUE (13, 29th; 50, 17th): Many modern visitors to all areas of the Great report a general sense of magic or mystery there. Lunn, who had "moments of intuition" in the Alps, believes that, for mountain lovers as for monks, "asceticism is the key to the higher forms of mystical experience." North Africa seemed to Bowles a "magic place" where nature communicated directly with consciousness. In Antarctica, Scott was piqued by a "sense of its mystery." Mystique's vagueness (like Fascination's) makes it difficult to place; most of its links are to the Spiritual Group. It can arise from a sense of Eternity or Infinity, and generate feelings of Incomprehension and Unreality.

NATURAL THEOLOGY (37, 13th; 12, 42nd): Most terms in the Spiritual Group decline in the modern period, but none more than Natural Theology, the idea of inferring God from nature; three-quarters of its occurrences predate Hardy's discussion of Egdon Heath. Muir, for whom mountains were "Nature's Bible," is a notable exception early in the period. Abbey calls the desert *locus dei*, "the place of God"; Lane would agree. About half of the modern usages come from poets and novelists. Natural Theology is closely associated with Awe, Power, and Sublimity in its own group, and with Grandeur, Infinity, and Eternity elsewhere.

NOBILITY (2, 39th; 10, 44th): A few men, mostly mountaineers, have pronounced the Great noble or dignified. Conway, an artist, is the chief exponent, finding "noble views" in the Alps and Andes and on Spitsbergen, whose dignity he derives from its "long sweeping lines," "simple forms and sombre colouring." Nobility's grammar is obscure; it usually accompanies Spacious or Spiritual responses (e.g. Grandeur, Sublimity), or Bareness and Simplicity in the Minimal Group.

OXYMORON (24, 21st; 39, 25th): One of the distinctive marks of the Great as an aesthetic category is its blending of pleasurable emotions with some that we normally seek to avoid, in the manner of poetic oxymoron. So Austin calls the Mojave desert "a lonely, inhospitable land, beautiful, terrible," to which one must return. Nansen was struck by the Arctic's mixture of beauty, death, and "endless sadness"; Muir notes that Mt. Shasta combines "sublime beauty" with danger. Oxymoron does not reside within a group, but links those to which its constituents belong: the Spacious, Spiritual, or Pleasure Group on one hand, and the Dark Group on the other.

PAIN FOR GAIN (5, 36th; 29, 31st): The idea that the hardships of exploring the Great are part of its value gains some strength in the modern period. Amundsen says that the suffering of the Franklin party first attracted him to polar exploration: he wanted to "endure those same sufferings." Doughty insists that the discomforts of travel sanctify the pilgrimage to Mecca, and that "pain enamours" the pilgrims of the trail. To the outsider this may look masochistic; to Habeler, climbing Everest without oxygen meant "a fruitful confrontation of human spirit and strength with nature." Pain for Gain belongs to the Dark Group, and is often associated with Asceticism and Challenge.

POWER (27, 18th; 39, 25th): An aura of might or strength around mountains and deserts is fairly widely attested, but its nature and source vary, or are obscure. Early examples may connect it with Divine power; later ones are usually secular, Muir being an exception. Smythe lists power, beauty, and grandeur as the chief sensations of Alpine climbs. Hedin pays homage to the Gobi Desert's "might and greatness." A few instances come from Antarctica; Gran noted how on a journey across the Barrier the Western Mountains grew daily in "beauty and might." Most of Power's associations are with qualities in the Spiritual Group, though it is also connected to Fear and to Grandeur.

PURITY (37, 13th; 79, 7th): One of the commonest reactions to the Great has been that it is extraordinarily pure. Muir saw Alaska's Fairweather range as "ineffably chaste and spiritual." Later visitors (e.g. Smythe) sometimes contrast Great landscapes with the foul civilization they have left. Thesiger recalls how the far-stretching Libyan desert meets the sky in "cleanness." Often human and natural purity are not distinguished; Cherry-Garrard calls Antarctica "pure," and remembers the "clean, open life" they lived on the Barrier. Purity, a quality of subtraction in which human impurities have been removed, is linked to responses in the Minimal (Ascetic, Bare) and Spiritual Groups (Holiness of Mountains, God in Desert).

REALITY (4, 37th; 22, 33rd): The Great gives some the sensation of touching a truth beyond disguise or appearance, a deeper reality, be it natural, personal, or metaphysical. On Annapurna, Herzog "seemed to discover the deep significance of existence"; Harvey learned to "see through the word to the thing" in Ladakh. Carl and Petit in the Sahara, and Peary in the Arctic, report that the Great brings out the true self. In Cather's *My Antonia*, a winter sunset is "like the light of truth," and a cold wind says, "This is reality." Depending on its trigger, Reality may take on the colouring of the Science, Space, Adventure, or Temporal Groups, but most examples belong to the Minimal Group in that they involve a stripping away to essences.

SELF-KNOWLEDGE (5, 36th; 17, 37th): A few travellers report a heightened sense of identity, self-reliance, or self-knowledge arising from contact with Great nature. Uwe George claims that the desert, "a landscape in which the human spirit can exult," helps us to "recapture" our identity. Habeler quotes Messner as saying that he climbs to "find himself." Self-Knowledge is difficult to place; it can be an aspect of Adventure, a kind of Pleasure, or part of Reality or Awareness. It often accompanies Mirror in the Metaphorical Group.

SEVERITY (0, -; 13, 41st): Some modern travellers say that deserts and mountains can be harsh, stern, or cruel without concluding that they should be avoided. Muir describes Yosemite's cliffs as "awful in stern majesty" and Wrangell Land as "severely solitary." To Diolé, the Tassili Mountains look "strangely cruel," yet the Sahara remains beautiful. The idea is usually that Severity is bracing. Eberhardt enjoyed the "harsher and wilder" parts of Algeria; for Smythe, Himalayan nature, "cruel" and beautiful, achieves harmony. Severity is closely related to other terms in the Dark Group, but also connects with Adventure and Pleasure.

SILENCE (36, 14th; 98, 5th): A good number of early visitors to Great landscapes of all kinds commented on their quietness, a quality even more praised by later travellers, many of whom contrast it with the noise they left behind. Polar explorers from Nansen and Amundsen to Messner value the soundlessness of high latitudes, the "perfect stillness" of the Barrier. Ratti loved the "solemn silence" of the high Alps (a theme of Smythe's books), and Bodley came to miss the "majestic silence of the Sahara." Silence, the absence of sound, is most closely related to other terms in the Minimal Group such as Emptiness and Solitude, and to Calm in the Pleasure Group.

SIMPLICITY (15, 27th; 44, 21st): Early theorists made simplicity of design a defining attribute of the Great, and travellers have endorsed the idea, especially in deserts and polar regions. Dr Cook was fascinated by the "strange simplicity" of the Antarctic in winter; Smythe, Shipton, and others have made similar remarks about mountains. Sometimes simplicity is existential: Stefansson noted the simple forms of Arctic life, and Thesiger concluded that the Bedu derived satisfaction from their lives' "bare simplicity," as did he. Simplicity is closely associated with Asceticism, Bareness, and Solitude in the Minimal Group. It often arises from a perception of Elements in a mood of Calm.

SOLITUDE (57, 8th; 114, 3rd): A sense of isolation or loneliness was always an integral part of contact with the Great. While a few found this oppressive, more affirmed its value. Solitude's appeal increased during the 20th century, with many seeking the Great for that quality and some trying to increase what they found. Adm. Byrd insisted on manning Advance Base alone in Antarctica, as did Courtauld in Greenland; Messner was determined to climb Everest solo. Austin's Mojave Desert, "the loneliest land that ever came out of God's hands," still - or therefore - "must be come back to inevitably." In the Sahara, Foucauld said, "It is good to live alone in the land." Solitude is closely related to Silence, Bareness, and Emptiness in the Minimal Group, as well as to Liberty, and sometimes Misanthropy.

SPIRITUALITY (67, 5th; 117, 2nd): Although the Spiritual *Group* shrinks and most religious responses decline in the modern period, the general piety or reverence towards Great nature implied by Spirituality grows. Ratti, a future pope, and Muir, a preacher's son, naturally took a spiritual view of mountains, but it also crops up in Herzog (who revered the Himalayas "with a monk's veneration of the divine") and Krakauer. For Tenzing Norgay, God is like a mountain; he felt a "closeness to God" atop Chomolungma. The pious Doughty found Arabian nomad life Biblical, but Austin, an agnostic, also says that the desert "favors the sense of personal relation to the supernatural." Most early polar explorers sensed spiritual energy in those regions, and Messner saw Antarctica as a Dantean landscape, "both Heaven and Hell." Spirituality, the central term of the Spiritual Group, is also related to Asceticism, Eternity, and Infinity.

SUBLIMITY (86, 2nd; 32, 28th): Before Hardy, Sublimity, the sense of being lifted up or expanded, was the second most popular response to the Great, but in the modern period it has had the second steepest decline in favour. Recent travellers hesitate to claim such emotional heights or repeat an old cliché, so most examples come early in the period, from Muir (who used it freely), Conway, Freshfield, Dutton, and Bird. Whitman called the prairies "sublime," and Twain conceded Mont Blanc's sublimity. It crops up occasionally later, in Smythe, Krutch, even Abbey and Messner, but is now rare enough to startle. Sublimity is related to other members of the Spiritual Group and to the factors of which it is a product, often Vastness, Infinity, or Eternity.

TIME (5, 36th; 13, 41st): Close contact with the Great gives some an altered sense of time or the illusion of time-travel. Alone in Antarctica, Adm. Byrd felt like "the last survivor of an ice age" and imagined that "This is the way the world will look … as it dies," ideas also found in Nansen. In the desert or the sea, says Diolé, we are suspended "above time and space"; a Saharan oasis is "a world forgotten outside time." Heyerdahl, crossing the Atlantic on a raft, also felt "outside time," and nights seemed to last forever. Time is related to other members of the Temporal Group and to Geology and Astronomy, often its source.

TOURISM (0, -; 13, 41st): A wholly modern category, Tourism here means the realization by travellers that hordes of visitors to Great landscapes can taint the experience and harm natural sites. In the 1890s, Conway chronicled the damage that tourists were doing to the Alps and Spitsbergen. Shipton found Chamonix "gross with tourism" in 1928, and Smythe's last books deplore Alpine development. Bonington, Krakauer, Thesiger, Messner, and others have extended these concerns to the Himalayas, Alaska, deserts, and polar regions. A member of the Dark Group, Tourism often occurs near Misanthropy.

UNREAL (28, 17th; 45, 20th): Some visitors to the Great find it so weird, uncanny, or deceptive as to constitute an "unreality." Dutton describes the Grand Canyon district as "transcending the power of the intelligence to comprehend it." Herzog says that on Annapurna he touched "the extreme boundaries of man's world." For Habeler, "the veil which hides the great beyond is particularly thin" at high altitudes. Polar explorers from Nansen onwards make similar remarks: Mear found the Antarctic "like a dream" and its beauty "surreal." Unreal (Uncanny in *The Road to Egdon Heath*) can accompany Fear or Incomprehension in the Dark Group, or shade towards Metaphysics in the Spiritual Group.

VASTNESS (83, 3rd; 147, 1st): Addison built magnitude into the idea of the Great ("a vast desert," "huge heaps of mountains," "a spacious horizon"). Some theorists questioned whether mere physical size could be "sublime," but many travellers have been deeply impressed by Vastness: the most frequent response by modern visitors in all areas. Uwe George recalls being alone in the Sahara, the "center of a vast, empty disk," and at night, the sense of "vast void." Scott, Shackleton, Amundsen, and later explorers have marvelled at the scale of Antarctica. Climbing in the Andes and looking out over the ocean, Conway glories in "the sense it gives of immensity ... beyond the reach even of imagination."

Vastness, the earthly regent of Infinity, is the central term of the Spacious Group. It may evoke feelings of Liberty, even Sublimity, or of Insignificance.

VOID (17, 25th; 47, 19th): The sense of Great spaces as Nothing, Nil, has grown since French poets gave the Void currency. It is strong among desert and polar travellers, and in literary work. Shackleton's *Heart of the Antarctic* notes, "Men go out into the void spaces of the world for various reasons." Moorhouse called his book on Saharan travel *The Fearful Void*; Asher first saw that desert as "a vast ocean of nothing." Logically Void belongs to the Minimal Group as an extreme form of Emptiness, and may connote Liberty, but it can also be part of the Dark Group and inspire Fear. For those receptive to a Buddhist Nothing, it may have spiritual and pleasurable associations.

WHITENESS (21, 23rd; 42, 23rd): The colour most often mentioned by writers on the Great is white, usually in connection with snow, well-lit deserts, or blankness. Amundsen evokes a tiny line of men and dogs on the "endless white surface" of Antarctica under "bright, white shining light." Some have used white as a tabula rasa symbolizing nature's inscrutability, or death. For Bell, desertic Palmyra was a "white skeleton." Kazantzakis sends his modern Odysseus to die in the "white, wretched bitterness" of southern seas. Whiteness is a member of the Metaphorical Group, but closely associated with Bareness and some other members of the Minimal Group, with Purity, and with Incomprehension in the Dark Group.

WILDNESS (36, 14th; 50, 17th): The Earl of Shaftesbury wrote in 1709, "The wildness pleases." The Great was often seen as wild, and opposed to civilized artifice. Climbers such as Muir, Conway, Smythe, and Shipton are especially apt to celebrate Wildness, but desert and polar travellers also praise it. Hudson wrote that the sweep of the Patagonian plains appeals to the wild side of our own natures. Messner comments that the worth of Antarctica may be seen in "the quality of its wildness." Wildness has connections to responses in various groups - Liberty, Misanthropy, Solitude, Emptiness, Chaos - but does not fit readily into any one group itself.

Works Cited

Abbey, Edward. *Desert Solitaire: A Season in the Wilderness*. 1968. New York: Simon and Schuster, 1970.

---. *The Monkey Wrench Gang*. 1975. New York: Avon, 1976.

Abley, Mark. *Beyond Forget: Rediscovering the Prairies*. Vancouver and Toronto: Douglas and McIntyre, 1986.

Adams, Robert Martin. *Nil. Episodes in the Literary Conquest of Void during the Nineteenth Century*. New York: Oxford UP, 1966.

Addison, Joseph. *Addison and Steele: Selections from* The Tatler *and* The Spectator. Introd. Robert J. Allen. New York: Holt, Rinehart and Winston, 1965.

Aesthetics. Ed. Susan L. Feagin and Patrick Maynard. Oxford and New York: Oxford UP, 1997.

Affelder, Paul. Liner notes. *In the Steppes of Central Asia* and other works by Borodin and Ippolitov-Ivanov. Philharmonic-Symphony Orch. of New York. Cond. Dmitri Mitropoulos. LP. Columbia CL 751, n.d. (1953?).

Albritton, Claude C., Jr. *The Abyss of Time. Changing Conceptions of the Earth's Antiquity After the Sixteenth Century*. 1980. Los Angeles: Jeremy P. Tarcher, 1986.

Alexander, Caroline. *The Endurance. Shackleton's Legendary Antarctic Expedition*. New York: Knopf, 2001.

Amundsen, Roald. *My Life as an Explorer*. New York: Doubleday, Page, 1927.

---. *The South Pole*. 1912. Introd. F. Nansen. Trans. A.G. Chater. 2 vols. in 1. London: Hurst, 1976.

Armstrong, Neil. Quoted in *TIME Magazine*. 25 July 1969: 12.

Asher, Michael. *Impossible Journey. Two Against the Sahara*. 1988. Penguin Books, 1991.

Assad, Thomas J. *Three Victorian Travellers*. London: Routledge and Kegan Paul, 1964.

Astill, Tony. *Mount Everest: The Reconnaissance 1935. The Forgotten Adventure.* Fwd. Lord Hunt. Introd. Sir Edmund Hillary. N.p.: The Author, 2005.

Atwood, Margaret. "Death By Landscape." *Wilderness Tips.* Toronto: McClelland and Stewart, 1991.

---. *Survival. A Thematic Guide to Canadian Literature.* Toronto: Anansi, 1972.

Auden, W.H., and Christopher Isherwood. *The Ascent of F.6 and On the Frontier.* 1937. London: Faber and Faber, 1958.

Auden, W.H. *Collected Poems.* Ed. Edward Mendelson. 1976. Rev. ed. London: Faber and Faber, 1991.

---. *The Enchaféd Flood; or, The Romantic Iconography of the Sea.* 1949. New York: Random House, 1950.

---, and Louis MacNeice. *Letters From Iceland.* 1937. New York: Random House, 1969.

Austin, Mary. *Beyond Borders. The Selected Essays of Mary Austin.* Ed. Reuben J. Ellis. Carbondale and Edwardsville: Southern Illinois UP, 1996.

---. *The Land of Little Rain.* Boston and New York: Houghton Mifflin, 1903.

Bachelard, Gaston. *The Poetics of Space.* Trans. Maria Jolas. New York: Orion Press, 1964.

---. *La Terre et les rêveries de la volonté.* 1948. Paris: José Corti, 1962.

Banff Festival of Mountain Books and Films. Panel discussion. "Beyond Imagining: The Next Great Projects." Banff, AB. Nov. 2003.

Barber, Noel. *The White Desert.* London: Hodder and Stoughton, 1958.

Barcott, Bruce. *The Measure of a Mountain: Beauty and Terror on Mt. Rainier.* New York: Ballantine Books, 1997.

Bate, Jonathan. *Romantic Ecology: Wordsworth and the Environmental Tradition.* London and New York: Routledge, 1991.

Battcock, Gregory, ed. *Minimal Art: A Critical Anthology.* New York: Dutton, 1968.

Beach, Joseph Warren. *The Concept of Nature in Nineteenth-Century English Poetry.* 1936. New York: Pageant, 1956.

Bell, Gertrude. *The Arabian Diaries, 1913-1914.* Ed. Rosemary O'Brien. Syracuse: Syracuse UP, 2000.

---. *The Letters of Gertrude Bell, selected and edited by Lady Bell.* 2 vols. London: Benn, 1927.

---. *Safar Nameh. Persian Pictures.* 1894. *Persian Pictures.* Pref. E. Denison Ross. London: Benn, 1928.

---. *Syria. The Desert and the Sown.* London: Heinemann, 1907.

Belloc, Hilaire. *Hills and the Sea.* London: Methuen, 1906.

---. *The Silence of the Sea and Other Essays.* 1940. Rpt. Freeport, NY: Books for Libraries Press, 1971.

---. "A Revelation of the Alps." In Lunn 1913.

Benoit, Pierre. *L'Atlantide.* Ed. Albin Michel. Paris: n. pub., 1919.

Berton, Pierre. *The Arctic Grail. The Quest for the Northwest Passage and the North Pole, 1818-1909.* 1988. Markham, ON: Penguin, 1989.

Bevis, Richard. *The Road to Egdon Heath. The Aesthetics of the Great in Nature.* Montreal and Kingston: McGill-Queen's UP, 1999.

Bevis, William W. *Mind of Winter. Wallace Stevens, Meditation, and Literature.* Pittsburgh: Pittsburgh UP, 1988.

---. *Ten Tough Trips. Montana Writers and the West.* Seattle and London: U of Washington P, 1990.

Bickel, Lennard. *Shackleton's Forgotten Men.* New York: Thunder's Mouth Press and Balliet & Fitzgerald, 2000.

Bietenholz, Peter G. *Desert and Bedouin in the European Mind: Changing Conceptions from the Middle Ages to the Present Time.* Khartoum: Khartoum UP, 1963.

Bird, Isabella L. *A Lady's Life in the Rocky Mountains.* 1879. Introd. Daniel J. Boorstin. Norman: U of Oklahoma P, 1960.

Birney, Earle. *David and Other Poems.* Toronto: Ryerson, 1942.

Blixen, Karen. See Dinesen, Isak.

Blunt, Anne. *Bedouin Tribes of the Euphrates.* Ed. W.S. Blunt. London: Murray, 1879.

---. *A Pilgrimage to Nejd.* Ed. W.S. Blunt. 2 vols. London: Murray, 1881.

Blunt, Wilfrid S[cawen]. *My Diaries.* Part One [1888-1900]. New York: Knopf, 1923.

Blyth, R.H. *Zen in English Literature and Oriental Classics.* Tokyo: Hokuseido, 1942.

Bodley, R.V.C. *Wind in the Sahara.* New York: Creative Age, 1944.

Bonington, Chris. *Everest the Hard Way.* 1976. London: Arrow, 1977.

Borchgrevink, C[arsten] E. *First on the Antarctic Continent ... The British Antarctic Expedition 1898-1900.* 1901. Montreal: McGill-Queens UP, 1980.

Borges, Jorge Luis. *Ficciones.* Madrid: Alianza, 1987.

Borodin, Alexander. *In the Steppes of Central Asia*. 1880. London: Eulenberg, n.d. See also Affelder, Paul.

Bourassa, Steven C. *The Aesthetics of Landscape*. London and New York: Belhaven, 1991.

Bowles, Paul. *Collected Stories 1939-1976*. Santa Barbara: Black Sparrow, 1979.

---. *Next to Nothing. Collected Poems 1926-1977*. Santa Barbara: Black Sparrow, 1981.

---. *The Sheltering Sky*. 1949. New York: Ecco, 1978.

---. *Their Heads Are Green and Their Hands Are Blue*. New York: Random House, 1963.

---. *Without Stopping*. New York: Putnam, 1972.

Bowman, Isaiah. *Desert Trails of Atacama*. New York: American Geographical Society, 1924.

Bridges, E. Lucas. *Uttermost Part of the Earth*. London: Hodder and Stoughton, 1948.

Bridges, Robert. *Poetical Works of Robert Bridges*. 2nd ed. London: Oxford UP, 1936.

Brockman, John, ed. *The Third Culture*. New York: Simon and Schuster, 1995.

Brown, Hamish. *Hamish's Mountain Walk*. 1978. London: Granada, 1980.

Bryson, Bill, ed. *The Best American Travel Writing 2000*. Boston: Houghton Mifflin, 2000.

Buell, Lawrence. *The Environmental Imagination: Thoreau, Nature Writing, and the Formation of American Culture*. Cambridge, MA, and London: Belknap/Harvard UP, 1995.

Burgoyne, Elizabeth. *Gertrude Bell From Her Personal Papers 1889-1914*. London: Benn, 1958. *1914-1926*. London: Benn, 1961.

Butala, Sharon. *The Perfection of the Morning. An Apprenticeship in Nature*. Toronto: HarperCollins, 1994.

Byrd, Richard. *Alone*. London: Putnam, 1938.

---. *Discovery. The Story of the Second Byrd Antarctic Expedition*. New York: Putnam, 1935.

Cameron, Ian. *Antarctica: The Last Continent*. Boston and Toronto: Little, Brown, 1974.

Cannon, Peter. *H.P. Lovecraft*. Boston: Twayne, 1989.

Caponi, Gena Dagel. *Paul Bowles: Romantic Savage*. Carbondale: Southern Illinois UP, 1994.

Carl, Louis, and Joseph Petit. *Tefedest: Méharée au Sahara Central.* 1953. *Tefedest: Journey to the Heart of the Sahara.* Trans. Stephen Becker. London: Allen and Unwin, 1954.

Carlson, Allen. "Aesthetic Appreciation of the Natural Environment." *Aesthetics.* Ed. Susan L. Feagin and Patrick Maynard. Oxford and New York: Oxford UP, 1997.

Carter, Paul. *The Road to Botany Bay. An Essay in Spatial History.* London and Boston: Faber and Faber, 1987.

Cather, Willa. *My Antonia.* 1918. Boston: Houghton Mifflin, 1949.

---. *The Song of the Lark.* Boston and New York: Houghton Mifflin, 1915.

Chadbourne, Richard, and Hallvard Dahlie, ed. *The New Land: Studies in a Literary Theme.* Calgary Institute for the Humanities. Waterloo, ON: Wilfrid Laurier UP, 1978.

Chadwick, Douglas H. "Our Wildest Wilderness." *National Geographic* Dec. 1979: 740-69.

Chapman, F. Spencer. *Memoirs of a Mountaineer. Helvellyn to Himalaya* ... [1940]. London: Chatto and Windus, 1951.

---. *Northern Lights: The Official Account of the British Arctic Air-Route Expedition.* Fwd. Richard E. Byrd. New York: Oxford UP, 1934.

Chatwin, Bruce. *The Songlines.* New York: Viking, 1987.

Cherry-Garrard, Apsley. *The Worst Journey in the World.* 1922. Harmondsworth: Penguin, 1970.

Clarke, Jamie. "Crossing the Rub al-Khali." Banff Festival of Mountain Books and Films, Banff, AB. 4 Nov. 1999.

Conrad, Joseph. *Lord Jim.* 1900. Harmondsworth: Penguin, 1957.

---. *Nostromo. A Tale of the Seaboard.* 1904. London: Dent, 1947a.

---. *The Portable Conrad.* Ed. Morton D. Zabel. New York: Viking, 1947b.

Conway, William Martin. *Aconcagua and Tierra del Fuego.* London: Cassell, 1902.

---. *The Alps from End to End.* 1895. London: Constable, 1904.

---. *The First Crossing of Spitsbergen.* London: Dent, 1897.

---. "First Vision of the Snows." In Lunn 1913.

Cook, Frederick A. *Return from the Pole.* Ed. Frederick J. Pohl. London: Burke, 1953.

---. *Through the First Antarctic Night, 1898-1899: The Voyage of the "Belgica".* 1900. Montréal: McGill-Queens UP, 1980.

Cooper, James Fenimore. *The Prairie.* 1827. Ed. James P. Elliott. Albany: State U of New York P, 1985.

Courtauld, Augustine. See Wollaston.

Crane, Hart. *The Poems of Hart Crane*. Ed. Marc Simon. New York: Liveright, 1986.

Dana, Richard Henry. *Two Years Before the Mast*. 1840. New York: Random House, 1936.

Daudet, Alphonse. *Tartarin sur les Alpes*. 1885. Trans. Henry Frith. New York and London: Dent-Dutton, 1910.

Dean, Dennis. "'Through Science to Despair': Geology and the Victorians." *Victorian Science and Victorian Values: Literary Perspectives*. Ed. James Paradis and Thomas Postlewait. *Annals of the New York Academy of Science* 360 (20 Apr. 1981): 111-36.

De Beer, Gavin. *Early Travellers in the Alps*. London: Sidgwick and Jackson, 1930.

Debenham, Frank. *Antarctica. The Story of a Continent*. London: Herbert Jenkins, 1959.

Delius, Frederick. *The Song of the High Hills*. 1911. Vienna: Universal Editions 13875, n.d.

Demars, Stanford E. *The Tourist in Yosemite, 1855-1985*. Salt Lake City: U Utah P, 1991.

[de Mille, James]. *A Strange MS. Found in a Copper Cylinder*. 1888. Toronto: Macmillan of Canada, 1910.

Dent, Clinton T. "The Conquest of the Dru." 1885. In Lunn 1913.

---, ed. *Mountaineering*. 1892. 3rd ed. London: Longmans, Green, 1901.

Deresiewicz, William. "Adaptation." Rev. of six books on Literary Darwinism. *The Nation* 8 June 2009: 26-31.

Le Désert. Spec. issue of *Moebius* 45 (Été 1990): 1-152.

Le Désert. Spec. issue of *Traverses* 19 (Juin 1980): 1-148.

Develing, E[nno], intro. *Minimal Art*. Exhibition catalogue. N.p. [The Hague]: gemeentemuseum, 1968.

Didion, Joan. *Play It as It Lays*. 1970. New York: Bantam, 1971.

Dinesen, Isak [Karen Blixen]. *Out of Africa* [1937] and *Shadows on the Grass* [1960]. Harmondsworth: Penguin, 1985.

Diolé, Philippe. *Le Plus beau désert du monde*. 1955. *Sahara Adventure*. Trans. Katherine Woods. New York: Julian Messner, 1956.

Doughty, Charles M. *Adam Cast Forth*. London: Duckworth, 1908.

---. *Travels in Arabia Deserta*. 1888. 2 vols. in 1. New York: Random House, n.d.

Douglas, Ed. *Tenzing: Hero of Everest. A Biography of Tenzing Norgay*. Washington: National Geographic Society, 2003.

Douglas, Norman. *Fountains in the Sand*. 1912. Oxford: Oxford UP, 1986.

Dufek, George J. *Operation Deepfreeze*. New York: Harcourt, Brace, 1957.

Durrell, Gerald. *The Corfu Trilogy*. London: Penguin, 2006.

Dutton, Clarence E. *Tertiary History of the Grand Cañon District with Atlas*. U.S. Geological Survey Monographs, vol. 2. Washington, DC: Government Printing Office, 1882.

Dutton, Geoff. *The Hero as Murderer. The Life of Edward John Eyre*. Sydney: Collins, 1967.

Dyott, G.M. *On the Trail of the Unknown*. London: Butterworth, 1926.

Eastlake, William. *Portrait of an Artist with Twenty-Six Horses*. 1958. New York: Simon and Schuster, 1963.

Eberhardt, Isabelle. *Prisoner of Dunes: Selected Writings of Isabelle Eberhardt*. Trans. Sharon Bangert. London and Chester Springs, PA: P. Owen, 1995.

Ehrlich, Gretel. *The Solace of Open Spaces*. 1985. New York: Penguin, 1986.

Eliade, Mircea. *The Sacred and the Profane. The Nature of Religion*. 1957. Trans. Willard R. Trask. New York: Harcourt, Brace, 1959.

Eliot, T[homas] S[tearns]. *The Complete Poems and Plays 1909-1950*. New York: Harcourt, Brace, 1952.

Engel, Claire-Éliane. *La Littérature alpestre en France et en Angleterre aux XVIIIe et XIXe siècles*. Chambéry: Dardel, 1930.

---. *Mountaineering in the Alps: An Historical Survey*. London: Allen and Unwin, 1950. Rev. ed., 1971.

Evans, Edward R.G.R. *South with Scott*. Glasgow: Collins, n.d. [1921?].

Ewart, Arthur. "John Muir and Vertical Sauntering." In Muir 1999.

Farquhar, Francis P. "John Muir and the Range of Light." In Muir 1999.

Fedden, Robin. *English Travellers in the Near East*. London: Longmans, Green, 1958.

Finch, David. *R.M. Patterson: A Life of Great Adventure*. Calgary: Rocky Mountain Books, 2000.

Finch, Edith. *Wilfrid Scawen Blunt*. London: Cape, 1938.

Fitter, Chris. *Poetry, Space, Landscape: Towards a New Theory*. Cambridge and New York: Cambridge UP, 1995.

Flecker, James Elroy. *Collected Poems of James Elroy Flecker*. London: Martin Secker, 1932.

Fletcher, Colin. *The Man Who Walked through Time*. 1967. New York: Random House, 1972.

Fletcher, John Baylis. *Up the Trail in '79*. Ed. Wayne Gard. Norman: U Oklahoma P, 1968.

Flores, Dan. *The Natural West: Environmental History in the Great Plains and Rocky Mountains*. Norman: U Oklahoma P, 2001.

Foucauld, Charles de. *Lettres et carnets*. Ed. J[ean]-F[rançois] Six. Paris: Seuil, 1966.

---. *Spiritual Autobiography of Charles de Foucauld*. Ed. Jean-François Six. Trans. J. Holland Smith. New York: P.J. Kenedy, 1964.

Fowles, John. *The Collector*. 1963. London: Pan, 1973.

---. *Daniel Martin*. 1976. Boston: Little, Brown, 1977.

---. *The French Lieutenant's Woman*. 1969. Toronto: New American Library, 1970.

---. *The Magus*. 1965. Rev. ed. 1978. New York: Dell, 1979.

Freshfield, Douglas W. *The Exploration of the Caucasus*. 2nd ed. 2 vols. London: Arnold, 1902.

---. *The Life of H[orace] B[énédict] de Saussure*. London: Arnold, 1920.

---. "Lombard Peaks" and "The Adamello." In Lunn 1913.

Frost, Robert. *The Complete Poems of Robert Frost*. New York: Holt, Rinehart, and Winston, 1949.

Fuchs, Vivian, and Edmund Hillary. *The Crossing of Antarctica*. London: Cassell, 1958.

Garland, Hamlin. *Boy Life on the Prairie*. 1899. New York: Washington Square, 1965.

---. *Main-Travelled Roads*. 1891. New York: Harper and Row, 1956.

Gautier, É[mile] F. *Sahara: The Great Desert*. 1923. 2nd ed. 1928. Trans. Dorothy Ford Mayhew. 1935. New York: Hippocrene, 1987.

George, Uwe. *In the Deserts of This Earth*. 1976. Trans. Richard and Clara Winston. New York and London: Harcourt, Brace, Jovanovich, 1977.

Georgi, Johannes. *Mid-Ice ... The Wegener Expedition to Greenland*. Trans. F.H. Lyon. New York: Dutton, 1935.

Gerster, Georg. *Sahara*. 1959. Trans. Stewart Thomson. London: Barrie and Rockliff, 1960.

Gide, André. *The Immoralist*. 1921. Trans. Dorothy Bussy. New York: Vintage, 1956.

Gilbar, Steven, ed. *Natural State ... California Nature Writing*. Berkeley: U California P, 1998.

Glacken, Clarence J. *Traces on the Rhodian Shore*. Berkeley: U California P, 1967.

Gore, Rick. "What *Voyager* Saw: Jupiter's Dazzling Realm." *National Geographic* Jan. 1980: 2-29.

Govinda, Lama Anagarika. *The Way of the White Clouds*. London: Hutchinson, 1966.

Gran, Tryggve. *The Norwegian with Scott: Trygge Gran's Antarctic Diary 1910-1913*. 1915. Ed. Geoffrey Hattersley-Smith. Trans. Ellen J. McGhie. N.p.: National Maritime Museum, 1984.

Gregory, Derek. *Geographical Imaginations*. Cambridge, MA, and Oxford: Blackwell, 1994.

Grofé, Ferde. *The Grand Canyon Suite*. 1931. New York: Robbins, 1943.

Grove, Frederick Philip. *In Search of Myself*. Toronto: Macmillan, 1946.

---. *Over Prairie Trails*. 1922. Toronto: McClelland and Stewart, 1957.

---. *Settlers of the Marsh*. Toronto: Ryerson, 1925.

Guthrie, A.B., Jr. *The Big Sky*. 1947. New York: Pocket Books, 1949.

Habeler, Peter. *Everest: Impossible Victory*. 1978. Trans. David Heald. London: Sphere, 1979.

Hamilton, Elizabeth. *The Desert My Dwelling Place: A Study of Charles de Foucauld 1858-1916*. London: Hodder and Stoughton, 1968.

Hammond, Alan. *To Climb a Sacred Mountain*. Menlo Park, CA: Illuminated Way Press, 1979.

Hardy, Thomas. *The Complete Poetical Works of Thomas Hardy*. Ed. Samuel Hynes. 5 vols. Oxford: Clarendon, 1982-95.

---. *The Return of the Native*. 1878. London: Zodiac, 1980.

---. *Tess of the D'Urbervilles*. 1891. Introd. A. Alvarez. Ed. David Skilton. Harmondsworth: Penguin, 1978.

---. *Two on a Tower*. 1882. New York and London: Harper, 1900.

---. *The Well-Beloved*. 1892. New York and London: Harper, 1900.

Harvey, Andrew. *A Journey in Ladakh*. London: Cape, 1983.

Heaney, Seamus. "The Sense of Place." *Preoccupations: Selected Prose 1968-1978*. London and Boston: Faber and Faber, 1980.

Hedin, Sven. *Across the Gobi Desert*. Trans. H.J. Cant. 1931. New York: Greenwood, 1968.

---. *A Conquest of Tibet*. Trans. Julius Lincoln. 1934. Garden City, NY: Halcyon House, 1941.

---. *My Life as an Explorer*. Trans. Alfhild Huebsch. Hong Kong: Oxford UP, 1991.

Heil, Nick. *Dark Summit: The True Story of Everest's Most Controversial Season*. N.p.: Random House Canada, 2008.

Hemingway, Ernest. *Green Hills of Africa*. 1935. N.p.: Perma, 1954.

---. "The Snows of Kilimanjaro." 1936. *The Snows of Kilimanjaro and Other Stories*. Harmondsworth: Penguin, 1963.

Henson, Matthew A. *A Negro Explorer at the North Pole*. 1912. *A Black Explorer at the North Pole*. Fwd. Robert E. Peary. Introd. Booker T. Washington. New York: Walker, 1969.

Herbert, Frank. *Dune*. 1965. New York: Berkley, 1980.

Herbert, Wally. *Across the Top of the World*. London: Longman, 1969.

Herzog, Maurice. *Annapurna*. 1952. Trans. Nea Morin and Janet Adam Smith. Introd. Eric Shipton. New York: Dutton, 1953.

Hesse, Hermann. *Blick ins Chaos: drei Aufsätze*. Bern: Seldwyla, 1922.

Heyerdahl, Thor. *The Kon-Tiki Expedition*. 1948. Trans. anon. Allen and Unwin, 1950. Harmondsworth: Penguin, 1963.

---. *The Ra Expeditions*. 1970. Rev. ed. Trans. Patricia Crampton. New York: New American Library, 1972.

Hichens, Robert. *The Garden of Allah*. London: Methuen, 1904.

Hillary, Edmund, ed. *Challenge of the Unknown*. New York: Dutton, 1958.

---, and Desmond Doig. *High in the Thin Cold Air*. New York: Doubleday, 1962.

---. "Hillary's Firsthand Account." *LIFE* 13 July 1953: 124-38.

---. *No Latitude for Error*. London: Hodder and Stoughton, 1961.

Hillerman, Tony. *Coyote Waits*. 1990. New York: Harper, 1992.

Hogarth, David G. *Accidents of an Antiquary's Life*. London: MacMillan, 1910.

---. *The Life of Charles M. Doughty*. New York: Doubleday, 1929.

---. *The Penetration of Arabia*. 1904. Beirut: Khayat, 1966.

Holst, Gustav. *Egdon Heath: Homage to Thomas Hardy*, op. 47. 1927. London: Novello, 1928.

---. *The Planets*. 1921. Introd. Vally Lasker. London: Boosey and Hawkes #15970, n.d.

Holthaus, Gary, and others, ed. *A Society to Match the Scenery*. Boulder: Colorado UP, 1991.

---. *Wide Skies: Finding a Home in the West*. Tucson: U Arizona P, 1997.

Hopkins, Gerard Manley. *The Poems of Gerard Manley Hopkins*. 1918. Ed. W.H. Gardner and N.H. MacKenzie. 4th ed. corr. London and New York: Oxford UP, 1970.

Hovhaness, Alan. *Mysterious Mountains*. Notes by Hinako Fujihara Hovhaness. Royal Liverpool Philharmonic Orchestra. Cond. Gerard Schwarz. Telarc CD-80604, 2003.

---. *Symphony #7 (Nanga Parvat) for Wind Orchestra*, op. 178. New York: Peters, 1960.

Howard-Bury, Charles. See Keaney, Marian, ed.

Hudson, W.H. *Idle Days in Patagonia*. 1893. Berkeley, CA: Creative Arts, 1979.

---. *The Purple Land That England Lost*. 1885. 2 vols. in 1. London: Sampson Low, 1887.

Hulme, T[homas] E[rnest]. *The Collected Writings of T.E. Hulme*. Ed. Karen Csengeri. Oxford: Clarendon, 1994.

Humphreys, Christmas. *Buddhism*. 1951. Rev. ed. Harmondsworth: Penguin, 1955.

Hunt, John. *The Ascent of Everest*. 1953. Reset ed. London: Hodder and Stoughton, 1957.

Huntford, Roland, ed. *The Amundsen Photos*. New York: Atlantic Monthly Press, 1987.

Huth, Hans. *Nature and the American*. Berkeley and Los Angeles: U California P, 1957.

Ibsen, Henrik. *Little Eyolf*. 1894. Trans. Michael Meyer. London: R. Hart-Davis, 1961.

Ippolitov-Ivanov, Mikhail M. *Caucasian Sketches*, op. 10. 1894. See Affelder, Paul.

Irvine, Demar, ed. *Anton von Webern. Perspectives*. Seattle and London: U Washington P, 1966.

Iseman, Peter A. "The Arabian Ethos." *Harper's* Feb. 1978: 37-56.

James, Henry. *The Short Stories of Henry James*. Ed. Clifton Fadiman. New York: Random House, 1945.

James, Lawrence. *The Golden Warrior. The Life and Legend of Lawrence of Arabia*. 1990. Rev. ed. London: Little, Brown, 1995.

James, William. *William James: The Essential Writings*. Ed. Bruce W. Wilshire. Albany: State U of New York P, 1984.

Jeans, James. *The Mysterious Universe*. Cambridge: Cambridge UP, 1930.

Jeffers, Robinson. *Dear Judas and Other Poems*. New York: H. Liveright, 1929.

---. *Roan Stallion. Tamar. And Other Poems*. New York: Modern Library, 1935.

Jerome, John. *On Mountains*. New York and London: Harcourt, Brace, Jovanovich, 1978.

Kattam, Naïm. "Le Thème de l'espace dans la littérature canadienne-française." In Chadbourne and Dahlie, ed.

Kazantzakis, Nikos. *The Odyssey: A Modern Sequel*. Trans. and introd. Kimon Friar. New York: Simon and Schuster, 1958.

Keaney, Marian, ed. *Everest Reconnaissance: The First Expedition of 1921*. Narratives of Charles Howard-Bury and George Leigh-Mallory. London: Hodder and Stoughton, 1991.

Kerouac, Jack. *Vanity of Duluoz: An Adventurous Education, 1935-46*. New York: Coward-McCann, 1967.

Kipling, Rudyard. *Kim*. 1900. Vol. 19 of *The Writings in Prose and Verse of Rudyard Kipling*. New York: Scribner's, 1902.

Kloss, Phillips [Wray]. *Arid*. New York: Macmillan, 1932.

Kluckhohn, Clyde. See Roberts.

Kobak, Annette. *Isabelle: The Life of Isabelle Eberhardt*. London: Chatto and Windus, 1988.

Kodas, Michael. *High Crimes: The Fate of Everest in an Age of Greed*. New York: Hyperion, 2008.

Kohak, Ezerim. *The Embers and the Stars. A Philosophical Enquiry into the Moral Sense of Nature*. Chicago: U Chicago P, 1984.

Koyré, Alexandre. *From the Closed World to the Infinite Universe*. Johns Hopkins UP, 1957.

Krakauer, Jon. *Eiger Dreams: Ventures Among Men and Mountains*. 1990. New York: Random House, 1997a.

---. *Into Thin Air*. New York: Random House, 1997b.

---. "Queen Maud Land." *National Geographic* Feb. 1998: 46-69.

Kreisel, Henry. "The Prairie: A State of Mind." 1968. *Canadian Anthology*. Ed. Reginald E. Watters and Carl F. Klinck. 3rd ed. rev. Toronto: Gage, 1974.

Kroetsch, Robert. *Badlands*. 1975. Toronto: General Publishing, 1982.

Krutch, Joseph Wood. *Baja California and the Geography of Hope*. San Francisco: Sierra Club, 1969.

---. *The Desert Year*. 1951. New York: Viking, 1963.

---. "The Eye of the Beholder." *American West* May 1967: 18-20.

---, ed. *Great American Nature Writing*. N.p.: Sloane, 1950.

---, introd. *In Wildness Is the Preservation of the World*. San Francisco: Sierra Club, 1962.

---. *The Voice of the Desert: A Naturalist's Interpretation*. 1954. New York: Sloane, 1955.

Landscape, Natural Beauty and the Arts. Ed. Salim Kemal and Ivan Gaskell. Cambridge: Cambridge UP, 1993.

Lane, Belden C. *The Solace of Fierce Landscapes: Exploring Desert and Mountain Spirituality.* New York: Oxford UP, 1998.

Langbaum, Robert. "The New Nature Poetry." *The American Scholar* Summer 1959: 323-40. Rpt. in *The Modern Spirit.* New York: Oxford UP, 1970.

Langone, John. *Life at the Bottom: The People of Antarctica.* Boston and Toronto: Little, Brown, 1977.

Lawrence, D[avid] H[erbert]. *Phoenix: The Posthumous Papers of D.H. Lawrence.* 1936. Ed. Edward D. MacDonald. New York: Viking, 1972.

---. *The Plumed Serpent.* 1926. Harmondsworth: Penguin, 1950.

---. *Sea and Sardinia.* 1921. London: Heinemann, 1956.

---. *The Spirit of Place.* Ed. Richard Aldington. 1935. London: Readers Union, 1944.

Lawrence, T[homas] E[dward]. *Selected Letters of T.E. Lawrence.* Ed. David Garnett. 1938. London: The Reprint Society, 1941.

---. *Seven Pillars of Wisdom: A Triumph.* 1926 (pvt.); 1935. New York: Garden City Publishing, 1938.

Laxness, Halldór. *Independent People.* 1946. Trans. J.A. Thompson. Introd. Brad Leithauser. New York: Random House, 1997.

Leepa, Alan. "Minimal Art and Primary Meanings." In Battcock.

Leigh-Mallory, George. See Keaney, Marian, ed.

Leopold, A. Starker. *The Desert.* New York: TIME, Inc., 1961.

Leopold, Aldo. *A Sand County Almanac: With Essays on Conservation from Round River.* 1949; 1953. New York: Random House, 1970.

Lévi-Strauss, Claude. *Tristes tropiques.* 1955. *A World on the Wane.* Trans. John Russel. New York: Criterion, 1961.

Lhote, Henri. *The Search for the Tassili Frescoes.* 1958. Trans. Alan Houghton Brodrick. 2nd ed. London: Hutchinson, 1973.

Lindqvist, Sven. *Desert Divers.* 1990. Trans. Joan Tate. London: Granta, 2000.

Longenbach, James. "A Music of Austerity." Rev. of *Wallace Stevens. Selected Poems,* ed. John N. Serio. *The Nation* September 2009: 25-30.

Lopez, Barry H. *Arctic Dreams.* New York: Scribner's, 1986.

---. *Crossing Open Ground.* 1988. New York: Random House, 1989.

---. *Desert Notes.* 1976. New York: Avon, 1981.

Loti, Pierre. *Le Désert.* 1895. *The Desert.* Trans. Jay Paul Minn. Salt Lake City: U Utah P, 1993.

---. *Pêcheur d'Islande.* 1886. *Iceland Fisherman.* Trans. W.P. Baines. London: Dent, 1935.

---. *Vers Ispahan*. 1904. Exeter, UK: Exeter U Publications, 1989.

Love, Glen. "Revaluing Nature: Toward an Ecological Criticism." *Western American Literature* 25.3 (1990): 201-15.

Lovecraft, H.P. See Cannon.

Lowenthal, David. "The American Scene." *Geographical Review* 58 (1968): 61-88.

---. "Awareness of Human Impacts: Changing Attitudes and Emphases." In *The Earth as Transformed by Human Action*. Ed. B.L. Turner II. Cambridge: Cambridge UP, 1990.

Lowry, Malcolm. *Hear Us, O Lord from Heaven Thy Dwelling Place*. Philadelphia: Lippincott, 1961.

Lunn, Arnold, ed. *The Englishman in the Alps: ... a Collection of Prose and Poetry* .... London: Oxford UP, 1913.

---. *Mountain Jubilee*. London: Eyre and Spottiswoode, 1943.

---. *Mountains of Memory*. London: Hollis and Carter, 1948.

MacDiarmid, Hugh [C.M. Grieve]. *The Complete Poems of Hugh MacDiarmid*. Ed. Michael Grieve and W.R. Aitken. Vol. 1. Harmondsworth: Penguin, 1985.

MacEwen, Gwendolyn. "Terror and Erebus." *Afterworlds*. Toronto: McClelland and Stewart, 1987.

---. *The T.E. Lawrence Poems*. Oakville, ON: Mosaic Press/Valley Editions, 1982.

MacLeish, Archibald. "Voyage to the Moon." 1969? *Collected Poems, 1917-1982*. Boston: Houghton Mifflin, 1985.

Mallet, Thierry. *Glimpses of the Barren Lands*. New York: Revillon Frères, 1930.

Mallory, George Leigh-. See Keaney, Marian, ed.

Marin, John. Quoted in *Artists on Art, from the XIV to the XX Century*. Ed. Robert Goldwater and Marco Treves. 3rd ed. New York: Random House, 1958. P. 468.

Markham, Clements. *The Lands of Silence: A History of Arctic and Antarctic Exploration*. Cambridge: Cambridge UP, 1921.

Marsh, George Perkins. *Man and Nature*. 1864. Ed. David Lowenthal. Belknap/Harvard UP, 1965.

Matthiessen, Peter. *The Snow Leopard*. 1978. New York: Bantam Books, 1979.

Maupassant, Guy de. *Mont-Oriol*. 1887. Paris: Conard, 1910.

Mauriac, François. *Le Désert de l'Amour*. 1925. *The Desert of Love*. Trans. Gerard Hopkins. London: Eyre and Spottiswoode, 1949.

McCarthy, Cormac. *All the Pretty Horses*. 1992. New York: Random House, 1993.

McCourt, Edward A. *The Canadian West in Fiction*. Toronto: Ryerson, 1949.

Mear, Roger, and Robert Swan. *A Walk to the Pole: To the Heart of Antarctica in the Footsteps of Scott*. New York: Crown, 1987.

Meredith, George. *Poems and Lyrics of the Joy of Earth*. London: Macmillan, 1883.

---. *A Reading of Earth*. London: Macmillan, 1888.

Merton, Thomas. *The Asian Journal of Thomas Merton*. Ed. Naomi Burton, Patrick Hart, and James Laughlin. 1968. New York: New Directions, 1973.

---. *The Wisdom of the Desert: Sayings from the Desert Fathers of the Fourth Century*. Trans. and introd. Thomas Merton. New York: New Directions, 1960.

Messner, Reinhold. *Antarktis - Himmel und Hölle zugleich*. 1990. *Antarctica: Both Heaven and Hell*. Trans. Jill Neate. Ramsbury: Crowood Press, 1991.

---. "At My Limit." *National Geographic* Oct. 1981: 552-66.

Millgate, Michael. *Thomas Hardy. A Biography*. New York: Random House, 1982.

Mitcham, Allison. *The Northern Imagination: A Study of Northern Canadian Literature*. Moonbeam, ON: Penumbra, 1983.

Mitchell, W.O. *Who Has Seen the Wind*. 1947. Toronto: Macmillan of Canada, 1972.

Moldenhauer, Hans, and Rosaleen Moldenhauer. *Anton von Webern*. New York: Knopf, 1979.

Moorhouse, Geoffrey. *The Fearful Void*. 1974. St Albans: Granada, 1975.

Morris, William. *The Collected Works of William Morris*. 24 vols. London and New York: Longmans, Green, 1910-15.

Moss, John. *Enduring Dreams: An Exploration of Arctic Landscape*. Concord, ON: Anansi, 1994.

Motte, Warren. *Small Worlds: Minimalism in Contemporary French Literature*. Lincoln and London: U Nebraska P, 1999.

Mowat, Farley. *The Polar Passion*. 1967. Vol. 2 of *The Top of the World* trilogy. Rev. ed. Toronto: McClelland and Stewart, 1973.

---. *The Snow Walker*. 1975. Toronto: McClelland and Stewart/ Bantam Ltd, 1977.

Muir, John. *The Cruise of the Corwin*. 1881. Ed. William F. Badè. Dunwoody, GA: Berg, 1974.

---. *John of the Mountains: The Unpublished Journals of John Muir*. 1938. Ed. Linnie Marsh Wolfe. Madison: U Wisconsin P, 1979a.

---. *Mountaineering Essays*. Ed. and introd. Richard F. Fleck. Salt Lake City: U Utah P, 1997.

---. *The Mountains of California*. 1894. Berkeley: Ten-Speed Press, 1977.

---. *Sacred Summits: John Muir's Greatest Climbs*. Ed. Graham White. Edinburgh: Canongate, 1999.

---. *Travels in Alaska*. 1915. Introd. Edwin Way Teale. Boston: Houghton Mifflin, 1979b.

---. *The Yosemite*. 1912. Introd. Frederic R. Gunsky. New York: Doubleday Anchor, 1962.

Mulhallen, Karen. "Schaferscapes/Wolfbound. Twelve Notes toward a New View of Camping." *Descant* Spring 1995: 133-76.

Mummery, A.F. See Lunn 1913.

Murry, John Middleton. "Arabia Deserta." *The Adelphi* Mar. 1926: 657-65.

---. "Charles Montagu Doughty." *Countries of the Mind*. London: Milford and Oxford UP, 1931.

Nabhan, Gary P. *The Desert Smells Like Rain*. San Francisco: North Point Press, 1982.

Naess, Arne. *Ecology, Community and Lifestyle. Outline of an Ecosophy*. Trans. and rev. David Rothenberg. Cambridge: Cambridge UP, 1989.

Nansen, Fridtjof. *Farthest North*. Appendix by Otto Sverdrup. 2 vols. London: Macmillan, 1897.

---. *The First Crossing of Greenland*. Trans. H.M. Gepp. 2 vols. London: Longmans, 1890.

---. *In Northern Mists*. Trans. Arthur G. Chater. 2 vols. London: Heinemann, 1911.

Nash, Roderick F. *The Rights of Nature: A History of Environmental Ethics*. Madison: U Wisconsin P, 1989.

---. *Wilderness and the American Mind*. 1967. 3rd ed. New Haven: Yale UP, 1982.

New, W[illiam] H. *Land Sliding: Imagining Space, Presence, and Power in Canadian Writing*. Toronto: U Toronto P, 1997.

Newby, Eric. *A Short Walk in the Hindu Kush*. 1958. Oakland: Lonely Planet, 1998.

Nicolson, Marjorie Hope. *Mountain Gloom and Mountain Glory. The Development of the Aesthetics of the Infinite*. 1959. New York: Norton, 1963.

Nietzsche, Friedrich. *Beyond Good and Evil: Prelude to a Philosophy of the Future*. 1886. Trans. Walter Kaufmann. New York: Random House, 1966.

Norgay, Jamling Tenzing, with Broughton Coburn. *Touching My Father's Soul*. 2001. San Francisco: Harper, 2002.

Noyce, Wilfrid. *The Scholar Mountaineers: Pioneers of Parnassus*. London: Dobson, 1950.

---. *To the Unknown Mountain: The Ascent of Trivor*. London: Heinemann, 1962.

Nye, Robert. "Rhapsody in Black." Rev. of *The Sheltering Sky*, by Paul Bowles. *Manchester Guardian Weekly* 9 Aug. 1981: 22.

Odell, Noel. "Mallory and Irvine's Attempt." In Roberts 161-72.

Oelschlaeger, Max. *The Idea of Wilderness. From Prehistory to the Age of Ecology*. New Haven and London: Yale UP, 1991.

Oliver, Harold H. "The Neglect and Recovery of Nature in Twentieth-Century Protestant Thought." *Journal of the American Academy of Religion* Fall 1992: 379-404.

Ostenso, Martha. *Wild Geese*. 1925. Toronto: McClelland, 1961.

Ousland, Børge. "Crossing Patagonia's Ice Field." *National Geographic* Aug. 2004: 62-79.

Patterson, R[aymond] M. *The Dangerous River*. 1954. Sidney, BC: Gray's Publishing, 1966.

Peary, Robert E. *The North Pole*. 1909. Introd. Theodore Roosevelt. Fwd. Gilbert Grosvenor. 2nd ed. New York: Stokes, 1910.

Perkins, Robert. *Into the Great Solitude: An Arctic Journey*. New York: Henry Holt, 1991.

Perse, Saint-John [Alexis Saint-Léger]. *Exil*. 1941. *Exile and Other Poems*. Trans. Denis Devlin. 1949. 2nd ed. 1953. New York: Pantheon, 1962.

Philby, H. St. John B. *Arabian Days*. London: R. Hale, 1948.

---. *The Empty Quarter*. New York: Holt, 1933.

Pinter, Harold. *Landscape* and *Silence*. London: Eyre Methuen, 1976.

---. *No Man's Land*. London: Methuen, 1975.

Powell, John Wesley. *Canyons of the Colorado*. 1895. New York: Argosy-Antiquarian, 1964.

Proulx, Annie. *Close Range. Wyoming Stories*. 1999. New York: Simon and Schuster, 2000.

Purdy, Al. *The Collected Poems of Al Purdy*. Ed. Russell Brown. Toronto: McClelland and Stewart, 1986.

Quartermain, L.B. *South from New Zealand: An Introduction to Antarctica*. Wellington, NZ: Government Printer, 1964.

---. *Two Huts in the Antarctic*. Wellington, NZ: Government Printer, 1963.

Raban, Jonathan. *Bad Land: An American Romance*. New York: Pantheon, 1996.

Rasmussen, Knud. *Across Arctic America. Narrative of the Fifth Thule Expedition*. New York and London: Putnam, 1927.

Ratti, Abate Achille [Pope Pius XI]. *Climbs on Alpine Peaks*. Trans. J.E.C. Eaton. Fwd. D. Freshfield. London: Benn, 1923.

Rees, Ronald. *New and Naked Land: Making the Prairies Home*. Saskatoon: Western Producer Prairie Books, 1988.

Reisner, Mark. *Cadillac Desert: The American West and Its Disappearing Water*. 1986. Rev. ed. Harmondsworth: Penguin, 1993.

Richardson, Henry Handel, pseud. [Ethel F. Lindesay Richardson] *Ultima Thule: Being the Third Part of the Chronicle of the Fortunes of Richard Mahoney*. Toronto: Doubleday, Doran and Gundy, 1929.

Ricou, Laurence. *Vertical Man/Horizontal World: Man and Landscape in Canadian Prairie Fiction*. Vancouver: U British Columbia P, 1973.

Rihani, Amin. *The Book of Khalid*. N.p.: Dodd, Mead, 1911.

Roberts, David, ed. *Points Unknown. A Century of Great Exploration*. New York: Norton, 2000.

Robinson, Edwin A. *The Man Against the Sky, a Book of Poems*. New York: Macmillan, 1916.

Rölvaag, O[le] E[dvart]. *Giants in the Earth*. 1924. Trans. by the author and others. 1927. New York: Harper, n.d.

Roosevelt, Theodore. "Address at the Grand Canyon." See Krutch 1967.

---. *African Game Trails*. 1909. New York: Scribner's, 1910.

Ross, Sinclair. *As for Me and My House*. 1941. Introd. Roy Daniells. Toronto: McClelland and Stewart, 1970.

Roy, Gabrielle. *Le Pays de bonheur d'occasion*. Montréal: Boréal, 2000.

Rule, Jane. *Desert of the Heart*. 1964. Vancouver: Talonbooks, 1980.

Ruskin, John. *Deucalion and Other Studies in Rocks and Stones*. 1875-83. *The Works of John Ruskin*. Ed. E.T. Cook and Alexander Wedderburn. Vol. 6. London: Allen, 1906.

Rutland, William R. *Thomas Hardy, a Study of His Writings and Their Background*. 1938. New York: Russell, 1962.

Rutter, Eldon. *The Holy Cities of Arabia*. 1928. 2 vols. in 1. London and New York: Putnam's, 1930.

Ruttledge, Hugh. *Everest 1933*. 1934. London: Hodder and Stoughton, 1936.

Ryan, Simon. "Exploring Aesthetics: The Picturesque Appropriation of Land in Journals of Australian Exploration." *Australian Literary Studies* Oct. 1992: 282-93.

Sackville-West, V[ita]. *Passenger to Teheran*. London: Hogarth Press, 1926.

Saint-Exupéry, Antoine de. *Courrier sud*. Paris: Gallimard, 1929.

---. *Le Petit prince*. 1943. Vol. 2. *Oeuvres complètes*. N.p.: Gallimard, 1999.

---. *Terre des hommes*. Paris: Gallimard, 1939.

---. *Vol de nuit*. Paris: Gallimard, 1931.

---. *Wind, Sand and Stars*. Trans. Lewis Galantière. New York: TIME, 1965.

Sartre, Jean-Paul. *L'Etre et le néant*. 1943. *Being and Nothingness*. Trans. Hazel Barnes. New York: Philosophical Library, 1956.

---. *Huis clos suivi de Les mouches*. 1944. Paris: Gallimard, 1947.

Sayre, Woodrow Wilson. *Four Against Everest*. Englewood Cliffs, NJ: Prentice-Hall, 1964.

Schaeffer, Jean-Marie. *Adieu à l'esthétique*. Paris: Presses universitaires de France, 2000.

Schafer, R. Murray. *Patria. The Complete Cycle*. N.p.: Coach House Books, 2002.

Schaller, George B. "In a High and Sacred Realm: Tibet's Remote Chang Tang." *National Geographic* Aug. 1993: 62-87.

Schama, Simon. *Landscape and Memory*. New York: Knopf, 1995.

Scott, Robert F., and others. *Scott's Last Expedition*. 1913. London: Murray, 1923.

---. *Voyage of the Discovery*. 1905. 2 vols. London: Nelson, n.d. [1929].

Seaton, Dorothy. "The Post-Colonial as Deconstruction: Land and Language in Kroetsch's 'Badlands'." *Canadian Literature* Spring 1991: 77-89.

Severin, Tim. *The Brendan Voyage*. 1978. London: Hutchinson/ Collins, 1979.

---. *In Search of Genghis Khan*. 1991. London: Random House UK, 1992.

Shackleton, Edward. *Arctic Journeys*. London: Hodder and Stoughton, n.d. [1936].

---. *Nansen the Explorer*. London: Witherby, 1959.

Shackleton, Ernest H. *The Heart of the Antarctic: The Story of the British Antarctica Expedition 1907-09*. 1909. London: Heinemann, 1932.

---. *South: The Story of Shackleton's Last Expedition 1914-1917*. 1919. New York: New American Library, 1999.

Shepard, Paul. *Man in the Landscape: A Historic View of the Esthetics of Nature*. New York: Knopf, 1967.

Sheridan, Clare. *Nuda Veritas*. 1927. *Naked Truth*. New York and London: Blue Ribbon, 1928.

Sherman, Paddy. *Cloud Walkers: Six Climbs on Major Canadian Peaks*. Toronto: Macmillan, 1965.

---. *Expeditions to Nowhere*. Toronto: McClelland and Stewart, 1981.

Shipton, Eric E. *Mountains of Tartary*. London: Hodder and Stoughton, n.d.

---. *That Untravelled World: an Autobiography*. London: Hodder and Stoughton, 1969.

---. *Tierra del Fuego: The Fatal Lodestone*. London: Knight, 1973.

Simmons, James C. *Passionate Pilgrims: English Travelers to the World of the Desert Arabs*. New York: William Morrow, 1987.

Skrede, Wilfred. *Across the Roof of the World*. Trans. M.A. Michael. London: Travel Book Club, 1954.

Smith, Henry Nash. *Virgin Land: The American West as Symbol and Myth*. New York: Random House, 1950.

Smith, Herbert F. *John Muir*. New York: Twayne, 1965.

Smythe, Frank S. *Again Switzerland*. London: Hodder and Stoughton, 1947.

---. *Climbs in the Canadian Rockies*. London: Hodder and Stoughton, 1950.

---. *Edward Whymper*. London: Hodder and Stoughton, 1940a.

---. *The Kangchenjunga Adventure*. London: Gollancz, 1930.

---. *The Mountain Vision*. London: Hodder and Stoughton, 1941.

---. *Mountaineering Holiday*. London: Hodder and Stoughton, 1940b.

---. *Over Tyrolese Hills*. 1936. 4th ed. London: Hodder and Stoughton, 1938a.

---. *The Valley of Flowers*. London: Hodder and Stoughton, 1938b.

Solotaroff, Theodore. "The Desert Within." Rev. of *The Time of Friendship*, by Paul Bowles. *New Republic* 2 Sep. 1967: 29-31.

Spender, Stephen. *Collected Poems 1928-1985*. New York: Random House, 1986.

Spufford, Francis. *I May Be Some Time: Ice and the English Imagination.* London: Faber and Faber, 1996.

Staib, Bjørn. *Nanok.* 1962. Anon. trans. *Across Greenland in Nansen's Track.* London: Allen and Unwin, 1963.

Stark, Freya. *Journey's Echo.* Fwd. Lawrence Durrell. London: Murray, 1963.

---. *The Valleys of the Assassins.* London: Murray, 1934.

---. *A Winter in Arabia.* 1940. London: Murray, 1948.

Starkell, Don. *Paddle to the Arctic.* Toronto: McClelland and Stewart, 1995.

Stefansson, Vilhjalmur. *The Friendly Arctic: The Story of Five Years in Polar Regions.* 1921. New York: Macmillan, 1922.

Stegner, Wallace. *Beyond the Hundredth Meridian. John Wesley Powell and the Second Opening of the West.* Introd. Bernard de Voto. Boston: Houghton Mifflin, 1954.

---. *Mormon Country.* New York: Duell, Sloan and Pearce, 1942.

---. "Wilderness as Idea." In "Wilderness Conservation." *Sierra Club Bulletin* Dec. 1967: 12-20. Pp. 12-13.

Stephen, Leslie. *Men, Books, and Mountains.* Introd. S.O.A. Ullmann. London: Hogarth Press, 1956.

Stevens, Holly, ed. *Letters* [of Wallace Stevens]. New York: Knopf, 1966.

Stevens, Wallace. *Collected Poetry and Prose.* Ed. Frank Kermode and Joan Richardson. New York: Library of America, 1997.

Stevenson, Lionel. *Darwin Among the Poets.* Chicago: U Chicago P, 1932.

Stevenson, Robert L. *From Scotland to Silverado: The Amateur Emigrant.* Ed. James D. Hart. Cambridge, MA: Belknap/Harvard UP, 1966.

---. *Travels with a Donkey in the Cevennes.* 1879. London: Chatto and Windus, 1912.

Storrs, Ronald. "Charles Doughty and T.E. Lawrence." *The Listener* 25 Dec. 1947: 1093-94.

Stow, Randolph. *To the Islands.* London: MacDonald, 1958.

Strauss, Richard. *Eine Alpensinfonie*, op. 64. 1915. Introd. Adolf Aber. München-Leipzig: Leuckart, n.d.

Sutherland, Ronald. "La Terre abandonnée." In Chadbourne and Dahlie, ed.

Swinburne, Algernon Charles. *Poems by Algernon Charles Swinburne.* Introd. Ernest Rhys. New York: Modern Library, n.d.

Tabachnick, Stephen. *Charles Doughty.* Boston: Twayne, 1981.

---, ed. *Explorations in Doughty's* Arabia Deserta. Athens and London: U Georgia P, 1987.

Taylor, A.J.P. *The First World War: An Illustrated History*. 1963. Harmondsworth: Penguin, 1966.

Taylor, Griffith. *Journeyman Taylor*. London: Hale, 1958.

---. "The Western Journey." In *Scott's Last Expedition*.

Tennyson, Alfred. *Tennyson's Poetry*. Ed. Robert W. Hill, Jr. New York: Norton, 1971.

Tenzing Norgay, in collaboration with James Ramsey Ullman. *Tiger of the Snows: The Autobiography of Tenzing of Everest*. New York: Putnam's, 1955.

Thesiger, Wilfred. *Arabian Sands*. 1959. Harmondsworth: Penguin, 1964.

---. *The Marsh Arabs*. 1964. Harmondsworth: Penguin, 1967.

Thomas, Bertram. *Arabia Felix: Across the Empty Quarter of Arabia*. Fwd. T.E. Shaw [Lawrence]. Oxford: Readers' Union, 1938.

Tilman, H.W. *Mount Everest 1938*. Cambridge: Cambridge UP, 1948.

Tippett, Maria, and Douglas Cole. *From Desolation to Splendour: Changing Perceptions of the British Columbia Landscape*. Toronto: Clarke Irwin, 1977.

Tomlinson, H.M. *The Sea and the Jungle*. 1912. New York: New American Library, 1961.

Toynbee, Polly. "Eyes to the Hills." *Manchester Guardian Weekly* 20 Apr. 1980: 19.

Treneer, Anne. *Charles M. Doughty: A Study of His Prose and Verse*. London: Cape, 1935.

Tuan, Yi-Fu. "Desert and Ice: Ambivalent Aesthetics." In *Landscape, Natural Beauty and the Arts*. 1993.

---. *Space and Place: The Perspective of Experience*. Minneapolis: U Minnesota P, 1977.

---. *Topophilia: A Study of Environmental Perception, Attitudes, and Values*. Englewood Cliffs, NJ: Prentice-Hall, 1974. Rev. 1990.

Twain, Mark [Samuel Clemens]. *A Tramp Abroad*. 1880. New York: Limited Editions Club, 1966.

Ullman, James Ramsey, comp. and ed. *Kingdom of Adventure: Everest. A Chronicle of Man's Assault on the Earth's Highest Mountain*. New York: Sloane, 1947.

van der Post, Laurens. *Venture to the Interior*. 1951. Harmondsworth: Penguin, 1957.

Verhaeren, Émile. *Oeuvres de Émile Verhaeren*. Paris: Mercure de France, n.d. [1914]

Verne, Jules. *Le Sphinx des glaces*. 1897. *The Sphinx of Ice, or An Antarctic Mystery*. Vol. 14. *Works of Jules Verne*. Ed. Charles F. Horne. New York and London: Parke, 1911.

Vieuchange, Michel. *Smara: The Forbidden City*. Introd. Paul Claudel. Ed. Jean Vieuchange. Trans. Fletcher Allen. London, Methuen, 1933.

Vigneault, Giles. "Mon Pays." *Avec les vieux mots*. Ottawa: Editions de l'arc, 1964.

Wald, Beth. "Patagonia." Banff Festival of Mountain Books and Films. Banff Centre for the Arts, Banff, AB. 4 Nov. 1999.

Wallach, Janet. *Desert Queen: The Extraordinary Life of Gertrude Bell*. Toronto: Nan A. Talese/Doubleday, 1996.

Watson, Jane W. *Deserts of the World*. New York: Putnam, 1981.

Webb, Francis. "Eyre All Alone." 1961. *Collected Poems*. Sydney: Angus and Robertson, 1969.

Webern, Anton von. See Irvine and Moldenhauer.

Webster, Harvey C. *On a Darkling Plain. The Art and Thought of Thomas Hardy*. 1947. London: Cass, 1964.

Weigall, Arthur E.P. *Travels in the Upper Egyptian Deserts*. London: Blackwood, 1913.

Weiner, Jonathan. *The Beak of the Finch: A Story of Evolution in Our Time*. 1994. New York: Random House, 1995.

Wellard, James H. *The Great Sahara*. New York: Dutton, 1965.

Wells, H[erbert] G[eorge]. *The Time Machine*. 1895. *The War of the Worlds and The Time Machine*. New York: Doubleday, 1961.

White, Lynn, Jr. "Historical Roots of Our Ecological Crisis." Address. American Academy for the Advancement of Science. *Sierra Club Bulletin* Oct. 1967: 123-7.

White, Patrick. *A Fringe of Leaves*. 1976. New York: Avon, 1978.

---. *The Tree of Man*. 1955. New York: Avon, 1975.

---. *Voss*. 1957. Harmondsworth: Penguin, 1981.

Whitman, Walt. *The Works of Walt Whitman. The Deathbed Edition*. Introd. Malcolm Cowley. 1948. 2 vols. New York: Funk and Wagnalls, 1968.

Whymper, Edward. *Travels Among the Great Andes of the Equator*. 1892. Introd. Loren McIntyre. Salt Lake City: Smith, 1987.

Wiebe, Rudy. *Playing Dead: A Contemplation Concerning the Arctic*. Edmonton: NeWest, 1989.

Williams, Ralph Vaughan. *The Film Music of Ralph Vaughan Williams.* Vol. 1. BBC Philharmonic and Sheffield Philharmonic Chorus. Cond. Rumon Gamba. Notes by Michael Kennedy. Chandos 10007, 2002.

---. *Sinfonia Antartica.* Symphony #7. London: Oxford UP, 1953. London Philharmonic Orchestra and Choir. Cond. Adrian Boult. Notes by Michael Kennedy. LP. Angel S-36763, n.d.

Willis, Clint, ed. *Epic. Stories of Survival from the World's Highest Peaks.* New York: Thunder's Mouth Press, 1997.

Winn, Michael. "A Taste for Freedom." *Aramco World* July-Aug. 1981: 3-7.

Wollaston, Nicholas. *The Man on the Ice Cap: The Life of Augustine Courtauld.* London: Constable, 1980.

Wood, Susan. *The Land in Canadian Prose 1840-1945.* Ottawa: Carleton UP, 1988.

Woodin, Ann. *Home Is the Desert.* Introd. Joseph Wood Krutch. New York: Macmillan, 1964.

Woodrow, Alain. "Alone in the Sahara." *Manchester Guardian Weekly* 7 Jan. 1979.

Worsley, F[rank] A[rthur]. *The Great Antarctic Rescue: Shackleton's Boat Journey.* Rpt. of 1st ed. London: Times Books, 1977.

---. *Under Sail in the Frozen North.* Philadelphia: McKay, 1927.

Young, G[eoffrey] W[inthrop], ed. *Mountain Craft.* London: Methuen, 1920.

---. *On High Hills. Memories of the Alps.* 1927. 5th ed. London: Methuen, 1947.

Zen Buddhism. Mt. Vernon, NY: Peter Pauper Press, 1959.

Index

This is principally a names-and-titles index of the main text, from Introduction through Conclusion. It does not cover the Preface (which pursues a separate argument), Chronology, Lexicon – itself an index of sorts – or, of course, the footnotes or bibliography. With a few exceptions, it does not list ideas and feelings that appear in the Lexicon, or the places visited by travellers, whose inclusion would have lengthened it by many hundred entries. In a book devoted largely to "the Great," indexing that term poses special problems of volume and usefulness. Where a range of pages (e.g. 36-9) is given, it may be taken as indicating a more concentrated interest in that area.

Borodin, Alexander, 88, 166, 255; *In the Steppes of Central Asia*, 88-9, 92, 167

Bowers, Lieut. H. R., 73, 75

Bowles, Paul, 243-6, 248, 249; *Collected Stories*, 244, 245; *Next to Nothing*, 245; *The Sheltering Sky*, 243, 244-5; *Their Heads Are Green...*, 246; *Without Stopping*, 243, 244, 246

Bowman, Isaiah, *Desert Trails of the Atacama*, 107-8

Bridges, Lucas, 205-6, 211; *Uttermost Part of the Earth*, 205-6

Bridges, Robert, "Wintry Delights," 91-2

Brown, Hamish, *Hamish's Mountain Walk*, 218-19

Bruno, Giordano, 2

Bryce, James, 44

Buddha, 25, 215; Buddhism, 155, 167, 169, 174-5, 178, 194, 199, 205, 212-16, 264; Buddhists, 82, 204, 206, 207, 209, 212-16, 221, 224; Zen Buddhism, 38, 94, 155, 174-5, 198, 203, 213, 214, 216, 221, 236, 267

Buell, Lawrence, *The Environmental Imagination*, 180, 268

Bunyan, John, *Pilgrim's Progress*, 78, 196

Burckhardt, John Lewis, 11

Burke, Edmund, 31, 40, 56, 82, 126, 136, 263, 267; *A Philosophical Enquiry into the Origin of our Ideas of the Sublime and the Beautiful*, 2, 202

Burnet, Thomas, 99; *The Sacred Theory of the Earth*, 2

Burton, Richard, 5, 7, 9, 11, 18, 33, 100, 177, 193

Butala, Sharon, *The Perfection of the Morning*, 201

Butler, Samuel, *Erewhon*, 86

Byrd, Adm. Richard, 141, 145, 149-50, 151, 154, 162, 170, 226; *Alone*, 149-50; *Discovery*, 149

Byron, George Gordon, Lord, 5, 18, 35, 43, 49, 139

Cage, John, 12

Calvino, Italo, 190

Camus, Albert, 12, 177, 197, 207, 245

Carl, Louis, *Tefedest*, 185

Carlyle, Thomas, 39, 91, 252; *Sartor Resartus*, 146

Cather, Willa, 157; *My Antonia*, 160; *The Song of the Lark*, 87-8

Chapman, F. Spencer, 138, 206-7; *Helvellyn to Himalaya*, 138, 207; *Lhasa, the Holy City*, 207; *Memoirs of a Mountaineer*, 138, 207; *Northern Lights*, 145-7

Chatwin, Bruce, *The Songlines*, 257-8

Garland, Hamlin, *Boy Life on the Prairie*, 87; *Main-Travelled Roads*, 87

Gautier, Emile, *Sahara*, 108

Geikie, Archibald, 263

Geology, geologists, 11, 12, 14, 15-17, 20, 21, 35, 36, 37, 41-2, 44, 73, 78, 80, 83, 92, 96, 104, 107, 108, 109, 121, 128, 153, 196, 201, 216, 219, 254, 266

George, Uwe, *In the Deserts of This Earth*, 187-8

Georgi, Dr Johannes, *Mid-Ice*, 148, 149, 150

Gerster, Georg, *Sahara*, 186-7

Gide, André, 114, 190; *L'Immoraliste*, 159-60

Gilbar, Steven, *Natural State ...*, 220, 261

Gill, John, 221

Goethe, Johann Wolfgang von, 168

Golding, William, 261

Govinda, Lama Anagarika, 215; *The Way of the White Clouds*, 213

Gran, Tryggve, 73, 74

Great, the, 1, 2, 4-6, 9, 17, 18, 20-3, 28, 32, 33, 36-9, 41, 46, 48, 49, 53-7, 61, 63, 64, 73, 74, 76, 80-5, 87, 88-95, 97, 100, 105, 108, 112, 114, 115, 117-21, 125, 126, 131, 136, 137, 141, 144, 146, 152, 153, 155-7, 160-3, 166, 168-70, 173, 175, 177, 181, 186, 191, 197, 199-203, 205, 216, 221, 228, 230, 232, 234, 236-8, 240, 241, 243, 245, 247, 250-3, 256, 257, 259, 261, 263-7, 269

Greely, Adolphus, 59, 87

Greene, Graham, 123

Greenpeace, 236

Gregory, Derek, 269

Grieg, Edvard, *Peer Gynt Suite*, 63, 89

Grofé, Ferde, *Grand Canyon Suite*, 168-9, 254, 255

Grove, Frederick Philip, 160-1; *In Search of Myself*, 242; *Over Prairie Trails*, 160-1; *Settlers in the Marsh*, 161

Guthrie, A. B., Jr, *The Big Sky*, 247

Habeler, Peter, 221, 222, 265; *Everest: Impossible Victory*, 217-18

Hammond, Alan, *To Climb a Sacred Mountain*, 215

Hardy, Thomas, 2-6, 7, 8, 14, 17, 21, 27, 31, 36, 41, 53, 59, 60, 64, 70, 72, 77, 79-81, 82, 85, 91, 98, 103, 115, 122, 141, 145, 153, 157, 161, 164, 167, 183, 186, 205, 223, 241, 263-70; "chastened sublimity," 3-4, 6, 8, 17, 36, 76, 80, 83, 87, 201, 241, 251, 263; Egdon Heath, 3-5, 7, 17, 32, 35, 36, 55, 78, 79, 80, 116, 152, 161,

340

162; *Wind, Sand and Stars*, 117-19

Waugh, Evelyn, 210

Webern, Anton von, 12, 167-8, 169, 200; *Im Sommerwind*, 168; *Tot*, 168

Wegener, Prof. Alfred, 147-8

Weigall, Arthur, *Travels in the Upper Egyptian Deserts*, 32

Weiner, Jonathan, 267; *The Beak of the Finch*, 180

Wellard, James, *The Great Sahara*, 187, 188

Wells, Herbert G., 104, 154; *The Time Machine*, 58, 81-2

Weston, Jesse, *From Ritual to Romance*, 153

White, Lynn, Jr, "Historical Roots of Our Ecological Crisis," 179-80, 269

White, Patrick, *A Fringe of Leaves*, 256; *The Tree of Man*, 256; *Voss*, 257

Whitman, Walt, 8, 22, 89, 253

Whymper, Edward, 50, 51, 83, 123, 124, 131, 137; *Scrambles Among the Alps*, 7, 35; *Travels Amongst the Great Andes of the Equator*, 35

Wiebe, Rudy, 259

Wilkins, G. H., 141

William of Rubruck, 194

Williams, Ralph V., *A Sea Symphony*, 253; *Scott of the Antarctic* (film score), 253; *Sinfonia Antartica*, 253-4

Wills, Alfred, 44, 45, 51, 123

Willumsen, Rasmus, 148

Wilson, Dr E. A. (Bill), 73, 75

Wilson, Maurice, 134

Wollaston, Nicholas, *The Man on the Ice Cap*, 146-7

Wollheim, Richard, 12, 105

Wood, Gareth, 235

Woodin, Ann, *Home Is the Desert*, 197-8, 203

Woodrow, Alain, 197

Woolf, Virginia, 114

Wordie, James, 146-7, 227

Wordsworth, William, 28, 36, 50, 125, 157, 175, 268; *The Excursion*, 82

Worsley, Frank, 141-2; *The Great Antarctic Rescue*, 97-8, 141, 234; *Under Sail in the Frozen North*, 142

Wyckoff, Jerome, 219

Yeats, William B., 212, 248; "Easter 1916," 121

Young, Geoffrey W., 51, 124, 129-30, 131, 138, 139; *Mountain Craft*, 124; *On High Hills*, 129-30

Younghusband, Sir Francis, 132, 155

Zen: see Buddha, Buddhism